The ÜberReader

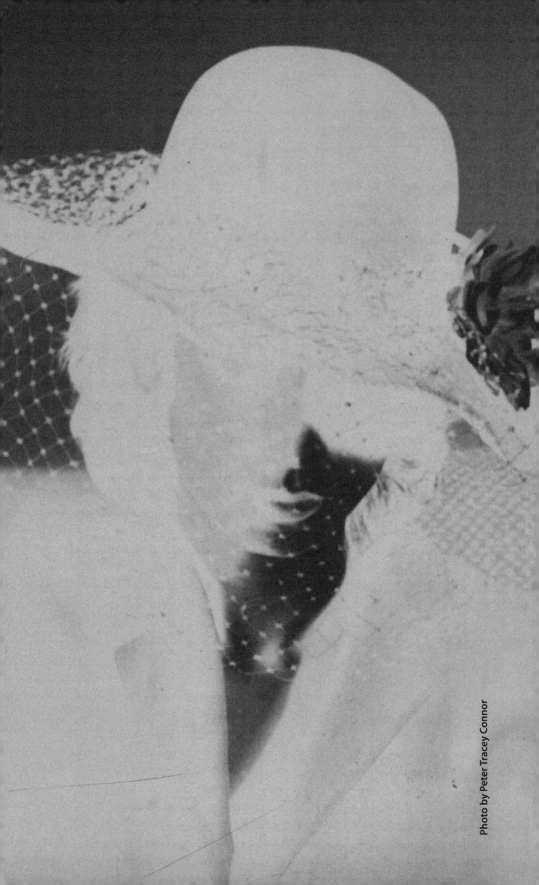

The ÜberReader

Selected Works of
AVITAL RONELL

Edited by Diane Davis

University of Illinois Press
Urbana and Chicago

Introduction © 2008 by
the Board of Trustees
of the University of Illinois
All rights reserved
Manufactured in the
United States of America
1 2 3 4 5 C P 5 4 3 2 1
∞ This book is printed on
acid-free paper.

Library of Congress
Cataloging-in-Publication Data
Ronell, Avital.
The ÜberReader : selected
works of Avital Ronell / edited
by Diane Davis.
p.   cm.
Includes bibliographical
references and index.
ISBN 978-0-252-03066-6
(cloth : alk. paper)
ISBN 978-0-252-07311-3
(pbk. : alk. paper)
1. Popular culture—United States—
History—20th century. 2. Avant-
garde (Aesthetics)—United States.
3. Literature, Modern—20th
century—History and criticism.
I. Davis, Diane II. Title. III. Title:
Über reader. IV. Title: Selected
works of Avital Ronell.
E169.Z83R66   2008
809'.04—dc22   2007030327

From the very first day that I was directed by Dr. Willis Regier to contact him, Richard Eckersley became a destination, if not a destiny, for my writing. He was reader, chief hermeneut, translator, and graphic transformer of the texts that were submitted to him in varying states of anxious readiness. Often, Richard would "see" language in a way that put wings on words, originating my intention and inflecting my thought in fresh and bracing ways. His interventions allowed for the most rigorous and also kindest forms of expropriation that one could hope for—unfolding the drama of dispossession to which he was attuned. Richard would seize on meaning, develop a field of intention, or invent an underground semantics, copiloting some of the most recalcitrant passages of my work to relative safety: he was never satisfied with some sort of soft safety but he conducted the work to the zone of its unrelenting positing, where it could fly with nearly Nietzschean freespiritedness and develop the characteristics of an altogether singular textual-graphic character. As for our "relationship," I was lulled and comforted by Richard's voice on the telephone, the site of our intense work; I was held by his patience and enlivened by his complicity with ethical pressure points of our reciprocal commitment. The last work he did with me involved the cover for this book. Unknowingly, we were already pointing to the beyond of spiritual expanses and scouting for the possibility of transcendental reading. Diane Davis and I counted on Richard's engagement with this work and were devastated when he was forced to withdraw his hand. Bereft and grieving, we dedicate the *ÜberReader*

to the memory of

RICHARD ECKERSLEY

Contents

Photo album follows page xxxvi

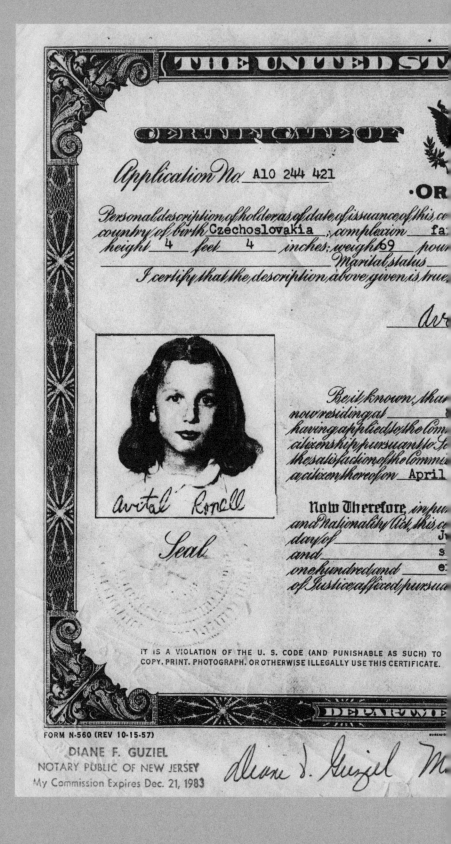

THE UNITED ST

CERTIFICATE OF

Application No. A10 244 421

·OR

Personal description of holder as of date of issuance of this ce
country of birth Czechoslovakia ; *complexion* fa
height 4 *feet* 4 *inches; weight* 69 *pour*
Marital status
I certify that the description above given is true

Av

Be it known, that
now residing at
having applied to the Com
citizenship pursuant to So
the satisfaction of the Commi
a citizen thereof on April

Avital Ronell

Now Therefore, *in pu*
and Nationality Act, this ce
day of J
and s
one hundred and e
of Justice affixed pursua

Seal

IT IS A VIOLATION OF THE U. S. CODE (AND PUNISHABLE AS SUCH) TO
COPY. PRINT. PHOTOGRAPH. OR OTHERWISE ILLEGALLY USE THIS CERTIFICATE.

DEPARTME

FORM N-560 (REV 10-15-57)

DIANE F. GUZIEL
NOTARY PUBLIC OF NEW JERSEY
My Commission Expires Dec. 21, 1983

Diane F. Guziel   M

No.   A-417481

CITIZENSHIP

NAL·

te:Sex   female   ;date of birth April 15, 1952 ;

;color of eyes   brown   ;color of hair   blond ;

sible distinctive marks   none

gle

hat the photograph affixed hereto is a likeness of me.

Ronell

(Complete and true signature of holder)

----AVITAL RONELL---- .

43rd Street, Brooklyn, New York

er of Immigration and Naturalization for a certificate of

41 of the Immigration and Nationality Act having proved to

hat (s)he is now a citizen of the United States of America, became

1961 and is now in the United States:

of the authority contained in Section 341 of the Immigration

e of citizenship is issued this   12th

in the year of our Lord nineteen hundred

one and of our Independence the

-fifth , and the seal of the Department

alute.

J. M. Swing

30, 1980

Acknowledgments

Grateful acknowledgment is made for permission to reprint the following: "Deviant Payback: The Aims of Valerie Solanas" appeared as the introduction to the twenty-fifth anniversary issue of *SCUM Manifesto* (London and New York: Verso, 2004): 1–31. "The Experimental Disposition: Nietzsche's Discovery of America (Or, Why the Present Administration Sees Everything in Terms of a Test)" first appeared in *American Literary History* 15, no. 3 (2003): 560–74. "State of the Art: Julia Scher's Disinscription of National Security" was published in *Julia Scher: Always There,* edited by Caroline Schneider and Brian Wallis (New York: Lukas & Sternberg, 2002): 17–21. The photo accompanying this piece, "Always There—Interactive Surveillance Zone, 1994" was taken by Joseph Cultice and also appears here by permission of the publishers. "On the Unrelenting Creepiness of Childhood: Lyotard, Kid-Tested" appears in *Minima Memoria: Essays in the Wake of Jean-François Lyotard,* edited by Claire Nouvet, Zrinka Stahuljak, and Kent Still, © 2005 by the Board of Trustees of the Leland Stanford Jr. University (simultaneously printed here by permission of the publishers). Portions of "The Sacred Alien: Heidegger's Reading of Hölderlin's 'Andenken,'" were published in *PMLA* 120, no. 1 (2005): 16–32, under the title "On the Misery of Theory without Poetry: Heidegger's Reading of Hölderlin's 'Andenken.'" "Koan Practice or Taking Down the Test" was published in *Parallax* 10, no. 1 (2004): 58–71. "Delay Call Forwarding" is the opening chapter of Ronell's *The Telephone Book: Technology, Schizophrenia, Electric Speech* (Lincoln: University of Nebraska Press, 1989): 1–25. "A Note on the Failure of Man's Custodianship," "Support Our Tropes," and "TraumaTV" appear in *Finitude's Score: Essays for the End of the Millennium* (Lincoln and London: University of Nebraska Press, 1994): 269–91, 305–27, and 41–46, respectively. "Toward a Narcoanalysis" is from *Crack Wars: Literature Addiction Mania* (Lincoln and London: University of Nebraska Press, 1992): 47–64. The "Preface" to *Dictations* originally appeared in the 1993 edition of *Dictations: On Haunted Writing* (Lincoln and London: University of Nebraska Press, 1993): ix–xix. "'Is It Happening?'" appears in *The Test Drive* (Urbana and Chicago: University of Illinois Press, 2004):107–9. Both "Slow Learner" and "The Disappearance and Returns of the Idiot" are from *Stupidity* (Urbana and Chicago: University of

Illinois Press, 2002): 1–33 and 170–196. And "Confessions of an Anacoluthon: Avital Ronell on Writing, Technology, Pedagogy, and Politics," excerpts from which are peppered throughout this volume, appeared in *jac: A Journal of Composition Theory* 20, no. 2 (2000): 243–81.

Publication of this book was supported by a University Cooperative Society Subvention Grant awarded by the University of Texas at Austin.

Introduction

Diane Davis

Gustave Flaubert once said "the worth of a book can be judged by the strength of the punches it gives and the length of time it takes you to recover from them."[1] According to this calculus of evaluation, typically reserved for literary texts, Avital Ronell's exceptionally hard hitters are works of inestimable value. It's not unusual to take tiny hits in a critical work that advances a specific position or viewpoint; however, the distinguishing feature of the Ronellian punch is that it's the effect of *no* positive knowledge claim. Ronell's critical texts operate not as formal arguments but as the obliteration of any possible argumentative ground, and that's what delivers the KO blow.

Each of Aristotle's twenty-eight general *topoi* or commonplace strategies of argumentation—argument from opposites or analytic division or cause and effect, etc.—presumes some steady ground, some prior knowledge against which to push off. And indeed, Ronell's texts are seductively oriented around sites of apparent familiarity: who doesn't suppose s/he knows a little something about the telephone, drugs, writing, opera, or military maneuvers? But rather than building an argument or inquiry on that potential point of *stasis,* Ronell's texts abruptly dissolve it, generating such a tight zoom on the putative object of knowledge that it slips from your appropriative grasp, withdrawing into a foreign space. The telephone Ronell analzyes, for example, turns out to be something unfamiliar, unlocatable, uncanny—not an originary site at all but a *haunted* one, a presence that cannot be situated securely within the present. The destabilizing force of Ronell's extreme close-ups institutes a break, an interruption in inherited meaning. And the punch takes place in this feat of ironic destruction, in or *as* this devastating withdrawal of understanding that leaves you with no recourse to anything like counterargument. "Nevertheless," Ronell reminds us, "interruption may always be a sign of life."[2] Inasmuch as the deracinating suspension is also an opening, it aligns itself with futurity and the sober potentiality of Nietzsche's "open sea." Ronell's punch is simultaneously her gift: wherever knowing falters, thinking and reading can begin.

• • •

*The editor's introduction is typically responsible for situating the force and sig-
nificance of an author within a philosophical, political, or historical framework.
Anyone familiar with Avital Ronell's oeuvre will, however, appreciate my dilemma:
How to situate a writer whose signature move is to sweep away the grounds by
which one might do so? How to locate on an intellectual map these texts devoted
to radical remappings, including those urged by "literature and psychoanalysis
but also by the logic of teletopical incursions that has supplanted ground and
grounding"?[3] I have no excuse, nothing to say for myself about what follows except
that attending faithfully to a body of work like this one may mean breaking here
and there with generic expectations.*

Brief Overview

Ronell's work has a sharp ironic edge and is, in this sense, reminiscent of the
works and inroads of the great German ironists. Although she likes her theory
"with a French accent" and is considered one of America's leading deconstruc-
tionists, she is first of all a Germanist whose approach and perspective owes
a great deal to her studies in German philosophy, music, and literature. She
often claims to have a dusty philological side, and indeed her work is, we might
say, solidly grounded in this rich tradition, many of the underlying histories
and presumptions of which she nonetheless disrupts—an effect of what she
calls her "irreverent type of reverence."[4] Ronell's intellectual trajectories are
extremely complex, and one finds in her work an extraordinary confluence of
several distinct scholarly traditions: it's tempting to suggest that she does French
theory American-style within a Germanic frame and marked by a Talmudic
meticulousness.[5] But that description wouldn't begin to cover it because, among
other things, in Ronell's texts "scholarly tradition" is itself endlessly hassled
and interrupted by ironic asides and biting critiques that constitute a kind
of a chorus of street-level resistance. At once a consummate scholar and the
anti-scholar, Ronell can be read as another double-edged figure punctuating
the German tradition.

In the early 1980s, Ronell's translations of Jacques Derrida's work helped
to introduce deconstruction to the American academy, and today her own
texts—intriguing works of art as well as exacting works of scholarship—have
been translated into several languages, including French, German, Spanish,
Polish, Norwegian, Swedish, Hebrew, Arabic, Danish, and Japanese.[6] Critically
engaged with pressing social issues, Ronell was the first to theorize rigorously
the new technologies and the first to write philosophically about AIDS.[7] At

the height of the war on drugs, she undertook the first sustained and comprehensive—philosophical, literary, and psycholanalytic—inquiry into drugs and addiction, opening and sketching the possible trajectories for what we now call addiction studies.[8] Ronell has performed dazzling (re)readings of everything from schizophrenia, Rodney King, and the Gulf War to *Being and Time, the SCUM Manifesto,* and *Madame Bovary.* Throughout her extensive oeuvre, and with her trademark style and wit, she has offered up jaw-dropping redescriptions that unsettle the language of certitude and judgment: for example, she has defined Moses and Aaron as a telephone, portrayed testimonial video as television's "voice of conscience," depicted "Goethe" as an effect largely produced by the "lip-syncher" Johannes Peter Eckermann, and described writing as a certain form of drugging, offering Emma Bovary (the first "trash body") as an exemplary figure for the so-called "geniune" writer.[9]

Ronell's texts operate against the grain and in the face of the most outspoken authorities, complicating presumptions of certainty by unworking the work of the concept with fearless tenacity. Within a political and philosophical climate still disproportionately given to Enlightenment values, Ronell dared to spring stupidity from conceptual confinement, exposing it not simply as the other of intelligence, but as both *our* transcendental predicament and philosophy's abject and largely repressed condition of possibility.[10] And in response to the contemporary conviction that nearly everything must be tested—from weapons systems, elementary school teachers, and paternity to hair products, urine samples, and loyalty oaths, including those of friendship—Ronell zeroed in on the figure of testing itself, scrutinizing its effects and exposing the terrible ambiguity of a will to test that constitutes ever-new realities but that also, as Nietzsche warned, tends to leave uninhabitable test sites in its tracks, making "the wasteland grow."[11]

As this random sampling already indicates, it's not possible to situate Ronell's pioneering oeuvre securely within disciplinary borders. Not simply philosophy or literary theory or media studies, her work also relinquishes safe harbor in critical theory, political theory, legal theory, and cultural studies. In fact, her thoroughly transdisciplinary interventions overflow the boundaries of the academy, earning her the acclaim of a radically diverse network of outlaw writers, filmmakers, digital artists, painters, photographers, and musicians.[12] Her work stubbornly resists—by exceeding—established classification systems and ready-to-hand labels, including those with which it is most often tagged: deconstructive, psychoanalytic, (post)feminist, Derridian, Heideggerian, Nietzschean, and so on. Although Ronell's texts openly discourse with and operate within a circuit of voices that is only partially indicated by these labels, they nonetheless retain an undeniable singularity, which is as impossible to ignore as it is to grasp and articulate. There is, in other words, a kind of resolute quality to Ronell's texts that keeps labels from sticking, and this quality invites some pause or stammering among those of us who attempt to write about her work. It is also at times responsible for prompting astonishing feats of competitive mimesis. In the introduction to a special section devoted to Ronell in the journal *diacritics*, Jonathan Culler notes that, among other things, her work "is striking . . . for the response it evokes, as those who write about it seek to imitate or outdo her in discussing the texts she and they engage."[13]

A Question of Style

Culler proposes that Ronell has "put together what must be one of the most remarkable critical oeuvres of our era," and he locates the ungraspable difference within the strange and powerful force of her language: "Avital Ronell produces sentences that startle, irritate, illuminate. At once hilarious and refractory, her books are like no others." He doesn't attempt to articulate what it is about her writing that makes it so remarkable, but he does point to this specific aspect of her unprecedented style: "[Ronell yokes] the slang of pop culture with philosophical analysis, forcing the confrontation of high literature and technology or drug culture." Even a quick glance through her major works indicates that this confrontation very often takes place visually, as well; the visual and the textual operate synergistically to forge explosive connections that challenge established distinctions between so-called high thought and marginal notation—between philosophy and rumor, literature and headline news, revelation and chatter. Already at the level of style, Ronell's work threatens the very divisions on which the university sustains itself—which may account, at least in part, for her large and fiercely loyal extra-academic following. It's also one reason that her texts tend to hit so hard within the academy, where they have set off some very powerful reactions.

Ronell's writing is characteristically *tough* in both senses of that term: it's difficult because of its theoretical sophistication, its philosophical and psychoanalytic vocabulary, and its enormous scope and depth; and it's also edgy, gutsy, and rough, slipping seamlessly in and out of a street vernacular that's relentlessly shrewd and cutting. Within Ronell's texts, sophisticated theory-head meets wise-ass street punk, and an odd scuffle breaks out. Or, in a recent interview, Ronell describes it more precisely as a "class struggle":

There is a class struggle in my texts: there's the girl gang speaking, the little gangster, the hoodlum; there's the high philosophical graduate student who studied at the Hermeneutics Institute in Berlin; and there's the more sophisticated Parisian, and so forth. There are different voices, compulsions, denials, and relations that emerge in the texts. But there is the continuity of the more "prolo," proletariat, and very often wise-ass girl who is watching this stuff happening and commenting on it—again, like the chorus or the buffo—who's ironic and whose narcissism involves a kind of sarcastic, biting, meta-critique of what is going on but without ever becoming anti-intellectual.[14]

Still, the intimidating hardness of Ronell's work is also cut here and there with a level of humility and compassion unprecedented in scholarly texts. And the synesthetic impact of this strange mix is intensified by the fact that Ronell has a buffo-like tendency to break suddenly with the conventions of scholarly distance to speak to "you," addressing you directly and putting you on the spot. Sometimes this abrupt address is gentle: "I have gotten into the habit of tagging my moods and monitoring the energy channels as I approach you, every day, a few hours every day, trying to figure you out."[15] Other times it's not so gentle: "This sounds very remote indeed from the lofty peaks that you thought philosophy was scaling. You were wrong. You didn't read close enough, with your nose to the ground."[16] Either way, things suddenly seem very close-range and onto you, and this effect can be somewhat jarring, perhaps especially because you weren't ready for it, because it wasn't supposed to happen to you in a scholarly work.

The visual performance that takes place in so many of Ronell's texts can be jarring, as well. *The Telephone Book* was her first and most intense visual production, and when the University of Nebraska Press first released it in 1989, its outrageously unconventional layout and design were unprecedented in the American academy.[17] *The Telephone Book* instantly became a collector's item, valuable both for its artistic and its scholarly performances. A product of Ronell's first collaboration with award-winning page and graphics designer Richard Eckersley, this oddly sized tome eschews standardizing templates, granting each individual page the freedom to perform a reading of the text it presents. The exploding typography sometimes flows over the expected margins of the printed page, graphics occasionally substitute for letters, and every now and then the text itself becomes visually unreadable, blurry, before slipping into various static symbols that are followed, at times, by gigantic periods that amplify the click of disconnection. Legitimate scholarly texts generally sport a clearly contained and orderly layout designed to silence the noise and interference out of which any writing emerges; offering a sense of clarity and closure, they confirm the author's mastery. *The Telephone Book,* on the other hand, scandalously performs the noise, cranking it up and allowing it to rattle the pages of the text.

The twin aims of this extravagant performance, as Ronell herself puts it in the User's Manual that opens the work, are to "engage a destabilization of the addressee" and to "crack open the closural sovereignty of the Book":

> *The Telephone Book* is going to resist you. Dealing with a logic and topos of the switchboard, it engages the destabilization of the addressee. Your mission, should you choose to accept it, is to learn to read with your ears. In addition to listening for the telephone, you are being asked to tune your ears to noise frequencies, to anticoding, to the inflated reserves of random indeterminate-ness—in a word, you are expected to remain open to the static and interfer-ence that will occupy these lines. We have attempted to install a switchboard which, vibrating a continuous current of electricity, also replicates the effects of scrambling. At first you may find the way the book runs to be disturbing, but we have had to break up its logic typographically. Like the electronic impulse, it is flooded with signals. To crack open the closural sovereignty of the Book, we have feigned silence and disconnection, suspending the tranquil cadencing of paragraphs and conventional divisions. At indicated times, schizophrenia lights up, jamming the switchboard, fracturing a latent semantics with multiple calls. You will become sensitive to the switching on and off of interjected voices. Our problem was how to maintain an open switchboard, one that disrupts a normally functioning text equipped with proper shock absorbers.

If *The Telephone Book* comes equipped with any sort of shock-absorbing mecha-nism, it is certainly not a proper one. Unapologetically putting forth the lowly image of telephone chatter as a frame through which to approach this highly philosophical work, Ronell orchestrates an industrial-sized collision between high thought and small talk. Figuring the author as an addressee struggling to take the multiple and static-filled calls that it visually depicts, *The Telephone Book* shatters the very concept of an original work and, in the process, throws a wrench into the academy's credentialing machine.

Each of Ronell's later books—*Crack Wars, Finitude's Score, Stupidity,* and *The Test Drive*—engages its own very distinct visual performance, and each one orchestrates, in its own way, a certain high–low collision. *Crack Wars,* for example, allows a street-drug trope to introduce the intellectual inquiry: the book opens with a section called "Hits," which delivers mostly single-para-graph doses of mind-blowing insights, each individually packaged in its own double-page spread. *Stupidity* evokes a powerful nocturnal theme and threat via altering typefaces, pitch black pages, and illustrations of the sun, the moon, satellites, and so on. Star constellations precede the surprisingly revealing autobiographical segments throughout the book, acknowledging that the author herself remains mostly in the dark, even when telling her own story. The book opens with the dramatic image of a full solar eclipse, and most of the four chapters and three satellites are separated by images of the progressively emerging sun. What becomes scandalously apparent, however—visually and textually—is that the light of clarity cannot be simply opposed to the night of stupidity, that the latter is the former's very condition of (im)possibility.

Via both visual and verbal channels, Ronell's texts offer up a disjunctive mix of philosophical reasoning and street savvy, of critical discourse and contemporary slang, of power and vulnerability. And at times they address it all very directly to "you," putting the personal pronoun into play even as they shatter the very notion of the "personal." Although Ronell threads the address through a Heideggerian and Derridian circuitry that pluralizes its articulation and destination, in other words, she nonetheless leaves it undecidable whether she's maintaining a steady course on these complicated registers or if she's heading straight for you, according to another, altogether jolting calculus of encounter. In her texts, the second-person pronoun both singularizes and disseminates, calling you up only to spread "you" out, and the destabilizing effect often provokes impassioned responses from readers. This passion is evidenced most explicitly in reviews of Ronell's work, which are themselves a fascinating study: her reviewers are rarely able to maintain a scholarly composure, dropping suddenly into nasty personal attacks or, equally as often, into celebratory effusions.

Eating Well: The Practice of Reading

> "One must eat well" does not mean above all taking in and grasping in itself, but learning and giving to eat, learning-to-give-the-other-to-eat. One never eats entirely on one's own: this constitutes the rule underlying the statement, "One must eat well." It is a rule offering infinite hospitality. And in all differences, ruptures, and wars (one might even say wars of religion), "eating well" is at stake.
> —Jacques Derrida, "Eating Well"

> [W]e may never learn how to read AR, how to listen to her, without engaging her practice of reading, a practice of reading that at the same

time names not only another practice of writing but also another conception of the self and its responsibilities.
—Eduardo Cadava, "Toward an Ethics of Decision"

Ronell's singular style is not solely responsible for the powerful reactions she
provokes within the academy, however. There is also the issue of her approach,
and in the interview cited above, she offers a sense of what's involved in it:

> I never embrace the anti-intellectual tendencies of the American academy.
> But, then, my boundaries for what is intellectual are very, very generous, I
> think. A lot belongs to that space. Indeed, I am always questioning what
> is proper to meaning and what is propertied by our estates of meaning, of
> teaching, and so on.[18]

According to Ronell, the American academy's "anti-intellectual tendencies"
go hand in hand with a presumption of mastery, and for her the rather liberal
boundaries of intellectual engagement include most anything for which academic discourse refuses to make a space, including the most difficult regions
of thought. It is actually considered impolite in the American academy, Ronell
maintains, to engage highly ambiguous, resistant textual challenges. But in this
case, she's willing to risk rudeness: Ronell's work could itself be described as
a sheltering site for the casualties of certitude's strictures, for whatever must
be evicted/evacuated for a discourse of mastery to sustain itself. A few of the
most explicit Ronellian rescue missions—"Minority Reports"—are collected
in Part 2, which follows, but this is a defining aspect of her entire oeuvre: her
work operates as an embrace of the excluded. In Ronell's case, however, this is
never (simply) a matter of championing the loser side of any given dichotomy;
it does not amount, that is, to the standard privilege-flippings associated with
reactionary (identity) politics. The force of Ronell's sometimes excessive hospitality collapses the dichotomous (identity-producing) structure itself, effectively
annulling the grounds for masterful posing and "calling thought back to the
sting of the unsayable," as she has put it, "where phrasing, each time anew,
stunned and dazed, begins to s-crawl."[19]

In her commentary on Lyotard's *The Différend,* Ronell offers a rare glimpse
into the motivations and the hopes accompanying her singular approach:

> Philosophy has to stop testifying for the institutionally self-satisfied controllers,
> stop kissing up to state-sanctioned power plays, and instead get into the un-
> tested regions of new idioms, new addresses, new referents; it has to abandon
> its conciliatory habits. Rather than continue its traditional pursuit of concili-

ation, philosophy, more or less according to Lyotard, needs to be invaded by new inconsistencies and to saturate itself with the *feeling* of the damaged. The differend must be put into phrases with the understanding that such an act cannot yet be accomplished: In sum, philosophical thought must come up with a link to the feeling-tone of the unaccounted for and offer privileged protection to the unaccountable refugees of cognitive regimens.[20]

Ronell's work attempts, each time and in various ways, to link up with this "feeling-tone" for which "cognitive regimens" cannot account, to call thought back to what unsettles it. This involves releasing the hostages of the concept—or, perhaps, in Roland Barthes's terminology, it involves "free[ing] the prisoners":

> When I used to play prisoner's base in the Luxembourg, what I liked best was not provoking the other team and boldly exposing myself to their right to take me prisoner; what I liked best was to free the prisoners—the effect of which was to put both teams back into circulation: the game started over again at zero.
>
> In the great game of the powers of speech, we also play prisoner's base: one language has only temporary rights over another; all it takes is for a third language to appear from the ranks for the assailant to be forced to retreat: in the conflict of rhetorics, the victory never goes to any but the *third language*. The task of this language is to release the prisoners: to scatter the signifieds, the catechisms.[21]

Because it's not possible simply to *account* for the unaccounted for, because this is not merely a question of adequate representation, it would be a mistake to presume that the prisoners, once released, are free to live happily ever after. Ronell's work demonstrates that the hostages of the concept require unending solicitation, and "free[ing] the prisoners," in the sense I'm borrowing from Barthes, signifies not the end of the game but its perpetual rebeginning, a way of trying, each time, to start "it over again at zero."

According to Barthes, the intervention of a "third language" frees the prisoners, but in Ronell's work the release takes place more generally as an effect or a function of reading. Attuned to an/other kind of reading protocol—attuned, that is, to the protocols of reading rather than interpretation—Ronell approaches her various objects of attention in a posture of extreme humility, remaining open to the ways in which they exceed conceptualization and so resist pre-understanding's interpretive grids. Whereas interpretation sets out to master "interference and the contingencies of textual disturbance," Ronell explains in *Stupidity*, "[r]eading enters the zone of non-understanding and tries at some level to manage the distress which the text releases." Proceeding "according to the logic of disturbance," reading casts "the drama of understanding against the comforting smoothness of interpretive synthesis." So whereas interpretation's job is to absorb the noise that betrays the limits of understanding, reading already means reading the static, welcoming the "rush of interference that produces gaps and unsettles cognition."[22] A certain understand*ing* is the goal, either way, but Ronell observes that "having understood, or thinking one has understood, stands precisely on a refusal to read."[23] Reading demonstrates that there is no ethical or logical past tense to understanding; guaranteed to shatter prejudgment structures and overwhelm cognition, it offers no comforting end point, no refuge of mastery or payoff of certitude. Reading really takes guts. And Ronell is a reader, an obsessive reader, the over and über-reader, who struggles with the "aboutness" ("über," about) of reading and the threat of its near extinction ("vor-über," over) on page after page and at every step of the way.

Reading well is a form of "eating well," which, as Derrida suggests, involves not merely consumption but a learning and a giving, a "learning-to-give-the-other-to-eat." It is first of all because Ronell reads well that her writing gives (us) to read not simply an identifying appropriation of the other but a sense of the other's radical inappropriability; she gives the other to be read *as* other. Very often she accomplishes this at the level of structure, producing explicitly genre-busting texts. *Crack Wars,* for example, operates simultaneously as literary analysis, philosophical inquiry, psychoanalytic examination, and biting cultural/political critique. The sections titled "EB on Ice," "The Doctor's Report," and "Cold Turkey" are themselves independent literary works ranging from science fiction to a sort of street theater. And this collision of frames is inevitable, Ronell says, because if the work were to perform itself strictly "in the genre of the philosophical essay, psychoanalytic interpretation, or political analysis—it would be expected to make certain kinds of assertions which obey a whole grammar of procedure and certitudes." Any one of these methods of inquiry, she acknowledges, "would have secured the project within a tolerably reliable frame." However, each one already presumes a level of understanding that is, for her, *in*tolerable: "[I]t's too soon to say with certainty that one has fully understood how to conduct the study of addiction and, in particular, how it may bear upon drugs. To understand in such a way would be to stop reading, to close the book, as it were, or even to throw the book at someone."[24] Ronell will not stop reading or giving-the-other-to-be-read. Her uncompromising texts endlessly crack open the book, taking us back to zero and, in this sense, making readers of us all. Tracing with exceptional precision the complicated and each time singular trajectories of certitude's withdrawal, she holds and abandons us to meaning's open*ing*.

This may be her signature approach: whereas scholarly tradition posits and propagates a causal link between rigor and certitude, the former leading to the latter, Ronell's work takes what Levinas might call the "fine risk" of offering instead an exceptionally rigorous interruption of certitude. Rather than closing in on her object of attention, attempting to fix and represent its meaning, Ronell traces and amplifies its proliferations in meaning, producing a nonrepresentational analysis that loosens our grip on it, releasing it from conceptual arrest. Rigorously interrogating a specific conceptual "object," she zooms us in so close to it that it overflows its object-status—the figure defigures—leaving a radical and inassimilable singularity in its tracks. When Ronell reads "stupidity," for example, she slips into detective mode and tails it through its various engagements with eighteenth-century and contemporary poets, novelists, philosophers, literary/critical theorists, and preschoolers; but the closer she brings us to it, each time—the more meticulously she examines it—the less knowable it appears, and so the less representable, leaving us feeling utterly stupid about stupidity. And therefore about knowledge, too: "As long as I don't *know* what stupidity is, what I know about knowing remains uncertain, even forbidding."[25]

Whenever and whatever Ronell reads, she frees. Her work has sprung from conceptual confinement and intellectual erasure the telephone, the television, writing, testing, and addiction, for example. In her work even the facticity of corporeal existence is defamiliarized, exposing body, too, as a site of sheer uncanniness. Foregrounding the stupefying conditions of corporeality, Ronell offers startling close-ups of body freezing and seizing, starving and binging, erupting and collapsing. Whereas Heidegger somehow manages to engage a thinking of finitude that nonetheless steers clear of body's depropriating imperatives—Levinas notes that in *Being and Time* Dasein is never shown eating or feeling hungry—Ronell, by contrast, zooms in on "the body as an organic, finite, damageable, eviscerable, castratable, crushable entity."[26] She never goes orthodox empiricist on us, though; she is ever the reader, and her exceptional attunement exposes us to the ways in which body operates as a "massive disruption of inherited meaning." When Ronell reads and gives us to read corporeal existence, what becomes clear is that there is no way to secure knowledge about the body, not even your *own* body: "there is no epistemological stronghold, no scientific comfort or medical absolute by which to grasp your body once and for all, as if it were ever merely itself, once and for all." Body, Ronell shows us, "never stays put long enough to form self-identity."[27] Relentlessly delocalizing and defamiliarizing whatever is closest and most familiar to us, Ronell's writing gives us to read the distance already inherent in proximity, the infinity already inherent in finitude. And in the process, it blows the whistle on a prevalent kind of academic discourse, exposing the metaphysical prejudices that it proffers—and releasing its prisoners.

Haunted Writing: On Being-Called

It would be a mistake, however, simply to figure Ronell as the Author of these interruptive performances, as if the author(ity) function itself were not radically disrupted in her writing. As *The Telephone Book* explicitly demonstrates, for her, writing is not an expression of interiority but—to the extent that such oppositions work—an exposition of exteriority; it's less a matter of will and skill than of extreme surrender and of being-called. Inasmuch as a writer is first of all called to write, writing necessarily involves exposure to an outside, an openness to the other's affection and effraction, which suggests that writing is not so much an appropriation of the other as it is a depropriation of the self, a being put "on assignment" by the other's call, as Ronell, alongside Levinas, likes to put it:

> I don't feel contemporaneous with the one who writes because, as we discussed earlier, writing is a depropriative act; it always comes from elsewhere. One is body-snatched, in a trance, haunted. Or, one is on assignment. I use that sense of being on assignment to emphasize how I am "called" to writing. I don't know how to locate its necessity. And one doesn't know where the imperative comes from. Nevertheless, one is assigned to it, so that one is always writing at the behest of the Other.[28]

"My" writing doesn't originate with me but takes place in response to a call that comes from elsewhere, and the assignation to respond is nonnegotiable: prior to every decision, I am exposed to and called by the other, whose demand for a response "does not leave any place of refuge," Levinas writes, "any chance to slip away." One writes in response to the other and because there are others. And inasmuch as "my" writing is always already a response to the other's call, it is made, as Levinas says, "despite the ego, or, more exactly despite me." To this call continually put forth, only a "'here I am' (*me voici*) can answer"; however, in this case "the pronoun 'I' is in the accusative, declined before any declension, possessed by the other."[29] When one is on assignment, I marks a site of extreme surrender; strictly speaking, the one who responds is not an ego but me under assignation, me deprived of first-person status, me without an I—or more carefully: my I sans full-blown ego/ism.

In *Dictations: On Haunted Writing*, Ronell figures writing as a mode of conversation, which "tells us, among other things, that writing never occurs simply by our own initiative: rather, it sends us."[30] Responding to something like an ethical summons, the writer first of all receives, writing only inasmuch as s/he is written, addressing only inasmuch as s/he is addressed: "writing always comes from elsewhere, at the behest of another, and is, at best, a shorthand transcription of the demand of this Other whose original distance is never altogether surmounted."[31] Conversation, which takes place in the between of the I and the you, holds an us together only by keeping the "I" and the "you" separate, exposing within an experience of profound intimacy an infinite distance, an uncrossable abyss. So long as we are engaged in conversation, I can't get a fix or a grasp on you—you remain both unbearably close and inaccessible. Though I can neither appropriate nor fuse with you, however, I must respond to you, orient myself toward you with seemingly boundless generosity. This generosity does not come from me, as if it were simply my choice, but overwhelms me, possesses me: "even where there is generosity," Ronell writes, "it is somehow compelled; it is the command performance issued by some unknown force that we can only welcome."[32]

In this sense, any true conversation involves a kind of haunting; and writing, which amounts to a conversation with the departed (dead or alive), is necessarily an experience of hauntedness: "Once we are so related and drawn to what withdraws, we incline ourselves in fateful submission to a power which comes from far away and for which writing is an offering."[33] Writing, responding to the call of an inappropriable other, already indicates that my presumed spontaneity has been interrupted; being-called drops me into response-only mode, putting my I on assignment and indicating, more significantly, that I may have no other mode. In any case, as long as I am/is conversing with you—responding to you, writing for and from you—I remain(s) your addressee, which means that I am/is ejected from the addressor slot. In the conversation we call writing, my I has no nominative form; it *is* only inasmuch as it responds to the other's call, inasmuch as it is both host and hostage to the other, as Levinas puts it. There is nothing weirder or more depropriating than conversation's apportionment, and the we that it generates never attains anything resembling equality: I always owe(s) you exorbitantly.

Inasmuch as it requires a donation of the I, writing involves a kind of dispossession, a mode of self-departure that can never be quite sure where it's headed. This is why Ronell suggests that to write is, among other things, to be "body snatched." Her work is packed with images of somatic abjection, of the writer's body being taken over by the writing, "overwritten," "hijacked," exploited by

Q. *You've had a great deal to say about "the writer" and "writing," and because what you've said problematizes both concepts, it'll be important for us to tease them through very carefully. Do you consider yourself a "writer"?*

A. In a certain way that question might be too masculinist for me because it suggests some kind of volition, agency, control at the wheel of fortuna or destiny. I would say that I have figured myself as a kind of secretary of the phantom. I take dictation. I would say also that one doesn't call oneself a writer: one is called, or one is convoked to writing in a way that remains mysterious and enigmatic for me. There was nothing that was going to determine this kind of activity or passivity—we still have to determine what writing is, of course. But sometimes I can, in a way, identify with the figures of "writerly being" (*Schriftstellersein*) that Kafka threw up. For example, that of Gregor Samsa, who is this little unfigurable, monstrous fright for his family and workplace, and who has to stay in his room, kind of locked up, flying on the ceiling and attached to the desk. Here is a figure with which I have repeatedly identified—which is to say, there's something monstrous and a little shameful involved in writing, at least in terms of social pragmatics. This sort of logic of the parasite is probably eventually why I wrote about the drug addict and the writer as figures, often paradoxically, of social unreliability, even where their greatest detachment produces minor insurrections, political stalls, and stammers in any apparatus of social justice.

From "Confessions of an Anacoluthon" (pp. 247–48).

writing's expropriating force. Ronell demonstrates, in other words, that writing is often a debilitating and abject experience, that it does not occur without a (physical) price. In stark contrast to romanticized images of the writer as an autonomous and heroic creator, Ronell proposes that the writer, like the addict, operates according to a parasitic logic: s/he is caught up in, even produced by, a network of other voices. "This is why every serious war on drugs comes from a community that is at some level of consciousness also hostile to the genuine writer," she writes, "the figure of drifter/dissident, which it threatens to expel."[34]

According to dominant humanist standards and values, Ronell observes, the writer, although often admired, is also something of a threat and an embarrassment; disabling the action hero, s/he is a little "monstrous" and "shameful," fragilized in some ways, a kind of dip in the road of social pragmatics. Indeed, one figure of writerly-being with whom Ronell identifies is Gregor Samsa, Kafka's enigmatic nonfigure who is a "fright for his family and workplace" and who must remain locked in his room, "under house arrest."[35] Another writerly figure in Ronell's Rolodex of provisional identifications is Emma Bovary, whose generalized abjection, Ronell proposes, is not something from which one can presume to detach but instead "reflects the writer's *common* lot":

On some level, this phasing out of oneself is what happens to all who write, or to all who are inclined toward writing or who are written up by writing—even written *off* by writing. There is no way for you to think, really, that you know to whom you are writing, or that you are going anywhere, or that you are doing anything, in the classical sense of those terms. Emma's housewifely psychosis, her loser's sense of having no one to write to, no audience, is to be honored for its particular scenography of abjection, for its critically depressive qualities and properties.[36]

Confounding "hubristic humanist assumptions," Ronell honors the predicament of radical passivity to which writing attests, embracing this scene of depleted grace as the site of an exceptional responsiveness: writing responds to a responsibility that exceeds the constricted bounds of the subject's intentions.[37] The ethical and writing dispositions are indissociably linked in this responsibility, which, etymologically speaking, comes from *respondere* (to respond) and suggests the (interminable) obligation to respond to the call of the other.

Still, the question that remains for the infinitely obligated addressee (in this case, "the writer"), as Lyotard suggests, is whether what is currently coming through as a call is *really* a call—rather than, for example, a "fantasy."[38] And according to Ronell, this is a permanent question: given the complexity of its destination and destiny, there will be no way to know for sure that a call has been put out, or that it's meant for you, that *you* are the one called. Responding, therefore, cannot be contingent on knowing; indeed, Ronell proposes that the writer's predicament consists simultaneously in a deracinating experience of being-called that interrupts the presumption of spontaneity or self-sufficiency *and* in an experience of undecidability, of radical uncertainty about whether you're being called in the first place.

Ronell's resolutely anxious stance and political edginess result in part from her resistance to any politics of election, to any presumption that the call could be received with certainty, "[a]s if it were ultimately possible to clear the static."[39] According to her, inasmuch as the call prompts an interruption in certitude, it demands not some nihilistic freeze but extreme caution and suspicion: one of the things that the call calls for is a pause in the blind urge to respond as if one were elected. In "The Experimental Disposition: Nietzsche's Discovery of America (Or, Why the Present Administration Sees Everything in Terms of a Test)," Ronell offers George W. Bush as one example of the insolence of uninterrogated response. Invoking a rhetoric of testing—his first remarks on the evening of 9/11 indicated that "we, as a nation, are being tested"—Bush answers what he presumes to be the divinely appointed call by putting out a call to arms. Ronell observes that although he was elected by dubious means, he feels that he is called upon to answer a call: he thus metaleptically ratifies his election by producing the fiction of a static-free call. Ronell, for her part, repeatedly challenges such fictions, homing in on the doubly depropriating predicament of being-called.

In *The Telephone Book,* Ronell boldly proposed that any call, including the "call of conscience," could be a kind of prank call.[40] Two of her more recent meditations on the problematics of the call are collected here, "Slow Learner" and "On the Unrelenting Creepiness of Childhood," both of which spotlight "the performance of a colossal blunder" involving "the naïve and insolent arrogance that consists in responding where no response is invited."[41] Along with Flaubert and Kafka, Ronell acknowledges that such uncalled-for responses "are reflexes of stupidity." Nonetheless, inasmuch as you can never be sure the call is a call or that it's meant for you ("How, precisely, can we *know?*"[42]), she indicates that *any* performance of the inscription involves an "immersion in stupidity": to write, to be "on assignment," is to respond to a call that you can't be certain was sent out.[43]

• • •

As we're on the subject of writing's abjection, I want to admit that I initially imagined that *The ÜberReader* would constitute volume one of Ronell's greatest hits. However, the task of producing such a collection quickly proved impossible for me, first, because I turned out to be incapable of making such fine distinctions among Ronell's radically diverse texts, of distinguishing the great*est* from the merely great. But also because, in any case, such a volume would be huge and daunting. The task of a reader—even if it should be *The ÜberReader*—I finally decided, must be to offer up a manageable and semirepresentative sampling of texts that will appeal both to the new and to the seasoned readers of this oeuvre. I should also note that many of Ronell's most amazing earlier essays are already collected in *Finitude's Score,* and I felt that *The ÜberReader* should clearly distinguish itself from that effort. Therefore, for those just entering Ronell's orbit, I've included at least one selection from each of her books and two classic selections from *Finitude's Score,* which together provide a fairly solid introduction to her work —maybe a kind of gateway drug into the hard stuff. And then for those loyal Ronell fans who have devoured each of her books and collected essays, one by one, I've included a handful of her newest uncollected works and also, as a kind of reward, some of her most kickass talks.

I also want to acknowledge up front that the thematic headings around which these selections are organized do not adequately indicate Ronell's astonishing range, nor do they begin to exhaust the major themes addressed in her work. Several of the texts presented here could easily fit under more than one heading, and the group of texts together suggest many more thematic possibilities. I would like to have found a way to foreground her work on the experience of abandonment, for example, and on cryptonymy. I'd like to have signaled her extraordinary approach to biography more explicitly, as well—you'll understand why when you read the selections collected here on Valerie Solanas and Kathy Acker. I did attempt to include sections organized around her (post)feminist interventions, her nonhumanist reflections on ethics, and her explorations of the politics of contamination—but these turned out to be impossible headings because they describe almost every text Ronell has produced.

In any case, all disclaimers aside, I do think the headings that survived all the tests and cuts offer a kind of sampling of Ronell's most celebrated achievements: She's recognized, for example, as the post-Heideggerian thinker of the call and of its troubled rapport with technology (Part I, "The Call of Technology"). She is known for her fearless examinations of the limits of cognition (Part 5: "The Fading Empire of Cognition") and for her stunning explorations of the meeting ground where psyche runs into soma (Part 3: "Psyche–Soma: The Finite Body"). Both in and out of the academy she is acknowledged for her thoroughly nonreactive analyses of minoritized and/or persecuted figures (Part 2: "Freedom and Obligation: Minority Report on Children, Addicts, Outlaws, and Ghosts"), and Ronell is one of only a small handful of contemporary American thinkers recognized for her deliberations on the nonappropriative, nonfusional relation, on the (im)possible relation with the other *as* other (Part 4: "*Danke! et Adieu:* On Hookups and Breakups").

I'm deeply grateful to Avital Ronell for her inspiring texts and for her responsiveness to my questions and quandaries. I'm also grateful to her for lending me her photo albms and allowing me to select a handful of fabulous shots to share with you here.[44] I'd like to thank Dr. Willis Regier, director of the University of Illinois Press, as well, not only for his wisdom and guidance but also for taking a chance in the late 1980s on a brilliant and outrageous young Germanist who was, at the time, at work on a seemingly improbable book about the telephone and facing considerable institutional static. Thanks also to Gregory Ulmer, Jeffrey Nealon, Shireen Patell, Patrick Helikson, Gil Anidjar, Eduardo Cadava, Victor J. Vitanza, Michelle Ballif, Cynthia Haynes, Rebecca Sabounchi, and Bill Endres for helpful feedback and discerning insights.

Notes

1. Cited in Francis Steegmuller's *Flaubert and Madame Bovary: A Double Portrait* (Chicago: University of Chicago Press, 1977), 283. Ronell cites Steegmuller's citation in *Crack Wars: Literature Addiction Mania* (Lincoln: University of Nebraska Press, 1992), 58.

2. *Finitude's Score: Essays for the End of the Millenium* (Lincoln: University of Nebraska Press, 1994), 3.

3. Ibid., ix.

4. "Confessions of an Anacoluthon: Avital Ronell on Writing, Technology, Pedagogy, and Politics." Interview with Diane Davis in *jac: A Journal of Composition Theory* 20, no. 2 (2000): 248.

5. It would be irresponsible to subject a writer like this one to biographical appropriation, but at this point Ronell's thoroughly cosmopolitan roots do seem to merit a certain consideration: Born in Prague to German-Jewish parents, she spent her early childhood in Ramat Gan, a kind of suburb of Tel Aviv, and then immigrated with her family to New York City by way of Mexico. (Levinas once said to her, "Yes, yours is a familiar itinerary.") On the more scholarly map, she earned her doctorate at Princeton University, studied with Jacob Taubes at the Hermeneutics Institute in Berlin, and then worked with Jacques Derrida and Hélène Cixous in Paris before returning to the States.

6. A few of Ronell's early translations of Derrida's work include "The Law of Genre," *Glyph: Textual Studies* 7 (1980): 202–29; "All Ears: Nietzsche's Otobiography," *Yale French*

Studies 63 (1982): 245–50; "My Chances/*Mes Chances:* A Rendezvous with Some Epicurean Stereophonies," with Irene Harvey, in *Taking Chances: Derrida and Psychoanalysis* (ed. Joseph H. Smith and William Kerrigan, Baltimore: Johns Hopkins University Press, 1984), 1–32; "Otobiographies: The Teaching of Nietzsche and the Politics of the Proper Name," in *The Ear of the Other: Otobiography, Transference, Translation: Texts and Discussions with Jacques Derrida* (ed. Christie V. McDonald, New York: Schocken Books, 1985), 1–38; "A Peine," in *Mémoires: For Paul de Man* (Ed and trans. Cecile Lindsay, Jonathan Culler, and Eduardo Cadava, New York: Columbia University Press, 1986), xxiii–xxv; and "Devant la loi," in *Kafka and the Contemporary Critical Performance: Centenary* (ed. Alan Udoff, Bloomington: Indiana University Press, 1987), 128–49.

7. For her work on the new technologies, see, for example, "Trauma TV: Twelve Steps beyond the Pleasure Principle" (1992) and "Activist Supplement: Papers on the Gulf War" (originally "Support Our Tropes II," 1992)—the former is reprinted here, and both are collected in *Finitude's Score: Essays for the End of the Millennium,* 305–27 and 293–304. For her early essays on AIDS, see "Queens of the Night" (1983) and "The Worst Neighborhood of the Real" (1989)—a selection from the former is reprinted here as "A Note on the Failure of Man's Custodianship," and both are collected in *Finitude's Score.*

8. The text, of course, is *Crack Wars,* the lexicon and trajectory of which inspired, in large part, the recent collection *High Culture: Reflections on Addiction and Modernity* (ed. Anna Alexander and Mark S. Roberts, Albany: State University of New York Press, 2002). The editors of that volume describe Ronell and Derrida as "innovators in the field of rhetoric and addiction," noting that Ronell both facilitated the translation of Derrida's "La rhétorique de la drogue" and "extended it to produce an important theoretical site for addiction studies in America" (xii). Derrida later extended *Crack Wars,* as well: in a lecture given at New York University in 2001, he proposed that the fate of the hospital is intricately connected to the addicted body that emerges in "Ronell's pathbreaking reflections" ("Substitution: La drogue, l'hôpital, l'hospitalité").

9. These redescriptions take place, respectively, in *The Telephone Book: Technology, Schizophrenia, Electric Speech* (Lincoln: University of Nebraska Press, 1989); "Trauma TV: Twelve Steps beyond the Pleasure Principle," in *Finitude's Score: Essays For the End of the Millennium* (Lincoln: University of Nebraska Press, 1994); *Dictations: On Haunted Writing* (Bloomington: Indiana University Press, 1986/Lincoln: University of Nebraska Press, 1993); and *Crack Wars: Literature Addiction Mania.*

10. See *Stupidity* (Urbana: University of Illinois Press, 2002).

11. See *The Test Drive* (Urbana: University of Illinois Press, 2005).

12. Ronell has been the subject of numerous independent films and documentaries, and she has been interviewed in a variety of forums, from the glossy pages of *Mondo 2000* ("Avital Ronell: On Hallucinogenres," issue no. 4, 63–69) to the airwaves of the BBC (*BBC Cultural Critique,* radio interview, March 1, 2002, London and New York). A few

of Ronell's more recent film appearances include Kirby Dick and Amy Ziering Kofman's *Derrida* (California and Sundance, 2002), Arno Boehler's *The Call* (Vienna, 2001), and Caspar Stracke's *The Circle's Short Circuit* (Berlin, 1998/99), the latter two of which spotlight her work on "telephonic logic." Another recent testimony to Ronell's cult status is Jonathan Lethem's recent novel, *The Fortress of Solitude* (New York: Doubleday, 2003), in which she debuts as Avital Rampart, one of Berkeley's pantheon of theory stars:

> Guy d'Seur was more than Abigale Ponders's thesis advisor, he was a Berkeley celebrity. Forget being a rock critic—forget even being a rock musician. The professors of the various graduate departments were the stars that wowed this burg. To walk into a Berkeley cafe and find seated before a latte and scone one of the Rhetoric or English faculties' roster of black-clad theorists—Avital Rampart, Stavros Petz, Kookie Grossman, and Guy d'Seur formed the current pantheon—was to have your stomach leap up into your throat. In Berkeley these were the people who hushed a room. (313)

13. *diacritics* 24.4 (winter 1994). All of Culler's comments, here and following, are from page 3.

14. "Confessions of an Anacoluthon," 273–74.

15. *Stupidity*, 63.

16. "The Worst Neighborhoods of the Real," 223.

17. Derrida's *Glas* had not yet been translated. It came out in English a year later, in 1990, also with the University of Nebraska Press and courtesy of Ronell's editorial and design team: Willis Regier and Richard Eckersley, the former now with the University of Illinois Press.

18. "Confessions of an Anacoluthon," 274.

19. "Is It Happening?" 325, this volume.

20. Ibid., 324.

21. *Roland Barthes by Roland Barthes* (trans. Richard Howard, Berkeley: University of California Press, 1977), 50.

22. *Stupidity*, 101–5.

23. Ibid., 156.

24. "Toward a Narcoanalysis," 128, this volume.

25. *Stupidity*, 4–5.

26. "Activist Supplement," 300. For Levinas's comment, see *Totality and Infinity: An Essay on Exteriority* (trans. Alphonso Lingis, Pittsburgh: Duquesne University Press, 1961), 134.

27. "The Disappearance and Returns of the Idiot," 169, this volume.

28. "Confessions of an Anacoluthon," 259–60.

29. *Otherwise than Being: Or beyond Essence* (trans. Alphonso Lingis, Pittsburgh: Duquesne University Press, 2000), 141–42.

30. *Dictations,* 149, this volume.

31. Ibid., 150.

32. Ibid., 150.

33. Ibid., 149.

34. *Crack Wars,* 106.

35. "Confessions of an Anocoluthon," 256.

36. Ibid., 255.

37. Ibid., 258. When asked about her decidedly post-humanist approach, Ronell responded: "[T]here are different protocols of marking experience, and to arrive at some sensible reading of those protocols, one should no longer be tethered irrevocably to humanist delusions—delusions for which I have the greatest respect, of course. But humanism often functions like a drug that one really ought to get off of in order to be politically responsible" ("Confessions," 258–59).

38. *The Differend: Phrases in Dispute* (trans. Georges Van Den Abbeele, Minneapolis: University of Minnesota Press, 1988), 107–8.

39. "On the Unrelenting Creepiness of Childhood: Lyotard, Kid-Tested," 116.

40. "So the voice that comes from me and from beyond me can be a phony one, it can miss the point, performing and inducing fraud, putting a metaphysics of identity on hold" (45).

41. "Slow Learner," 268, this volume.

42. Ibid., 269.

43. Ibid., 269.

44. A few of my favorite photos did turn out to be unreproducible, too dark or too light, and I regret the loss of four in particular: one of Avital walking with Larry Rickels to Heidegger's Hütte in Todtnauberg in 1984, another of her with Pierre Alferi in Tübingen near the Hölderin Tower around the same time, one of her decked out in a punkish mini-skirt in Santa Barbara with Shireen Patell and John Muse in 1989, and a rather famous shot of Avital with Kathy Acker on Kathy's motorcycle in the early 1990s.

Front cover: "Avi Goes to Princeton, "
photo ID with Kafka's top hat, '74.

Jacques and me — testing out a new theory on the Master, '04.

Photo by Jean-Luc Nancy

After a seminar at Berkeley—
Philippe Lacoue-Labarthe, Ann Smock,
Chris Fynsk, Katherine Rudolph,
and me, '89.

Marguerite, Jacques, me, and Jean—
Strangers in Beverly Hills '88
Photo by Jean-Luc Nancy

With Jean-Luc:
Being Singular Plural
at Pis Orangis '04.

Photo by Hélène Nancy

Punning on the
palms in
Miami '02.

Photo by
Mario Lozano

Climb Every Mountain — Judith Butler,
me, and Diane Davis reading one another's'
work in the Alpine regions of Switzerland.

Photo by Kiri Close

Pierre captures the historical moment:
me, Suzanne Doppelt, and Peter Connor, '86.
Photo by Pierre Alferi

Portrait of family stability
in the World Trade Center, '96, Tom, Ami,
Mom, Littik, me, & Astrid von Chamier.

Photo by an obliging waiter.

Koan lecture at the European
Graduate School, '03.
Photo by Diane Davis.

The ÜberReader

Part One
The Call of Technology

Q. *Would you characterize your approach to technology as posthumanist?*

A. Yes, I certainly would, though I might have to pause and explicate the meaning of "post." Still, I look to technology to affirm those aspects of posthumanism that are more liberatory and politically challenging to us. As I said, one of my concerns has been with television. Beyond the thematizations of crime, murder, and the production of corpses that don't need to be mourned, I am very interested in the way television stages and absorbs trauma, the way it puts in crisis our understanding of history and the relation of memory to experience. All of these aspects of the televisual that I have tried to read, as you indicate, presuppose a posthumanist incursion into these fields or presume that a posthumanist incursion has been made by these technological innovations (or philosophemes, as I like to call them). On a terribly somber note, I don't see how, after Auschwitz, one can be a humanist.

My work has concerned itself with the Nazi state as the first technologically constellated polity as well as with the fact that technology is irremissible. Mary Shelley projected this view of technology with her massive, monumental, commemorative work on the technobody, which was the nameless monster. The problem with (or opening for) technology is that no one is or can stay behind the wheel, finally, and no one is in charge. And the way I have tried to route and circuit the thinking of technology—indeed, in a posthumanist frame—exposes the extent to which it belongs to the domain of testing. This view has little to do with hubristic humanist assumptions. . . .

Technology has produced different registers of being, or is reflective of different registers of being, and even our rhetoric of desire has been steadily technologized. We say we're "turned on," we're "turned off," and so on. We also say we "had a blast," which indicates a nuclear desire in desire. Nonetheless, there are different protocols of marking experience, and to arrive at some sensible reading of those protocols, one should no longer be tethered irrevocably to humanist delusions—delusions for which I have the greatest respect, of course. But humanism often functions like a drug that one really ought to get off of in order to be politically responsible. I think it is irresponsible not to be Nietzschean in this sense of risking the greatest indecency, of crossing certain boundaries that have seemed safe and comfortable and are managed at best by general consensus. Posthumanism is not necessarily popular with those who hold the moral scepter at this point. But I think it would be regressive and cowardly to proceed without rigorously interrogating humanist projections and propositions. It would be irresponsible not to go with these irreversible movements, or "revelations of being," so to speak. That sounds a little irresponsible, too, since it's a citation of Heidegger. But that's just it: one is precisely prone to stuttering and stammering as one tries to release oneself from the captivity of very comfortable and accepted types of assignments and speech. An incalculable mix of prudence and daring is called for.

From "Confessions of an Anacoluthon" (258–59).

Delay Call Forwarding

. . . . And yet, you're saying yes, almost automatically, suddenly, sometimes irreversibly. Your picking it up means the call has come through. It means more: you're its beneficiary, rising to meet its demand, to pay a debt. You don't know who's calling or what you are going to be called upon to do, and still, you are lending your ear, giving something up, receiving an order. It is a question of answerability. Who answers the call of the telephone, the call of duty, and accounts for the taxes it appears to impose?

The project of presenting a telephone book belongs to the anxiety registers of historical recounting. It is essentially a philosophical project, although Heidegger long ago arrested Nietzsche as the last philosopher. Still, to the extent that Nietzsche was said to philosophize with a hammer, we shall take another tool in hand, one that sheds the purity of an identity as tool, however, through its engagement with immateriality and by the uses to which it is put: spiritual, technical, intimate, musical, military, schizonoid, bureaucratic, obscene, political. Of course a hammer also falls under the idea of a political tool, and one can always do more than philosophize with it; one can make it sing or cry; one can invest it with the Heideggerian *cri/écrit,* the *Schreiben/Schrei* of a technical mutation. Ours could be a sort of tool, then, a technical object whose technicity appears to dissolve at the moment of essential connection.

When does the telephone become what it is? It presupposes the existence of another telephone, somewhere, though its atotality as apparatus, its singularity, is what we think of when we say "telephone." To be what it is, it has to be pluralized, multiplied, engaged by another line, high strung and heading for you. But if thinking the telephone, inhabited by new modalities of being called, is to make genuinely philosophical claims—and this includes the technological, the literary, the psychotheoretical, the antiracist demand—where but in the forgetting of philosophy can these claims be located? Philosophy is never where you expect to find it; we know that Nietzsche found Socrates doing dialectics in some backstreet alley. The topography of thinking shifts like the Californian coast: "et la *philosophie* n'est jamais là où on l'attend," writes Jean-

Luc Nancy in L'oubli de la philosophie.[1] Either it is not discoverable in the philosopher's book, or it hasn't taken up residence in the ideal, or else it's not living in life, nor even in the concept: always incomplete, always unreachable, forever promising at once its essence and its existence, philosophy identifies itself finally with this promise, which is to say, with its own unreachability. It is no longer a question of a "philosophy of value," but of philosophy itself as value, submitted, as Nancy argues, to the permanent *Verstellung,* or displacement, of value. Philosophy, love of wisdom, asserts a distance between love and wisdom, and in this gap that tenuously joins what it separates, we shall attempt to set up our cables.

Our line on philosophy, always running interference with itself, will be accompanied no doubt by static. The telephone connection houses the improper. Hitting the streets, it welcomes linguistic pollutants and reminds you to ask, "Have I been understood?" Lodged somewhere among politics, poetry, and science, between memory and hallucination, the telephone necessarily touches the state, terrorism, psychoanalysis, language theory, and a number of death-support systems. Its concept has preceded its technical installation. Thus we are inclined to place the telephone not so much at the origin of some reflection but as a response, as that which is answering a call.

Perhaps the first and most arousing subscribers to the call of the telephone were the schizophrenics, who created a rhetoric of bionic assimilation—a mode of perception on the alert, articulating itself through the logic of transalive coding. The schizophrenic's stationary mobility, the migratory patterns that stay in place offer one dimension of the telephonic incorporation. The case studies which we consult, including those of the late nineteenth century, show the extent to which the schizo has distributed telephone receivers along her body. The treatment texts faithfully transcribe these articulations without, however, offering any analysis of how the telephone called the schizophrenic home. Nor even a word explaining why the schizo might be attracted to the carceral silence of a telephone booth.

But to understand all this we have had to go the way of language. We have had to ask what "to speak" means. R. D. Laing constructs a theory of schizophrenia based, he claims, on Heidegger's ontology, and more exactly still, on Heidegger's path of speech, where he locates the call of conscience. This consideration has made it so much the more crucial for us to take the time to read what Heidegger has to say about speaking and calling, even if he should have suspended his sentences when it came to taking a call. Where Laing's text ventrilocates Heidegger, he falls into error, placing the schizo utterance on a continent other than that of Heidegger's claims for language. So, in a sense, we

6

never leave Heidegger's side, for this side is multifaceted, deep and troubling. We never leave his side but we split, and our paths part. Anyway, the encounter with Laing has made us cross a channel.

Following the sites of transference and telephonic addiction we have had to immigrate in this work to America, or more correctly, to the discourse inflating an America of the technologically ghostless above. America operates according to the logic of interruption and emergency calling. It is the place from which Alexander Graham Bell tried to honor the contract he had signed with his brother. Whoever departed first was to contact the survivor through a medium demonstrably superior to the more traditional channel of spiritualism. Nietzsche must have sensed this subterranean pact, for in the *Genealogy of Morals* he writes of a telephone to the beyond. Science's debt to devastation is so large that I have wanted to limit its narrative to this story of a personal catastrophe whose principal figures evolved out of a deceased brother. Add to that two pairs of deaf ears: those of Bell's mother and his wife, Mabel Bell.

Maintaining and joining, the telephone line holds together what it separates. It creates a space of asignifying breaks and is tuned by the emergency feminine on the maternal cord reissued. The telephone was borne up by the invaginated structures of a mother's deaf ear. Still, it was an ear that placed calls, and, like the probing sonar in the waters, it has remained open to your signals. The lines to which the insensible ear reconnects us are consternating, broken up, severely cracking the surface of the region we have come to hold as a Book.

Even so, the telephone book boldly answers as the other book of books, a site which registers all the names of history, if only to attend the refusal of the proper name. A partial archivization of the names of the living, the telephone book binds the living and the dead in an unarticulated thematics of destination. Who writes the telephone book, assumes its peculiar idiom or makes its referential assignments? And who would be so foolish as to assert with conviction that its principal concern lies in eliciting the essential disclosure of truth? Indeed, the telephone line forms an elliptical construction that does not close around a place but disperses the book, takes it into the streets, keeping itself radically open to the outside. We shall be tightroping along this line of a speculative telephonics, operating the calls of conscience to which you or I or any partially technologized subject might be asked to respond.

The Telephone Book, should you agree to these terms, opens with the somewhat transcendental predicament of accepting a call. What does it mean to answer the telephone, to make oneself answerable to it in a situation whose gestural syntax already means yes, even if the affirmation should find itself followed by a question mark: Yes?[2] No matter how you cut it, on either side of the line, there is no such thing as a free call. Hence the interrogative inflection of a yes that finds itself accepting charges.

To the extent that you have become what you are, namely, in part, an automatic answering machine, it becomes necessary for questions to be asked on the order of, Who answers the call of the telephone, the call of duty, or accounts for the taxes it appears to impose? Its reception determines its *Geschick,* its destinal arrangement, affirming that a call has taken place. But it is precisely at the moment of connection, prior to any proper signification or articulation of content, that one wonders, Who's there?

Martin Heidegger, whose work can be seen to be organized around the philosophical theme of proximity, answered a telephone call. He gave it no heed, not in the terms he assigned to his elaborations of technology. Nor did he attempt in any way to situate the call within the vast registers of calling that we find in *Being and Time, What Is Called Thinking?,* his essays on Trakl or Hölderlin, his Nietzsche book. Heidegger answered a call but never answered to it. He withdrew his hand from the demand extended by a technologized call without considering whether the Self which answered that day was not occupied by a toxic invasion of the Other, or "where" indeed the call took place. We shall attempt to circumscribe this locality in the pages that follow. Where he put it on external hold, Heidegger nonetheless accepted the call. It was a call from the SA Storm Trooper Bureau.

Why did Heidegger, the long-distance thinker par excellence, accept this particular call, or say he did? Why did he turn his thought from its structure or provenance? Averting his gaze, he darkens the face of a felt humanity: "man is that animal that confronts face to face" (I, 61). The call that Heidegger did but didn't take is to take its place—herein lies the entire problematic: where is its place, its site and advent? Today, on the return of fascism (we did not say a return to fascism), we take the call or rather, we field it, listening in, taking note. Like an aberrant detective agency that maps our empirical and ontological regions of inquiry, we trace its almost imperceptible place of origin. Heidegger, like the telephone, indicates a structure to which he has himself only a disjunctive rapport. That is to say, both the telephone and Martin Heidegger never entirely coincide with what they are made to communicate with; they operate as the synecdoches of what they are. Thus Heidegger engineers the metonymical displacements which permit us to read National Socialism as the supertechnical power whose phantasms of unmediated instantaneity, defacement, and historical erasure invested telephone lines of the state. These lines are never wholly spliced off from the barbed wires circumscribing the space of devastation; calls for execution were made by telephone, leaving behind the immense border disturbances of the oral traces which attempt to account for a history. Hence the trait that continues to flash through every phone call in one form or another, possessing characteristics of that which comes to us with a receipt of acknowledgment or in the hidden agency of repression: the call as decisive, as verdict, the call as death sentence. One need only consult the literatures trying to contain the telephone in order to recognize the persistent trigger of the apocalyptic call. It turns on you: it's the gun pointed at your head.

This presents the dark side of the telephonic structure. Kafka had already figured it in *The Trial, The Castle,* "The Penal Colony," "My Neighbor." The more luminous sides—for there are many—of grace and reprieve, for instance, of magical proximities, require one to turn the pages, or perhaps to await someone else's hand. Take Benjamin's hand, if you will, when he, resounding Bell, names the telephone after an absent brother ("mein Zwillingsbruder"). The telephone of the Berlin childhood performed the rescue missions from a depleted solitude: Den Hoffnungslosen, die diese schlechte Welt verlassen wollte, blinkte er mit dem Licht der letzten Hoffnung. Mit den Verlassenen teilte er ihr Bett. Auch stand er im Begriff, die schrille Stimme, die er aus dem Exil behalten hatte, zu einem warmen Summen abzudämpfen.[3] So even if you didn't catch the foreign drift, and the telephone has no subtitles, you know that the danger zone bears that which saves, das Rettende auch: calling back from exile, suspending solitude, and postponing the suicide mission with the "light of the last hope," the telephone operates both sides of the life-and-death switchboard. For Benjamin, for the convict on death row, for Mvelase in Umtata.[4] Let it be said, in conjunction with Max Brod's speculations, that the telephone is double-breasted, as it were, circumscribing itself differently each time, according to the symbolic localities marked by the good breast or the bad breast, the Kleinian good object or bad object. For the telephone has also flashed a sharp critique at the contact taboos legislated by racism. We shall still need to verify these lines, but let us assume for now that they are in working order and that the angel's rescue is closely tied to the pronouncement of killer sentences.

Just as Heidegger, however, by no means poses as identical to that for which he is made to stand—as subject engaged on the lines of National Socialism—so the telephone, operating as synecdoche for technology, is at once greater and lesser than itself. Technology and National Socialism signed a contract; during the long night of the annihilating call, they even believed in each other. And thus the telephone was pulled into the districts of historical mutation, making epistemological inscriptions of a new order, while installing a scrambling device whose *décryptage* has become our task. Never as such on the side of truth, the telephone became an open accomplice to lies, helping to blur sentences that nonetheless exercised executive power. Don't get me wrong. The asserted side of truth was even more pernicious, sure of its aim and the aims of man. Activated as truth's shredding machine, the telephone, at this moment, became the channeling mechanism for massive disowning. To a large extent, the calls were unsigned.

This work, which was written before the Heidegger affair became an issue of general concern, anticipates some of the urgency with which one tries to grasp the political seduction of a Heidegger. However, where Victor Farías has scrambled connections, largely reducing technology to a mere mention, he sets up a roadblock to *thinking* National Socialism and its others.* To the extent that we continue to be haunted by National Socialism and are threatened by its return from the future, it seems necessary to open the question of politics beyond a proper name that would displace thinking to a subjective contingency. I am less curious about Mr. Heidegger's fantasy of becoming the Führer's Führer—he momentarily wanted to teach and inflect "destiny"—than compelled to recognize in Heidegger's thinking the ineluctable signaling of democracy's demise. Heidegger failed democracy (the way a teacher fails a class, but also the way one fails a task, an *Aufgabe*) on the grounds of technology. His thinking of the *essence* of technology, for which he claims a different status than technology, forces us to consider how the human subject has been refashioned in the "current talk about human resources, about the supply of patients for a clinic," and body count.** It is Heidegger who poses the greatest challenge to those of us who want to shatter the iron collar of fascism's continued grip on the world. By naming technology the greatest danger that democracy faces, Heidegger, citing Hölderlin, has tried to locate the saving power, too ("das Rettende auch"). Heidegger's crucial questioning concerns the possibility for a free relation to technology. We shall have to backtrack scrupulously in order to discover the unfreedom for which he became a loudspeaker. He was not the only one, nor certainly the crudest of those who were hooked onto a state apparatus of disastrous technological consequences. Heidegger saw the danger, and he called it. And yet, Heidegger experienced the danger too late, which is why we have had to route his thinking on the essence of technology—this has everything to do with death machines—through a delay-call-forwarding system. That is

---

*See in particular the interview with Victor Farías conducted by Crocker Coulsen for *Minerva: Zeitschrift für Notwehr und Philosophie*, no. 93/4 (Summer 1988): 25. When asked whether he perceives a link between Heidegger's critique of technology and National Socialism, Farías responds with a series of reckless cliches that serves to close off rather than expand the field of unprobed intensities shared by technology and the terroristic state.

**The Question Concerning Technology* (New York: Harper and Row, 1977), 18.

to say, the asserted origin of Heidegger's relation to National Socialism began with the call of technology that has yet to get through to us.

The German telefilm *Heimat* (1987) organizes part of its narrative around the erection of a telephone system. The telephone connects where there has been little or no relation, it globalizes and unifies, suturing a country like a wound. The telephone participates in the myths of organic unity, where one discerns a shelter or defense against castration. A state casts a net of connectedness around itself from which the deadly flower of unity can grow under the sun of constant surveillance. In contract, we have tried to locate telephones that disconnect, those that teach you to hang up and dial again. Of course the telephone does not "explain" National Socialism or, for that matter, any state in its totality; rather, it offers a certain untried access code to a terrorism that, in the first place, is technologically constellated. It is in any case my only inroad, for I can't get any closer. And yet, in defense of my project, I might say that this length of distance is something which totalitarianism could not ever hope to take. When it zeroed in on meaning and confined signification to a tightly throttled regimen, submitting it to the sting of imposed sense, totalitarianism was also making an attempt to crush the real. But existence absolutely resists such an imposition of close range signification. In a genuinely revolutionary text, Jean-Luc Nancy links fascism and Nazism precisely to phantasms of immediacy which are opposed to indefinite mediation. Our telephone junction, at points along its trajectory, tries to dialogue with Nancy's "présence-à-distance," the questions linking freedom to long-distance and other modulations of the call.

These are some of the historical and theoretical premises that have made it seem desirable to dissolve the Book into a point of contact with the Bell system—something that in itself reflects an uncanny history which I felt compelled to trace. Still, with the telephone on the line, one could not simply write a biography as if nothing had come between the *bios* and the graph. One had to invent another form, that of biophony, where the facts of life fall into a twilight zone between knowing and not knowing, between the rather crude ground of empiricity and the more diaphanous heights of speculation. If anything, we have invited Bell and his assistant Watson to speak in order to put a stop sign before technological machismo, and to ask one to listen again to the eerie and altogether hair-raising beginnings forming the implacable fact of the telephone. As proof of the good faith that has guided this procedure, I offer a portion of our biophony, prior to the Survival Guide, appended as a story without specularity and one in fact that, like the telephone, is pregnant with this other. It was a path cut between orality and writing on the edge of a dispersion where absence and exile became the rule.

11

Why the telephone? In some ways it was the cleanest way to reach the regime of any number of metaphysical certitudes. It destabilizes the identity of self and other, subject and thing, it abolishes the originariness of site; it undermines the authority of the Book and constantly menaces the existence of literature. It is itself unsure of its identity as object, thing, piece of equipment, perlocutionary intensity or artwork (the beginnings of telephony argue for its place as artwork); it offers itself as instrument of the destinal alarm, and the disconnecting force of the telephone enables us to establish something like the maternal superego. Of course Derrida and others cleared the way. They built the switch. For Freud, the telephone, while exemplifying unconscious transmissions, set off the drama of an unprecedented long distance. There is always a child left behind, or the face of a distant friend translated sonically into a call. And there was always a Heidegger pulled into fascism by the strangulating umbilicus of a telephone cord whose radius he failed to measure. There were other orders of strangulations for which the telephone was made to feel responsible, and these, too, shall fall under our gaze. To trace these calls, the conditions of a long distance that speaks, and the many toxic invasions waged by telephone, it seemed necessary to start with the absolute priority of the Other to the self, and to acknowledge the constitutive impurity that obliges a self to respond to its calling .. ..
.. ..
.. .. **AR**.. .... **AREA CODE 415**

The scopic field narrows,   music accompanies

some of these figurations.　　　　Lights dimming.　　　　Another foreign tongue.

LA VOIX HUMAINE

——*Si, mais très loin. . .*

　　　　　　　　　　　　　　　　—*Toi, tu m'entends?*

—*Ce fil, c'est le dernier qui me*
　rattache encore à nous.

　　　　　　　　　　　　　　　　—*Je m'étais couchée*
　　　　　　　　　　　　　　　　avec le téléphone—

—*Si tu ne m'aimais pas et si*
　tu étais adroit, le téléphone
　deviendrait une arme effrayante.
　Une arme qui ne laisse
　pas de traces, pas de bruit.

A terrifying weapon leaving no traces. Her fear of being cut off from him intensifies. She wraps the cord around her neck.

—*J'ai ta voix autour de mon cou.*

Is she hanging or strangling herself? You can't decide, you can't cut it. The
receiver falls to the ground.

. . . .

. . . . **"It's for You"**

A structure that is not equivalent to its technical history, the telephone, at this stage of preliminary inquiry, indicates more than a mere technological object. In our first listening, under the pressure of "accepting a call," the telephone in fact will emerge as a synecdoche of technology. As provisional object—for we have yet to define it in its finitude—the telephone is at once lesser and greater than itself. Perhaps because the telephone belongs as such to no recognizable topos or lends itself to an *athetic* response, picking it up, especially in Heidegger and in World War II, can by no means produce a reading without static on the line. We shall constantly be interrupted by the static of internal explosions and syncopation—the historical beep tones disruptively crackling on a line of thought. To sustain our reading against the crush of repressive agencies, busy signals, and missed connections, something like the "rights of nerves" will be newly mobilized.[5] Suppose we begin by citing Heidegger in a decidedly aphilosophical mood when, in angry reaction to a reporter's persistent claims, he responds to a certain genre of transmission problems:

HEIDEGGER:
Das ist eine Verleumdung.
That's a slander.

SPIEGEL:
Und es gibt auch keinen
Brief, in der dieses Verbot
gegen Husserl ausgesprochen
wird? Wie wohl ist dieses
Gerücht wohl aufgekommen?
And there is no letter
in which such a prohibition is
recorded? How did the
rumor come about?

HEIDEGGER:
Weiss ich auch nicht, ich finde
dafür keine Erklärung. Die
Unmöglichkeit dieser ganzen
Sache kann ich Ihnen
dadurch demonstrieren, was
auch nicht bekannt ist. *(I,9)*
It's beyond me. I've no
explanation for it. I can show you
the unlikelihood of the
accusation.[6]

To be sure, Husserl's name is doubly cut off when it finds itself missing in the translation. And perhaps because Heidegger is about to "demonstrate," his mood is not so aphilosophical after all. Heidegger poses himself as a kind of unscrambling device for a massively entangled historical narrative whose other end somehow involves a telephone call. In the passage cited the call is being set up; Heidegger has not yet made the connection, technologically fitted, to the hollow of the state. What does it mean to begin a telephone call by quoting the rumor? Or rather, by having Heidegger quoted? Not just Heidegger whose proper name resonates with imperial dignity but the Heidegger cited above (the interview appeared when Heidegger was no longer here)—to borrow a subtitling phrase from Nietzsche, the Heidegger "for everyone and no one," the philosopher who put himself into circulation after his death.   Part of his destinal mark was to have been made in a newspaper article, the space of *Gerede's* loudspeaker, which, roughly speaking, refers us to the lower agencies of language transaction. It is beyond Heidegger, the speaker is quoted as saying. We all know what "the rumor" concerns. More or less. In any event, its epistemological authority is such that no further naming seems necessary in order to establish a ground of sound referential effects. In a gesture that rumorological paranoia exacts, the subject will want to settle his debt with rumorous transmissions in a structure of "after-my-death," in the very fragile place where rumor encounters itself, the supplementary issue, in this case, the *Spiegel.* To quell "the rumor" in a weekly journal, Heidegger turns it over to a telephone system for declassification. This is the line that will engage us here. Throughout the ensuing conversations we shall wonder whether there is not something perturbing about the philosopher's explication with a forum of public opinion which splices answerability into the technological instances that Heidegger himself regarded with suspicion. Has Heidegger wanted to bequeath his most urgently authenticated confession to a discourse of *Gerede?* In other words, is Heidegger's last word, made to be articulated after his death, a stroke against his philosophy, a woundingly ironic utterance made against the grain of his thinking (what does it mean for a Heidegger to intend to tell the truth in a newspaper?), or will his afterworldly in-the-world discourse force a rethinking of language's housing projects?   It is not that we are listening for a prior continuity which telephone wires would cable into the language of Heidegger, his War Words or *Spiegel* reflections. In some respects, Heidegger's work including his final interview, hooks up the telephone as if to simulate answerability where it in fact creates a scrambling device whose decoding strands it nonetheless enjoins us to follow. It is Heidegger himself who poses the telephone. He poses it at this junction, almost as if he wished to supply the want of an ethics. It has been said that Heidegger has no Ethics. This brings us to the problem to be raised by the Central Exchange of our system, where empirical guilt and the Heideggerian theory of guilt seem to share the same operator.   This is a serious problem promoted by an oeuvre that provides itself with a manual, a directory assistance that makes such connections inevitable, at once calling them forth and wanting to annul them. Yet, if the interview containing the telephone call is a ruse or a scrambling device intentionally installed by the philosopher, then he still isn't given over to laughter. Whether this is because Heidegger would never strike such a pose of subjective mastery—perhaps he would not wish to assert, in the sense of Baudelaire, the idea of a superior being—or whether nonlaughter marks a more sinister conviction will have to remain open to an answer temporarily out of service. While it is necessary to elude the confusion of situating a purely empirical/anthropological reading of guilt within a theoretically grounded one, it must be recognized that for Heidegger the relations between anthropology and ontology are not simply external ones. Indeed, Philippe Lacoue-Labarthe has shown the thematization in Heidegger of the empirical and historical figure cut by the philosopher.[7]

The time has come to record the message, to listen in a gathering way to what has been said within the interstices of two beep tones.

Let us wind up this recording around the major points it appears to have urged. Heidegger accepted a call. In Lacan's sense we call this predicament the transfer of power from the subject to the Other.[8] In this case, the other happens to be the top command of the Storm Trooper University Bureau. Heidegger traces his relationship to National Socialism to this call, asserting thereby the placeless place where the other invaded him, the nondiscoverable place or moment when the connection was to have taken place. He does not report a face-to-face meeting, but we shall arrange this momentarily. The scene can be teletyped for review according to two preliminary aspects. First, Heidegger's compromise with National Socialism marks an arrangement with a supertechnical power. Second, Heidegger in fact elaborates an idea of *techné* that largely stands under the shadow of the negative. It has a contract out on Being, tightening its corruption, its veiling and forgetting. The coherency of these two aspects will lead us to examine whether it is not precisely owing to his theory of technology (*Technik*) that Heidegger was engaged on the Nazi Party line. Later, Heidegger would locate himself at a remove from National Socialism by linking the movement to technology. But if Heidegger can be embarked in the adventure of National Socialism in the first place, this occurs to the extent that there is something which he resists in technology, hoping it can be surmounted like the grief or pain one feels in the human realm over a loss. We shall have to put a search on this unmarked grief through which Heidegger mourns the figure of technology. Or even more to the point, Heidegger *wants* to mourn technology, but it proves to be unmournable as yet, that is, undead and very possibly encrypted.   In large, constative terms, we shall have to concern ourselves here with the contours of another, somewhat displaced horizon through which it may be claimed that no fundamental distance establishes itself between the technical, natural, human, or existential worlds, no purity or absolute exteriority of one of these to the other. But Heidegger has produced, let us say quickly, a naive reading of technology whose philosophically inflected and historical effects require rigorous examination. It is as if he thought there were something beyond the radical rupture in Being which technology involves—another relation to Being, more original than that supplied by a technological emplacing; and this possibility he identifies at one point with the Nazis. Still, what is nazism if not also the worst moment in the history of technology?[9] "Worst" can serve as a rhetorical qualification of "moment," which may not be restricted or an indication of closure. The worst moment in the history of technology may not have an off switch, but only a modality of being on. Let me formulate this pointedly so that the telephone can begin its job of condensing and displacing questions of desire and extermination, war machines and simulators, within the apparatus of a peace time: before the time of *Gelassenheit,* when Heidegger fails to consider that technology cannot be surmounted, surpassed, or even perhaps sublated, he walks into a trap. I want to trace this trap to one day, one event. I am going to take the same call several times, and then try to move beyond it.

18

Rector's Office

Rector's Office

Husserl, whose name suffered erasure by Heidegger under the same regime—Heidegger had deleted the dedication to *Sein und Zeit*—was removed from the offices which Heidegger now occupies. Husserl was not there to answer; he would not even answer to his name. The mentor had had his telephone removed. During Heidegger's tenure a telephone was reinstalled.[10] These gestures are connected to the paternal belly of the state by the umbilical of the telephone. The scene was technologically set for Heidegger to take the call. Preliminarily we shall argue that what came through on that day was a certain type of call of conscience. Why did he answer precisely this call? Or say he did? Is he not trying to give it the same existential legitimacy, trying to make it the same type of call that *Sein und Zeit* describes? Simply asked, what is the status of a philosophy, or rather a *thinking,* that doesn't permit one to distinguish with surety between the call of conscience and the call of the Storm Trooper? This raises a first point.   The other point is organized around Heidegger's technological blind spot as concerns the telephone, which can be grasped as a way to measure his commitment ontologically to divest technology. Accepting the call by missing the point—that is to say, missing the appointment of the other call, its "significance"—Heidegger thus demonstrates the force by which to gauge his attempt to secondarize, ontologically speaking, technology. To the degree that his concept of technology is blind or lacking, it is guilty of his alliance of power with nazism. Of course, to the extent that he underreads technology, Heidegger cannot be identified, purely and simply, with the self-constitution of National Socialism. He himself says that he was accused by the party for his "private National Socialism." But the status of what he says is shaky, particularly since it has run on rumorological grounds, a history of dissimulation and silence. On his own subject, on the subject of the Third Reich, Heidegger never stopped playing telephone. The mark to be made here, the incision, indicates the surface of a weakly held limit between technology and Being. Technology, while by no means neutral, but a field of fascination, is viewed as potentially covering an authentic relation to Being. It is from this point onward that claims are made for a relation to Being more original than the technically assumed one.[11]   To be sure, the notation of a Being that would enfold technology only by hesitant parasitical inclusion, has received expression from the "other" side of the line. In a recently disclosed letter to Heinrich Vangleer, Einstein wrote from Berlin in 1917: "All our lauded technological progress—our very civilization—is like the axe in the hand of the pathological criminal."[12] The aberrant course traced by technopathology engages a risk of blindness as if the axe could be surrendered and the criminal appeased, as if, indeed, there were a truer law

21

of Being into which technology were cutting a pathology. However, Einstein was not instituting an ontology—a discourse on Being which presupposes the responsibility of the "yes," as Derrida writes: "Yes, what is said is said, I respond or 'it' responds to the call of Being."[13] Einstein, then, was not taking on an ontology or saying yes to a call, he was definitively disconnected from the supertechnical powers which drew the open ear of Heidegger. In addition, he only took a call from Princeton . . . .

. . . . **The Maternalizing Call**

As we heard ourselves say, the telephone is a synecdoche for technology. It is less than itself but also the greater, as in the maternalizing call of *What is Called Thinking?* A number of things might be put on this account. Lecture 5 of this text opens the telephone book. It is mysterious and compelling. It wants to teach teaching. The mother calls her boy home, opening his ears but also teaching him a lesson. She appears, if only sonically, at a long distance. A certain oedipedagogy is taking shape here—the restoration of contact is in the making, initiated by a mother whose navel, in Joycean terms, would emit signals. The navel is the third eye, closed, knotted, the eye of blindness. Whatever the lesson of the mother, which turns into a desemanticized Nietzschean scream, telephonic logic means here, as everywhere, that contact with the Other has been disrupted; but it also means that the break is never absolute. Being on the telephone will come to mean, therefore, that contact is never constant nor is the break clean.   Such a logic finds its way through much of the obliterature that handles these calls. Heidegger's *What Is Called Thinking?* names Nietzsche in the passage to the ear canal. In a way that comes through clearly, this call has been transferred from Nietzsche before it is returned to him. One should think of Nietzsche on the mother tongue.[14] Deformed by the educational system whose condition she remains, she makes you become a high-fidelity receiver on a telephonic line rerouted by interceptors to the state. This is the telelogic of the Nietzschean critique whose access code runs through "On Redemption." The bildopedic culture has produced itself out of a combinatory of lack ("for there are human beings who lack everything") and excess ("one thing of which they have too much"); it constellates the human subject telephonically.[15] Figuring the human thus first undermines visual security: "for

22

the first time I did not trust my eyes and looked and looked again, and said at last, 'An ear! the tremendous ear was attached to a small, thin stalk—but this stalk was a human being! If one used a magnifying glass one could even recognize a tiny envious face; also that a bloated little soul was dangling from the stalk.'"[16] That Nietzsche's texts are telephonically charged is clarified in *Genealogy of Morals,* where he writes of a "telephone to the beyond," which arguably is the case with every connection arranged by such a switchboard.[17] It is Joyce who excites the hope that an explicit link might be forged between the call to the beyond and a maternal connection which we hear enunciated in Heidegger's exposition:

Boys, do it now. God's time is 12.25 [twenty-five minutes past the Nietzschean mid-day, therefore]. *Tell Mother you'll be there. Rush your order and you play a slick ace. Join on right here! Book through eternity junction, the nonstop run.*[18]

The little boys tell mother they'll be there. While here, which is never "here," they are booking it through eternity junction, cathecting onto the gamble of the book. All the while mother is on the line. What links this act to the calling apparatus of state? Don't forget, though: we are not reading an indifferently occupied state but one which destined itself to the ear, in terms achieved by Hélène Cixous, to the jouissance of the ear.[19] The ear has been addicted, fascinated. And just as Hamlet's father, head of state, overdosed on the oto-injection ("in the blossoms of my sin"), the ghostly *Spiegel*-interlocutor, speaking from the beyond, utters the news of technology's infectious spread, beginning with a phone call. Again, and forever, why did Heidegger accept this particular call? Through which orifice did nazism pass in Heidegger? He has already told us. In terms of an entirely different intensity (but is it so different?), in "The Madonna's Conception through the Ear" Ernest Jones convincingly shows the ear to cover for the displaced anus.[20] This demonstration has received security clearance from subsequent psychoanalytic claims on the matter. Yet, we are not addressing a multiplicity of ears but one ear, technologically unified against the threat of a narcissistic blowout. The jouissance of the ear was felt by a whole nation, whether it was listening to Wagner or to the constant blare of the radio, which is said to have hypnotized a whole people, a tremendous national ear.[21]   Heidegger's ear was trained on the telephone. It was what Maurice Blanchot calls "fascinated." He answered the call. The blindness associated with any call assumes proportions that are difficult to name but which nonetheless can be circumscribed. A problematics of image obliteration engages the telephone, and even the rhetoric surrounding it. The telephone sinks away as a sensory object, much as the mother's figure disappears. When Heidegger mentions being-on-the-telephone, it is not meant to coagulate into an image. The call was fleetingly arranged, like a sonic intrusion. The Nazis were not in sight, they were the hidden and private eyes to whom Heidegger spoke. Visual apprehension on the retreat, supplanted by the dead gaze: these constitute elements brought together in "The Essential Solitude" of Blanchot. A dead gaze, "a gaze become the ghost of eternal vision," stares fixedly from his text, which listens to the Heidegger text which it quietly repeats.[22] In a way, the call of *What Is Called Thinking?* is taken up, transferred or translated to "the force of the maternal figure," which itself gradually dissolves into the indeterminate They (33). Following the telepath of Heidegger, Blanchot induces a stage of telephonics in which he regards the vanishing image. The mark of a maternalized hearing which blinds all imaging, he call this "fascination." Why fascination? Seeing, which presupposes distance, a decisiveness which separates, fosters a power to stay out of contact and in contact, to avoid confusion. But he writes of a manner of seeing which amounts to "a kind of touch, when seeing is *contact at a distance*" (32). His focus, if that is the proper way of putting it, fixes fascination—something allows sight to be blinded into a neutral, directionless gleam which will not go out, yet does not clarify. "In it blindness is vision still" (32). This vision has been perturbed; it is a "vision which is no longer the possibility of seeing" (32). Fascinated into the dead gaze, one retreats from the sensory and sense: "What fascinates us robs us of our power to give sense. It abandons its 'sensory' nature, abandons the world, draws back from the world, and draws us along" (32).   Now the transfer or transit is made to the other woman, the one about to speak to us, teachingly, in Heidegger. The habit-forming mother freezes the image into the blinding absence which we have come to call the telephone. Alongside Heidegger's little boy, we encounter the child of Blanchot, transfixing and fascinated, unseeingly drawn by the enchantment of the mother. Blanchot takes a step in the direction of Heidegger by fading a mother into the They, the neutral, impersonal "indeterminate milieu of fascination" (32). As if responding to a query coming from elsewhere, he offers: "Perhaps the force of the maternal figure receives its intensity from the very force of fascination, and one might say then, that if the mother exerts this fascinating attraction it is because, appearing when the child lives altogether in fascination's gaze, she concentrates in herself all the powers of enchantment. It is because the child is fascinated that the mother is fascinating, and that is why all the impressions of early childhood have a kind of fixity which comes from fascination" (33). Blanchot's evocation continues to withdraw itself from sight, effecting a sense of immediacy complicit with absolute distance. The sequence releases the mother, letting her drop out of sight while the subject appears to have achieved cecity: "Whoever is fascinated doesn't see, properly speaking, what he sees. Rather, it touches him in an immediate proximity; it seizes and ceaselessly draws him close, even though it leaves him absolutely at a distance. Fascination is fundamentally linked to neutral, impersonal presence, to the indeterminate They, the immense, faceless Someone. Fascination is the relation the gaze entertains—a relation which is itself neutral and impersonal—with sightless, shapeless depth the absence one sees because it is blinding" (33). We should like to retain the neutral gleam, the sightless depth that sees—a tele-vision without image, not very distant from the annihilating gaze of Lacan, though perhaps less in arms. The texts of Heidegger and Blanchot are not merely practicing the oedipal blindness with which the maternally contacting child is menaced—even if, indeed, it is the mother who calls first. With the possible exception of Cixous's words, little has been said about Jocasta's call, the way she secretly calls the shots and her responsibility. If these texts were repeating the gesture according to which the oedipal gaze is averted, then we should remember that every repetition, to be what it is, brings something new with it. The child has disappeared in the mother. This disappearance or traversal also devours the mother—each the absolute hostage of the Other, caught in a structure that inhibits the desire to cancel a call. Once made, the call indicates the mother as *aufgehoben,* picked up, preserved, and canned. "L'Imprésentable" is the name Philippe Lacoue-Labarthe gives to the essay which shows how the female figure has always been one that Western thought has attempted to "overcome" or wind down (*überwinden*) in its philosophical, aesthetical, and physical dimensions.[23] The child, like philosophy, gains on the mother. The child, as we said, has disappeared in the mother. He is, in Blanchot, there and not there. He has arrived, if sightlessly averting his gaze henceforth, to face the immense, faceless Someone. In Heidegger, though Blanchot does not simply contradict him in this, the child maintains a long distance. Even though it was a local call. The remoteness of the child to the place from which the call was issued is never collapsed into the "immediate proximity" felt, if evanescently, by the Blanchot text. The invading Other doesn't arrive at touching, contaminating the one that is called or in the ontic enclosure that separates the caller from the called; the one is never held hostage by the Other, fascinated or derailed. The Heideggerian remoteness from the call's source guarantees that it will avoid being danger zoned, for it masquerades as the purity of a long-distance call. This detoxified scene of calling is what, in Heidegger, we call into question. In this light, one of the things that we shall need to ponder concerns a tranquil assertion such as one finds in *Being and Time:*

"Being towards Others is ontologically different from Being towards Things which are present-at-hand" (*BT*, 124). While this articulation involves a complex series of designations whose elaborations would require a patient tapping of each term ("Being towards. . .," "present-at-hand"), it can nonetheless be seen to assume a clean ontological separation of Others and Things wherein the Other, as Heidegger states in the same passage, would be a duplicate (*Dublette*) of the Self. The question that we raise before any approach can be made toward this passage or the locality of Other suggests a disposition other than the one disclosed in Heidegger's assertion. The mood we wish to establish is not one of reactivity but of genuine wonder and bewilderment before the statement. At first sight the statement asserts itself as constatively unproblematic: Being towards Others is ontologically different from Being towards Things which are present-at-hand. What is supposed, however, regards not only the difference between modes of "Being towards" but the aim or destination which would know the gap separating Others from Things. Now, what if Others were encapsulated in Things, in a way that Being towards Things were not ontologically severable, in Heidegger's terms, from Being towards Others? What if the mode of Dasein of Others were to dwell in Things, and so forth? In the same light, then, what if the Thing were a *Dublette* of the Self, and not what is called Other? Or more radically still, what if the Self were in some fundamental way becoming a Xerox copy, a duplicate, of the Thing in its assumed essence? This perspective may duplicate a movement in Freud's reading of the uncanny, and the confusion whirling about Olympia as regards her Thingness. Perhaps this might be borne in mind, as both Freud and Heidegger situate arguments on the Other's thingification within a notion of *Unheimlichkeit*, the primordial being not-at-home, and of doublings.   The second type of question, which nags critical integrity, having received only an implicit formulation, concerns the history of, let us say provisionally, a subject of the private sector who normally would be granted diplomatic immunity, sheltered as he is by the structures regulating philosophical politesse. A transgression, authorized by Nietzsche, has permitted us to view the life of a philosopher not as so many empirical accidents external to the corpus of his works. But where Nietzsche constantly affirms the value of dissimulation, including self-dissimulation, Heidegger does not.[24] Thus it is not clear that we already know what, in this instance, involves self-presentation and a statement of identity. In Nietzsche's heterobiography, *Ecce Homo*, we know that the self will fail to reappropriate itself; in Heidegger's journalistic disclosures we know no such thing. At any event, the referential pathos of this explication leaves room for serious refutation. This order of bewilderment, granted a Nietzschean pass, has permitted us to open the case on two infinitely non-reciprocal texts, linking *Sein und Zeit* (henceforth *SuZ*) and the *Spiegel* interview. Is the call of conscience readable in terms of a telephone call? We suggest this to be the case. More precisely, perhaps, can one rigorously speaking utter Dasein's anonymous calling in the same breath with the call taken by a historical subject whose identity papers, civil status, and telephone personality name a "Martin Heidegger"? A receptionist must know how connections are tolerably made, determining which opening will establish communication between two parties or two things—in brief, she must understand how to manipulate the switchboard or she would lose her post ....

.. ..
....
.. ..
.. ..
....,, ...
....
....
.. ..
....
.. ..
....
....
.. ..
....
....
.. ..
.. ..
....
....
....
.. ..
....
.. ..
....
....
.. ..
.. ..
....

Classified

1. Jean-Luc Nancy, *L'oubli de la philosophie* (Paris: Galilée, 1986), 56.

2. Laurence A. Rickels, in *Aberrations of Mourning: Writing on German Crypts* (Detroit: Wayne State University Press, 1988), 395, offers a line on the yes-saying that accrues to the telephone by treating the postulation of a no: "Freud argues that there is no *no* in the unconscious: instead, things are more or less cathected—*besetzt* (occupied). According to both Freud and Kafka, there is no *no* on the phone." The yes which the telephone calls to itself should at no point be confused with Nietzschean affirmation, however, which requires a double yes threaded through the eternal return of the Same. This is why it is necessary to begin with the telephone as the pose of reactivity—a suspension, as Rickels argues, of the *no*.

3. Walter Benjamin, "Berliner Kindheit um Neunzehnhundert: Telephon," in *Illuminationen,* Ausgewählte Schriften (Frankfurt: Suhrkamp, 1961), 299–300.

4. See the syncopated drama of frantic telephone calls and incarceration in Janet Levine's "Out of South Africa," *New York Times Magazine,* September 20, 1987, section 6.

5. The topos of *enervation* as critical impetus can be situated within a historical typology of mood, or *Stimmung*. The age of nerves, while no doubt beginning to stir in the corpus of Nietzsche's works, has acquired its peculiar heuristic value through Walter Benjamin, who has introduced the "rights of nerves" as a principle of reading and valuation in his essay on Karl Kraus: "He found that (the nerves) were just as worthy an object of impassioned defense as were property, house and home, party, and constitution. He became an advocate of nerves" (*Reflections,* trans. Edmund Jephcott [New York: Harcourt Brack Jovanovich, 1978], 261; *Illuminationen* [Frankfurt: Suhrkamp, 1955]). And if we were to follow a reading that creates a kind of strategic enervation?

6. *I,* 12. The translation repeats the exclusion of Husserl. The relationship of rumor to a telephonic logic is by no means contingent, as Rickels, *Aberrations of Mourning,* 288, confirms: "*Gerücht* (rumor) is linked etymologically to *Ruf* (call) and even in the sixteenth century, for example, was virtually synonymous with *Geschrey* (scream). That is, *Ruf,* which means not only call but also name and reputation, is related to *Gerücht* which, as a collective noun, signifies a great many, if not too many, calls."

7. Philippe Lacoue-Labarthe presented as supplement to his thesis an interpretation of Heidegger's politics (*La fiction du politique: Heidegger, l'art et la politique* [Strasbourg: Association de Publications près les Universités de Strasbourg, 1987]) which further permits us to understand Heidegger's engagement in terms of the call: "Les énoncés (sur l'Allemagne, sur le travail, sur l'Université, etc.) sont purement et simplement programmatiques et s'organisent du reste en de multiples 'appels' [The statements (on Germany, on work, on the University, etc.) are purely and simply programmatic; these

28

statements are organized, moreover, according to multiple 'calls']" (18). Before considering the question of Heidegger's calls, Lacoue-Labarthe elects to situate a reactivity of deafness: "Etre ou se dire 'heideggérien' ne signifie donc rien, pas plus qu'être ou se dire 'anti-heideggérien.' Ou plutôt cela signifie la même chose: qu'on a manqué, dans la pensée de Heidegger, l'essentiel; et qu'on se condamne à rester sourd à la question qu'à travers Heidegger pose l'époque [To be or to consider oneself a "Heideggerian" does not mean a thing, not more than being or considering oneself "anti-Heideggerian." Or rather, this means the same thing: that one has overlooked what is essential in the thinking of Heidegger, and that one is thus condemned to remain deaf to the question that made its mark through Heidegger]" (16). See also his review of Victor Farías's *Heidegger et le Nazisme* in *Le Journal Littéraire*, no. 2 (December 1987–January 1988): 115–118, which in more general terms argues that Heidegger's political involvement with fascism is neither an accident nor an error but ought to be treated first of all as a fault in thinking. Heidegger, however, began establishing a philosophical distance to the state in *Introduction to Metaphysics* (1935) and through his *Schelling* (1936), where he very clearly disputes the confusing mergers of the official philosophy of value, the concept of world and lived experience (*Erlebnis*), as well as anti-Semitic discrimination in philosophical thought (particularly in terms of Spinoza). Lacoue-Labarthe reminds us of Mrs. Heidegger's article on girls in the Third Reich, which, if you ask me, is laced with some of Mr. H.'s rhetoric.

8. Jacques Lacan, "The field of the Other and Back to the Transference," *The Four Fundamental Concepts of Psycho-Analysis*, trans. Alan Sheridan (New York: Norton, 1977), 203–260; *Le séminaire de Jacques Lacan, Livre XI, 'Les quatre concepts fondamentaux de la psychanalyse'* (Paris: Seuil, 1973).

9. A number of somewhat unmapped access roads to fascism have been discovered by way of the aestheticization of forms in the totalitarian state. An aesthetic will to power has been most recently treated in Lacoue-Labarthe's *Fiction du politique*, where the author discerns the roots of a "national aestheticism." Our decoding systems are engaged here on a more technological register of commanding utterance. We attempt to situate the peculiar idiom of nazism—as does, no doubt, Lacoue-Labarthe—historically after the death of god, when the transcendental ceiling came crashing down and every body was on the line. The telephone installs itself as directory assistance for all other technological executions, asserting a place of a nearly traceless politics of denunciation, ideological clarification (Heidegger on the phone to Jaspers praising the Führer's beautiful hands), extermination. The committee for the Wannsee Conference of 1942, where the "final solution" was passed, depended on the telephone, initiating a whole politics of telephone ordering systems. For a well-considered reading of the Third Reich and general technology, consider Jeffrey Herf, *Reactionary Modernism: Technology, Culture, and Politics in Weimar and the Third Reich* (Cambridge: Cambridge University

Press, 1984). The detail of Herf's book is presupposed by our argument, of which two phrases can be provisionally isolated at this time: "Although technology exerted a fascination for fascist intellectuals all over Europe, it was only in Germany that it became part of the national identity" (10). "German anticapitalism was anti-Semitic but not anti-technological" (9). See also Gert Theunissen, "Der Mensch der Technik," in *Der Deutsche Baumeister,* no. 2 (Munich, 1942), and L. Lochner, *Goebbels Tagebücher* (Zurich, 1948), to get a sense of the "pure present" and abolition of History desired by National Socialism. In his review of Suzanne Lorme's translation of J. P. Stern, *Hitler—Le Führer et le peuple,* introduced by Pierre Aycoberry (Paris: Flammarion, 1985), Eric Michaud suggests nazism's desire for disjunctive instantaneity and the technological imperative. The Führer's rhetoric, though full of jarring contradiction (his discourse concerning "the Jews in each of us," his *speeches* against speaking and for pure action, etc.), in its perlocutionary character, tended to stress a "Führer-unmittelbarer Entscheidung," a kind of unbendable immediacy (1030). This immediacy tends to be held together by a notion of magic and the "magic vision" that the Führer attributes to himself and grafts onto technology. Michaud makes a footnote out of this link which needs a magnifying gaze to set it in relief. After citing Herman Rauschning's *Hitler m'a dit* (Paris: Coopération, 1939) on Hitler's surpassingly magic vision which allows him to overcome the Christian God, he adds: "Il est vrai que la technique a permis cette illusion de toutepuissance et surtout d'*omniprésence* divine du Führer: de l'automobile à l'avion, de l'effigie infiniment reproduite à la transmission radiophonique, la technique pouvait donner ce sentiment de l'immédiat propre à la fulgurance de l'action magique, qui dissout les barrières de l'espace et du temps sensibles [It is true that technology allowed for this illusion of the divine omnipotence, and especially the divine *omnipresence* of the Führer: from the automobile to the aeroplane, from the infinitely reproducible effigy to radiophonic transmission, technology could give that feeling of immediacy known in the fulguration of the magic act which could dissolve the sensible barriers of space and time]" (1029; trans. Peter T. Connor, hereafter PTC). Michaud links the irrepresentable space of a pure present to the devouring fire of an "immediate action." From this angle it might be offered that, in the Nazi state, even art is submitted to technology to the extent that it has always ever been a "tool": "C'est aussi pourquoi il n'y a pas d' 'art nazi': il n'y a qu'un usage de l'art, de la médiation de l'art et de la pensée pour contraindre les hommes à l'action immédiate, de même qu'il y a, dans les camps de la mort, usage des victimes pour leur propre anéantissement [This is also why there is no "Nazi art." There is only a use of art, a mediation of art and thought so as to force men into immediate action, in the same way that, in the death camps, the victims were used for their own annihilation]" (Eric Michaud, "Nazisme et représentation," In *Critique: Revue générale des publications française et étrangères* 43, no. 487 [December 1987]: 1034; trans. PTC).

While nazism was phantasmatically invested in technology, a nuance should be signaled: Hitler himself apparently lagged behind the projects and projections of his scientific subordinates. To his comparative "naiveté" in the regime of potential technologies, we seem to owe the suspension in Germany of plans to build an atomic bomb and advances in aviation. The representations which Hitler understood and to which he had access were, in terms of what was projected as possible—if necessary, global destruction—relatively crude and simple. It should be clear that we are not speaking here of the effects of Hitlerian death machines, but merely pointing out his limited technovision in terms of what was asserted to be materially at hand. Laurence A. Rickels's "Final Destination," in *Aberrations of Mourning*, discovers the body counts that will help future researchers link Hitler's rapport to technology with his bunker/crypt (161–162).

10. In the section of his article entitled "Der Einsatz des Mediums: Schalten" in "Pronto! Telefonate und Telefonstimmen" (*Diskursanalysen 1: Medien*, ed. F. A. Kittler, M. Schneider, and S. Weber [Opladen: Westdeutscher Verlag, 1987]), Rüdiger Campe produces evidence for Husserl's telephobic strain. "Edmund Husserl hat das Telefonieren offenkundig nicht geliebt. Der Philosophieprofessor in Göttingen besass (1900–1916) keinen Anschluss, der Ordinarius in Freiburg hatte von 1916–1920 eine Nummer, dann schaffte er sie für beinahe die ganze übrige Amtszeit ab [This information has been retrieved from state and university libraries in Karlsruhe, Hannover, and Göttingen.] Wenn die These vom impliziten Thema Telefon bei Husserl gehalten werden kann, deutet das auf eine 'hinterhältige Verwandschaft' der Phänomenologie zwar nicht zu den 'empirischen Analysen des Menschen,' aber zum medientechnischen Alltag des philosophen [It was publicly known that Edmund Husserl had no love for telephoning. This professor of philosophy in Göttingen (1900–1916) did not own a hookup; this Ordinarius in Freiburg had a number between 1916 and 1920, but then disconnected it for nearly the entire remainder of his tenure. If the thesis can be maintained that there exists an implicit telephone theme in Husserl, this points to an 'underhand relationship' of phenomenology not to the 'empirical analyses of a person' but rather to the quotidian media-technical life of the philosopher]" ("The Engaging of the Medium: Switching on [the Line]" in "Pronto! Telephone Calls and Telephone Voices," trans. Anna Kazumi Stahl, hereafter AKS).

11. A mode of revealing, technology models different readings in the so-called early and later Heidegger. *Die Technik und die Kehre* did not appear until 1962 (Pfullingen: Günther Neske), while *Vorträge und Aufsätze*, containing "Die Frage nach der Technik," was published in 1954, also by Günther Neske. By the time of this essay, Heidegger asserts: "Everywhere we remain unfree and chained to technology whether we passionately affirm or deny it. But we are delivered over to it in the worst possible way when we regard it as something neutral; for this conception [*Vorstellung*] of it, to which today we particularly like to do homage, makes us utterly blind to the essence of technology" (*TQCT*, 4). Early in the essay, building his way to the place of questioning technology,

Heidegger raises the issue of "being responsible and being indebted." "Today we are too easily inclined either to understand being responsible and being indebted moralistically as a lapse, or else to construe them in terms of effecting. . . . In order to guard against such misinterpretations of being responsible and being indebted, let us clarify the four ways of being responsible in terms of that for which they are responsible" (*TQCT,* 9). Still, the chief characteristics of technology as that which Heidegger comes to call "the challenging revealing" is that "everywhere everything is ordered to stand by, to be immediately at hand, indeed to stand there just so that it may be on call for a further ordering" (*TQCT,* 17). He calls whatever is ordered about this way the "standing-reserve" (*Bestand*). Whatever "stands by in the sense of standing-reserve no longer stands over against us as object" (*TQCT,* 17). Yet "an airliner that stands on the runway is surely an object. Certainly. We can represent the machine so. But then it conceals itself as to what and how it is. Revealed, it stands on the taxi strip only as standing-reserve, inasmuch as it is ordered to ensure the possibility of transportation. For this it must be in its whole structure and in every one of its constituent parts, on call for duty, i.e., ready for takeoff. . . . (Seen in terms of the standing-reserve, the machine is completely unautonomous, for it has its standing only from the ordering of the orderable.)" (*TQCT,* 17). Near the end of the essay Heidegger evokes the essence of technology in a mood of apprehension, "holding always before our eyes the extreme danger. The coming to presence of technology threatens revealing, threatens it with the possibility that all revealing will be consumed in ordering and that everything will present itself only in the unconcealedness of standing-reserve. Human activity can never directly counter this danger. Human achievement alone can never banish it," and so forth (*TQCT,* 33). This comes on the footsteps of the hierarchical difference that Heidegger has installed to protect technology against another abyssal risk, that of parasitic contamination, or what Derrida calls an "anoppositional differance" (*Memories for Paul de Man,* trans. Cecile Lindsay, Jonathan Culler, and Eduardo Cadava [New York: Columbia University Press, 1986], 140).

> "What is dangerous is not technology, there is no demonry of technology, but rather there is the mystery of its essence. The essence of technology, as a destining of revealing, is the danger. . . . The threat to man does not come in the first instance from the potentially lethal machines and apparatus of technology. The actual threat has already affected man in his essence. The rule of Enframing threatens man with the possibility that it could be denied to him to enter into a more original revealing and hence *to experience the call of a more primordial truth*" (*TQCT,* 28; italics added and trans. modified).

It would be compelling to trace the calls that explicity are placed in *TQCT,* of which we engage only one instance: the moment in which Heidegger has Plato accepting the call of Ideas for which he cannot claim the right of invention, as he only responded to them. "The thinker only responded to what addressed itself to him" (*TQCT*, 18). One trait that will distinguish Heidegger's later take on technology resides in the *Ge-stell*, translated by William Lovitt and others as "Enframing," which, fundamentally, is a calling forth. It is, writes Lovitt, a "challenging claim," a "demanding summons that 'gathers' so as to reveal" (*TQCT*, 19). I feel that it becomes necessary not to bypass Heidegger's memory of *Gestell*, something that we might assign to the bodybuilding of Mary Shelley's *Frankenstein*, whose "frame" occupies scenes of nomination. Listen: "According to ordinary usage," starts Heidegger, "the word *Gestell* (frame) means some kind of apparatus, e.g., a bookrack. *Gestell* is also the name for a skeleton. And the employment of the word *Ge-stell* (Enframing) that is now required of us seems equally eerie, not to speak of the arbitrariness with which words of a mature language are thus misused. Can anything be more strange? Surely not. Yet this strangeness is an old usage of thinking" (*TQCT*, 20). Even though it is elsewhere achieved in the spirit of denial, there is no reading of technology that is not in some sense spooked, even when Heidegger displaces the focus to *Ge-stell*, at whose basis a skeleton rises. The eerie, uncanny dimension of technology is precisely what engages us, as is the rapport to grief or loss within Heidegger's techno-hermeneutics of mourning: In "The Turning," writing on the restorative surmounting of the essence of technology, Heidegger uncharacteristically designs a wounding (*wunden*) which is to be dressed, covered over, overcome: "the coming to presence of technology will be surmounted (*verwunden*) in a way that restores it into its yet concealed truth. This restoring surmounting is similar to what happens when, in the human realm, one gets over grief or pain" (*TQCT*, 39). The surmounting of Enframing, as a surmounting of a destining of Being, is precisely what causes us to pause and wonder. Perhaps "the essence" of Heidegger's dream of restorative overcoming might be located in this sheltered allusion to a grief or pain under promised anesthesia. What would constitute the successful mourning but another forgetting? What was this thinking trying to overcome, subdue, and carry over to a convalescent home of Being?

To resume, Heidegger, in *TQCT*, wants to bring to light our relationship to its essence. The essence of modern technology, he writes, shows itself in *Ge-stell*, Enframing. But simply to indicate this still fails to answer the question concerning technology, "if to answer means to respond, in the sense of correspond" (*TQCT*, 23). You see, *TQCT* is itself posed as a call to which Heidegger responds in the sense of correspond. So much is by this time on call: "It is stockpiled; that is, it is on call" (*TQCT*, 15). The split, however, is a bit too clean, for Enframing is "nothing technological, nothing on the order of a machine. It is the way in which the real reveals itself as standing-reserve. . . ." Above all, "never too late comes the question as to whether and how we actually admit ourselves into that wherein Enframing itself comes to presence" (*TQCT*, 24). As if elaborating the problematic within which we, like Kafka's land surveyor, wander, Heidegger articulates the lesson of discernment now, as if, again, he responds to our call; this time he picks up the relay saying yes, OK, I see your point: "For man becomes truly free only insofar as he belongs to the realm of destining and so becomes one who listens and hears [*Hörender*], and not only one who is simply constrained to obey [*Höriger*] (*TQCT*, 25). Finally, we note Harold Alderman's conclusion of his essay "Heidegger's Critique of Science and Technology," which ends on a sense of futurity that, once again, promises a beyond technology to which we raise our questions: "We are all finally technicians and if we are to be at home in our own world we must learn to accept that fate as both a gift and a burden. With this acceptance will come the chance of moving beyond technology. Thus the burden of science and technology lie not in their calculative style but rather in their insistent and aggressive spirit. It is, surely, part of Heidegger's point that the same trait would be pernicious in any style of thought" (In *Heidegger and Modern Philosophy: Critical Essays*, ed. Michael Murray [New Haven: Yale University Press, 1978], 50). Beginning with Heidegger's unpublished essay, "Die Gefahr" (Danger), Wolfgang Schirmacher reflects some of these concerns by writing: "Seine radikale Analyse der modernen Technik entdeckt uns auch einen Ausweg aus ihr [His radical analysis of modern technology also discloses for us a way out]." See his impressive reading of how metaphysics fulfills itself in modern technology in *Technik und Gelassenheit: Zeitkritik nach Heidegger* (Freiburg/München: Verlag Karl Alber, 1983), 21.

12. Albert Einstein, *The Collected Papers of Albert Einstein*, vol. 3, *The Berlin Years: 1914–1933*, ed. John Stachel (Princeton: Princeton University Press, 1987). At about the same time, Norbert Wiener initiated a profound discussion of the fundamental revolution in technique in which he links telephonic theorems to cybernetics. See *Cybernetics, or Control and Communication in the Animal and the Machine* (Cambridge: Technology Press of M.I.T., 1949) and *The Human Use of Human Beings: Cybernetics and Society* (Boston: Houghton Mifflin Company, 1950).

13. Jacques Derrida, *Ulysse gramophone: Deux mots pour Joyce* (Paris: Galilée, 1987), 108.

14. See Jacques Derrida, "Otobiographies: The Teaching of Nietzsche and the Politics of the Proper Name," trans. A. Ronell, in *The Ear of the Other: Otobiography, Transference, Translation*, ed. Christie V. McDonald (New York: Schocken Books, 1985), 21–22; originally *L'oreille de l'autre*, ed. Claude Lévesque and Christie V. McDonald (Montreal: Vlb Editeur, 1982): "Today's teaching establishment perpetrates a crime against life understood as the living feminine. . . . There has to be a pact or alliance with the living language of the living feminine against death, against the dead. The repeated affirmation—like the contract, hymen, and alliance—always belongs to language: it comes down and comes back to the signature of the maternal, nondegenerate, noble tongue. . . . History or historical science, which puts to death or treats the dead, which deals or negotiates with the dead, is the science of the father. . . . the good master [teacher]

trains for the service of the mother whose subject he is; he commands obedience by obeying the law of the mother tongue and by respecting the living integrity of its body" (21–22).

15. Friedrich Nietzsche, "On Redemption," in *Thus Spake Zarathustra* (New York: Penguin Books, 1987), 138; *Also Sprach Zarathustra, Friedrich Nietzsche Werke III* (Berlin: Ullstein, 1969), 321.

16. Nietzsche, "On Redemption," 138.

17. Nietzsche evokes the telephone, a kind of transcendental SPRINT to the beyond, in *Genealogy of Morals;* but already in the stages of foreplay that figure "the seduction of the ear," Nietzsche, in *The Birth of Tragedy,* starts wiring his texts telephonically. In the competition between phenomenal image and the sonic blaze, who would be so petty as to deny the possibility that Dionysus is a telephone? "The Dionysian musician is, without any images, himself pure primordial pain and its primordial re-echoing" (*The Basic Works of Nietzsche,* trans. Walter Kaufmann [New York: Random House, 1969], 50; *Die Geburt der Tragödie, Werke in zwei Bänden* vol. 1 [Munich: Carl Hanser, 1967]).

18. James Joyce, *Ulysses* (New York: Random House, Vintage Books, 1961), 153. I offer thanks to my colleague, Professor John Bishop, for the discussion we had in the summer of 1987, tapping into Joycean telephonics and the absent tense. *Notes from my stenopad:* "Origin of space in the maternal body. Origination, Genesis beginning: 'Hello Hibernia! Matt speaking. Lucas calling, hold the line.' 'Spraining their ears, listening and listening to the oceans of kissening, with their eyes glistening. *psadatelopholomy, the past and present (Johnny Mac Dougall speaking, give me trunks, miss!) and present and absent and past and present and perfect *arma virumque romano. (Finnegan's Wake* [New York: Viking Press], 258) 'phone man on mogapnoised (technical term for difficulty in speaking). remarkable clairaudience. I am amp amp amplify. 77 saywhen saywhen static Babel whoishe shoishe, (499–500). Priority call clear the line. Joyce talking to son in NY—the devil was playing havoc with static. 'moisten your lips for a lightning strike and begin again. TELLAFUN BOOK.' breaks, ruptures abortive attempts for connection. supernatural access to the world. Television kills telephony in brothers' broil. 'Our eyes demand their turn. Let them be seen!' Cut to Balbec. Proust's grandmother. spectral agents like nymphs of the underworld who conduct spirits of humans into the flickering present. phone as umbilicus. conversation broken off. Premonition of her death. // killer telephones catalyst: bomb explosions. phone-booth confessional: phones within phones. Musil's man. Also *Der Schwierige.*"

19. This was first emitted in Hélène Cixous's lecture of November 15, 1982, at the "Colloque pour James Joyce" at the Centre Georges-Pompidou, and can now be read as "Joyce: The (R)use of Writing" in *Post-Structuralist Joyce: Essays from the French,* ed. Derek Altridge and Danie Ferrer (Cambridge: Cambridge University Press, 1984). Derrida's commentary runs: "pour relancer ce qu'Hélène Cixous vient de nous dire; la

scène primitive, le père complet, la loi, la jouissance par l'oreille, *by the ear* plus littérale-
ment, par le mot d' 'oreille,' selon le mode 'oreille,' par exemple en anglais et à supposer
que jouir par l'oreille soit plutôt féminin [To bring up again what Hélène Cixous has
just said to us: the primal scene, the complete father, law, coming through the ear, more
literally *by the ear,* through the word 'ear,' as in English for example, and which leads
one to suppose that the ear's coming actually belongs to the *feminine* registers].

20. Ernest Jones, "The Madonna's Conception through the Ear," in *Essays in Applied
Psycho-Analysis* (London: Hogarth Press, 1951); originally in *Jahrbuch der Psychoanal-
yse,* vol. 6 (1914). No attempt will be made to resume this richly connoted essay. Jones
addresses the ear and its position of privilege as receptive organ (273), treating among
other elements the pneuma that generates thought and semen (298), noise, Christian
Logos, and "an old German picture which was very popular at the end of the fifteenth
century" (reproduced by P. C. Cahier, *Caractéristiques des Saints dans l'art populaire,*
1867): "In this the Annunciation is represented in the form of a hunt. Gabriel blows the
angelic greeting on a hunting horn. A unicorn flees (or is blown) to the Virgin," etc. A
second example is even less ambiguous, for in it the passage of God's breath is actually
imagined as proceeding through a tube; over a portal of the Marienkappelle at Würzburg
is a relief-representation of the Annunciation in which the Heavenly Father is blowing
along a tube that extends from his lips to the Virgin's ear, and down which the infant
Jesus is descending (reproduced by Fuchs, *Illustrierte Sittengeschichte; Renaissance;
Ergänzungsband* [1909, S. 289]), (331). Further along (345) we read: "We are not told
whether Jesus was actually born, like Rabelais's Gargantua, through his mother's ear,
as well as being conceived through it. . . . That the danger of this form of conception is
regarded by Catholics as not having entirely passed is shown by the custom with which
all nuns still comply of protecting their chastity against assault by keeping their ears
constantly covered, a custom which stands in a direct historical relation to the legend
forming the subject of this essay (see Tertullian, *De Virginibus Velandis*)." We have
isolated the more telephonically constructed illustration of the ear's pregnancy from
which Jones extrapolates anal origins for the immaculate aural conception, the sacred
ear overwhelming the repressed body of earlier anal-sadistic zoning laws.

21. Consider, for example, Alice Yaeger Kaplan's argument in *Reproductions of Banality:
Fascism, Literature, and French Intellectual Life* (Minneapolis: University of Minnesota
Press, 1986), where, in a discussion of radiophony, she momentarily smuggles in the
telephone. It should be noted that Kaplan assimilates a notion of "telephonocentrism"
to a primary model of radiophony, leaving the telephone somewhat out of the order:

> The administrators of fascist radio stations sometimes connected their broadcasting
> success to real crowd-gathering. In the Italy of the 1930s, Mussolini organized a radio
> show called the "Workers, Ten Minutes" that interrupted all activity in factories,

unions, and public squares. But there were other ways to spread the consumption of sound. In Germany, the government imposed mass production of a seventy-six-mark Volksradio, then sold 100,000 of them in one evening at a nationally organized Radio Fair. What about radio in the house? As of 1933, and in the same month that Le Poste Parisien (a French radio station) initiated the first daily "wake-up" weather and news program directed at the private listener, that station also began, as part of its morning diet, a translation of the radio speeches of Hitler, the new chancellor. By 1937, the Popular Front government was aware of radio's potential. . . .

The tension between the radio experience as a private experience and as a public one is at the heart of radio ideology. Radio and telephone were the first electrical "personal appliances," the first electric machines to leave the factories and become "part of the furniture." Radio gave people a sense of intimacy with electricity, a sense of control over technology; at the same time, radio's "wirelessness," the invisibility of its method, made it subject to the greatest mystifications. . . .

It is into this radio world, this ideologically vulnerable space of listening, that Rebatet, as fascist reader, receives the texts of Céline. . . . In a prophetic misreading, the American Federal Communications Commission officials who monitored and transcribed the Italian broadcasts didn't recognize the word Céline and recorded it as Stalin, thus substituting a political totalitarian label for what is now recognizable as the quite specific telephonocentric of a French fascist aesthetics. (135–137)

Kaplan points us to Pierre Sansot's *Poétique de la ville,* which describes "the revolution in perception that accompanied the appearance of radios, telephones, and refrigerators in daily life. . . . His distinction is crucial for an understanding of the fascist as someone excited by the extension of perceptual powers that comes with radio-hearing, aerial viewing, and so on" (141).

22. Maurice Blanchot, *The Space of Literature,* trans. Ann Smock (Lincoln: University of Nebraska Press, 1982), 32; *L'espace littéraire* (Paris: Gallimard, 1955). Page numbers in parentheses refer to Blanchot's chapter, "The Essential Solitude," 19–34.

23. Juliet Flower MacCannell, "Oedipus Wrecks: Lancan, Stendhal, and the Narrative Form of the Real," in *Lacan and Narration: The Psychoanalytic Difference in Narrative Theory,* ed. Robert Con Davis (Baltimore: Johns Hopkins University Press, 1983), 911. Phillippe Lacoue-Labarthe "L'Imprésentable," in *Poétique* 1975): 53–95.

24. See Derrida, *The Ear of the Other,* p. 10: "Forcing himself to say who he is, he goes against his natural *habitus* that prompts him to dissimulate behind masks."

Support Our Tropes

READING DESERT STORM

GOING DOWN IN HISTORY: According to one version, there was a telephone call that did not take place. This is the version of Saddam Hussein. If the Iraqi troops were remarkably immobilized when they were ordered by George Bush to withdraw from Kuwait, this was because Saddam (so the version goes) was stationed at the reception desk of international politics, waiting for Bush's call. Had that call been completed, claimed Saddam on several occasions, he would have honored the demand of the community of nations for which Bush was the principal operator. But George Bush never placed that call, and Saddam Hussein refused to budge. Instead, Bush called in the tropes—or the armies of metaphors and metonymies, as Nietzsche would say, that were to justify war.

If we begin by establishing the story of a disconnected telephone line, this is for a number of reasons. None of these has much to do with the question of credibility on either side because that line of questioning has been scrambled by all parties concerned: the war was less a matter of truth than of rhetorical maneuvers that were dominated by unconscious transmission systems and symbolic displacements but which nonetheless have produced material effects. In the first place, the missed telephone appointment that Saddam Hussein has placed at the origin of the war signals at a primary level the electronic impulses that were flowing between the powers. Whether or not the crucial telephone call was to be made—Bush was relating full on to telephonics for the duration of the war—the atopos of the telephone created a primal site of technological encounter.[1] This was going to be a war of teletopologies, presence at a distance, a war which could have been averted, according to the one version, by a telephone call. Saddam Hussein said he would have transferred the locus of power to the Other, provided the Other wasn't going to be a specular other, a mere counterpart and double. No, Saddam Hussein had to hear himself speak through the locus of the Other if he was to cooperate, or at least feign cooperation with the community of nations. This is precisely what a telephone call accomplishes: it allows transference to take place in a manner that would supercede a stand-off between two egological entities or two continuous subjects; in sum, it programs another algorithm of encounter.

Saddam Hussein, inscribed by Western teletopies and coded by our projection systems, would have answered to his name, he says: he was bound to accept the call, if not the charges. That call, which Saddam said would have made a critical difference in the way the two parties subsequently engaged their lines, never came through. The telecommunicational cast of the Gulf War remains enigmatic (despite so much focus on the participating media technologies), and seems to admit no simple reconstitution of its vicissitudes. For its part, the United States did not put that call through, preferring instead to answer a clearer call to arms. The question is how to trace this call within the dense network of motivation, parapraxes, conscious and unconscious national maneuvers, or even international strategies. The missed call to which Saddam has pointed by no means places him as the principal agency of our inquiry. The point, since there must be one in matters of war, is to take seriously that which disrupted the possibility for communication between US and Them, and between us and us. There is something at play here that goes beyond the desire to institute international law, or even beyond our oil addiction. It has to do with compulsion in politics—something that belongs to another scene of articulation. So, in the first place, why did we refrain from including Iraq on the circuit of collective calls? In part because of the different time zones that rendered any simple connection impossible. For George Herbert Walker Bush is a haunted man, and the Middle East, a phantom territory between the West and its others.

Not that the Middle East was noiseless—ghosts always make their presence known, and sometimes they seem real enough. Except in photo shoots. The call that never came through nonetheless exists. It follows the contours of a disrupted loop or a broken circuit. It presents for us, though in a fugitive manner, an allegory of nonclosure. The Middle East marks the spot to where World War II was clandestinely displaced when its history refused to close upon itself. Political scientists and historians can fill in the blanks better than I could ever hope to, so I will restrict my contribution to pointing to certain mappings of the rhetorical unconscious. This time, when history repeated itself, it was not a joke, but the production of a haunted man to whose systems of repetition compulsion we were all assigned. There was the matter of resurrecting Hitler in the Middle East, and a felt need to control the airspace. The Patriot missile system perforated two phantasmic oppressions: the Germans had never lost air control in World War II, and George Herbert Walker Bush's was the only one of the three planes on mission to go down that day. When the Avenger plunged into the ocean, young Bush, the youngest fighter pilot in the U.S. Navy, lost two close friends. Puking from fear and endless seawater, the youngest pilot started attending a funeral whose site he would never be able to pinpoint.

SON OF SAME: Let me back up. It is not the case *empirically* that the Germans retained air control. But only a naive historicist perspective would disallow the speculative impact historicity genuinely involves. In this analysis, we feel called upon to locate the Gulf War, or the return of the figure of war as such, in the disjunction between empirical history and speculative prolepsis. If we maintain that a major phantasm bequeathed by the Second World War consists in the desire for a certain closure of air, as it were, this is because one of the dimensions of the war that was left unresolved—unmourned—was both generally, and in the particular case of George Bush, located off the map, in the air.

How is it that war has returned as the excess of plenitude and the exercise of sovereignty? To be sure, every war is about the presencing of sovereignty which modern humanism's peace plans, with their absence of grandeur or divine manifestation, have never been able to secure. There is no war—the extreme exercise of sovereign right—that does not claim to disclose a transcendental trace. In this case, technology carried the message from God. But what allowed the sudden remotivation or legitimation of war as privileged space of national sovereignty? The return of war as a sanctioned figure has everything to do with the return call that at once bypassed Saddam Hussein and destined him as proxy and stand-in for an unresolved break in world history. What was it about World War II that was called back at this time? What called scores of military phantoms back into action?

World War II invented carpet bombing, creating fire storms. After the experience of mass destruction and victory, the Allies however concluded that the air war had been ineffective, even to the point of having extended the duration of the war. The scope of destruction and random targetting would remain in holding pattern until, at the time of the Gulf War, we took recourse to nuclear and smart bombs, legitimating, that is, their usage. Not only had the air war been ineffective, but it had created immense resentment among the civilian populations to whom we henceforth owed restitution. Something else came down from the air as well. When it was decided that the atomic bomb would be deployed, this event was not expected to take on a morally ambiguous cast. The atomic bomb was to accomplish what normally, in the course of carpet bombing, would take three days. The atomic bomb was understood merely to amplify the effects of these fire storms. When WWII left the air wide open, therefore we could say that it morally gave notice of an unpaid debt, an account to be settled. For the air had to be disambiguated, rescued and reterritorialized to a just cause. If a just war were ever to be fought again, it would have to restitute to the skies a moral horizon which would communicate with a failure to close WWII. The smart bomb, which addresses itself to that failure, would outsmart the inerasable error of WWII, in other words, it would not *smart*. This is not a play on words, though our war included playing and games. What I am trying to get at is precisely the signifying chains that the phantom of WWII keeps rattling.[2]

• • •

The American unconscious has everything to do with riding signifiers on the re-bound which, subject as they are at times to retooling, nonetheless return to the haunts of the Same. By retooling, we mean that, while increasingly technologiz-ing death, the fundamental idiom hearkens back to the tropes instituted in this century by modern warfare. Thus "collateral damage," for instance, refashions the industrial production of corpses which Martin Heidegger signaled after WWII, where "friendly fire," while minted by the death denial inclination of California, points to the Pacific and the suicide pact which that side of the war staged through the kamikaze. By the Same, we are indicating on another level of discourse that we are guilty of reducing everything to an order of sameness. This is why the very thing responsible for the excess of meaning or the sense of otherness which occupies the Middle East is being systematically obliterated along the same lines of arrest that has kept Mr. Bush in a forty-year daze. The incredible fact that the Iraqi leader was prompted to pose as Hitler's double (Same), in other words, as a by-product of the Western logos (it is grotesque to forget that Adolf Hitler was a *Western* production), in itself demonstrates the compulsive aspect of this war.

We are reading a case study of history that presents itself as a symptom. The symptom is that of historical nonclosure and seems in itself to be arrested within a predicament of nonclosure. This war, which masquerades as being "over" (Joyce: "he war," to be read in the Anglo-Germanic space that is opening up before us),[3] has not properly begun to situate its effects: in short, everything was left in the air. This is one reason the war cannot be read according to tradi-tional protocols of historical investigation, or even along the lines of strategic or tactical analyses. I am tracing a *phantasmic history*. This is not the result of a whim or an effect of subjective contingency. The phantasmic control systems are out of my hands just as this war left a number of us disarmed. On the eve of German reunification, Goebbels's phrase "new world order" leapt out of his diaries to be recircuited through the ventrilocating syntax of George Bush. If

Saddam Hussein was a prop, it is also the case that this concept functionally suited George Bush. Indeed, we are faced here with the projections of a somewhat more original prop who, in order mythically to fill himself out, needed to rerun through the same war that had knocked him out. This corresponds to a mythic structure of return and second chance which, in life, tends to revert either to the happy few or to the severely neurotic. George Bush was one of them—or rather, two of them. At any rate Bush had always been second and secondary. This was his nature, to be a second nature.

Too young at the advent of World War II, he was destined to be late on arrival. Known as the son of Pres Bush, vice prez to the undead Reagan, a simulating machine par excellence, he was to become the uncanny president of the near end of the millennium. Something went into suspense or responded to the clandestine command "Freeze!", when he lost his two friends. It was as if George Bush had been arrested, which is why his iconic relation to his wife, for instance, looks as though he had struck a deal with a soul murderer, giving the couple the disjunctive look of a moment in *Dorian Gray*.

It has been suggested that George Bush had the luck of encountering the Oedipal taboo head on: he was permitted actually (symbolically) to marry his mother, thus turning back the interdictory power of the law. With paternal law falling down, crashing out of the sky, the symbolic register is exposed to the most serious effects of scrambling. In the first place, this predicament maintains him in the position of son, ever competing with an ineffectual father (this was played out with Reagan, whom he all but banished from the White House). Secondly, the prez will have experienced fusional desire and the illicit communions which will have proliferated from this "experience"—we are referring to his special missions directed by God, represented here on earth on the eve of the Gulf War by Billy Graham, with whom Bush spent the night. Perhaps we need to take a closer look at the situation. This look will not constitute the voyeur's gaze into a privately circumscribed space, but will open out onto the unconscious mappings which we are endeavoring to retrieve.

The Bush couple is proud of the generational difference that their union appears to mark. Barbara refuses to mask or suppress the mark of difference that in fact exposes a fusional desire. I am not saying that the male subject should abstain from locating his desire in an "older woman"; that would be absurd and out of sync with the times. I am saying rather that the first couple stages its communion within the precincts of nonhistorical difference. While Barbara Bush has grown into her age—the end of the twentieth century—George Bush will not grow, he cannot age, and this in turn reflects the ahistorical fusions which his tenure accomplishes. (The scandal of difference which the first couple inscribes is displaced on to the family pet, Millie. After Bush was elected prez, the first couple announced the ritual copulation of Millie with a pure breed, which, in dog language, means Aryan. Hence the "Millie-Vanilli" prez who would fuse and simulate histories was to oversee pure generational evolution. Indeed, Millie was so exceptionally evolved that she wrote the autobiography ventriloquized by Barbara Bush. Millie shared not only the couple's secrets but their diseases as well. The phantasms of which Millie Bush is sole receptacle will have to be treated elsewhere.)

While Bush stands arrested, his language spinning accidentally out of control, Barbara withers. She is the figure in the couple who mourns: attributing her gray hair—an overnight job—to the grief she suffered over a deceased child (a Robin), she also took a downward plunge a week before the bombing of Iraq started. Sliding downhill on a sled, Barbara Bush breaks a hip joint. The couple is disjointed, a connection dislocated. With the guilty part and partner externalized and maternalized, George Bush can go on with his business unfeelingly. If he cried uncontrollably at the event of his crash, his language oddly obsessed on his unwillingness to shed a single tear over the dead of the Gulf War (he shared this charming attribute with General Schwarzkopf). There is a whole history of pressing tears here on which Barbara bloats and George—well, he sees, he says, he feels, no reason to grieve. With Barbara as shock absorber and Millie as totemic father or expulsed superego, GeoBush somnambulizes as he occupies uninterrogated lands of the dead. (Only after the replay, in Christian rallies, he lets drop a tear: major breakthrough for the one who could not mourn.) One thing, perhaps, has become clear for us: The way the first couple presents itself is not merely a matter for quirky pomo readability. Everything that Bush does is a matter of presencing for a dead center that keeps on replicating itself. Catching up to first place, first couple, first superpower, Bush is still running behind, fluttering and second. America is losing the races; like Bush, it is losing heart, faltering in full regression. Everything that George Bush does is intended to efface history, or to bring it back to pre-civil rights days, and so on, in other words to bring it back to the day of the crash.

With GeoBush at the helm we can only go down, crash—or turn around. This is the field of his rhetorical unconscious. Hence the strange and belated evocation of the "line in the sand" which, presenting itself spatially as a deadline, came too late. All of Bush's politics depends on reversing the order of the "too late," reproducing the deadline after it has passed, going back on history.

ON RAISING THE PARATAXES: George Bush's couplifications appear to demonstrate the principle of nonlinkage. In other words, the other is a locus of profound connectivity which first has to be articulated in order to be disavowed. His history as vice prez is summed up in the notorious avowal of May 1988: "For seven and a half years, I have worked along side [Reagan] and I am proud to be his partner. We have had triumphs, we have made mistakes, we have had sex." Recovering this lapsus (he means "we have had setbacks"), he elaborates the scene of parataxes by comparing himself to a "javelin thrower who won the coin toss and elected to receive"[4] Others have adequately noted the "wimp factor" that dominated Bush's electoral anxieties—being second to the top, at the feminized receiving end, and now he has to turn things around via anal-sadistic military penetrations to equally feminized territories. Curiously, Bush's initial correction reveals the proximity of sex and setback, which is to say the backside of projected progress, the place of impasse. The substitution of "sex" for "setback," which in this context refers to Bush's secondary position within a structure of the couple, reveals as well the libidinal investment in the setback—which is to say, in the reversal, postponement, delay, which must be surmounted. It further shows that setback for Bush is beyond the pleasure principle and in the service of repetition and the death drive.

On the other end of Mr. Bush's couplifications, on the receiving end, we encounter the absolute dummy both in the Lacanian and popular senses of the term. The name of the symptom: Dan Quayle. As dummy par excellence, he ventriloquizes with exceptional precision the breaches in presidential linguistics. He exists, as Bush's political double or other, as that which cannot be; he scans as a sign for the impossibility of becoming president. As ventriloquizing locus and externalization of the president's inarticulable phantasmata, Dan Quayle dramatizes the executive desire for historical effacement. He is moreover the figure that George Bush has chosen to replace and repeat himself, to fill his space and articulate its contours. Where Bush restricts his elliptical performances of linguistic nonclosure to sex/setback sets, believing also that "comme ci, comme ça" is a popular Hispanic phrase, and other confusions that name themselves (George Bush's lapses are frequently metacommentaries: the setback names the lapsus he has just committed, comme ci comme ça designates the "undecideds" which can go either or both ways, and so on), Dan Quayle discloses himself as if to let the prez speak through an empty body-as-megaphone; he is a broadcast system switched on by the sinister vicissitudes of Bushian desire. When George Bush says, "Read my lips," he means look into the gaping abyss—the yawn—and listen to Dan Quayle. (In French, Bush is pronounced "bouche," mouth.) One could offer a compelling, if not compelled, reading of Bush and Quayle as a mutant breed of "cyburban" cowboys, particularly given Bush's simulated address in and from Texas, a hotel in Houston. For our purposes, however, I am going to treat the Bush-Quayle couple as a single entity or utterance machine with the sole purpose of analyzing their dehistoricizing desire. For all its emptiness and technobody hollows, the prez-vice presidential machine targets the lack in the Other in a continual setback of friendly fire.

Of the lapses that have been noted in the repertoire of the Bush administration, one in particular puts the achronos and atopos of the war in uncanny perspective: "The Holocaust was an obscene period in our nation's history. I mean this century's history. But we all lived in this century. I didn't live in this century."[5] The Bush-Quayle machine has produced a rich utterance which, at first sight appears to confirm Mary McGrory's insight that "the non sequitur is the one grammatical [sic] form Bush has mastered."[6] Clearly, there is some irony to this assertion, for the non sequitur is precisely that which eludes mastery, marking as it does a gap, the abyss of nonlinkage. Diane Rubinstein has identified this tendency to skip a beat semantically as the binary logic that would oppose the office of presidential speech to the couch of analysand: "For Bush's digressions, non sequiturs, lapses, repetitions recall those of an analysand rather than the narrative closure of an authorial subject (i.e., the President of the United States . . .). One of Bush's most interesting and parodied linguistic tropes is his use of the word 'thing.'[7] We shall get to thingification momentarily, though we are already following a logic of the automata. First let us gloss the slippage that locates the Holocaust on our shores. In fact the (vice-)presidential unconscious knows how to read, and like the essence itself of the unconscious it stakes out the timeless, refusing contradiction: the Holocaust was a moment in American history, says the (vice-)president of the United States. This general assertion is followed by a single subject's intentional inflection ("I mean this century's history"), then it reverts to the general assertion ("But we . . .") and reverts once more to a particularized subject's predicament ("I didn't live in this century"). This subject, as pure subject of enunciation and inscription, is a dead subject who makes claims for not having lived in this century, or rather, for not having lived according to calendrial or historical time. Everyone lived in this century ("we all lived") but the speaker himself did not experience this century, which in his transmission metonymically displaces "the Holocaust." The (vice-)presidential unconscious knows that it does not know the Holocaust, but this unknowing is obtained only as a condition of not having lived in this nation/century. The geo- and chronopolitical map of this administration's compulsion is being disclosed here. The confusion of space and time crucially underscores the possibilization of essential analogy. But beyond the structure that permits our nation to incorporate the grotesque history of Germany or Poland—an outstanding debt for which we inheritors of nazism still have to pay—Dan Quayle speaks for an administration that will not have lived. As Bush's hologram, this total recall machine (which lives with all memory but cannot live in time or with introjection) also prints out its participation in the presidential death drive.

If his compulsive program is associated with the death drive, this by no means constitutes a way of putting down Mr. Bush or that which lip syncs him. In fact, it offers a compliment, one that possibly overestimates the presidential reserve of libido. The death drive is understood both by Freud and Lacan as a normal paradox of bioinstinctual setback for our species. The Bush-Quayle entity may well extend beyond the death drive, which is to say, at the limit of the domain of drives [Triebe]. Going this way or that, they have mutated into a function of thingification where they are placed under instinctual arrest. I in no way intend simply to condemn one man or one man's symptomatology. It may be the case that one has to draw the line somewhere; but, as Heidegger has suggested in another contextual milieu, let us first contemplate that line. One might easily be drawn into the reactive posturing that elicits condemnation. And yet, this is precisely the time—most "moral" of times—to resist condemnation. Perhaps such a politics of utterance deserves some explanation. Having supplanted rigorous analysis, condemnation, as if to build a roadblock to thinking, has been expressed too often and possibly too recklessly with historically signified villains. I have no interest in attacking one man or his singular decoy—this would be too metaphysical a gesture, and would accomplish no more than locating the origin of event or History in a single (male) Subject. That would be the easy way out: to pin the blame on a proper name that is placeholder for an entire symptomatology of beings. the question has to be, rather: Why was it possible for George Bush to be president? Why was it possible, at this particular moment in history, for Saddam Hussein to pose as Adolf Hitler? Whether or not you voted, protested, freaked out, or elected one or another mode of passivity, it is a question of our history.[8] The war is what we share—even if this should be exercised in the mode of repression or according to the injunction to forget. As the (vice-)presidential utterance has disclosed, the boundaries around the place of occupation, according to spatial and temporal determinations, are difficult to fix. This is why it is necessary to resist condemning one person or even one form of substance dependency, such as oil, as having exclusive rights over catastrophic blindness, for condemnation has never brought any serious analysis to term. Thus Jean-Luc Nancy crucially observes that "condemnation, by itself, tells us nothing about what made possible that which is condemned. . . . con-demnation keeps at a distance, along with the condemned, the question of what it is that made their guilt possible."[9]

§: In an essay that resists treating but names the cases of Paul de Man and Martin Heidegger, Nancy argues that "it is our history as such that has been put in question and in abeyance" by such "cases":

> In any case it seems as if recent history were multiplying individual "cases," for all that they are very different, in order to force us to ask this question [Can our history continue simply to represent itself as History, as the general program of a certain Humanity, a Subject, a Progress—a program that would only have been, can still only be troubled by accidents, by foreign bodies, but not *in itself* and as such?]. It is surely not by chance. For thirty years, self assurance preserved or achieved at the conclusion of the war (assurance, or the fierce will to be reassured) has caused us to misconstrue the question. In the first place, a marxist self-assurance, whatever its form or consistency. But also, a techno-scientific one; and a democratic-progressivist one. In one way or another, it was the assurance of a certain "destination," come from way back, able to lead us far. But these assurances have worn away, or collapsed, and our history asks how we ever came to this point. The question can no longer be avoided. We cannot be content with affirming that there were "errors," and "mistakes," nor be content with denouncing them. Fundamentally, we all know that very well. Everything that claims to escape this knowledge is only pitiful dissimulation.[10]

Our history asks how we ever got to this point. We are responsible to our history, for which we have to answer. Setback. Cutback. Finback. The call for spiritual renewal "already had a certain history behind" it. In the West, history has always been a history of reappropriated crashing—something we still need to explain, or rather, to respond to as the desire of metaphysics.

The chain of certitudes through which it is transmitted destines metaphysics, in its last spasm, to the objectification of world in technology. When Heidegger writes about our unshieldedness, he recruits Rilke, perhaps the last mortal to have experienced in nature the Open. In the grips of technological dominion, where no mark can be zoned outside of us to land in some circumscribed area of noncontamination, man now negotiates the mutation of metaphysics and History at the unmarked frontiers of the technosphere. Since WWII, technology—including computer technology—and the promise of spiritual renewal have been going steady. Can we take a closer look at this hypothetical assertion? FREEZE FRAME BLOWUP: George Herbert Walker Bush in the open seas, the Navy will not come back for him, they were on their last mission and were moving out. Endless open sea. Leo Nadeau used to say the Avenger could fall faster than it could fly. Nothing works—even the parachute proves defective.

"By rote, he found the rip cord, and the chute opened, but it was torn. . . . He was falling fast . . . bleeding. . . . —Doug West. He'd seen the blood on Bush's face, dropped a medical kit. Bush hand-paddled for it. . . . There was no paddle. There was no fresh water. The container in the raft had broken in the fall. Bush was paddling with both hands, puking from fear and seawater, bleeding from the head. He got his med kit and with a shaky left hand swabbed at himself with iodine. He got out his .38 revolver and checked it."[11] He is bleeding. And then it happens, something that will recur incessantly through the peculiar circuitry of the unconscious. In the Open, George Herbert Walker Bush discovers God in technology. The submarine which emerged out of nowhere, the apparition of pure delivery, rose out of the infinite sublime. When the sky crashed into the ocean, God answered the call technologically. God's name, at that moment, flashed on to the sideboard of the metallic surge; it was *Finback*.

Finback was the name of the sub that rescued George Bush. Three thousand miles of ocean. They came to get him. And they filmed him. "And the seaman he saw was standing there, watching with this thing up to his face, a camera, a movie camera. They were filming."[12] It was known that the men on the crew loved their job. An unconscious pilot would awaken; he'd learn that he was alive, rescued. The future would happen. But George Bush was in a sense destined to remain unconscious. When he awoke, for a brief spell, back then, he cried, he was delirious. He wanted his friends. He was young, he was *hysterical*. No matter what they did, George Bush would never learn that he was alive after that day.

Finback will be the name of this war, but also of the history of metaphysics. Read bifocally, in French and English, it refers us back to an end, the apocalyptic condition for any happening. The end will have come "back then," in the wake of an emerging submarine or in another version of *Finnegan's Wake*, in the endless parlor where WWII refused the movement toward its own burial. Finback is the promise of a comeback, a second coming that, like the promise of the infinite, can never as such take place in finity. Finback means that the end is behind us: "They had behind them, perhaps, in a sense, something that derived from our entire history. Did not the West begin by being, simultaneously, the acknowledgment of its own decline and the demand for its own renewal? Was it not Athens which longed for the time of Solon, and Plato who called for renewal?" This is a question of our own history, involving the production of our own identity, and the will to be origin and end to ourselves. "To inaugurate a new era in order to reanimate the breath of a spirit weakened by the accidents of an itinerary that is nevertheless its own, and underneath those accidents to recover a destiny, an epic, the organic growth of the spirit or of man—that is what it means or has meant to possess the *meaning* of history. . . . It knows accidents, precipitous declines, regressions, but its meaning is forever available to it, and it can always reconvoke itself once again to the undertaking of some renewal, some setting straight, some rediscovery."[13]

Locked into the pose of the one rescued, the guilty survivor—he had sent his boys to die—Bush was delivered to a history of denial and compulsive repetition. To be sure, death or pain or catastrophe, each in its singularity, does not possess any historicity whatsoever but can only retrospectively acquire enough velocity to constitute a narrative event. Taking refuge in submersion and repression, history was going to insinuate itself through the untapped disruption that punched a permanent hole in the real. Tight-fisted and knotted up by the near miss, George Bush would never depropriate his history enough in order to set forth those conditions which might guarantee a future-to-come. He would never be able to let go of the totalized, if lost, meaning which his "precipitous decline" immediately acquired. Instead, he got married real fast, graduated from Yale, and went into the oil business. But oil was not nowhere. Odessa, Texas, was a desert back then, a site of deprivation where George and Bar could repel the aggressive incursions of melancholia. If God and technology continued to go steady in those earth-poking days, there was no breakup in sight. In fact, they were to be engaged in the Gulf War.

EATING BROCCOLI:[14] George Bush connected the deserts in his life by a thin thread. The temporal structure of this connection was exposed when in January 1991 he drew a "line in the sand." What kind of figure did this gesture cut? At first glance, it seems straightforward enough. George Bush was issuing an ultimatum. Yet, what concerns us is the rhetorical dimension of this act. A rather ordinary performative speech act, it spatially meant to designate a point beyond which the Iraqis must not pass. The line was evoked, however, *after* Iraq had crossed the Kuwaiti border. The line in fact functioned less as a spatially conceived marker than as a temporally pointing one. What it was pointing at was a deadline. But what sort of contract was this line drawing up? It was a line that turned back upon itself because it was intended to designate Iraqi withdrawal, a double line of the *re-trait*. In ordinary language usage, a line in the sand does not mean that one is supposed to fall back on the other side of the line, but usually means its opposite. Figuring a deadline, expiration date, and promise, the line in the sand troped instead the time limit of an hour glass. Like an hour glass, however, it was about reversal and turning things around as a measure of time. The line in the sand, catechrestically deployed, posed an ultimatum for what already had transpired in the form of a morally inflected imperative: this boundary crossing should not have occurred. The line, as line of impasse or imperfect past, implemented the signature of reversal and repetition by means of which this war would be authorized. Still, what is a line in the sand but a sign of its own effacement, a writing of disaster that territorializes the past on the ground of shifting sands? Promised to erasure, the line in the sand figurally says the forgetting to which this was doubly committed. A figure of immediacy, masquerading in clarity of contour, the line, as word, is that which cannot be kept. In fact, it already points to a word not kept, for the Iraqis had already been granted permission, by diplomatic channels of ambiguity, to cross the line. This in part explains why the line can only point to the suspension of any clear demarcation. Ever pointing to its obliteration in time, it is not a line capable of guaranteeing even its own future, much less *the* future. Nonetheless, it is the line that we were fed.

To the extent that this line at all invites readability, it constitutes a catechrestic metalepsis—arguably the structure itself that dominated the "events" of the Gulf War, where nothing was new under the sky. Let us recapitulate: as a boundary not to be crossed, the line in the sand presented itself as moot, for the war was said to have originated in a crossed boundary. It therefore inscribes a boundary that ought not to have been crossed, a moral line, in fact, that says: this is where America draws the line. As Mad Maxed out as it may have seemed in the inscription of its fury and spontaneity, this line in the sand pointed us to the past in general, and to the phantom double of this line that ought not to have been crossed. George Bush, youngest fighter pilot of WWII, draws the line at this time; he comes of age. Which age?

The line in the sand is, we shall see, not drawn across an indifferently figured body. This body was named a feminine body time and again, a mother's body, and a body subject to rape. A psychology of international relations is taking shape (this is not my invention but a contribution of those who have psychologized and pornographized the "enemy," the invention of those who have made this a war, once again, of the sexes). Where has this land feminization (be)gotten us? Somewhere between the realignment of reunified Germany and Japan, prior to the sexual warfare that informed the Clarence Thomas hearings, George Bush drew a line in the sand. As America, a faltering empire, loses its bearings the president, an eternal son not up to the task, will also have traced out a line of castration. But I want at all costs to prevent precipitous decline and to steer us slowly over this heavily symbolized terrain. A great deal has returned to haunt us now, making it hardly surprising that we are inundated by a rhetoric of restoration and reversal. The phantomic return triangulating—once again—Germany, Japan, and America, has motivated the pathos with which this administration goes about restoring the national phallus to its proper place.

The narrative of purloined oil wells crudely illustrates the stakes of this dramatic replay. Indeed, as slippery as this may seem, the possession of oil wells marked in the 1940s a critical moment in the strategies of national desire. In the 1940s the State Department described Middle East oil as "a stupendous source of strategic power, and one of the greatest material prizes in world history," "probably the richest economic prize in the world in the field of foreign investment." After the war, Eisenhower called the Middle East the "most strategically important area in the world." Further, at "the end of World War II, when immense petroleum deposits were discovered in Saudi Arabia, Secretary of the Navy James Forrestal told Secretary of State Byrnes, 'I don't care which American companies develop the Arabian reserves, but I think most emphatically that it [sic] should be American.'" After World War II the Americans acquired Saudi concessions for themselves, freezing out the British and French.

Regardless of the real import of oil, there is no economy that is not also a libidinal economy, or that does not resignify symbolic deposits of national desire. Z magazine reminds us that in the view of the New York Times, "a heavy cost must be paid" when an oil-rich Third World nation "goes berserk with fanatical nationalism."[15] Z justly remarks that going "berserk" with "fanatical nationalism" is the Times's way of describing a Third World nation expecting to benefit from its own resources. In part, though, ownership—the values ascribed to property, propriety, the proper—has gone largely symbolic, which is why the so-called Third World slips into an altogether different space of engagement. This is not to deny the value of those discussions organized around capital motivation—but that alone is not what resurrected the respectability of warfare or created the referential indetermination of what is going on. While Japan, Germany, and America triangulate into a new phase of Oedipal self-patterning—one that does not permit genuine ambivalence but is staked on repression and obsessive replay—we must not allow ourselves to forget the fourth term, or the displacement to what is being called the Middle East—at once the most artificial and originary of historical mappings.

"IT IS TRUE THAT TROPES ARE THE PRODUCERS OF IDEOLOGIES THAT ARE NO LONGER TRUE":[16] We have until now considered the question from the side of war. Is there another side?

In a sense, this war declared itself, when it declared itself, as a war about forgetting war. It was as if it wanted to play itself out as impasse, something accomplished by pressing the record and erase functions at once. In any case,

this reflects the way the war was "covered" by the media, simultaneously recording and erasing its referential track. At the same time as past wars were
being done with, this war opened the line of vision for the institution of future
wars. A war to end War in order to begin wars, this one wanted to start from
scratch (chicken scratch or turkey shoot). It is a matter of civility to declare
each gruesome war the last one. Modern warfare has largely been conducted
with the stated aim of ending war or of safety checking democratic roadways.
Now America is chattering openly about future wars and what we learned
from the test site called Iraq. Let us take a brief technological reality check:
third-rate Patriot missiles encountered fifth-rate, merely *ballistic* SCUD missiles, triggering mythic defense narratives. This is like getting off on a nightstick.
Obviously, there were a couple of smart bombs on the loose, promoting the
fiction that a missile always reaches its destination.[17] This fiction is of course
crucial: it upholds our history, our metaphysics, our appropriated meaning—all
of which are about to meet their destination. But what if they've got the wrong
address, and what if the future is not about restoring the phallus—or, for that
matter, woman—to a "proper" place? What is the proper place of this war in
our destiny? Why have we mortals never been able to act nonteleologically?
And why did destiny shift its site to the nomadic desert spaces where it is said
that Moses once broke the tablets of the Law, Jesus of Nazareth was pinned to
the cross, and the Sphinx asked you, What is man?

There is no discourse or act of war that can put an end to war. War offers
community the image of its sovereign exposition to death. Because it stages the
infinity of a finitude that encounters its end, war collectivizes and stimulates to
life by its horror. Little has matched the pure excess that war draws to its occurrence, as a kind of ransom for the future. As the literature of virility and heroism,
war is "the monument, the feast, the somber and pure sign of the community
expressing its sovereignty."[18] Each time it arrives as the "once and for all" of a
promised catharsis. Except, possibly, in Vietnam, where war became shameful,
and our boys, abject. A kind of *conscientious abjection* took hold, and this ran
interference with the loaded circuits that coded World War II.

If war has meant so much to us, how are we to let go of its power to fascinate
and entrance? There is only the imperative ideal of peace. Peace is not the opposite of war, but its absolute other—something that we have never as such
experienced. This in part is because peace, to be what it is, predicates the infinite
where war is finite. War in fact aligns itself with the Western appropriation of
meaning. Establishing epistemic breaks, a radical possibilization of the Idea
in history, exacting decision, war has functioned as the special megaphone of
the Western logos. It has been, in our history, a way of achieving resolution

through finitizing acts of containment. Thus even this war was waged against the nonfinite, uncontrolled effects of past wars in recent history. War has articulated a readable mode of *decision* to whose cause God, nation, and other transcendental recruits have been called. It is the way the West was won. This has everything to do with truth and the apocalyptic conditions for revealing truth in its transparency. In the history of beings and the history of Being, war is truth. At least, it has been inscribed unfailingly as the necessary road to truth or to a justice rendered beyond the suspension and constitutive blindness that justice in fact figures. The decisive truth of war locates the premises upon which justice can no longer be suspended. This has been our history's way of putting behind us the undecidables. It amounts to nothing less than the Western compulsion to "finish with," that is, to reach the finish line. But this finish line, and the arrogant impatience that drives us toward it, is, we have seen, nothing but a line in the sand. Still, it has been drawn by language and logos. Precisely because war feeds the truth machine, aiming for truth, destinal arrival and the clean cut of history, it is our task as thinkers to decelerate finitude's thrust and abide with the inconceivable horizon of an infinite unfinished. What would it mean *not* to close a deal with transcendence, or to desist from following a path of resurrected war aims? What would it mean to follow a politics of radical nonclosure, leaving time as well as borders open to the absolute otherness that must accompany genuine futurity? The line in the sand, as the sign of the figural deconstruction of its literal meaning, promises divisibility as well as infinite granules of pathless randomness and essential aberration which can never be simply appropriated to the sure movement of a path, whether or not it leads "nowhere." The desert commits itself to the abolition of path.

Just as we have to renounce "finishing with" and dealing final notice, Western logos must learn to open its Faustian fist, indeed, to desert the explosions of otherness that the logos has always detonated. For these reasons I have relied upon psychoanalysis to help us count the losses. For psychoanalysis, besides reading war, has taught us in this century to be wary of the desire for termination and has exemplarily, if relentlessly, advocated the interminable nature of working through. While it nonetheless posits a term, psychoanalysis also knows about the production of unknown meaning and the ineluctable deviancy inflecting normal self-constitution, be this of a nation state or the human subject. In an uncharacteristically simple formula, psychoanalysis has known from the start that it may be, for us in our history, a matter of choosing either interminable or exterminable. But psychoanalysis has also met the limits of theorizing its knowledge. It reads from layerings of silence and repression, if only to slow down the inclines of the death drive, with which we'll never be finished. Like a woman, psychoanalysis's job is never done. In the future, I daresay, the prereq-uisites for presidential candidacy, will include, beside the restrictions pertain-ing to age and citizenship, a growing demand for health checks and balances, namely, in addition to doctors' reports, appropriate certificates of therapy.

The Gulf War, which was meant to put to rest other wars whose wounds would not close, resurrected the respectability of war as a moment in West-ern discourse or polemics. While we obviously resisted opening diplomatic channels, it is not simply the case that we refused to negotiate. Rather, quick polemological tactics supplanted negotiation as a more efficient means of finish-ing with the problem. Yet to the extent that the war followed, at least in stated principle, strict guidelines, United Nations discussions, telephone treaties, and the Geneva Convention, the war as it was conducted cannot be seen in simple opposition to diplomacy. Of course, as Nietzsche has said about history, it is all a matter of dosage.

DOWNLOADING: It was Kant who tried to teach us that peace must be rigor-ously established. In his uncannily timely *To Perpetual Peace: A Philosophical Sketch* (1759), Kant outlines the dangers of a progressive technologization of the troop, anticipating the rhetoric of collateral damage and surgical strike ("man is thrown into the same class as other living machines," "paying men to kill or be killed appears to use them as mere machines and tools," "subjects are used and wasted as mere objects," and so on).[19] In its delicacy of operation and telescoping futural vision this work evokes an emphatic sense of being "on location." It is, when reading the *Perpetual Peace,* as if Kant had been piloting Finback that day, looking forward and back, reading a special clarity from the skies whose open-endedness ought never to have obscured our history. Among the critical interventions that his text makes on behalf of an enduring peace, he warns:

> A war of punishment [*bellum punitivum*] between nations is inconceivable (for there is no relation of superior and inferior between them). From this it follows that a war of extermination—where the destruction of both parties along with all rights is the result—would permit perpetual peace to occur only in the vast graveyard of humanity as a whole. Thus, such a war, including all means used to wage it, must be absolutely prohibited. But that the means named above inexorably lead to such war becomes clear from the following: Once they come into use, these intrinsically despicable, infernal acts cannot long be confined to war alone. This applies to the use of spies [*uti exploratori-bus*], where only the dishonorableness *of others* (which can never be entirely

eliminated) is exploited; but such activities will also carry over to peacetime and will thus undermine it. (109)

It is interesting to note that Kant counts the necessity for ensuring the survival of peoples along with that of rights, offering them each the same ontological peace dividend. This suggests that war exceeds rights while it nonetheless, as the prerogative of power, proceeds from a concept of the rights of sovereignty. As long as there is a national entity, war is within the realm of rights, even though it threatens the survival of individual rights or a more transcendental bill of rights. The nation enjoys a sovereign right to go to war, and thus to destabilize the rights for which it may be ostensibly fighting. This contradiction belongs to the essence of the nation state. War, according to Jean-Luc Nancy, in fact exposes the "sovereign exception" that it institutes within the realm of rights. Clearly, what needs to be rethought is the legitimacy of national sovereignty and of everything that is implied thereby. But as long as national identity continues to assert its historical "necessity," what becomes of the ideal of sovereign peace?

The problem that Kant faces in the entire essay involves the deflection of perpetual peace from its semantic hole in the graveyard: could there be a movement of peace that is unhitched from the death drive? Must the duty we have toward peace necessarily have as its background music that radical tranquility which resonates with "rest in peace"? If Kant can only draw a philosophical sketch of peace, this is because his leanings push him toward the edge of undecidability where absolute peace, like war, means you're dead. To get out of this peace cemetery, Kant will have to institute performative speech acts; in other words, he will have to declare a certain type of war on war. Kant is perfectly aware of the rhetorical difficulties that face any linguistic mobilization on behalf of peace. To preempt the inevitable strike of war (we earthlings have not known, empirically or historically, a warless time zone), he will begin parergonally with ironic deterrents. Later on, the argument will move into more transcendental fields when, for instance, Kant proposes "the transcendental principle in publicity," which basically opposes all forms of secrecy, saying, "if I cannot *publicly acknowledge* it without thereby inevitably arousing everyone's opposition to my plan, then this necessary and universal, and thus *a priori* foreseeable, opposition of all to me could not have come from anything other than the injustice with which it threatens everyone" (135–36). The transcendental formula of public right comes down to this maxim: "All actions that affect the rights of other men are wrong if their maxim is not consistent with publicity." It is only under the transcendental concept of public right, linked to publicity, that an agreement can be reached between politics and morality. To guarantee this agreement Kant initiates "another transcendental and affirmative principle of public right" whose explanation he however indefinitely postpones, breaking off the essay with the promise for a future unfolding of perpetual peace ("I must postpone the further development and explanation of this principle for another occasion"). The principle in question reads:

> All maxims that *require* publicity (in order not to fail of their end) agree with both politics and morality. (135)

Though unfinished, the essay nonetheless names the fulfillment of its terms, namely, the establishment of "perpetual peace, which will follow the hitherto falsely so-called treaties of peace (which are really only a suspension of war)" (108). This replacement of the peace treaty with genuine, lasting peace, Kant assures, "is no empty idea, but a task that, gradually completed, steadily approaches its goal." But was not the hope for peace staked in the abandonment of goal or teleological fulfillment? The disjunction, I believe, accounts for the constitutive incompletion of the text which performs its inability to reach an end or fulfill a goal, consequently swerving in its performance from the finite repetition of war. Postponing itself perpetually, the text opens out to meet the starry sky that Kant saw above his head, granting tensed suspension. It is within this pause between the performative inauguration of peace and the postponement to which its fulfillment is subject, that Kant can make out the fragile sketch of a perpetual peace. Refusing to end, Kant sends us back to the beginning of this text which never quite gets off the ground but is all the more powerful for it.

The problem for Kant, and for us, is getting started on the peace march. Kant enumerates in the first section his war grievances and prepares the ground for the installation of a perpetual peace. The first section issues as an instituting injunction that "1. No treaty of peace that tacitly reserves issues for a future war shall be held valid" (107). Kant explains: "For if this were the case, it would be a mere truce, a suspension of hostilities, not *peace*, which means the end of all hostilities, so much so that even to modify it by 'perpetual' smacks of pleonasm" (107). In sum, a peace treaty would be self-annulling to the extent that its raison d'être is expected to crumble. A true peace treaty would constitute the war on war par excellence, and therefore suspend its function as a mere contractual deal amongst nations. A contract, as Benjamin will later point out in his *Critique of Violence*, always implies its own suspension, or a return to violence in the event that one of the parties should fail to honor its terms.[20] A contract or treaty therefore belongs to the pervasive logic of war, offering little to effect the disinstallation of war in our history.

But if we choose to cite Kant at the unclosing end of the Gulf War, it is also in order to retrieve his frame. For who has not suffered despondency these past several months (the manic victory allowances are in fact part of the experience of despondency, though on the more unsavory side of disavowal). Who has not felt the *paradox of abortion* performed on the body of history, pregnant with the future?

Kant's frame, in any case, contains its own ironic destruction. If it is to be part of the experience of knowing peace, the essay nonetheless forces him to deliver a few punchlines. The doubling up in laughter (or in pain) marked by the initial breakthrough accompanies the mood of essential peace-making. The initial breakthrough quickly stalls, however. "To Perpetual Peace," the essay's dedication begins; but this beginning is also an end, shadowing as it does the death of that which has not as yet come to be. One can never be sure if we are engaged in a ceremonial performative of clinking champagne glasses or if we are not saying, rather, "In Memorium: To PP." Precisely because of this chasm of indecision, it is necessary to follow Kant, repeating his gesture, if only to inscribe ourselves by *affirming* castration, which is to say, by putting ourselves in the place of the destitute other without displacing or colonizing this other. Kant's question begins with the undecidable nature of PP. Is it beyond the pleasure principle, on the side of death and absolute quiescence, or can it be achieved by finite beings? "To PP," as it turns out, is a citation that opens up the undecidable:

> Whether this satirical inscription on a certain Dutch shopkeeper's sign, on which a graveyard was painted, holds for *men* in general, or especially for heads of state who can never get enough of war, or perhaps only for philosophers who dream that sweet dream, is not for us to decide. (107)

Nonetheless, or even because we cannot decide the readability of the inscription—which is generalizable to the sign of signs, the ensepulchered *seme*—thinking, as if heeding an impossible injunction, must intervene. And what it does when it is called upon to intervene at the scene of absolute undecidability, in the crossfire of life and death, the real and the dream, reading and the impossible, is to name the strength of its own impotence. Writing to peace, as if this were the true but unknown address of the philosopher's dreamwork, exposes the empty phallus:

> However, the author of this essay does set out one condition: The practical politician tends to look down with great smugness on the political theorist, regarding him as an academic whose empty ideas cannot endanger the nation [*Staat*] since the nation must proceed on principles [derived from] experi-

57

ence [*Erfahrungsgrundsätzen*]; consequently, the theorist is allowed to fire his entire volley, without the worldly-wise statesman becoming the least bit concerned. (107)

The theorist, then, can fire away precisely because his words are from the start diverted from a teleological path or aim. But if Kant seems to be launching a war of the worlds between politician and theorist, it is in order strategically to avert the assaults which theorizing peace ineluctably attracts. In fact, Kant's project in the set up of his essay is to ensure the immunocompetence of his text, which is to say, he is sending out antibodies to neutralize the war utterance of the political body. For, in times of trouble—and thinking's business concerns making trouble by responding authentically to trouble—the political body always sends in troops to subdue the critical intervention that true philosophical mobilization must contemplate. Kant allows himself to "fire his entire volley" because they are blanks; they are the stuff of dreams and address themselves to that which does not exist in the present. Kant's army of metaphors and metonymies, while participating in the structure of destination, cannot touch the statesman and therefore arrives, if it arrives, as a blank flag of surrender. It is a surrender that protects by establishing the terms of an absolute *différend:*

> Now if he is to be consistent—and this is the condition I set out—the practical politician must not claim, in the event of a dispute with a theorist, to detect some danger to the nations in those views that the political theorist expresses openly and without ulterior motive. By this *clausula salvatoria,* the author of this essay will regard himself to be expressly protected in the best way possible from all malicious interpretation. (107)

Theorists, behold! In German, Kant writes that the theorist will know [*wissen*] protection. Where does this knowledge come from? In order to pass beyond the limits of the peace treaty, Kant must initially draw up this legally articulated contract with the politician. Its detachability from the body of the text—the threat of beheading or castration—always attends this essay which in fact sets out to abolish the conditions for instituting a peace treaty. Because the theorist is fundamentally disarmed by the state, and barred by the nature of philosophizing from producing a referential dent in policy, the politician will have to desist from waging war or polemics on theoretical activity. Nonetheless, what this essay makes clear from the start is that the state practices the duplicitous policy of remaining at once unconcerned with theoretical reflection while menacing it with reprisal for betraying the interests of national security. What is sad for us today, is that institutions of learning, linked as they are to the state and other corporate configurations, have tended to internalize this threatened and threatening posture. Hence the myth or, depending on which side you find yourself, the wish fulfillment of "tenured radicals."

Well, at any rate, Kant, in order to protect his text from malicious interpretation, heads up his essay with a joke, a dream, castration, and contract. The detachable introduction, which nonetheless enables reflection on a lasting peace to occur at all, ends with a kind of proxy signing. For, as we know, the politician will not then and not now cosign this contract which Kant, in his own and our defense, draws up. That is why I, Immanuel Kant, "the author of this essay," will regard myself to be "expressly protected" by my performative declaration which, alas, may only be a decoy. From what is he performatively protecting himself? From that part of war that politicians have consistently waged on reflection ("in the event of a dispute"). But this is not merely a professional suit that he brings to bear. What politics may justly deem threatening is the interminable, morally anxious, and genuinely ambivalent cast of speculative analysis.

Perhaps the most serious challenge that Kant poses to us today does not so much concern a regional or local disturbance (wherever that may be) but one that requires us to reflect upon the repressed disjunction of freedom and democracy:

> Among the three forms of government, *democracy,* in the proper sense of the term, is necessarily a *despotism,* because it sets up an executive power in which all citizens make decisions about and, if need be, against one (who therefore does not agree); consequently, all, who are not quite all, decide, so that the general will contradicts both itself and freedom. (114)

Whether standing alone to mark the cleave in which freedom breaks off from itself, or drawing up an unabating contract with the political statesman, the theorist constitutes that figure which cuts into the idealized imaginary of state politics. Indeed, the theoretical imperative consists principally in making the state back off from its disavowal systems—particularly in moments when a nation's predicament reflects a mode of psychotic disassociation.

Notes

1. I have treated the technologically constellated state and the telephone in *The Telephone Book: Technology—Schizophrenia—Electric Speech* (Lincoln: University of Nebraska Press, 1989). Consider George Bush's departure from the White House. His stoicism collapses only when he has to separate from the telephone operators: "He

thought he could handle the farewell to the White House operators. But, as he put it, 'I overflowed.' They had been for so long, so diligent, so patient. John Kennedy had said, 'they could raise Lazarus.' They had hooked Bush up to the far world's leaders like no other president" (Hugh Sidey, "Bush's Flight into the Sunset," *Time*, 1 Feb. 1993, 47). One might also consider, in the context of the telephone and the technologically constellated state, the terror of Stalin's nocturnal phone calls.

2. In "The *Differends* of Man" (in *Finitude's Score*), an essay on Lyotard, deconstruction and Heidegger, I have tried to reveal historical woundings that will not heal.

3. Derrida has explored the polysemous aspects of James Joyce's "he war" in "Two Words for Joyce," in *Acts of Literature: Jacques Derrida,* ed. Derek Attridge (New York: Routledge, 1992).

4. On Bush's discourse, see the challenging readings produced in Diane Rubinstein's essay, "This Is Not a President: Baudrillard, Bush and Enchanted Simulation," in *The Hysterical Male: New Feminist Theory,* ed. Arthur and Marilouise Kroker (New York: St. Martin's Press, 1991), 259ff. The principle of nonlinkage belongs to psychoanalytical investigations. Consider in this regard the definition of "isolation" in J. Laplanche and J.-B. Pontalis, *The Language of Psycho-Analysis,* trans. Donald Nicholson-Smith (New York: W. W. Norton and Company, 1973).

5. Cited in Paul Simms, "How to Become President," *Spy,* Nov. 1988, 128.

6. Mary McGrory, *Washington Post,* 29 Sept. 1988, A2.

7. Rubinstein, "This Is Not a President," 264.

8. See Jean-Luc Nancy, "Our History," trans. Cynthia Chase, Richard Klein, and A. Mitchell Brown in *diacritics* 20 (Fall 1990). I am also following the protocols established by Nancy for considering this war. See "Guerre, Droit, Souvraineté—Techné," *Les Temps modernes* 539 (June 1991).

9. Nancy, "Our History," 107.

10. Ibid., 101.

11. Richard Ben Kramer, "How Bush Made It: A Portrait of the President as a Young Man," *Esquire,* June 1991, 82.

12. Ibid., 83.

13. Nancy, "Our History," 108.

14. When George Bush proudly proclaimed that he could now abandon the odious burden, imposed by his mother, of eating broccoli, he signaled the decline of the super-egoical function for him. As prez nothing would be forced down his throat any longer; he could expulse the law without remorse. Elsewhere I have shown what it means for Freud "to learn to love spinach"—an unbearable internalization of mucosity. For Freud's table of laws, this turn toward the totemized spinach meant he had successfully integrated the superego and lawgiver. I analyze the utterance "Eat your spinach!"—a once common injunction issued by parents to their children—in *Dictations: On Haunted Writing*

(Lincoln: University of Nebraska Press, 1993). The spinach episode in Freud's oeuvre functions as an exemplary passage through Oedipus. The more phallically organized broccoli, which Bush has graduated into not eating, suggests rather a refusal of castration: the classical Freudian condition of disavowal, which forms his major character traits.

15. Cited in Joel Beinin, "Origins of the Gulf War," *Open Pamphlet Magazine Series* 3 (February 1991): 32.

16. Paul de Man, *Allegories of Reading: Figural Language in Rousseau, Nietzsche, Rilke, and Proust* (New Haven, CT: Yale University Press, 1979), 157.

17. This argument implies some familiarity with the debates figured by Derrida and Lacan in the case of Edgar Allan Poe's "The Purloined Letter." For this discussion, see Lacan's "Le Séminaire sur 'La Lettre volée,'" *Écrits* (Paris: Éditions du Seuil, 1966); an English translation is available in *The Purloined Poe: Lacan, Derrida and Psychoanalytic Readings,* trans. Jeffrey Mehlman, ed. John P. Muller and William J. Richardson (Baltimore: Johns Hopkins University Press, 1988); and Derrida's "Le Facteur de la vérité," in *The Post Card: From Socrates to Freud and Beyond,* trans. Alan Bass (Chicago: University of Chicago Press, 1987) and also his "My Chances/ *Mes Chances:* A Rendezvous with Some Epicurean Stereophonies," trans. I. Harvey and A. Ronell, in *Taking Chances: Derrida, Psychoanalysis, and Literature,* ed. Joseph H. Smith and William Kerrigan (Baltimore: Johns Hopkins University Press, 1984).

18. See Nancy's work on Georges Bataille and community in *The Inoperative Community and Other Essays,* trans. and ed. Peter T. Connor (Minneapolis: University of Minnesota Press, 1991), 17–23.

19. Immanuel Kant, *Perpetual Peace and Other Essays,* trans. Ted Humphrey (Indianapolis: Hackett, 1983).

20. Derrida has evoked some of these motifs in his treatment of Benjamin's essay in "Force of Law: 'The Mystical Foundation of Authority,'" trans. Mary Quaintance, *Deconstruction and the Possibility of Justice,* special issue of *Cardozo Law Review* 2 (July–Aug. 1990).

TraumaTV

**TWELVE STEPS BEYOND THE
PLEASURE PRINCIPLE**

CHANNEL TWELVE: Ethics has been largely confined to the domains of doing, which include performative acts of a linguistic nature. While we have
understood that there is no decision which has not passed through the crucible
of undecidability, ethics still engages, in the largest possible terms, a reflection on doing. Now what about the wasted, condemned bodies that crumble
before a television? What kinds of evaluations, political or moral, accrue to
the evacuated gleam of one who is wasting time—or wasted by time? There
is perhaps little that is more innocent, or more neutral, than the passivity of
the telespectator. Yet, in *Dispatches,* Michael Herr writes, "it took the war to
teach it, that you were as responsible for everything you saw as you were for
everything you did. The problem was that you didn't always know what you
were seeing until later, maybe years later, that a lot of it never made it in at all,
it just stayed stored there in your eyes."[1] What might especially interest us here
is the fact that responsibility no longer pivots on a notion of interiority. Seeing
itself, without the assistance of cognition or memory, suffices to make the subject responsible. It is a responsibility that is neither alert, vigilant, particularly
present, nor in-formed.

HEADLINE NEWS: *Testimonial video functions as the* objet petit a *for justice
and the legal system within which it marks a redundancy and of which it is the
remainder.*

CHANNEL ELEVEN: The defense team takedown involved approaching George
Holliday's video tape by replicating the violence that had been done to Rodney
King.[2] The unquestioned premise upon which the team of lawyers based their
defense of the police called for an interpretation of video in terms of a "frame-
by-frame" procedure. No one questioned this act of framing, and the verdict
which ensued unleashed the violence that would explode the frames set up by
the court. In the blow-by-blow account, counting and recounting the event

of the beating, the defense presented a slow-mo sequencing of photographs whose rhythm of articulation beat a scratchless track into the court records. The decisive moves that were made on video require us to review the way in which media technology inflects decisions of state. That would be the larger picture. The smaller picture, encapsulated by the larger one, concerns the legal ramifications of distinct interpretive maneuvers. Thus, the chilling effects of warping video into freeze-frame photography cannot be overlooked—even where *overlooking* can be said to characterize the predicament in which testimonial video places the law. For the duration of the trial, the temporization that reading video customarily entails was halted by spatial determinations that were bound to refigure the violence to which King was submitted. No one needs to read Derrida's work on framing in order to know that justice was not served in Simi Valley, California. But, possibly, if one had concerned oneself with the entire problematic of the frame, its installation and effects of violence—indeed with the *excessive force* that acts of framing always risk—then it would have been something of an imperative to understand what it means to convert in a court of law a video tape into a photograph. For the photograph, according to the works of Walter Benjamin, Roland Barthes, Jacques Derrida, and a number of others, draws upon phantomal anxieties as well as the subject's inexorable arrest. I need not stress to what extent the black body in the history of racist phantasms has been associated with the ghost or zombie. Perhaps we ought to begin, then, with the astonishing remarks of Jacques Lacan when he was on *Television*:

—*From another direction, what gives you the confidence to prophesy the rise of racism? And why the devil do you have to speak of it?*

—Because it doesn't strike me as funny and yet, it's true.

With our *jouissance* going off the track, only the Other is able to mark its position, but only insofar as we are separated from this Other. Whence certain fantasies—unheard of before the melting pot.

Leaving this Other to his own mode of *jouissance,* that would only be possible by not imposing our own on him, by not thinking of him as underdeveloped.[3]

It would appear that, in *Television,* the incompletion of our *jouissance* is marked with some measure of clarity only by the Other; or, at least its off-track predicament engages a boundary that exposes the Other to the projections of racist fantasies. Claiming the relative stability of a position, the Other becomes the place which failed *jouissance* targets, if only because it provides a range of separation. This separation, this *tele-,* constitutes the distance we have to travel,

64

whether this be accomplished hand-held or alone, on the streets or *in camera*. Of the fantasies that set off the signals for mutilating the body of Rodney King, one involved precisely a kind of tele-vision that could see little more than the *jouissance* of the Other, a night vision flashing a second degree of self that emerges with destructive *jouissance:* the night blindness that operates the intricate network that is responsible for the policing of drugs. In order to get in gear, the police force had to image their suspect on PCP; and they fantasized, they claimed, that they were considerably threatened by the solitary figure, "buffed out" as he was perceived to be. What does it mean to say that the police force is hallucinating drugs, or, in this case, to allow the suggestion that it was already in the projection booth as concerns Rodney King? In the first place, before the first place, they were watching the phantom of racist footage. According to black-and-white TV, Rodney King could not be merely by himself or who he was that night. In order to break Rodney King, or break the story, the phantasm of the supplemented Other—on junk, beside himself, not himself, more than himself, a technozombie of supernatural capabilities—had to be agreed upon by the police force. The police reached such a consensus on location. So, in the first place (we are reconstructing the politicotopography slowly), the Rodney King event was articulated as a metonymy of the war on drugs; this war, ever displacing its target zones, licenses acts of ethnocide by hallucinating mainstreamers. But there are other places and other types of projections that come to light here: the Rodney King event is equally that which opens the dossier of the effaced Gulf War. When television collapses into a blank stare, whiting out the Gulf War, nomadic video in turn flashes a metonymy of police action perpetrated upon a black body. I would like to argue these points with as much clarity as the blurs and the static allow. While things and connections should be encouraged to become clear, they should not perhaps hold out expectations of becoming, once and for all, "perfectly clear"—an idiom which has all too often served as a code for the white lie.

The empirical gesture through which the violence erupted on 3 March 1991 was linked to Rodney King's legs. Did he take a step or was he charging the police? The footage seemed unclear. The defense team charged that King had in fact charged the police. "Gehen wir darum einen Schritt weiter," writes Freud in *Beyond the Pleasure Principle*—a text bringing together the topoi of charges, repetition compulsion, violence, and phantasms. Let us take another step, and another, and as many as it takes, in order to read the charges that are electrifying our derelict community.

HEADLINE NEWS: *Read the step digitally: crime serials/serial murders.*

CHANNEL TEN: Unlike telephony, cinema, or locomotion, television emerged as a prominent figure of our time only after the Second World War. There are many reasons for this (the Nazis voted in radio as the transferential agency par excellence; television was canceled out of the secret service of fascisoid transfixion). The mass invasion of television occurred after the war; it was served on the cold-war platter, which is to say that, in one way or another, TV is not so much the beginning of something new, but is instead the residue of an unassimilable history. Television is linked crucially to the enigma of survival. It inhabits the contiguous neighborhoods of broken experience and rerouted memory. Refusing in its discourse and values to record, but preferring instead to play out the myths of liveness, living color and being there, television will have produced a counterphobic perspective to an *interrupted history*. I hope to scan the way TV acts as a shock absorber to the incomprehensibility of survival, and views being "live" or outliving as the critical enigma of our time.

Walter Benjamin theorized the difference between *überleben* and *fortleben*— surviving and living on. Television plays out the tensions between these modalities of being by producing narratives that compulsively turn around crime. These narratives, traveling between real and fictive reference, allow for no loose ends but suture and resolve the enigmas they name. Television produces corpses that need not be mourned because, in part, of the persistence of surviving that is shown. Still, television itself is cut up, lacerated, seriated, commercial broken, so that its heterogeneous corpus can let something other than itself leak out. I would like to explore in slow-mo, though scheduling always rushes us, the status of crime time which has saturated television, if only to name an unreadable relation to the incomprehensibility of survival and its relation to law.

CHANNEL NINE: The death of God has left us with a lot of appliances. Indeed, the historical event we call the death of God is inscribed within the last metaphysical spasm of our history as it continues to be interrogated by the question of technology. The event of the death of God, which dispersed and channeled the sacred according to altogether new protocols, is circuited through much of technology, occasionally giving rise to electric shocks. I am referring to God because, despite everything, He in part was the guarantor of absolute representability and the luminous truth of transparency. In an era of constitutive opaqueness—there is no transcendental light shining upon us; we dwell in the shadows of mediation and withdrawal; there will be no revelation, can be no manifestation as such—things have to be tuned in, adjusted, subjected to double takes and are dominated by amnesia. Without recourse to any dialectic

66

of incarnation, something however beams through, as though the interruption itself were the thing to watch.

CHANNEL NINE: Media technology has made an irreversible incursion into the domain of American "politics." The anxieties which have ensued concern not so much the nature of fictioning—politics has always been subject to representation, rhetoric, artifice—as the newly intrusive effects of law. This is not to say that the law has ever been zoned outside of us, but, thanks to the media, different maps of arrest have been drawn up; the subject is being arrested according to altogether new protocols of containment. And practically everybody in homeless America is under house arrest. In this restricted space (the "space allotted" by the conventions of an essay), it is possible to scan seriously only one episode in the relation of media to law. This episode is exemplary because it functions as an example—something that implies a generality of which it is a part; but at the same time one must not lose sight of the singularity it brings to bear upon our understanding of media and state politics. Few episodes have broken the assignments of their frames and exploded into the socius as has the Rodney King "event." Beyond the articulated outrage that this episode has produced, its persistent visibility has forced us to ask tough questions about American scenes of violence. When they pass into the media and graduate into "events" are these scenes already *effects* of the media? To what extent is serial killing an *effect* of serial television or its imprinting upon a national unconscious? Or, to return to our channel: What is the relationship between mutant forms of racism (today's racism is not the same as yesterday's; it is constituted by a different transmitter) and the media, which appears to resist older types of racism? I am merely trying to pose the questions, if only to adjust the proper channels through which they may be circuited. One may wonder why it was the case that the Los Angeles Police Department, and not an equally pernicious police force, became the object of coverage by television. On some crucial level, television owns and recognizes itself in the LAPD, if only because television first produced the mythic dimension of policing by means of "Dragnet" and the like. The LAPD is divided by referential effects of historical and televisual narration. That the one is constantly exposed by the other, flashing its badge or serial number, is something we now need to interrogate. But exposed as the LAPD appears to be, it is always covered by television. What is television covering? This seems to bring us a long way from the question of politics in America. Yet, owing to the teletopies created by television when it maps political sites, we no longer know where to locate the polis, much less "home." This is why we must begin with the most relentless of home fronts.

HEADLINE NEWS: *Some of you think that it is the hour of TV-guided destitution. Inside and outside the home, the time has come to think about the wasted, condemned bodies that crumble before a television.*

CHANNEL EIGHT: Among the things that TV has insisted upon, little is more prevalent than the interruption or the hiatus for which it speaks and of which it is a part. The television persists in a permanent state of urgency, whence the necessity of the series. The series, or seriature, extradites television to a mode of reading in which interruption insists, even if it does so as an interrupted discourse whose "aim is to recapture its own rupture."[4] If we are going to attempt to read the interruption as such, then we shall be reading something that is no longer appropriable as a phenomenon of essence. The question remains as to whether we can read the trace of interruption that is put into some sort of shape by a series or net, without having it be dominated by the logic of the cut but rather by tracking the intricacies of *destricturation;* that is, the interruptions which constitute a network where knots never land or tie up but cause traces of intervals to be indicated. Precisely such fugitive intervals—as elusive slip or trace of interruption—bind us ethically. Through its singular mode of persistence, the hiatus announces nothing other than the necessity of enhancing the moments, particularly the moments of rupture, albeit in a nondialectical fashion: it would be absurd to make claims for producing a dialectical summation of all the series, that is, interruptions, that tie up TV and its breaks. Where the effect of shock continues to jolt or to make the image jump, there is still the necessity of enchaining the moments and producing linkage.

So, in the space of interruption (an atopy or interruption that used to be called Television Land), there exists a muted injunction to read the hiatus and let oneself be marked by the hiatus—a necessity of negotiating the invisible lineage of the net.[5] To this end, it becomes necessary to displace the focus from television as totality to the seriality of derangement, a place of disturbance, something that can be designated as being "on location" only on the condition that it remain dislocated, disarticulated, made inadequate and anterior to itself, absolutely primitive with regard to what is said about it. If TV has taught us anything—and I think it is helpful to locate it somewhere between Kansas and Oz, an internal spread of exteriority, an interruption precisely of the phantasmic difference between interiority and exteriority—the teaching principally concerns, I think, the *impossibility of staying at home.* In fact, the more local it gets, the more uncanny, not at home, it appears. Television, which Heidegger, when he was on, once associated with the essence of his thinking, chaining you and fascinating you by its neutral gleam, is about being-not-at-home, telling you that you are chained to the deracinating grid of being-in-the-world. Perhaps this explains why, during his broadcast season, Lacan spoke of *homme*-sickness.[6] We miss being-at-home in the world, which never happened anyway, and missing home, Lacan suggests, has everything to do in the age of technological dominion with being sick of *homme*. In the closing words of *The Wizard of Oz*, "There's no place like home." So where were we? asks the scholar.

We have no way of stabilizing or locating with certainty the "in" of being-in-the-world, no matter how much channel surfing you are capable of enduring. Television exposes that constitutive outside that you have to let into the house of being, inundating and saturating you, even when it is "off." While television, regardless of its content or signified, tends toward an ontologization of its status—no matter what's on, I daresay, it is emptied of any signified; it is a site of evacuation, the hemorrhaging of meaning, ever disrupting its semantic fields and the phenomenal activities of showing—television traces an articulation of sheer uncanniness. This is what Heidegger understands as our fundamental predicament of being-not-at-home in this world (which we have yet to locate and which technology helps to map in terms of teletopies, which is of no help). While television's tendential urge guides it toward ontology, there are internal limits that, however, freeze frame the ontological urge into an ethical compulsion. One of these internal limits that is at once lodged outside *and* inside TV is a certain type of monitoring—the nomadic, aleatory, unpredictable eruption we sometimes call video.

CHANNEL SEVEN: TV has always been under surveillance. From credit attributions to ratings and censorship concessions, television consistently swerves from the ontological tendency to the establishment of legitimacy, which places it under pressure from an entirely other obligation. It is no wonder that television keeps on interrupting itself and replaying to itself the serial crime stories that establish some provisional adjudication between what can be seen and an ethicolegal position on the programs of showing. Oedipus has never stopped running through television, but I'll get to the violence of legitimation and patricidal shooting momentarily. At any rate, the crime stories that TV compulsively tells itself have been charged with possession of a mimetic trigger; in other words, as TV allegorizes its interrupted relation to law, it is charged with producing a contagion of violence. A perpetual matter of dispute, the relation of television to violence is, however, neither contingent nor arbitrary but zooms in on the absent, evacuated center of televisual seriature. At the core of a hiatus that pulses television, I am placing the mutism of video, the strategy of its silence and concealment. Though I recognize the radically different usages to which they have been put empirically and the divergent syntaxes that govern their behavior, I am more interested in the interpellation that takes place between television and video, the way the one calls the other to order, which is one way of calling the other to itself. In fact, where nomadic or testimonial video practices a strategy of silence, concealment and unrehearsed semantics, installed as it is in television as bug or parasite, watching (out) (for) television, it at times produces the Ethical Scream which television has massively interrupted.

This ethical scream that interrupts a discourse of effacement (even if that effacement should indeed thematize crime and its legal, moral, or police resolutions), this ethical scream—and video means for us "I saw it"—perforates television from an inner periphery, instituting a break in the compulsive effacement to which television is in fact seriously committed (I am not speaking of the politically correct gestures that TV has produced by star trekking interracial and interspecial specials: these are on the order of thematic considerations which have been sufficiently interpreted elsewhere). When testimonial video breaks out of concealment and into the television programming that it occasionally supersedes, it is acting as the call of conscience of television. This is why, also, when television wants to simulate a call of conscience (the call of conscience [Gewissensruf] is the aphonic call discussed in Heidegger's Being and Time), it itself reverts to video. The abyssal inclusion of video as call of conscience offers no easy transparency but requires a reading; it calls for a discourse. As we have been shown with singular clarity in the Rodney King case and, in particular, with the trial, what is called for when video acts as the call of conscience is not so much a viewing of a spectacle, but a reading, and, instead of voyeurism, an exegesis. On both sides of the showing of this video, we are confronted with the image of condemned and deserted bodies—what I try in Crack Wars to define as the "trash bodies," dejected and wasted—and this is why, when you're on television, as its spectral subject on either side of the screen, you've been trashed, even if watching television is only a metonymy of being wasted in the form, for instance, of "wasting time." To the extent that we, like Rodney King, are shown being wasted by the deregulation of force, and are left crumpled by the wayside, we know we are dealing with a spectral experience and the screen memory of the phantom. At the same time, we also must endeavor to understand why the generative impulse of the Rodney King story was pivoted on the misappropriation of drugs—by the police. TV on drugs, policing drugs: the working-out of a hallucinogenre in which the suspect is, on the surface, viewed as being on PCP, a problem relating alētheia to phantomal force. The collapse of police into television is only beginning to produce a history of phenomenal proportions. As the technical medium returns to the site of its haunted origins, it shows one of the more daunting aspects of the collaboration between law enforcement and performative television to consist in the growing number of arrests that the latter has made.[7]

• • •

Haunted TV: the phantom of the Gulf War, bleeding through the body of King. Haunted TV: showing by not showing what lay at our feet, the step out of line. Haunted TV: focusing the limitless figure of the police, this "index of a phantom-like violence because they are everywhere." The police aren't just the police "today more or less than ever," writes Derrida; "they are the *figure sans figure*."[8] They cut a faceless figure, a violence without a form as Benjamin puts it: *gestaltlos*. This formless, ungraspable figure of the police, even as it is metonymized, spectralized, and even if it installs its haunting presence everywhere, remains, for Benjamin, a determinable figure inextricably linked to the concept of the civilized state. This is why we are never going to be on furlough as concerns the necessity of reading the effects of haunted TV.

The Rodney King interruption of broadcast television not only forces a reading of force and enforcement of law, but requires citation and the reading precisely of the phantom body of the police. If anything, it announces the ubiquity of the police station identification. The police become hallucinatory and spectral because they haunt everything. They are everywhere, even where they are not. They are present in a way that does not coincide with presence: *they are television.* But when they come after you and beat you, they are like those televisions that explode out of their frames and break into a heterotopy that stings. Always on, they are on your case, in your face.

What video teaches, something that television knows but cannot as such articulate, is that every medium is related in some crucial way to specters. This ghostly relationship that the image produces between phenomenal and referential effects of language is what makes ethical phrasing as precarious as it is necessary. Because of its transmission of ghostly figures, interruption, and seriature, it would be hardly sufficient to assimilate television to the Frankfurt School's subsumption of it under the regime of the visual, which is associated with mass media and the threat of a culture of fascism. This threat always exists, but I would like to consider the way television in its couple with video offers a picture of numbed resistance to the unlacerated regimes of fascist media as it mutates into forms of video and cybernetic technology, electronic reproduction, and cybervisual technologies.

HEADLINE NEWS: *The disfiguring writing on the face of Rodney King.*

CHANNEL SIX: Television is being switched on out of a number of considerations. Despite and beside itself, TV has become the atopical locus of the ethical implant. Not when it is itself, if that should ever occur or stabilize, but when it jumps up and down on the static machine, interfering as an alterity of constant disbandment.

One problem with television is that it exists in trauma, or rather, trauma is what preoccupies television: it is always on television. This present us with considerable technical difficulty, for trauma undermines experience and yet acts as its tremendous retainer. The "technical" difficulty consists in the fact that trauma can be experienced in a least two ways, both of which block normal channels of transmission: as a memory that one cannot integrate into one's own experience, and as a catastrophic knowledge that one cannot communicate to others. If television cannot be hooked up to what we commonly understand by experience, and if it cannot communicate, or even telecommunicate, a catastrophic knowledge but can only—perhaps—signal the transmission of a gap (at times a yawn), a dark abyss, or the black box of talking survival—then what has it been doing? Also, why does it at once induce the response of nonresponse and yet get strapped with charges of violent inducement?

CHANNEL FIVE: I have to admit that initially, when adjusting myself to technology, I was more pointedly drawn in by the umbilicus of the telephone, whose speculative logic kept me on a rather short leash. On first sight, television seemed like a corruption, as in the case of many supersessions, of the serious lineage of telephony; it seemed like a low grade transferential apparatus, and I felt television and telephone fight it out as in the battle in *Robocop* between mere robot (his majesty the ego) and the highly complex cyborg (who came equipped with memory traces, superego, id, and—ever displacing the ego—a crypt). In yet another idiom, telephony was for me linked to the Old Testament (the polite relation to God, as Nietzsche says), whereas television seemed like the image-laden New Testament (where one rudely assumes an intimacy with God and makes one of His images appear on the screen of our historical memory). Needless to say, I was on the side of the more remote, less controlled, audible sacred, to the extent that its technical mutation can be figured as telephone. The Old Testament unfolds a drama of listening and inscription of law; in contrast, the New Testament produces a kind of videodrome revision of some of the themes, topoi, and localities of its ancestral text. Now, I am not referring us to these texts in order to admit a conversion of any sort, but merely for the purpose of turning the dial and switching the ways in which our being has been modalized by a technology that works according to a different protocol of ethical attunement. If I refer us to the twin Testaments, this in part is for the purpose of exploring the site of testimony that television, despite and beside itself, has initiated. It is no accident that television, in view of the dramas we have come to associate with the names of Lacan, Elvis, Heidegger, Anita Hill, Rodney King, Lee Harvey Oswald, Vietnam—fill in the blanks—and Desert Storm, has become the locus of testimony, even if we are faced with false testimony or resolute noncoverage. In a moment I will try to show, to the extent that anything can be shown, why the Gulf War was presented to us as a discourse of effacement; in other words, why at moments of referential need, the experience of the image is left behind. This has everything to do with the interruptive status of death, but also with the problematic of thematization. In other words, there is, I believe, a concurrent mark of an invisable channel in television that *says* the problematic of thematization, which makes the rhetoricity of the televisual image collapse into a blank stare.

At moments such as these—most manifestly, during the seriated nothing that was on at the time of the Gulf War—television is not merely performing an allegory of the impossibility of reading, because this would still be a thematizing activity (the problematic activity of thematizing will have been taken up again in the Rodney King case). During the Gulf War, television, as a production system of narrative, image, information flow, and so forth, took a major commercial break as it ran interference with its semantic and thematic dimensions. The interference that television ran with itself, and continues to rerun on a secret track, points us to something like the essence of television. I would like to argue that the Rodney King event, which forced an image back on the screen, presented that which was unpresentable during the war. Rodney King, the black body under attack by a massive show of force, showed what would not be shown in its generalized form: the American police force attacking helpless brown bodies in Iraq. Now it so happens that the Rodney King trial was about force itself. Thematically, what is being measured, tested, and judged in the televised trial, is the question of force as it eventuates in the form of excessive police force. And there's the catch. We saw it blown up and cut down in the Anita Hill case—force can never be perceived as such. This is a persistent question circulating in the more or less robust corpus of philosophical inquiry. The question now is: How can philosophy talk about force?

The "theme" par excellence in "Cops on Trial" produced arguments concerning the regulation of force, its constitution and performance, which proved to be thematically disturbed and could be scaled only in terms of an ethics of dosage (escalation and deescalation of force). This served to demonstrate that we still do not know how to talk about force with an assured sense of its value or implications for judgment. While TV was under the covers, nomadic video captured images of brute force committed by the LAPD. Anyone who was watching the trial knows that the referential stability of the images was blown out of the water. Witnesses were reading blurs and blurring images. The status of the image as a semantic shooting range has been severely undermined as TV conducts this interrogation of force. The interrogation was forced upon TV—it involves an interrogation, I would submit, about its own textual performance in the production of force. What comes out provisionally, at least, is the fact that video, *nomadic* video—aleatory, unpredictable, vigilant, testimonial video—emerges as the call of conscience of broadcast TV, including CNN, C-SPAN, and so on.

HEADLINE NEWS: *Expenditure, wasting time. Getting wasted. A bug or virus that started spreading after the war: the endless survival of what has not been fully understood. The circuits are loaded with the enigma of survival.*

CHANNEL FOUR: What interests me provisionally, today, concerns the two eyes of television. TV is always watching, always involved in or subjected to monitoring and surveillance when it has two eyes, one of which can be the eye donated by video. I am not saying that video is the truth of television, nor its essence. Rather, it is what is watching television; it is the place of the testimonial that cannot speak with referential assurance but does assert the truth of what it says. This is why I want to focus it as the call of conscience, which is to say that video responds in some crucial sense to the call of television. Now, you have seen me play with the contrast and wave TV into the realm, or rather logic, of telephony. How can TV make a call, or more precisely, respond to a call? The way we call it is critical. (At the same time as TV is being watched by video and called to order, football has decided to dispense with instant replay. This decision, while made by team owners and not by media technologists, theorists, or media activists, nonetheless asserts that when it comes to calling it, TV withdraws its bid for claims made on behalf of referential stability.)

Let me try to unfold some of these points, and indicate where I think I'm going. On one level, television calls for a theory of distraction which appears to be rooted in the trauma that it is always telling, yet unable to fix. This suggests a complicated economy of visual playback and shock absorption, for trauma essentially involves an image without internalization. Recently, Cathy Caruth has argued that trauma does not "simply serve as a record of the past but pre-

74

cisely registers the force of an experience that is not yet fully owned. . . . this paradoxical experience . . . both urgently demands historical awareness and yet denies our usual modes of access to it. . . . while the images of traumatic reenactment remain absolutely accurate and precise, they are largely inaccessible to conscious recall and control."[9]

HEADLINE NEWS: *The relatedness of television to the end of history. Codes for such a reading were punched in when Benjamin and Freud discovered the experience of shock and the steps beyond the pleasure principle. This leads us to ask: What does it mean precisely for history to be the history of trauma?*[10] *It becomes necessary to translate the possibility of history by means of technology's flashback programming or the prerecorded logic of TV.*

Let me bring some of these strands into contact with one another. TV is irremissible; it is always on, even when it is off. Its voice of conscience is that internal alterity which runs interference with television in order to bring it closer to itself, but this closed-circuit surveillance can be experienced only in the mode of an estrangement. Television presents itself as being there only when it is other than itself: when it mimes police work or when, during the Gulf War, blanking out in a phobic response to the call of reference, it becomes a radio. And yet, it's not that simple: in this case it *showed* itself not showing, and *became* the closed, knotted eye of blindness. Within this act of showing itself not showing, posing itself as exposed, which is to say, showing that its rapport to the promise of reference is essentially one of phobia, it produces a dead gaze—what Blanchot would call "a gaze become the ghost of eternal vision." There is something in and from television that allows sight to be blinded into a neutral, directionless gleam. Yet, "blindness is vision still," "a vision which is no longer the possibility of seeing."[11]

In a sense, TV doubled for our blindness and in fact performed the rhetoric of blindness that guided the Gulf War. Television entered us into the realm of the eternal diurnal, night vision and twenty-four-hour operational engagement; its unseeing gaze was figured by the hypervision responsible for flaring TV-guided missiles that exploded sight at the point of contact. Television showed precisely a *tele*-vision, that is, a vision which is no longer the possibility of seeing what is at hand, and if it taught us anything, it was this: What fascinates us robs us of our power to give sense; drawing back from the world at the moment of contact, it draws us along, fascinated, blinded, exploded. Despite the propaganda contracts which it had taken out, television produced a neutral gleam that told us the relation between fascination and not seeing. If it showed anything, television showed a television without image, a site of trauma in which the experience of immediate proximity involved absolute distance. But it was through video, intervening as the call of conscience of TV, as foreign body and parasitical inclusion in broadcast television, that a rhetoricity of televisual blindness emerged. Marking the incommensurate proximity of the same, testimonial video split television from its willed blindness and forced it to see what it would not show. Something was apprehended.

There was the undisclosed Gulf War. Earlier I tried to read this according to Lacanian protocols of mapping the maternal body. The imaginary mapping of the primordial aggression of the subject reproduces the cartography of the mother's internal empire, marking the origin of all aggression, according to Lacan and, before him, Melanie Klein. This in part explains why mothers became such prominent figures in this war that refused to figure itself materially. Mother ("mother of all battles," "mothers go to war," and so on) was not only put on the map by this war; she *was* the map. Can't get into her now, though it can be said that all forms of (paranoiac) aggression are perpetrated upon a displaced cartography of the maternal or, in the case of white on black, upon a body mangled by the rage through which the Other is marked with lacerations in the feminine.[12] As crude as it may seem to recognize this—and yet who doesn't know it?—Rodney King was put upon and sodomized ("Saddamized" in the metonymic citation) by brutal hets.

CHANNEL THREE: So, as I was saying, the Gulf War was blanked out, put into a position of latency. As with all unsuccessful attempts at repression, the symptoms were bound to come rocketing from a displaced area of the vast televisual corpus. The Rodney King event of 3 March 1991 stages the survival of the Gulf War in its displaced form. Indeed, on his last day in office, on television, Chief of Police Gates blamed the media for precisely this type of displacement: "You made it [the Rodney King beating] into something bigger than the Gulf War" (broadcast news reports, 27 June 1992). This holds for the beating, but when the troops were sent into L.A. to subdue the targeted population, the media reverted to their failure to show, recovering in essence their rerunning away, or the structural relation to the whited-out war.

What we call "Rodney King" has brought the question of force, or, officially, that of excessive use of force, to a hearing; it has placed police action on trial. Desert Storm was time and again understood as police action. Whether or not this represents a conceptually correct assessment in terms of strategy, buildup, tactical maneuvers, declarations of intent, and so on, it remains the case that at this instance the national unconscious inscribed the collapse of police action and military intervention. "Rodney King" (who in fact never presented himself in the first trial that refers us to him) names the hearings which never took place for war crimes committed in the Persian Gulf War. Condensed and displaced to the beating of Rodney King, the televised trial, subtitled "Cops on Trial," thematized unthematizable force fields of intensity, while studying the problem of impact and the incitement to brutality with which TV has always been, in one form or another, associated. What is the relation between TV and violence? Hasn't this been television's only question when you get down to it?

COMMERCIAL BREAK: "That's not the way force is studied," retorted use of force expert Robert Michaels several weeks into the trial. Bringing to the fore a study of force impact involving the difference between incapacitating strikes and pain compliance impact devices (in particular the electric Taser gun), upper-body control holds, theories of escalation and deescalation of force, the trial induced by Rodney King showed how television, forced by video, was hearing out arguments organized around its own essence. This essence was shown to be critically linked to questions concerning trauma control and the administration of force. As the use of force expert tells it, on the first level the "empirical" force spectrum entails evaluations of verbal communication and effects of presence, while the second level involves responsiveness to pain compliance impact devices, including upper-body control holds and the chokehold (whose routinely racist applications the police recognizes and hence avoids using when beating King). Resolutely uninterrogated, the force spectrum however fails to provide a reliable grid for evaluating force because it has not been tapped by theoretically sound means that would throw some light on what constitutes "effects of presence," "responsiveness," "communication," and the like. I am not so foolish as to prescribe a mandatory reading list of Heidegger, Wittgenstein, Deleuze, Foucault, and Derrida for police training, though it would not hurt (their victims). But once the police started reading or knowing what they were doing, or whom they were representing and why, they would no longer be the police, the phantom index to which Benjamin's argument pointed us. At the very least they would be, as readers, essentially detectives (and only *essentially*): those loners who, resisting group formation, sometimes have to turn in their badges or cross an ethicolegal line in order to investigate, piece together, read, and scour unconscious densities of meaning. It's not a pretty job, and it's generally managed according to a different time clock than that which the police regularly punches. To the extent that pedagogy was blamed for the failure of the police to understand the scene of arrest or to control the usage of brute force, and teachers were asked to speak about teaching, certain questions of how to read, or, at least, how to produce effects of learning, were emphatically focused in the trial. While the introduction of the "force spectrum" was never in itself reflected upon or theorized, it nonetheless serves to circumscribe such levels of responsiveness as law enforcement and television, each in the idiom peculiar to it, attempt to elicit and regulate. Working over the arrested body, each inscribes and wastes it, making it do time, sometimes along the lines of teaching a lesson.

HEADLINE NEWS: *If television and the police are experiencing some kind of shared predicament of being on call, it is necessary that we understand how these calls are circuited through the transmission systems of police force. The circuits are loaded: they range from the call of duty, to which an officer is likely to respond with violence, to highly suspect considerations of what constitutes responsiveness. (The defense's refusal to interpret King's calls as cries of pain was maintained throughout the trial.) Yet, the motif of the call ambiguates the scene of violence, for the possibility of appeal and the call of conscience are logged on to the same systems.*

One would have to bring to bear a critique of violence in the manner of Benjamin, if it were not that TV was itself trying to tell us something about the status of legal and social fictions. TV does not know what it knows. In the idiom of Heideggerian insight, TV cannot think the essence of TV which it is however constantly marking and remarking. Television's principal compulsion and major attraction comes to us as the relation to law. As that which is thematized compulsively, the relation to law is at once there and not there, cancelling its program by producing it. (Hence the proliferation of police shows, from "Dragnet" to "Perry Mason," "911," "Hard Copy," "Top Cops," "FBI," "Law and Order," and courtroom dramas; even westerns with their lone law enforcer and inevitable sheriff belong to this topos.) This relation to law which television compulsively repeats as its theme is simultaneously presented as the unthematizable par excellence—that is to say, this is a relation that cannot be presented as such but can only be appealed to or offered up as metonymic citation. Television is summoned before the law, but every attempt to produce the relation to law on a merely thematic level produces instead a narrative which is itself metonymic; the narrative is metonymic not because it is narrative, but because it depends on metonymic substitution from the start.[13] In other words, television cannot say the continuity of its relation to itself or its premier "object," which can be understood as force. This is why Rodney King's show, "Cops on Trial," is about television watching the law watching video, its call to order, a figure of order

78

that tries to find the language by which to measure out an ethical dosage of force. At no point do television or policing delude themselves into assuming they can do without force, but they do not question this essential supplement. (Concerning supplement and dosage, Television, as a drug, is also a tranquilizing force, regularly absorbing and administering hits of violence. After a hard day's work on *Psycho,* Alfred Hitchcock used to doze off in front of TV, claiming that TV, unlike film, was soporiferous.) Alternately stimulating and tranquilizing, ever anxiety producing, television belongs to the domain of the internalized *Ge-Stell* or "posure" of drugs, which is why, once again, the Rodney King event has to start its narrative engine with a false start acknowledged by all—everyone involved in the chase had to start by assuming that they were pursuing a PCP suspect. Without technology's relation to the asserted effects of drugs, hallucination and supernatural force, there would be no act of television reading itself, which is to say reading images of a phenomenal "self" pumped up on the supposition of drugs but without any substance behind it.[14]

HEADLINE NEWS: *Implicit difference between tele-vision and video according to chapter seven of* Sein und Zeit. *Heidegger comments that the* scheinen *of semblance, in its various forms, "is founded upon pure* phainesthai, *in the sense of phenomenal presencing. The Greek sense of phainetai," he notes, "differs from that of the Latin* vidētur, *even where mere semblance is denoted, for the Latin term is offered from the perspective of the observer, rather than from out of the unconstrained spontaneity of presencing."*[15]

HEADLINE NEWS: *The disruption of experience and comprehension that trauma involves.*

What, then, were the charges made in the Rodney King trial? The defense has tried to show that, following the car chase, King took a step which in fact was a charge—he was said to be charging the LAPD. The countercharges, made by the defense in this case, pivot on the difference between a subject who is taking a step and one who is charging. If King was charging, then the force used to subdue him would have been justified. The distinction between taking a step and charging could not be determined with certainty by the footage provided in the George Holliday video tape. There seems to be an impasse, even though a phenomenal imaging of this scene exists. Repeated several hundred times in court, the frame-by-frame analyses explicitly raise questions about the relation between video recording and human memory. When witness David Love relies on his own memory of the beating he feels the violence to have been entirely

79

justified; however, when he is asked to interpret the video he finds the "same" scene to display an excessive and altogether inexplicable use of force. Throughout the testimony it is asked of this witness to express "what the video does and does not say." The entire problematic of witnessing comes into play. An assertive if provisional conclusion nominates the video as "the best witness"; but video, it is further argued, "doesn't tell the whole story" because it cannot reveal "state of mind." There were no strong readers around, at least none were called in. Superior Court Judge Weisberg rules out the expert testimony even of psychologists (who perhaps should not be confused with strong readers).

Is there a whole story, a totality of a story that eludes the video scope but can be located elsewhere? Is there a state of mind, a clarity of intention, an interpretation with its totalizing impulses, upon which the LAPD can confidently count?[16] We know that a "strong reading" (one should measure how much force strong reading requires) of the tapes would need first to account for these metaphysical ploys and rhetorical deceits, if only to discern the axiology upon which the constitution of force could be thought. What the video cannot in any case show, states the court, concerns an interiority which it cannot inscribe; the video is pure surface without depth, running a mystifying release precisely because it fails to record inner perceptions. Unfueled by metaphysics, video is running on empty. Without access to interiority, the videotape deflects the scene from its locus in truth. This is why the court rules in favor of human memory of violence, the flaws and gaps in recall notwithstanding. Precisely where human memory of experience fails to achieve cognition—so the logic seems to go—it captures the "whole story." The court depends upon this evacuated site in order to retrieve a sense of the totality of the scene. This explains how the videotape's excess weighs in as deficiency in court. A mere machine, simply present while at the same time devoid of presence, it originates in a place without truth. As pure surface, the videotape effaces interiority as a condition of running. This is why the police give it chase—but they are also chased down by this suprapolice tape; on and off the streets, in your face and behind your back, the tape indifferently keeps running.

But let us keep in line with the first step of this process. Did Rodney King charge or step? The video that records this moment does not tell. The phenomenal instability of the image is staggering; there is no assured way to read the syntax of the move on a literal level. This step, which is out of line with all the certitudes we think we have about documenting the real, is in sync with Lacan's assertion that our encounter with the real is a missed appointment. In terms of the reading protocols that make up our legacy, the step that hesitates referentially between a step and a charge, tripping up the case as it does, is also a Freudian slip, a lapsus and collapse in the grammar of conscious imaging. So the television watches as the video is on compulsive replay, tripping over this unreadable scene that it has witnessed. "Gehen wir darum einen Schritt weiter," writes Freud in *Beyond the Pleasure Principle*. Freud, like the video on compulsive instant replay, reruns this step throughout the text that goes beyond the pleasure principle. Let us take another step.

HEADLINE NEWS: *Implications for memory: the difference between internalized memory and Memorex clips that run along the lines of flashback and other intrusive phenomena.*

It is as if Freud is watching us watching this scene that returns incessantly. Running through psychoanalysis, we learn that vectorizing our thoughts toward "current events" means that we are in fact looking at recurrent events whose eventuation cannot as such be easily located. Trauma reduces us to scanning external stimuli whose signals beam out a density of materials for historical reconstitution: "Solche Erregungen von aussen, die stark genug sind, den Reizschutz zu durchbrechen, heissen wir traumatische. . . . Ein Vorkommnis wie das äußere Trauma wird gewiß eine großartige Störung im Energiebetrieb des Organismus hervorrufen und alle Abwehrmittel in Bewegung setzen [We describe as 'traumatic' any external stimuli which are powerful enough to break through the protective shield [layering]. . . . The occurrence of a trauma externally induced is bound to create a major disturbance in the functioning of the organism's energy and to set in motion every possible defensive measure]."[17] What I would like to suggest is that the Rodney King trial in its particularity constitutes a moment when television reads itself, and, staging itself reading itself, it is prompted by the interpretation of force set out in *Beyond the Pleasure Principle,* where the death drive kicks in by taking repetitive steps toward a beyond. It was Derrida who first noted, in *La Carte postale,* how Freud keeps on trying rhetorically to take another step in an attempt to get beyond a textual impasse. But going nowhere on a fast and invisible track, Freud steps up the momentum of external force, eventually achieving what he sees as the phenomenon of "breaking into the psychic layer that protects against excessive force." The dramatic incursion of excessive force peels down this protective layering, radically exposing the subject to the domain of the traumatic. In the realm of media technology, such a structure of protective layering has been historically provided by television which, up to a point, manages the scenography of external stimuli. The excess of the Rodney King intrusion upon broadcast television dramatized the rupturing of the protective film with which television

THE CALL OF TECHNOLOGY

habitually covers itself by showing and producing the traumatic scene of "excessive force." Broken in upon by testimonial video, television ceased to protect against that very thing which it is intended to regulate. Formally on par with television, what Freud calls the domain of the traumatic is not as such a domain according to classical calculations of space and time but that which opens up a site of tremendous disturbances ("wird gewiß eine großartige Störung . . . in Bewegung setzen") whose limits are difficult to discern. Like television, the "domain" of the traumatic, while producing historical effects of reference, cannot be located in the world, but points instead to paradoxes of temporal complexities. We are on location, dislocated to the site of a provocation from the past that stammers over the "pas au delà"—that Blanchotian space where the step can and cannot go beyond, restricted by a prohibitory injunction that points us backward as we attempt to trace the future of a step. The step beyond also involves the tripping that made it possible for the taped brutalization of King to blow out of teleproportion and into the streets.

HEADLINE NEWS: *"The historical power of trauma is not just that the experience is repeated after its forgetting, but that it is only in and through its inherent forgetting that it is first experienced at all."*[18]

What urges us on, and motivates linkage between the Freud text and Rodney King event text and with the discourse underlying the war on drugs, and all the steps we have been impelled to take beyond the pleasure principle, involves the same break in consciousness. We now encounter the fact of fundamental disruption in traditional modes of consciousness and understanding, a disruption that occurs traumatically in the very experience of our history. This invasion of consciousness, a type of break in the possibilities traditionally allowed for experiencing experience, is what Benjamin called the *Chockerlebnis*—a jolt which occurs when an event is dissociated from the understanding that might attach itself to it; shock produces a split of memory from consciousness, often triggering technologically morphed mechanisms on the order of flashback or hallucination.

CHANNEL TWO: The trial has produced a number of maps, photographs, and flowcharts of chronological time sequences; yet these common devices for capturing empirical parameters of events have failed to prove much of anything. Except, possibly, that we are dealing here with a type of experience that eludes temporal and spatial determinations altogether—something that can bust into a scene at any time, any place, miming the experience of the police.

If the Rodney King beating figures the survival of the effaced Persian Gulf War, then its principal "object" of projection would involve the phantom text of a trauma. Precisely because the trauma is hidden from televised view—the Rodney King beating is a metonymy of a hidden atrocity, be this the unshown war or the atrocities to which African-Americans are routinely subjected—it is accessible only by reading. The spectral trauma remains hidden even to the hidden camera that blindly captures it. Yet, capturing the hidden trauma—and not the suspect called Rodney King or even the police out of line—is the way that video has participated in focusing the disruption of experience and comprehension that Trauma TV involves. Under nocturnal cover, nomadic, guerrilla video captures no more than the debilitating discrepancy, always screened by television, between experience and meaning which Freud associated with trauma. This is why it could prove nothing but this discrepancy in a court of law. "Gehen wir darum einen Schritt weiter."

When the trial tries to number the blows, count the strikes and determine the velocity of force, all it can do is attempt to parry the shock that "in modernity dissociates once and for all the traditional cohesion of experience and cognition."[19] The repeat performance of a frame-by-frame blow shows how this text became nothing more than the compulsive unfolding of a blank citation. In this instance, video intervened as a distance that separates the witness's knowledge of the traumatic occurrence from the sheer repetitiveness which marks the experience of its telling.

CHANNEL ONE: Is it accidental if one refers to the function of witness repeatedly by using the masculine pronoun? Or is it perhaps an "accident" of such magnitude that its enigmatic character has been somewhat effaced? Testimony, as Freud knew, reverts to the privilege of testicles, engendering truth within the seminal flow of testimonial utterance. Let's take this a few steps further. Standing as witness, in step with Freudian logic, and bearing testimony [*Zeug, zeugen*], swearing in the truth of one's testimony upon one's testicles, implies that the subject before the law comes under the threat of castration. The truth is related to this threat. Oedipus the video, lagging behind, limping out of step and out of line, plucking his eyes out when he sees the truth—this is the truth of video, the site of the neutral gleam that knows something which cannot be shown. When Freud traces testimony back to testicles he is also severing truth from any security net that might underlie cognition. Testimony, and that which it begets, is linked not so much to perception but to speculation. When Roman jurists swore upon their testicles they were swearing upon a truth that could never be known for sure, to whose resolution no amount of evidence could do

83

more than swear. Swearing, bearing witness, producing the testimonial—these constitute acts of language that, unfounded (that is, neither "founded" as in poetic speech nor "grounded" as in philosophical speech nor even secured by "ordinary language" usage), rely upon the vagaries of speculation, displacing the *testi*mony to the fragility of the eyes: the two eyes of television and video, which are committed to the uncertain rigors of reading. Whether you are making sense or semen, you can never know for sure whether you are indeed the father of truth. Thus, in its essence and logic, testimonial is fragile, uncertain, performative, speculative. (In this regard, the one who is feminized, on the side of sense certainty, penetrated by force, the figure of excluded negativity, is bound to lose out to the symbolic inscription of the testimonial.) The legal mode of the trial "dramatizes . . . a contained and culturally channelled, institutionalized crisis of truth. The trial both derives from and proceeds by a crisis of evidence, which the verdict must resolve."[20] As a sentence, the verdict is a force of law performatively enacted as a defensive gesture for not knowing.

FACE THE NATION: To this end, the Clarence Thomas hearings say more about that which cannot be presented, the relation between phallus and castration, the unrelenting crisis of evidence, and the nature of the testimonial as the drama by which the symbolicity of testicles come to be marked. These hearings bore witness to the powerful but empty phallus that could not be summoned to appear but around which the hearing was organized. This was not a negligible testimonial but one addressing itself to the essence of a supreme organ of state, namely, the Supreme Court of the United States. In this case, which tested the case of the case—the essence of testimony and the rectitude of justice—race, I daresay, initially disguised the sexual difference upon which legal testimony is erected and judgment based. It will not do to simplify the case by stating that Justice Thomas is a black man; identified as such, the African-American nominee carried with him phantasms of the *jouissance* of the Other and effects of the phallus. In this regard, race aggravated the demand for presenting the phallus; but, like the phantom it is when presentation is beckoning, the phallus was shown for what it is: *in camera* as on camera, it can only be nothing.

CHANNEL ZERO: My contention is (and others have argued this according to different impulses and grammars) that television has always been related to the law, which it locates at the site of crucial trauma. When it is not performing metonymies of law, it is still producing some cognition around its traumatic diffusions; thus even the laugh track, programming the traumatic experience of laughter, can be understood to function as a shock absorber. It signals the obsessive distraction that links laughter to a concept of history within which Baudelaire located the loss of balance and, indeed, "mankind's universal fallen condition" ("On the Essence of Laughter"). With the loss of balance and the condition of falling, we are back to that unreadable blur that is said to project the step—or the charge—taken by Rodney King on 3 March 1991.

"Trauma stops the chronological clock," writes Lawrence Langer in 1991. This stopwatch configures, in fact, what makes television, despite the insistence of its "60 Minutes"–like ticking or the breathless schedule that it runs, freeze. Still, television stops the chronological clock which it also parallels in a fugitive, clandestine way and according to two modes of temporal assignment. Television stops time by interrupting its simulated chronology in the event of an "event" which is neither of time nor in time but something that depends upon repetition for its occurrence. The "event" usually enters television from a place of exteriority in which the witness is figured by an untrained video operator (consider here the footage of the collapsed Bay Bridge in the 17 October 1989 San Francisco earthquake). Television also stops the chronological clock by miming its regularity and predictability around the clock, running and rerunning the familiar foreignness of traumatic repetition. Indeed, one would be hard pressed to prove that the effectivity of TV was not a symptom of the traumatic stress which it also works to perpetuate. In their article on trauma entitled "The Intrusive Past," B. A. van der Kolk and Otto van der Hart describe trauma as if it were linked to the very functioning of the television apparatus, or, at least, as if the traumatized subject were caught in a perpetual state of internalized channel surfing: "He switches from one [existence] to the other without synchronization because he is reporting not on a sequence but a simultaneity. . . . A different state consists of a continuous switching from one internal world to another."[21] A monument to that which cannot be stabilized, television captures disruption, seriature, the effraction of cognition, and internal breaks—whether commercial or constitutive—and is scripted by a need to play out the difference between reference and phenomenality. On this score, there remains one more thing to be said about the relation of television to trauma. This has everything to do with the essential character of traumatism as a nonsymbolizable wound that comes before any other effraction: *this* would be TV's guide—how to symbolize the wound that will not be shown.

Of the symptoms that television most indelibly remarks, one is the alternation marked between hypermnesia and amnesia. What is the relation between amnesia and the image? We have observed in films such as *Total Recall* that, in order to discover the limits of any possible reality, acts of remembering are prompted by mnemonic devices along the lines of video implants. In fact, video has tracked considerable thematizations of internalized, commemorative memory (*Erinnerung,* in Hegel's vocabulary) that are nothing if not the literalization of *Gedächtnis,* an external memory prompter, a cue, or memo padding. While these video implants are often accompanied by nightmarish hues, they somehow remain external to the subject who needs these prompters to supplement an absence of memory. The image comes to infuse an amnesiac subject. "Total recall" is not the same as memory or recollection, and it is only total to the extent that it names the need for a prosthetic technology that would produce a memory track. In such films, the video transport—always pointing to a modality of transport, they constantly neurotransmit highs, crashes, incessant repetition or fuzzing, they combine the idioms of drugs and electronics—the technochip induces some sort of trip, a condition of memory seen as lapsus, stimulating the transmission of the slip. The video transport coexists with a condition of stated amnesia. It is to such intractable amnesia, channel surfing through blank zones of trauma, that television, sponsored by screen memories and forgetting, responds, secretly measuring the force of an unbearable history.

Notes

1. Cited in Cathy Caruth, "Unclaimed Experience: Trauma and the Possibility of History," in *Literature and the Ethical Question,* ed. Claire Nouvet, *Yale French Studies* 79 (1991): 181.

2. This essay was written while "Cops on Trial" was being aired on Fox Television, prior to the announcement of the Simi Valley's jury's verdict of not guilty. The logic of the ethical scream by which testimonial video is here understood appears to have stood its test: when the verdict of nonreading came out, the video produced effects of insurrection on the streets. It will not do to go with the unassailed diction of "burning down one's *own* neighborhood" when in fact it is a matter of radical expropriation and being not at home, which is the subject of this paper. Delivered in New York City, Oakland, Berkeley, and Los Angeles before and during the "riots," this paper retains stylistic traces of the circumstances in which it was first presented. (I am not as opposed to the usage of the word *riots* as others have been, no doubt because I am not seriously susceptible to supporting the order or logic of reason to which the riot addresses itself. As a type of noise and disturbance, *riot* belongs to the field of the ethical scream.) I have benefited greatly from the papers and discussions of Fred Moten, Peter Connor, and Shireen Patell.

3. Jacques Lacan, "Television," in a special issue, ed. Joan Copjec, of *October,* no. 40 (Spring 1987): 36.

4. On interruption and the logic of destricturation, I am following Jacques Derrida's argument in his discussion of Levinas in "En ce moment même dans cet ouvrage me voici," *Psyché: Inventions de l'autre* (Paris: Galilée, 1987), 159–202.

5. A number of works have provided the frame within which to cast the catastrophic topicalities of television/video. I have benefited from discussions with and papers by a community of media scholars, which includes Mary Anne Doane, Gregory Ulmer, Meghan Morris, Maggie Morse, John Hanhardt, Jonathan Crary, Mark Taylor, Patricia Mellencamp, David Levi Strauss, Gilles Deleuze, and others. I would also like to acknowledge a paper given by Deborah Esch, "No Time Like the Present: The 'Fact' of Television" at the University of California Humanities Research Institute, Irvine, March 1992. It was there, while participating in the "Future Deconstructions" conference, that I had the opportunity to watch intensive television and follow the Rodney King trial in detail.

6. I am implicitly networking through the signifying chain of home-*homme* and homophobia. The technical media has thrown into relief an unreadable line between sexual marking and racial identification. On the law and its relation to sodomy in Freud, see my "The *Sujet Suppositaire:* Freud and Rat Man" (*Finitude's Score*). In this essay I begin to develop a reading of the difference between detective and police work in terms of their relation to truth.

7. Television has made an increasing number of arrests in recent years; one show has recently celebrated its two-hundredth arrest.

8. See Jacques Derrida's remarkable discussion of Walter Benjamin's "Critique of Violence" in "Force of Law: The 'Mystical Foundation of Authority,'" trans. Mary Quaintance, *Deconstruction and the Possibility of Justice,* spec. issue of *Cardozo Law Review* 2:5–6 (July/August 1990): 1009.

9. Caruth, introduction to *Psychoanalysis, Culture, Trauma II*, ed. Caruth, special issue of *American Imago* 48 (Winter 1991): 417. On the relation of atopy and flashback, Caruth writes that what the "history of flashback tells—as psychiatry, psychoanalysis and neurobiology equally suggest—is, therefore, a history that literally *has no place,* neither in the past, in which it was not fully experienced, nor in the present, in which its precise images and enactments are not fully understood. In its repeated imposition as both image and amnesia, the trauma thus seems to evoke the difficult truth of a history that is constituted by the very incomprehensibility of its occurrence" (418).

10. On an urgent inflection of this question, see also Caruth and Thomas Keenan, "'The AIDS Crisis Is Not Over': A Conversation with Gregg Bordowitz, Douglas Crimp, and Laura Pinsky," in *Psychoanalysis, Culture, Trauma II,* 539–56.

11. Maurice Blanchot, "The Essential Solitude," *The Space of Literature,* trans. Ann Smock (Lincoln: University of Nebraska Press, 1982), 32.

12. See "Support Our Tropes (Reading Desert Storm)," esp. the "Activist Supplement" (*Finitude's Score*).

13. Consider Paul de Man's demonstration of metonymic substitution in "Time and History in Wordsworth," *Diacritics* 17 (Winter 1987): 4–17.

14. For two relatively new readings of technicity and *Ge-stell* in Heidegger, I would suggest Véronique Foti's *Heidegger and the Poets: Poiēsis/Sophia/Technē* (Atlantic Highlands, NJ: Humanities Press International, 1992), and, especially, Jean-Luc Nancy's title essay in *Une Pensée finie* (Paris: Galilée, 1990).

15. Foti, *Heidegger and the Poets*, 4.

16. The tensional relationship between interpretation and reading is drawn from Andrzej Warminski, *Readings in Interpretation: Hölderlin, Hegel, Heidegger* (Minneapolis: University of Minnesota Press, 1987).

17. Sigmund Freud, "Jenseits des Lustprinzips," *Psychologie des Unbewußten* (Frankfurt: Fischer Taschenbuch Verlag, 1975), 239. For the English translation see *Beyond the Pleasure Principle, Complete Psychological Works,* ed. James Strachey, 18:29 (trans. mod.).

18. Caruth, introduction to *Psychoanalysis, Culture and Trauma I,* ed. Caruth, special issue of *American Imago* 48 (Spring 1991): 7.

19. Kevin Newmark, "Traumatic Poetry: Charles Baudelaire and the Shock of Laughter," in *Psychoanalysis, Culture, Trauma II,* 534.

20. Shoshana Felman and Dori Laub, *Testimony: Crises of Witnessing in Literature, Psychoanalysis, and History* (New York: Routledge, 1991), 18.

21. B. A. van der Kolk and Otto van der Hart, "The Intrusive Past," in *Psychoanalysis, Culture, Trauma I,* 448, 449.

State of the Art

JULIA SCHER'S DISINSCRIPTION
OF NATIONAL SECURITY

When at long last he came out of hiding to offer a word of solace or an official statement of fact, the president of the United States said, "We are being tested." In the meanwhile the mayor of New York suddenly came alive with language and filled the telecommunicational spaces with quiet grandeur. Both understood that they were being tested—or more precisely, perhaps, *retested,* since they were riding waves of repetition compulsion and responding to some failed anteriority; they had both been subjected to the blows of delegitimizing narratives of which they were, for the most part, themselves the origin. On this day the president ducked out of sight for many crucial hours, withholding language and the semblance of public dignity. The other one, the mayor, on-site, rose to the occasion, offered language and future without, for once, compromising the exigencies of mourning. The prez, when he came back to something like language, repeated that the nation was being tested. He is said to have been transformed by the test, to have of a sudden understood his task and destiny, to have recognized the precise contours of evil. The calamity of September 11 marked, according to the national rhetoric, the beginning of a new test site. The internal folds of the new test site multiplied the stakes of constitutional democracy and threw its meaning, by the overwhelming pressure of emergency, into technological fast-forward—that is to say, into regression. Once again the engine of perfection that characterized the Gulf War—the technological theater of deployment, the unrivaled virtual sophistication—raged against recalcitrant landscapes. But more significantly, the state of exception provoked by the attacks on the World Trade Center and Pentagon decisively shifted the focus of state from conventional tropes of governance to those principally of security. The immeasurable grief caused by the missions allowed for the violence of the shift to pass with only a whimper. The modern state has always had a thing for security. Obviously. In an unpublished work of the 1970s Michel Foucault had outlined the gravity of such a shift, pointing, as Giorgio Agamben reminds us, to the fact that "security as leading principle of state politics dates back to the birth of the modern state.

THE CALL OF TECHNOLOGY

Hobbes already mentions it as the opposite of fear, which compels human beings to come together within a society."[1] But not until the eighteenth century did the thought of security come into its own. The concept of national security has made any lucid citizen and alien shudder with anxiety. It is the ironclad concept by which any number of abuses get smuggled into the precincts of an otherwise vigilant social expanse. It is so strong a concept, so powerfully allied with restorative efforts of symbolic repair, that it singularly resists demystifying incursions. Who could argue with a felt need for security? Who would be so mindless as to risk Bataillean derision at the very imposition of a possible security as something worthy, legitimate, and desirable? From the security blanket to unalloyed military assertions of urgent need, the regime of security holds sway over us unlike any other statement of irrefutable political purpose.

If there is one artist who has insisted with exemplary prescience on articulating the premises of such a political mutation, it is Julia Scher. Her work has consistently brought into focus the dependency of our nation on the complexity of surveillance systems and the persistent determinations of a security state which, her work argues, stands in a contestatory relation to democratic institutions and tropes. Agamben argues that the shift to the security state is irreconcilable with democracy. Scher, while relentlessly critical of the security tropes around which her thought is organized, offers an even more disturbing view.

She in effect meshes the deadly zones of security measures with the pervasive yet hidden problem of technological seduction. Hers is a site of acute political sensibility that remains open to infiltrations, psychic leakage, and unaccountable contaminations. Alongside the sinister crackdowns of state she locates life-forms of S/M wish fulfillment, entering a hypothesis of a Schreberesque reception system that uniquely welcomes the invisibly penetrating rays of high technology. Her insight does not stop at the intrusive probes of the security state or traumatic arrests of the electronic capture but explores the secret complicities, the unavowable concessions made to invasive control. She posits the nearly post-human body as that which blossoms open to the pulse of technological encroachment, as that which thrives on the intrusive threat and offers itself as test site for new transparencies. The bag and the body lean forward to receive the penetrating probes of a deceptively benevolent form of social engineering. The intrusive maneuvers of thoroughgoing inspection parallel the sexual instruction and are filtered on the whole by a reassuring idiom; thus the titles *Hardly feel it going in* and *I'll be gentle*.

Unlike political theorists, including Agamben, Scher is not shy about considering the fatal pleasure calls of the otherwise neutralized, globalized, and invading state of security. She reflects that which tracks and attracts, and offers us a way to read those who get off on being watched and punished, those who thrill to the inexorability of being caught on tape. In other words, Julia Scher stands alone as guard and guardian of an unstated perspective of what has befallen us: she uniquely has an angle on the future of the security state which takes into account the psychoanalytic predictions of a masochistic politics—something that might account for an unprecedented docility on the part of a highly technologized body politic. Scher's work in effect exposes a politics of submission that no longer belongs to any recognizable lexicon of oppression, poverty, or class determination. She discovers and marks another epoch of submission that flies beneath the radar of traditional theoretical protocols of political understanding. To be sure, she is clear about the murderous consequences of carrying out dubious police action in the name of security. She understands the regime of new teletopies, the disruption of political sites and the consistently morphing configurations of electronic disturbance. Yet, she leaves room for a study of scoptophilia, sexuality and surveillance, the seduction of cooing female voices—the phallic penetration of the ear—the punctual thrills of data harvesting, the singular abandon of batch recording, and the low-tech matter of commonly accessorized uniforms. There is nothing simplistic about Julia Scher's vision, nor does she revert to a peculiar brand of Deleuzian machismo fueled by legendary desiring machines.

Instead, Scher registers a different level of visual dissidence, prompting a minor insurrection each time she mobilizes the viewing body as part of the totality of her work. The viewer/citizen is fed into the installation by a field that mimes what can be seen as the municipal–clinical gaze, disrupting the ruling metaphors of autonomy and integrity of self. The viewer body submits to the calculative traversals associated with technology—a body probed, analyzed, sectioned and scanned, measured and standardized by the pressures of the technological grid. The viewers fail to reappropriate themselves by means of a solidifying image but see a representation gliding through the monitors, vaguely dislocating their whereabouts and furtive gestural expression. Unaccountably, one has opened an account with a bank of monitors. Like technology itself, video surveillance is henceforth irremissible. It is always on, on you, trained on you as part of the unbroken quotation of a certain grasp of reality. It is not as though one could turn away from technology at will or zone its incursions to a circumscribed space, a comfortably sealed Elsewhere. Ever probing, the security technology intensifies the body's sense of exposure, illuminating while denying its absolute fragility.

But what has become of the body, not to say the body politic, since it has come under the control and command of ever-encroaching surveillance systems?

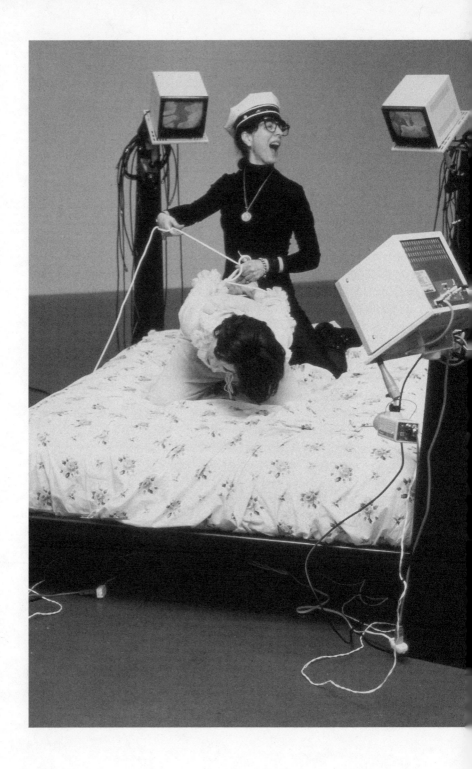

What has this to do with the province of so-called art? At least since Holbein's *Dead Christ in the Tomb* (Kunstmuseum, Basel), art has been fascinated by the portrayal of the body without transcendence, the pure corpse, mangled and mutilated, which has yet to be rescued by the promise of resurrection. The body surrendered to security technologies is reflected in the concerns of some of these installations which capture the inevitable instrumentality of unredeemed corporeality, whether dead or alive, though already deadened as it swipes through an otherworldly video corridor. The artist/guard becomes its amnesiac witness, capable of momentary attestations, observing and monitoring, unsure of ever recovering sense from the irruptions of total contingency, measuring out an endless unedited C-SPAN of corporeal manifestation. Sometimes the body is but a shadow on the work, a fragment, a vaguely contorted figuration; sometimes the space of an installation is emptied of the human body that nonetheless seems dispersed over its premises—there are room and spaces, prison cells, that have been traversed by somebody, even a phantom body, inscribing textures that open forgotten wounds and tag commemorative lesions. The body is there even when it is not there; and when it is there on the screen, it poses as a screen memory of another body, another regime of disclosure. The body is momentarily secured; it is cleared of transcendence as it gets searched for the lethal prosthesis or is simply recorded, reduced to a thumbprint, unique and concentrated, if largely irrelevant to mythemes of human striving.

Relentlessly engaging the catastrophic consequences of the uncritical use of the figure of security, Scher is herself a certified security expert; she operates a company called Safe and Secure Productions. Yet Julia Scher pumps her installations with irony, something that has prompted some controversy concerning the purported meaning of her work. It would be unreasonable to overlook the crucial dimensions of her ironic hold on things. In the first place she has addressed the way in which her installations produce an ironic double of the state premised on a rhetoric of national security. She copies that rhetoric in order to sculpt and inhabit a space of dissimilarity. Unlike more representational or regressive artists, Scher practices active forms of mimesis that depart from models or copies. She simulates the very structure that she criticizes, risking at every juncture to locate herself inside an apparatus whose hegemony she denounces. She does not occupy a comfortable outside, nor does she proceed with the unflappable certitudes of an insider's knowledge. There is always a traumatic residue that cannot be read, something that can slip away from signification or go out of control. She sits in the control room burdened by impotence, articulating a space of powerlessness that she nonetheless affirms. Thus in her talk "Transgressions," she asserts the movement of difference that defines her efforts to mime and dismantle. Having "gone where artists weren't supposed to go, infiltrated the deep bowels and hidden computer nets," she remarks that she has merely simulated a takeover. However:

> Oh no . . . un-uh . . . I haven't taken their space. I haven't gone where I wasn't wanted. I haven't. You and I have not taken space—we may have used space— we may have mused on its character but un-uh oh no—we haven't taken the space. I may have in some small way tried to copy those people that do take space—that take whole countries, that take whole peoples and move them around—that take their land. But no, I haven't done that. . . . I may have in a small way, tried to copy those who have infiltrated
>
> THE GOVERNMENT HAS INFILTRATED
> RCA HAS INFILTRATED
> THE CIA HAS INFILTRATED
>
> Have we ever taken away an identity, a country's country by infiltrating? You may have taken a site but you have never taken someone's home away. Have I ever done anything covert? No. I never did anything covert. . . . I have not documented sexually embarrassing facts and created opportunities for their documentation. . . . I may have feigned intimacy and deceived a bit . . . but I never put up for sale an entire people, entire country—I never sold out an entire generation of children for profit—I never destroyed the health of thousands to get my point across. . . . I've never given anyone space for genocide.

Affirming the work of a negative mimesis, Scher circumscribes a space of what is not, holding firmly to what she fails to perform yet steadily invokes in her acts. Sharing the same syntax and method as that of which she is critical, Scher performs a sort of Nietzschean destruction; that is to say, she destroys what is destructive in order to clear the way, in order to open another space for future—one or rather ones that are yet indeterminable and radically hospitable to genuine futurity. Here the Heideggerian distinction between destruction and devastation may prove useful. *Devastation* is foreclosive, it kills off the future—this is where Scher locates acts of government—whereas *destruction* is subjected to the exigencies of clearing away, opening paths for the future. One could say that all of Scher's work is hinged on the border between destruction and devastation, doubling the parameters of that which she destroys as she builds—or, in another, equally suggestive idiom, she *disinscribes* as she inscribes. The repetition of technological structures and designs, the unrelenting replication of immoderate security measures, produces a steady disinscription of the ideological premises on which they are set up. Scher does not turn away from that which impinges on Dasein ever more insistently but travels its edges in order to repeat and reflect the offending technosymptomatologies. In this sense she has always been an ironist, that is to say, she produces the ironic interruption, the caesura or hiatus within the smooth totality of a security state that contains her like a foreign body. Julia Scher not only monitors the museum space that she sets up to replicate corporate, government, and penal probes but, acting as an allegory for other spaces, she has placed the state under surveillance—she watches them watch, even if all she does is signal that watching slips by as a traumatic event—something we no longer see and that does not belong to the conventional categories of experience as such. Ever on the alert, her systems signal other, often more pernicious, acts of viewing, sometimes more sleepy forms of seeing, recording, inscribing. Henceforth, the techno-activity of state is on her watch. She may not hold the power to disable criminal excesses of state, but she is watching: Julia Scher has installed herself as the internal alterity of all security systems; she has become the call of conscience of surveillance technology. She inhabits, as trace or as ironic destruction, the surveillance apparatus fixed on Washington Square Park, in airports, at the ATM, in prisons, throughout department stores, in police vehicles, in your face and hidden from view. She is even, in her own view, an updated flâneur, cruising the streets with Walter Benjamin's ghost, sporting a suitcam, once in a great while a dresscam, and other hidden video cameras that capture the existential arcades.

The ironic doubling in which her work persists points to a type of historical activism that is situated with pressing clarity by Kierkegaard. For Julia Scher's efforts require us to situate the altogether provocative poses that her work assumes—somewhere between *prophesy* and *absolute negativity*, Kierkegaard's way of naming irony. Kierkegaard retains clear boundaries between prophesy and irony, which Scher can be seen to cross at crucial junctures. It will help us to address those who have an uninterrogated hankering for something "new" in art and installations. Discussing the significance of the *turning point* in history, Kierkegaard moves from the tragic hero (who battles for the new and strives to destroy what for him is a vanishing actuality, "but his task is still not so much to destroy as to advance the new and thereby destroy the past indirectly. . . . the old must be superseded") to the ironic subject, who does not possess the new.

> In one sense the ironist is certainly prophetic, because he is continually pointing to something impending, but what it is he does not know. He is prophetic, but his position and situation are the reverse of the prophet's. The prophet walks arm in arm with his age, and from this position he glimpses what is coming . . . The ironist, however, has stepped out of line with his age, has

turned around and faced it. That which is coming is hidden from him, lies behind his back, but the actuality he so antagonistically confronts is what he must destroy; upon this he focuses his burning gaze.

According to Kierkegaard, the ironist is also a sacrifice that the world process demands, not as if the ironist needed in the strict sense to fall as a sacrifice, but she is consumed by her own fervor in the service of the world spirit. This is where Kierkegaard famously locates irony as the infinite absolute negativity. "It is negativity because it only negates; it is infinite because it does not negate this or that phenomenon; it is absolute because that by virtue of which it negates is a higher something that still is not. The irony establishes nothing, because that which is to be established lies behind it."[2]

A rigorously disruptive formation that puts power hegemonies on trial, the work of disinscribing the art and language of today's security state, is, like a woman's work, never done. It is in any case not established in the comfortable performative sense, but she turns her back to what is coming, taking the blows, getting stabbed by the winds of an unknowable futurity, returning evermore to sender as she antagonistically confronts what must be destroyed. In this way, pointing to what is impending, the work produces a test site for a national rhetoric that claims to exceed its untractably vigilant scrutiny.

Notes

1. *On Security and Terror,* unauthorized translation by soenke.zehle@web.de, source: Frankfurter Allgemeine Zeitung, 20 September 2001.
2. Søren Kierkegaard, *The Concept of Irony, with Continual Reference to Socrates* (ed. and trans. Howard V. Hong and Edna H. Hong, Princeton, N.J., Princeton University Press, 1989), 260–61.

Part Two

Freedom and Obligation

Minority Report on Children,
Addicts, Outlaws, and Ghosts

Q. *In the introductory remarks to the interview you did with*
Andrea Juno in Research: Angry Women, *you are referred*
to as an "ivory-tower terrorist." Are you comfortable with
that label? Does it seem accurate?

A. These are questions about naming and location, and in
this regard neither term is acceptable. The ivory tower
is something that I have never been embraced by, or
possibly even seen; it is a phantasm. And "terrorist"
would imply a kind of being that is single-minded and
fanatically set on a goal. By contrast, I would be too
dispersed, self-retracting, and self-annulling in the way
I work to be considered a terrorist as such. If anything,
I would say that I am a counterterrorist. It is true that
I have called for something like an extremist writing.
And also I have made hyperbolic attempts to secure the
space of academia as a sheltering place of unconditional
hospitality for dissidence and insurrection, refutation
and undomesticatable explosions of thought. To the extent that the academy is a mausoleum, it tends to expect
the reverence due the dead, and my irreverent type of
reverence seems to set off, in those describing what I do,
some explosive language. But I would also say, in a more
general and gendered sense, that very often women
who have a somewhat original bent are institutionally
psychoticized and isolated. They tend to be structurally
positioned as dangerous creatures, so there is always a
SWAT team of academic proprietors closing in on them.
In this sense, I can see how the "terrorist" appellation
might have grown on me or been pinned on me. But it
comes from the institutional space and not from me. I
was tagged.

There's also this: While I was at Berkeley, I was close
friends with Kathy Acker and Andrea Juno. *Mondo 2000*

declared us the "deviant boss girls of a new scene," models of subversion, and so on. That little community may have provoked some politicized assertions, marking the way the three of us would stage ourselves publicly and "kick ass" in a certain way. In this regard, I think one would want to look more closely at the possibility or impossibility of friendship in academia, and what it implies. Who are your friends? How does friendship set up (or subvert) a transmission system for the kind of work you do and read? One is often judged by one's public friendships. I was friends with Kathy and A.J. And I think there was something scary about this little girl gang of troublemaker writers. Certainly, publishing with *Angry Women* did do momentary damage; it dented my career a bit—though it is laughable to offer up an imago of my career as a smooth surface to be dented. It was never not dented: one originary dent.

Q.   *What kind of damage did it do?*

A.   Well, I think colleagues were a little shocked to see me involved with performance artists, recontextualized and reformatted in the space of very angry, very outrageous, shit-covered, dildo-wielding, multisexual women. I think there was a gender-genre crossing that probably seemed a little excessive.

Q.   *Did you have tenure yet?*

A.   Yes I did.

From "Confessions of an Anacoluthon" (248–49).

On the Unrelenting
Creepiness of Childhood

LYOTARD, KID-TESTED

From Socrates' predatory urges to Locke's invention of the "Ideot" or Hegel's racist assignments—for the moment I shall take this no further—philosophy has demonstrated a need to impound those who could not speak for themselves, who had not reached a certain legislated majority. Under the reign of Locke, Hume, and Condillac, empirical philosophy assembled the figure of the idiot in order to put some reality behind established hypothetical assumptions.[1] The idiot pinned down the first folds of language in the essays on human understanding. Made to stand for an epoch, lost to civilization, of originary memory, the idiot spanned the chasm between nature and culture. His entry on philosophical pages helped, moreover, to rehabilitate the "empirical" basis of empiricism. Much can be said about the induction of wild children, savages, idiots, and infants into the realm of philosophical speculation, and it would be important to investigate more fully the peculiar yet crucial status of these minorities as philosophy conducts its adult raids. No doubt Nietzsche may be seen to have turned this state of affairs on its head when he invited the animals to participate in a new tropology.

Now comes Jean-François Lyotard, who talks to children. No matter how polymorphously perverse, punctually pampered, or pacified, these are the distressed among us, the fearful and hungry. They squeak and peek and try to get their meaning across. They panic, then smile and burble, then panic. Held in abusive custody by the laws of becoming, they hang on to your finger for dear life. From the get-go, the reality principle sneaks up on them to snap them out of the domain of the pleasure principle (of course this is a complicated relay, as Lacan has shown, for the reality principle is always in defeat; but still, it goes after you). As in Goethe's ballad, the Erlking is out to get them, poised to snatch the child from the arms of momentary reassurance. In the case presented by Lyotard we are faced with the figure of the minor, often oppressed, for whom language and representation may not be entirely foreclosed, though surrender, the predominance of muteness, and a repertoire of stammers often govern the thwarted scene of childhood. Still, there are reprieves and the event of memory; language, however jumbled, mimetic, deregulated, occurs and belongs to the existence to which childhood—something that eventually goes into remission but returns in waves throughout the lives of the wounded—is fitted. Interiority does not necessarily take hold at the early stages. Yet even when these children are silenced or a hand is laid on them, they are traversed by what Lyotard understands as sheer *feeling*—maybe a pinch of joy, a sting of melancholic regret, a straitening that cuts both ways, a body memory that trembles. With no language of interiority to vouch for feeling, the children are more or less stranded, bared to colonializing projection.

Vaulted and shut, their subjectivity—if there is one—offers little in the way of an account; even so, in most cases they surpass or at least scramble the master codes of philosophical claims made on their behalf and elude the cognitive scanners that try to detect and classify them. The child constitutes a security risk for the house of philosophy. It crawls in, setting off a lot of noise. The figure of the child, which in the end inserts an imaginary lesion in philosophy—a condition that calls out for endless symbolic repair—may be borne by the anguish of the *différend*. That is to say it enters, or is entered, into the places where speech falters and language chokes in the throat of a political body, where the question of fair representation is peremptorily dismissed or simply not addressed. But it is not as if the child had the means of representation at hand. The child is given over to extreme forms of defenselessness: dependency, Lyotard indicates, is too weak a word to describe the condition of such minority-being, the ever haunting condition of childhood.

How did they stumble into philosophical headquarters? Well, their prototype, the essential child—the idiot—appeared alongside or at the head of the train of blind, deaf, or mute subjects (whose implications for subjecthood, precisely, provoked crisis) and was most closely leagued with the prestige accorded to the construction of the wild child—the teachable idiot. They were pressed into service, assigned to uphold mythic assurances of the humanly clean slate, presenting such a possibility, in theory, at least, to the extent that they—idiots—donated their bodies to the cause of a science that staked everything on what appeared to constitute observable traits of human origins. Recruited to the cause of philosophy to make a philosophical point, the idiot belongs outside the philosophy whose integrity it promotes. The child, as I said, crawls in at unexpected moments or morphs, as in Kant's critical reflections, into the ambivalent purveyor of genius—the irresponsible, often puerile excess to which we owe the poetic word.

In *The Inhuman,* Lyotard, for his part, writes of the debt to childhood that is never paid off. A matter of the traces of an indetermination, childhood continues to hold us hostage. The obscure savageness of childhood reminds us that all education is inhuman "because it does not happen without constraint and terror" (4).[2] At once savaging and civilizing (there is never one without the other), education straitens the little one, who is cornered by cultural demand. Childhood, in any case, will leave us with inhuman surges of deregulation, with a level of fear and distress that can come up at any point in the trajectory of so-called human development. "Shorn of speech, incapable of standing upright, hesitating over the objects of its interest, not able to calculate its advantages, not sensitive to common reason, the child is eminently the human because its distress heralds and promises things possible" (3–4). Lagging behind itself, the child's "initial delay in humanity," moreover, "which makes it the hostage of the adult community, is also what manifests to this community the lack of humanity it is suffering from, and which calls on it to become more human" (4). The irrevocable creepiness of childhood is the place from which an ethical call is placed—be it made by the day-care crowd or the operators Antigone, Christ, and Isaac, all loyalists to the child's camp, even though their identity as children must remain at once undecidable and settled. (For some reason—or unreason—some figures of ethical calling are tagged essentially as children, even if by other measures they are plainly in midlife crises when they are tried.) Lyotard asks: "What shall we call human in humans, the initial misery of their childhood, or their capacity to acquire a 'second' nature which, thanks to language, makes them fit to share in communal life, adult consciousness and reason?" (3). Childhood enters a breach into the very concept of the human and makes us ask, once again, what it means to be human. Yet the decision to claim the human is split between the early episodes of initial desolation and the later cover-up schemes that language supports and the community payrolls.

More severe words are reserved for the provocation of childhood in another, later text. In "Mainmise" the child is lined up with the slave, with the one whose destiny is put in the hands of another.[3] Like the slave, the child does not belong to itself, having, Lyotard says, no claim to himself (there is no play of "/herself," so out of a sense of frustrated probity I will repeat the complete oppression of the girl-child): "He is in the hands of another. Dependency is too weak a word to describe this condition of being seized and held by the hand of the other" (1). By childhood Lyotard means that we are born before being born to ourselves. "We are born from others but also to others, given over defenseless to them. Subject to their *mancipium,* and to an extent that even they do not recognize" (2–3). The offense is such that even the offenders, by necessity repeat offenders, operate on the level of an unconscious siege. You may want to know when exactly the sneak attacks strike: Childhood is an age that is not marked by age—or rather, it does not age but recurs episodically, even historically. Childhood can last a whole lifetime if you find yourself throttled and unable to root out some representation of what is affecting you; this can happen every day. "I am speaking of this condition of being *affected* and not having the means—language, representation—to name, identify, reproduce, and recognize what is affecting us" (2). If I am not mistaken, Lyotard uses childhood to resist the modern Western ideal of emancipation; he manages to deflate the reverie that has you thinking you'll get out from under the grip of the *mancipium.*

The *mainmise,* which travels in many disguises (parental love "may have been a calamity—it may have engendered such a *mainmise* over the child's soul" [3]), often remains unknown to the child as an adult. Something is taking her down, even as she meets the world with measurable instances of "success." Under the thumb of an invisible yet persistent *mainmise,* the adult child regresses to minority following an unpredictable rhythm of being that beats the drum of an impossible emancipation—the emancipation promised by humanism, whether Christian or secular, which teaches that "man is something that must be freed" (3). As for the nature of this freeing, "there are many different possibilities, from Augustine up through Marx" (3). These promises say in effect that the *mainmise* can be thrown off, even dealt with definitively, according to some calculable program or redemptive ground plan. If we could get over it—this would suppose that we had a reciprocal grasp of what is keeping us down.

The *mainmise,* a condition of extreme captivity, can be so powerfully effective that, like the child, the adult has no access to it by means of memory or cognition. To bring the terms of this condition to bear on us, if only by projective inversion, it is almost as in those stories of *The Twilight Zone,* which end with a shot of a miniature house where normalcy was played out under the gaze of a giantess, a playing child. The shadow thrown on you was in a sense too big to be perceived, much less fought off. One is left dumb and unknowing about the *mainmise* that nonetheless accompanies your every move and persists in calling the shots. The imprint is so profound that the child, well, "it will not even occur to him to rebel, nor will he have received the gift or grace to pray that his *mainmise* be lifted" (3). Because of the untraceable fingerprints of the *mainmise*—I am surmising here, as Lyotard is unclear about how this works—the condition that he describes should not be subsumed merely by structures such as those underlying severe neuroses or psychoses ("I am not just talking about severe neuroses or psychoses" [3]). There is no account or narrative that could contain or point reliably to the *mainmise*, no anamnesis, as he likes to say. At the same time, the surrender is so pervasive that it need not be pathologized in order to be heard. One does not have to be psychotic to understand that you're barely out on bail on good days and back in the hovel of wretched captivity on other days of your so-called autonomous being. The possibility of a given freedom, freedom as unquestionably given, and before all else a given, thrown in with the *da* of our Dasein—in other words the kind of freedom that Jean-Luc Nancy with his Kantian signet posits—seems to be absent from the scene.[4]

The hold on the child translates into an irrevocable wounding on which childhood in fact depends. The timing may be slightly off, because in this instance Lyotard hints that pleasure may be felt prior to the wound, while elsewhere he indicated, I thought, that the wounding hold had first dibs on the child. To the extent that the rhythm of unconscious time bombing is included in the depiction of these experiences (which often bypass "experience"), it would be petty no doubt to insist on strict synchronicities. Lyotard offers this wo(u)nderful observation: "For the child, everything is a wound, the wound of a pleasure that is going to be forbidden and taken away" (3). The *mainmise* is raised as a sign of what is about to happen, namely, of what has always happened: it is raised to slap the pleasure out of the child. In this round the *mainmise* is, we could say, the hand of time. Time beating pleasure, given over to the stranglehold of the reality principle. "The suffering that results and the search for the object, something analogous, in short, to emancipation, arise out of this wound" (3). The emancipatory urge, prompted by the early experience of essential deprivation, starts with this figure of analogy, weak but soldering. (In Lacan's reading of Freud, the fundamental desire—the incestuous one—is prohibited in one of the starts of life: everything else flows from the initial withholding pattern, including the battering search for the object neither entirely lost nor altogether found.[5]) Alive with the memory trace of early forfeiture, the subject tries to free itself, at least enough to cover the losses. Thus originates the call, a call to emancipation or of exodus—a call, in any case, that initiates the movement of flight. The call positions the constrained child in relation to elsewhere. The children of Israel (why are they children?) are said to have taken the call as they headed for trouble or, rather, more trouble, and elsewhere.

Lyotard links the temporal wounding to the flight from Egypt. In the essay he observes, in reference to the exodus of the Hebrews, that they "escaped the Pharaoh's *mancipium* only by placing themselves under the *mancipium* of Yahweh" (2). The fantasy of a promising elsewhere is broken. It is not as though there would be a locatable exteriority to the primal hold. Permit me to introduce an analogy, another hand to play in the negotiations with the *mainmise,* for it is still necessary to elucidate the difficulty of ever obtaining a truly valid exit visa when it comes to the anticipation of an exodus. It is understood that every analogy ends in catechresis. Let us move on. As with the plight of addiction elaborated by Thomas de Quincey, one can move only from one addiction to the other, even if the second term is that of a cure; the oppression of dependency, the demand of adherence to the addiction or to that which opposes it, is structurally the same.[6] What joins the disparate events consisting in the *mainmise* of the child, the flight from Egypt, and the call from elsewhere (Lyotard persistently figures the flight from Egypt as a response to a call, a "vocation") is the unknowing in which they originate and continue effectively to hold sway. One is dumbstruck, somnambulizing, rising to a call that cannot be identified or in any meaningful way secured. Perhaps it comes from the past or resounds in a future dimly awaited. "It comes from beyond me and within me"—this is how Heidegger locates the call, the aphonic call of conscience in *Sein und Zeit.*[7] At any rate, one cannot account for the call that has a hold on me or, disrupting any conscious itinerary, that puts me on hold without my consent, surpassing my initiative or the knowledge I think I have about the way things go as I crawl through the playing fields of Being-in-the-world.

Attentive to that which, defying cognition and eluding memory, stultifies, Lyotard tries time and again to trace the call. There is something that grinds Being, knowledge, memory, as well even as health, to a level of indifference, something that defies all conceptuality or generalizable principle. He stays close to the ground and keeps his receptors open. There is a grand coherency in the fact that when his narrated *Lebenslauf,* his *curriculum vitae,* established in *Peregrinations,* evokes the call on an almost ontological frequency ("there is something like a call" [9]), Lyotard claims a lifelong interest in the notion and doctrines of indifference.[8] Something in Being menaces thought, undermines writing, with a quiet, sort of pernicious consistency. In the distant past, Lyotard offers, he was committed to the encounter with that to which we remain deaf and sluggish—to the "groundlessness of Being which constantly exerts a fascinating threat over thinking and writing" (9). He writes his MA dissertation on *Indifference as an Ethical Notion.* A paper investigating a kind of originary stupor that involved the Epicurean *ataraxia,* the Stoic *apatheia,* the extreme Stoic *adiaphora,* the Zen not-thinking, the Taoist nothingness, and so forth, it later on leads to considerations of other stultifying modalities of Being. I would not hesitate to go as far as grouping his concern with reflective judgment in this category or to mobilize for this thought-numbing area of the work his discussion of Freud's call to let the mind float: "You have to impoverish your mind, clean it out as much as possible, so that you make it capable of anticipating the meaning, the 'What' of the 'It happens . . .'" (18). The poverty leveling of mind does not oppose itself to thought but allows something to arrive, something that we associate with the possibility of meaning.

The advent of the event, moreover, is, as Lyotard contends, itself dependent upon the ability of mind to scale back its holdings, that is to say: "No event is at all accessible if the self does not renounce the glamour of its culture, its wealth, health, knowledge, and memory. . . . Let us make ourselves weak and sick the way Proust did, or let us fall truly in love." (18). The only possible existential glitch here resides in the suggestion that one would be positioned to *make* oneself fall ill or in love; this, no doubt, is said with that smile of irony for which Jean-François Lyotard was known by his friends. Still, it must be admitted that, in the strict sense, renunciation implies a supplement of will—the *ability*, precisely, to disable, when mind exercises its ability to disable the self. That is the only hurdle I see here, and perhaps I am placing it too firmly in this deserted landscape where debility rules. There is a splitting that seems to be at issue, an almost Fichtean split of self according to which one of the selves, the transcendental self, watches the other, more empirical one crash into the wall of necessary failure. It is hardly probable that Lyotard, smile or no smile, would permit such an Idealist formulation to prevail at this time. I will have to suppose that there is not a rescued self that survives the crash or that is shown determined to play the weak and sick card.

In order to attune one's being to the event, in order to prime for the advent of meaning, a thoroughgoing impoverishment, an extreme ascesis, needs to be welcomed and assumed. Yet, because it involves a supplement of will, this degree of ontological deflation still does not sink to the level of being that in "Mainmise" he later on associates with the *mancipium*. Acts of self-depletion are somehow engaged by the subject as it renews the encounter with the limit-experience of deficiency. The depleted condition,[9] which Lyotard eventually relates to the stakes of knowledge, opens the channels in his work of art and politics—inscriptions that run on empty, forfeiting the support of cognition and its corresponding power players. Another way of putting this is that art and politics are not simply rule-based or governed solely by preexisting contracts or criteria. In a Kantian turn, Lyotard thus argues that both art and politics are exempted from the hegemony of the genre of discourse called cognitive (21). In Kant's terms, such an exemption means that we have no use for the sort of judgment he called determinant judgment. Among other things, this explains why we are essentially bereft—left clueless in the end, off-base and in a cloud of obscurity.[10]

107

Reflective judgment implies the ability of the mind to synthesize data, be it sensuous or sociohistorical, without recourse to a predetermined rule. Lyotard writes: "Accordingly, thinking advances through clouds by touching them as enigmatic cases, the reason for which—their 'what they are'—is not given with them, with their 'that they are occurring'" (20). Determinant judgment operates differently. "The problem at the heart of the latter is the following: a concept being defined, one must find the available cases to be subsumed under it and so doing begin to validate the concept. In other words, understanding possesses a rule of explanation and is trying to select references to which it can be applied. This is a formidable way for wandering through thoughts; it is the way called science" (21). Determinant judgment gives way to the technoscientific universe, announcing the place of the Heideggerian *Gestell* as the modern way for thinking to be related to Being. It would appear that determinant judgment has won out by securing a type of cognitive base—a calculable grid—that compensates for the backsliding returns and depletions which were earlier at issue.

Lyotard shows that in spite of the triumph of determinant judgment in the contemporary world (in the values of programming, forecasting, efficiency, security, computing, and the like), "other games or genres of discourse are available in which formulating a rule or pretending to give an explanation is irrelevant, even forbidden" (21). This is particularly the case with aesthetic judgment, with taste, which introduces a kind of cognitive humbling, an essential passivity: "No concept, no external finality, no empirical or ethical interest is involved in the reception by the imagination of sensations coming from so-called data. There are only the most humble syntheses. . . . The conceptual rule under which the data could be subsumed must remain inactive" (22). Lyotard in fact ends the first lecture of *Peregrinations,* "Touches," by putting through a kind of ethical call—one might say, in keeping with the logic he unfolds, an ethical call without ethical interest or prescriptive pathos. He says, concluding the lecture, that to "respond to a case without criteria, which is reflective judgment, is itself a case in its turn, an event to which an answer, a mode of linking, will eventually have to be found. This condition may be negative, but it is the principle for all probity in politics as it is in art. I am also obliged to say: as it is in thinking" (27). No predetermination, Lyotard maintains, exempts any thinking from the responsibility of responding to each case. Thinking is responsible to the singularity of each case, being answerable to the unsubstitutable demand placed upon it. It is delusory to give a meaning to an event or imagine a meaning for an event by anticipating what that event will be in reference to a prior text. "But it is indeed impossible to avoid this way of thinking completely, because it offers security against the calls or touches of the big X"

(27). Traveling through a space between the active and unconscious breaches of mind, the big X marks the spot where sheer receptivity can be located, on the other side of any claim of knowability.

The big X has to do with the "something" that may occur—in the case of Cézanne under or on his eyes "if they make themselves receptive enough to it. This 'something' is a quality of chromatism, a color, timbre. To achieve this is a matter of a 'passivity' without pathos, which is the opposite of either the controlled or unconscious activity of the mind" (19). X addresses the uncanny "fact" that "there is" something here and now, regardless of what it is. "It is as if something hidden inside the Montagne Sainte Victoire, say Being, or that entity Kant calls 'the X in general,' was playing in a game against the painter by making 'moves' with chromatic material" (19). One cannot psych out the "X in general" or know what it's up to. On good days, one can simply acknowledge, follow, or, if one's name is Cézanne, somehow paint its disposition. Placing us in the grips of a major double bind, it lords over us like the immovable power play of the *mainmise*. On the one hand, we strive to let go in order to avoid being hard of hearing when the big X puts out a call: in order to be attuned to the call we are not supposed to know, grasp, or force subsumption on the uncanny fact that it occurs. It hits us as an appeal without precedent, a circumstance without cognitive netting. There is no other hand (which by no means lessens the grip of the double bind). Yet things go on as if there had always been another, perhaps a first hand—this turns us over to the shriveled authority of the *manchot* of which Lyotard writes, the missing hand ("By freeing himself from the tutelage of the other, the *manchot* takes back his hand, takes things back into his own hands. He thinks he is getting over his castration, that the wound is healing. This dream of being able to get over lack, over what is missing, is the very dream that gives rise to emancipation today" [5]). This missing other hand is the hand played by the supplement of will that we detected earlier, that is, by the action of self-mutilation that permits one to exercise control over a stretch of destiny. Like the crab that loses its claw or the animal tearing off a limb or paw in panic, the *manchot* takes things in hand, albeit in the clutch of a missing hand. The rhetoricity of this moment is impossible, for the *manchot* is shown taking back a hand that no longer is. The inexistent trophy dominates the promissory note of political rhetoric. According to Lyotard, the violence that suppresses castration dominates and blinds the politics of emancipatory struggle today.

Although his thought edges toward the chasms of absolute impoverishment, inscribing the mind and taking the body down with him, Lyotard often pulls back from his insight, in the end entrusting his elaboration to a surplus of linguisticity. He shares this tendency with Lacan. Lyotard, for example, has named a hole in being but then recoups by saying there are other games, other discursive genres. Yet he has himself traced a movement where no game plan or map of discursiveness would hold. This indemnifying gesture signals a tension in his articulation, which we have noted in his prescription for making oneself weak or rendering the mind inactive—as if the passivity without pathos that he equally promotes were not possibly coextensive with all the qualities of Being. For what is *mainmise* but an originary condition of oppression, a lower gear in the death drive that in fact tramples the subject-elect prior even to the irreversible alienation of language?

Now all this comes down to the ordeal or trial of the call, to the call of the big X, or Being, or the mountain, or God. On top of Being or God, or at their feet, even the mountain calls. The call is not necessarily of language or entirely without language. It is hard to situate with any certainty. In *Sein und Zeit* Heidegger had said of the call—the aphonic call of conscience—that it comes from within me and from beyond me. In order to heed the call, one has to have emptied oneself, have undergone a personal kenosis (which, to the extent that it empties, drops off the "personal"). In any case, there is nothing on the order of knowledge to guarantee the call or ensure its referential authority (we shall see how the call without knowledge or ascertainable origin becomes the call of the father). Lyotard himself began the essay with such a stamp, miming its necessity by splitting himself off from his own intention. He began in the twilight of unknowing. About the observations he was prepared to unfold, he said of their origin that they "do not come from the place of some presumed knowledge. For I know nothing of what I have to say here. Nothing of this love of knowledge and wisdom that the Greeks instilled in us under the name of philosophy" (1). In this sense, according to the logic of the argument he subsequently develops, Lyotard has worked through the seduction of woman. According to the biblical fable, she exists in order to make man forget that he does not know (you know, the fable of the apple: "woman's desire is that man forget that he cannot have knowledge" [8]). Correspondingly, there is something like a false call that is posited in the fable—a false and therefore also a true call, and primal man has been shown falling prey to the false call, the call to knowledge or to forgetting his castration (already in paradise there was castration!).

These calls test man, constitute his trial, ordeal ("[T]he letters of the Torah that designate God's asking find their best approximation in the German verb *versuchen*. This word means trial, attempt, tentative, even temptation. Yahweh tries Abraham by asking him for his son" [9–10]). The essential test of childhood, "a great uncertainty concerning childhood," writes Lyotard, involves the binding (*liaison*) and the unbinding or disconnection (*déliaison*): "That is to say, concerning the very core of what governs emancipation. This uncertainty concerns the status of the call and of that which calls, which is to say, the status of the father" (7). This goes very fast but we have already seen that the feminine can pull a fast one, and place a false call ("the evil that speaks in woman"). At the same time the *mainmise* is that of the father, even if he has engaged a wayward operator.

> Jesus' response to the question "Who is the greatest in the kingdom of heaven?" quivers like an arrow that has hit its target; it is the little one, the child (Matthew 18:1–5), *parvulus* in the Vulgate. That is why the child must not be "scandalized" [Gr. *skandalisei*: offended, made to stumble] (Matthew 18:6). Using the term *wound,* I said that this scandal or stumbling block (what Freud called seduction) is inherent to childhood insofar as it is subject to the *mancipium* of adults. And *mancipium* must be taken in both senses here: the one that the adult exercises over the child, and the one that their own childhood exercises over them, even while they are exercising it over the child. (7)

Reflecting the double track of *mancipium,* Lyotard understands the terms of "childhood" in two ways: the childhood that is not bound to this time but is "the celestial model of what has no need to be emancipated, having never been subjected to any other *mainmise* than that of the father; and the subject that is inevitably subjected to scandal, to stumbling blocks, and thus to the abjection of what does not belong to the truth of this call" (7). The scandal or stumbling block "is everything that sidetracks this call—violence, exclusion, humiliation, and the seduction (in the original sense) of the innocent child" (7). The one by means of whom the scandal or stumbling block occurs exercises a *mancipium* over the child, thereby misguiding and keeping the child away from his only *manceps,* the father. Splitting man from the father, Lyotard affirms the disturbing plight that pulls the child from the paternal domain: "This stumbling block and misguidance are necessary. It is necessary to be *bound,* expropriated, appropriated by man rather than the father" (7). Man in this case stands for woman, who intercepts the call and runs it through a scrambling device that endangers the man-child. "The woman's desire is that man stand up and rival the Almighty—thus no longer obeying the Almighty's call, no longer being bound to his *mancipium.* Such is the wicked emancipation that the hysteric whispers to her man: you are not castrated. This emancipation is paid for by suffering, labor and death" (8). Woman calls on man to block the call, to disconnect from the divine call-forwarding system in order to come into his own. She disrupts the Edenic paternal flow and throws her man to the winds of time, repetition, and death. Introducing pain into the destinal equation, she levels at the "beyond" of beyond the pleasure principle.

Somehow or other, the only two boys who will not have been led astray by the feminine, which Lyotard funnels into the maternal *mancipium,* are Isaac and Jesus, whose moms were not entirely or simply women ("Their mothers will have barely been women" [8]). This is so because of the effects of maternal time warp: one was with child too late, having checked out as barren, and the other too soon, having checked in as virgin. Sarah welcomes impregnation with a laugh that is to become the name of her child (Isaac: "he laughed"). Lyotard compares the incredulous, vengeful laughter of Sarah to the Virgin's simple faith, framed by a smile. Because of these traits that unwoman them, the Jewess who is on the mat too late and the Christian icon whose womb conceives too soon are granted a certificate of exemption from the sphere of endangering maternity. These two women, Sarah and Mary, are exempted "from the fate of the mother as seductress. Hence the two sons, Isaac and Jesus, will have been only slightly led astray, or perhaps not at all, by the maternal *mancipium*" (8). The barring of the women—barren or humanly inconceivable—allows for the unintercepted call to come through to these boys. "It is from the father himself that the trial of the binding and unbinding comes to the son" (8). Mother takes her place at the sidelines, steadily transforming herself into the figure of mourning. Always in the grips of a lose–lose situation, mother appears to have the choice between damning herself as invasive seductress or effacing herself under the insistent beat of a death knell.

Lyotard continues his reading of the fable, though he no longer signals its fabulous contextual hold. Instead he focalizes what he now regards as *good emancipation*—what amounts to an extreme form of paternal binding. "For the child, good emancipation has to do in both cases with rising to the call of the father, with being able to listen to it. It is not at all a matter of freeing oneself from this voice. For freedom comes, on the contrary, in listening to it" (8). Freedom is signaled, one could say, within the Heideggerian conjunction of *Hören* and *Gehorsam,* of hearing and adhering. Listening is an extreme form of obedience, of opening and giving oneself over to the voice of the other (8). Paul sketches the switchover from one master transmitter to another when he writes of an abiding enslavement within different registers of address: "For just as you once presented your members as slaves to impurity and to greater and greater iniquity, so now present your members as slaves to righteousness for sanctification" (Romans 6:19). Lyotard comments: "One is emancipated from death only by accepting to be 'enslaved to God,' for 'the advantage you get,' [Paul] continues, 'is sanctification. The end is eternal life' (Romans 6:22)

(8)." The enslaved may respond to a different master, but the condition of enslavement does not in itself undergo significant modification. Lyotard does not spend much time tracing the slippage from freedom to sanctification but concentrates instead on the emancipatory drive that may with more or less success satisfy its aims.

Jews and Christians have observed a tacit agreement in one area—the area that covers the reception of the other. They are similarly disposed at the reception desk of the transcendental intrusion, watchful and ready to take note or direct a command. For Lyotard, the Jewish side of things is unambiguous in terms of receiving the call. On the Jewish side, he writes, "there is no need to comment further upon the listening, which I would wish to call absolute or perfect (in the way one speaks of a musician having perfect pitch), that is, upon the ear that Abraham or Moses lends to the calling of his name" (9). I would like to ask that you lend your ears to this flattering mystification of the Jewish pitch. It grieves me to add a sour note to the assertion, yet how can one's ears, trained on the inaudible, not prick up when provoked by the friendly foreclosiveness of the utterance "there is no need to comment further"? Affirming Lyotard's own ethics of responsiveness, one must *enchaîner,* one must produce phrases around this silence, even if it should rest on the silence of presumed perfection. The statement calls for something of a midrashic intervention, for it may be wrong to stabilize the calling of the name or what Abraham thought he heard that day (we leave Moses to another treatment, perhaps a psychoanalytical one, as when Lacan, discussing *das Ding,* offers that the burning bush was Moses' Thing). Let us put this call momentarily on hold and proceed. Lyotard continues: "On this point Jews and Christians are in agreement—emancipation is listening to the true *manceps*" (9). Both sides of the divide agree upon the essential structure of subjection to a higher force, located in the commanding voice. This is the agreement that modernity disrupts when it tries to imagine and bring about an emancipation without an other. "Such an emancipation can only appear, in terms of the Scriptures, as weakness and impurity, a recurrence of the Edenic scene. The Jews and Christians agree on the impossibility, futility and abjection of an emancipation without *manceps,* without voice."[11] Nonetheless a profound disagreement divides them. It stems, Lyotard offers, from the value that each ascribes to sacrifice. Paul makes virtually no reference to the trial of Abraham, contesting instead the Jews' ritualistic faith which is commemorated in the annual sacrifice, marking the division of the Temple into two tabernacles, the second being reserved for the sovereign sacrificer. Paul omits mention, Lyotard points out, of the call that Abraham received—namely, the one by means of which Yahweh asks Abraham to offer up his son, or rather submits him to the test of sacrifice but then calls off the test. "There will be no sacrifice of the child. Only a perpetual threat. The threat that Yahweh may forget to send the ram" (10). (Lyotard invites another to speak: "As George Steiner puts it so well in his little book entitled *Comment taire?*,[12] every Jewish son knows that his father might be called to lead him up the hill that is now named *Adonai-Yerae*, that is 'God will provide' [Rabbinic translation], so that he may be sacrificed to Yahweh. Not being sure that God will provide" [10]. For what it's worth, I do not see the earth-shattering insight here; could one not say that every Christian son knows he might be nailed by his father? Is not every father, at least every imaginary father, the foster parent of child Oedipus, out to get him at some level of unconscious deliberation?) The necessary point here is that the bond fastened round the body of Isaac, its "binding," its *liance,* can be undone, "thus marking the precariousness of the binding, almost inviting the people of Israel to forget it, inviting renewed sin and trial, endless rereading and rewriting" (11). God backed off, the supreme hand desisted. Which is to say: He can always make a comeback. The Christians, on the other hand, went all the way on the issue of sacrifice. Even Jesus was surprised that he was not Isaac and that the game was not called off in the last moment. But just because the game was not called off and the sacrifice played itself out does not mean that this amounted to what Lyotard has called a "good emancipation." The transfiguration of suffering, humiliation, and death into passion is *already* emancipation. The flesh was redeemed or pardoned (*graciée*). In this regard, the sacrifice cut both ways.

"Certainly, this confidence in pardoning or remission can give rise to bad emancipation, to appropriation, privilege, and worldly powers. Protestants knew this and so protested" (11). Lyotard ends the elaboration by pointing to a *différend* between the Torah and the Christian testament, which pivots on the question of forgiveness. Hannah Arendt writes in *The Human Condition* that forgiveness is the remission granted for what has been done. "Not a forgetting but a new giving out, the dealing of a new hand. One would have to examine the relationship between this and emancipation" (12). The problem is, can *mainmise* play with a new deck or would such optimism merely set the stage for new *Deckerinnerungen* (screen memories) concerning the unrelenting terrorism of childhood?

There were two test sites for us Westerners, then, two figures of children who more or less transcended their putdowns. In a sense, however, testing in terms of the Christian reinscription was called off, or more precisely: it was rigged. Indeed, a *différend* has emerged in the Church's reappropriation of Christ precisely where it refuses the test. A genuine test has been denied consistently by the Church, called off or deemed out of line with the exigencies of erecting an untestable deity. The testing structure is repelled to such an extent that when the issue arises of Christ being put to the test, it becomes a marked scandal. There is the matter of the unavowable Temptation. Unsublatable, the Temptation fades under the worldly scepter of bad emancipation. Even when popular modes of expression try to put the trial back in the Passion—as in the filmic articulation, *The Last Temptation of Christ*—the Church sends out its delegation to make street noises and block entry into the body of a tempted, troubled, tested son of God. Christ untested guarantees a certain narrative stability, no doubt—the stability of repression—but it interrupts the disturbing fable of the becoming-god.

I want to stay on this side of the fence and leave the Xians to the transfiguring humiliations, the passions of which so much has been said and what Lyotard sees bolstered, I think, by dialectics, as so many counterfeit test sites. Let us, though, return to the trial of Abraham, if only to read, in response to Lyotard, the ambiguity of the call that came through on that fateful day. If rising to the call of the father offers a fighting chance for good emancipation, then let us check in on the way that call was placed—or, as the case may be, misplaced. Someone's father took the call, and some kid paid for it. . . . . Listen. . . . . . . :

"Abraham!
Abraham!". . . . . The call befalls you and you cannot prevent the "falling" which you are: it throws you. You are thrown (*geworfen*)—thrown off before any "I" can constitute itself or any subject can be thrown together. You are called to come to the world and answer for yourself. In fact "called" is your most proper name, prior to any nomination, any baptism. This is why the call concerns only you. Your being is being-called. But why, why did God call twice? This is a matter that Lyotard does not take up, but it has a bearing, I think, on the way we encounter—or fail to acknowledge—the *mancipium*. For if the oppressive hand weighs so heavily upon us and has left a lasting thumb print on our being, then it is necessary to recall that there is trouble on the line, and a difficulty in assigning the call with any certitude. Given the static, moreover, that harassed the line and lineage, it remains difficult to determine whether the position of father can be stabilized and does not itself jump, fall, leap back into childhood's regressive posturings. Even God had to double deal, or deal at least with two pressing moments, when placing the call. These two moments have divided God against Himself, effecting once again the weak point of the "big A," *Autre*, the so-called Other. While Lyotard allows for a false call inadvertently to come through in

his reading, and has something to say about that which sidetracks the call, he retains a sense of the truth in calling. As if it were ultimately possible to clear the static. God, for his part and party line, stutters: a hapax. Even though He is constantly repeating himself and renewing his threats, I do not believe that in order to make himself clear he has had to stutter the way he does over the name of our ur-patriarch.

"Abraham! Abraham!" Why did God have to call out the name twice? Why does God have to say Abraham two times? Or are there two of him? Had God surrendered from the start to the temporal predicament of the addressee, or was He Himself split by the destination of his call? In this double call or the call of the double, Kafka, as if fielding Lyotard's call, situates a parable.

"Abraham! Abraham!" The call came through as a gift that surpassed his initiative, indebting and obliging him before he could undertake any decision. I am not saying that the voice is a phenome or a *phoné sémantiké:* perhaps you hear it without hearing. Yet as inaudible and incomprehensible as it may be, it never lets up on calling you. . . . .

. . . . I want to consider in light of Lyotard's focus on the calling structure that held Abraham in thrall this virtually unknown text of Kafka. Titled "Abraham," it begins by splitting the addressee: "There must have been other Abrahams." My perspective, if that is what we can call it, would have been that of the child Isaac, switching, at times, also to that of Sarah. "And Sarah laughed," writes Kafka. But mostly I fell for the child Isaac, the one who was benched in the last minute of an ancient homegrown world series, where the trace of sacrifice, the sacrificial punt, still exists. Isaac, in any case, was benched, pulled off the playing field of a transcendental rumble: Isaac sacked. The story depicts him, if we need to find a cultural diagnosis, as a mostly masochistic lame loser. "Loser" may still imply too much agency, though. Kafka rereads the call that was taken on that fateful day in terms of a terror that was nowhere articulated in the sedimented responses that have accrued to it: the terror of becoming ridiculous. What could it mean to have to sacrifice your sacrifice, which is to say, the father's sacrifice to which you have been assigned—or rather, to find yourself stripped even of the sliver of volition that implicates you in his sacrifice, in the sacrificial act which is not even your own? The grammar of Isaac's failure to sacrifice, that is, to be sacrificed, is even more abject: what could it mean for us today that Isaac's sacrifice was sacrificed, called off? In *The Gift of Death,* Derrida writes that death is the place of one's irreplaceability, unsubstitutability, for "sacrifice supposes the putting to death of the unique in terms of its being unique, irreplaceable, and most precious. It also therefore refers to the impossibility of substitution, the unsubstitutable."[13]

Now we come to Lyotard's assertion of the Jewish perfect pitch as it may be exemplified by Abraham. Let us recall the resolute way in which Lyotard pitches—or rather, ditches—the problem. On the Jewish side, he writes, "there is no need to comment further upon the listening, which I would wish to call absolute or perfect (in the way one speaks of a musician having perfect pitch), that is, upon the ear that Abraham or Moses lends to the calling of his name" (9). At this point I want to convoke a counsel of elders, one from the field of literature, the other from the philosophical domain. Both are ironists who have reached deeply into abysses. They were fearless when it came to reporting what they had found. Kafka and Kierkegaard, on the trail of the great patriarch, shared an insight into the ridiculousness of Abraham. Kierkegaard's example of foolish faithfulness, which he takes up at length in *Fear and Trembling,* is Abraham: "Abraham believed and did not doubt, he believed in the preposterous."[14] Kafka's parable "Abraham," which ponders the possible deconstitution of the primal patriarch, evokes Kierkegaard (and Don Quixote). Multiplied and serialized, his several Abrahams are ridiculous creatures—the world would laugh itself to death at the sight of them, one of which is a harried waiter taking an order. Their performance of insurmountable foolishness inscribes them in an unforgettable saga, dividing while sealing a first letter to the Father.[15]

The great patriarch, the *Erzvater,* from whom, as Kafka reminds us, we are said to descend, shares decisive motifs with those figures of error and misconception that tend to be thematized in his stories and novels. Inevitably set to provoke the world's laughter, the retakes of Abraham begin by naming the spiritual poverty of the patriarch ("Abrahams geistige Armut") and the inertia it spreads, the indifference that clouds his ability to see the diversity of world. And then, outrageously, as if capable of sustaining a competition with the Almighty, the text itself conjures and calls up the man, the primal one, creating for itself another possibility of Abraham ("Ich könnte mir einen anderen Abraham denken—").[16] The "I" thinks up an Abraham who, though prepared to satisfy the demand for a sacrifice immediately, first freezes upon receiving his marching orders. This one stumbles, namely, over the constative utterance in the Bible, which unleashes a performative necessity: "He set his house in order."

The narrative can't get past the fact of this house, whose ordering it posits (the Bible does not set great store in having Abraham clean house, Kafka read it off some wall).[17] The parable insists: Abraham had some property. He had a house; moreover, it had to be set in order. The house of being or a small estate, this house already contained Abraham, bestowed upon him specific, worldly properties, and established somewhat of a prescriptive routine. He was bound by this house. It had to be put in order before any other, higher orders could be followed, much less heard. Housebound, this Abraham, who "certainly would have never gotten to be a patriarch or even an old-clothes dealer," was prepared to answer the call with the promptness of a waiter, but was unable to bring it off "because he was unable to get away, being indispensable; the household needed him, there was perpetually something or other to put in order, the house was never ready" (41). The issue of sacrifice implicates readiness, a giving up of property. The concern evinced by Kafka is presacrificial. How can a house be ready when the call comes through? A house needs to be ready so that a call can be received. The reception of the call would deliver the host to an outside that is more intimate than the hearth. What is the link between the call and the order of the house? There is the insinuation of a state of house arrest: he'll never leave the house, not even by leaping out the window. There is the other issue of the leap, Abraham's leap which does not appear to take place.

The problem with this Abraham, says the narrator, is that he already had the house, something to fall back on, something to leave: "if he had not had a house, where would he have raised his son, and in which rafter would he have stuck the sacrificial knife?" This Abraham who displays greater evidence of style than the more popular, the impoverished one, becomes a substitute, becomes the more "real Abraham" who, however, is "an old story not worth discussing any longer" (43). So why are we discussing it?

There is something about the old story that cannot be put to rest; it calls us, repeating itself ever as an old story whose recurrence marks it as a founding story, the story of Abraham, the one who received the call. This one "had everything to start with, was brought up to it from childhood—I can't see the leap." The narrator supplies logic where the leap is missing. If this Abraham already had everything, then something had to be taken away from him, "at least in appearance: this would be logical and no leap." Where is the famous leap of faith promoted by Kierkegaard, of a sudden, unaccountable narrative breakaway? The logic of sacrifice seems too close to calculative simplicity here, resembling in a prefigurative way that of Job, from whose vitality so much was taken. "It was different for the other Abrahams, who stood in the houses they were building and suddenly had to go up on Mount Moriah; it is possible that they did not even have a son, yet already had to sacrifice him. These are impossibilities, and Sarah was right to laugh." But Sarah's laughter is not addressed to the most ridiculous of possibilities, only to impossibilities that make sense and fail to produce a leap. What makes sense? There were Abrahams who were called before they were ready, that is, before their houses were readied, much less built. These were pure sacrificial beings who were prepared to surrender that which they did not have. This sacrifice, following the logic of the parable, is greater even than that of the Abraham who had someone to give up to a higher power. These Abrahams gave what they could not offer. Hence Sarah laughs at the gift which, never having been given, is already, "suddenly," given away and somehow redeemed. She laughs at the peculiar nothingness of the gift, the danger and disruption of the gift that bears no present. Her laughter, as Lyotard sees it, contrasts with the sublime smile of the Virgin. But he does not present the immaternal mother in a particularly theo-heretical light. Laughing, Sarah doubles the gift's unfathomable givens, for according to Freud and Nancy laughter "itself" would be gift as well—the *Geschenk* or *Gabe* inhering in the surrender of giving up (*Aufgabe*).[18] Laughing, she surrenders an unnameable gift. According to the program notes provided by Baudelaire, her laughter would be that of a she-devil, breaking and entering into the house of limits, bursting and busting (she bursts into laughter) the steeliness of man's calculative grid.

The narrator continues: "But take another Abraham" ("Aber ein anderer Abraham"), in which the "aber" and "abra" and "aba" converge, an other father, one who in principle inhabits the leap and passes through a loop of warping disjuncture, if only to be stopped at the moment itself of reception. This other one got everything straight, he "wanted to perform the sacrifice altogether in the right way and had a correct sense in general of the whole affair." There was a problem of address, however, scorched by an impossible presentation, the sheer negativity of exposition. He had the right sense of things, "but could not believe that he was the one meant, he, an ugly old man, and the dirty youngster that was his child. . . . He would make the sacrifice in the right spirit if only he could believe he was the one meant" (43). It is not the case that this one, he does not believe in God; no, what he does not believe is that the call was meant for him to take. He does not believe in himself as destination, he cannot believe that the call will have arrived if he were to respond to its demand. This might be an intercept, a matter of mistaken identity in the divine call forwarding system. In fact this Abraham, old and capable of presenting only his ugliness, fears mainly the metamorphosis. "He is afraid that after starting out as Abraham with his son he would change on the way into Don Quixote." He would turn into the ridiculed figure of the seeker, the improbable hero of thought, a fabulously bumbling tourist of the imaginary. Worse still, he would have turned into literature; that is, he would have turned himself into the authority of a literature which strip-searches the sacred, consistently enraging world. "The world would have been enraged at Abraham could it have beheld him at the time, but this one is afraid that the world would laugh itself to death at the sight of him" ("die Welt werde sich bei dem Anblick totlachen" [44]). The

119

other side of the world's rage at Abraham consists in this laughter, a laughter-to-death which threatens extinction. Kafka's text thus presents another version of *Totem and Taboo* where, instead of producing a blood-and-guts murder of the primal father, the world-horde emerges as capable of laughing itself to death, to his death, in a broad sweep of castrative derision. The trope of ridiculousness subverts the gravity of biblical patriarchy or shows what was always there, left untouched. It prepares the grounds for a world-class masochistic introject, for another internalization of the first father, humiliated and steadily miniaturized. Freud's horde got theirs, too. Conscience-bitten, they were felled by remorse in the end or rather, they were henceforth to stand by remorse and a father for whom love arrived in the ambivalent aftermath of an immemorial murder. Their father, however, stood tall, with haunting authority.

Reversing the flow, the new caller ID system puts the presumptive addressee on the line. The one who thinks the call is meant for him alone, and heading straight for him with his name on it, is subjected to particularly brutal forms of ridicule. ("And Sarah laughed.") We learn from Kafka's narrator that ridiculousness has power of agency and aging. It is not merely the case that his ugliness makes him ridiculous, but, more to the point, ridiculousness increases his age and ugliness, further sullying his son. Ridiculousness is imbued with divine powers of negation, and so a subtle tautology enters in a contest which resounds with laughter: "However, it is not ridiculousness as such that he is afraid of—though he is, of course, afraid of that too and, above all, of his joining in the laughter—but in the main he is afraid that this ridiculousness will make him even older and uglier, his son even dirtier, even more unworthy of being really called." The ridiculous is exposition: it will expose him, nearly eating into his skin, *making* him older and uglier, transforming him as it presents him, rendering unsightly as it inspects. It is, moreover, hereditary, for it exposes the son to even more dirt on his father, "his son even dirtier," tainted, destitute. An improper sacrifice acts in fact as the destruction of sacrifice (something that Kafka accomplishes but which, as we come to understand, God could not: the end of sacrifice). The son, Isaac, if he is to be offered, must be given up as a clean sacrifice, as that which is clean in itself, a clean cut, a proper offering. The parable takes up the other side of the biblical obsession with cleanliness, zooming in on a stain that cannot be removed: the possibility that Abraham was dirty, his child even dirtier. The proper mode of responsiveness depends upon erasing the stain that however proves to be ineffaceable. Under the circumstances, how can Abraham make the cut or take the call? Ridicule stalks him like a ghost.

Abraham finds himself in a bind: he must of course answer the call, because it addresses him; when rising to answer the call, he becomes ridiculous for responding to it as if it had been meant for him, Abraham. Ridiculousness, which comes after the call, reverses the charges, turning temporality around on itself, for it bestows upon Abraham the predicament of having not been called—not really called ("wirklich gerufen zu werden"). It has the ability to return the call on itself and re-originates it as mistaken, off range. The ridiculous diverts and cancels the call. So God "really" could have made the call to this Abraham, the call "nur für Dich bestimmt," intended only for you, as the doorkeeper in another parable says to the man from the country. This Abraham could have been God's intended, the intended destination of His call, which was to be canceled when the ridiculous supervened as a kind of devil on the line of divine transmission. But ridiculousness has effected a mutation in the addressee, who was no longer the same as the one called. Abraham did not become ridiculous until, believing in his own perfect pitch, he answered the call. Answering the call, he annuls it: "An Abraham who should come unsummoned!" (45).

The narrator of the parable fades the sequence into a pedagogical analogy of contemporary consequence, deriving a scene wherein the class dummkopf hears his name called on commencement day. An institutional ritual has been disrupted: the student body writhes in laughter. In order to understand the folly of Abraham's pitch, we are regressed into another childhood drama, another scene of humiliation. "It is as if, at the end of the year, when the best student was solemnly about to receive a prize, the worst student rose in the expectant stillness and came forward from his dirty desk in the last row because he had made a mistake of hearing, and the whole class burst out laughing." The dumbest of the dumb rises to the occasion of solemn bestowal, having heard his name and felt himself to be addressed. A notably Christian moment can be seen to occur when the meek comes up from educational death row, the last row and lowest rank, to inherit, unaccountably, the prize. He is crucified by class difference; betrayed within a different hierarchical standard by which he is downgraded, his insufficiency provokes a unanimous peal of laughter. The class dummkopf is too dumb to know that he cannot be the smart one beckoned forth on this day, he leaps up—here, finally, comes the leap—to claim the prize meant for the best student according to a scorecard that he proves unable to decipher. All he knows is that he heard his name called. Again, this morphed Abraham, the childish patriarch, is associated with the improper: his desk, dirty, has not been put in order, yet he hears himself being called. There is a film of disgust trailing Abraham, a minor dust storm kicking up in the wake of father. The solemnity of the event is broken. The unclean father, a constant Kafkan obsession, returns to its once auratic source exposing the father as reflected in a dirty child or lame student. There is one thing, *the Thing,* that occupies a shared imago and shatters its integrity. It arrests the stain, inevitably disfiguring the face of authority without lessening the severity of that authority—lending it rather the power to induce even more anxiety. Crumbs on a newspaper, dirty sheets, a tear in a picture: these lesions in being whose precise punctuation already marked Abraham. The presentation has been absolutely sacrificed, appearances materialized and degraded, beginning with the dirty desk in the back row, the loser's place. How could an Abraham, stained and disheveled, originate in the back row except by hearing impairment or random draw—the deformity—of an improper address?

One possibility remains constant: that his name had been called out, if only, the text says, in punishment. The contest of the faculties enfolds the question of contesting faculties, for if he can believe his ears maybe the teacher's understanding is at stake: "And perhaps he had made no mistake at all, his name really was called, it having been the teacher's intention to make the rewarding of the best student at the same time a punishment for the worst one." Kafka does a retake of the great Book, displacing and condensing the value of reward, the necessity of punishment. How was the truth of Abraham tested? There are two parts to this test. While in the Bible, Abraham's obedience was tested—he passed the test, won back the boy, got God on his side—in Kafka the test, though schooled and standardized, is scrambled, the test results rendered inconclusive. Did he pass? Did he fail? Did he not need always already to have failed in order to pass? Or did he think he passed but was failed by the multiplication of Sarah's laughter booming through the chorus of his classmates? Did he accidentally skip a grade when he was supposed to be left back?[19]

His faculties contested, little dumb dirty Abraham answers to the call of the faculty, a call meant as punishment but where no one can be entirely sure anymore who is being rewarded as best student or punished as the worst one. All we know is that the punished and rewarded are collapsed into the same figure that accounts for the fiction of the father. The most exalted and secretly ridiculed of beings owes his existence to the undecidable nature of the call, its meaning or address, its intention and value. By answering to his name, he has already offered his sacrifice, whether or not the teacher will call it off—whether or not it is even in the power of the faculty to recognize the difference. The final irony is that, having been called, Abraham comes unsummoned. As unforgettable source, seared by the trauma of universal laughter, he is measured in Kafka by the consistent shedding of self-worth, bowed by the incursion of unrelenting indignities. Consistently lapsing into the stupefying commands of childhood, he remains hostage to those subliminal acts—they are a matter largely of passivity, of following a sacrificial order—which risk exposing him primordially to the most naked core of sheer ridiculous being.

The teacher, the master, or God play their part in the sullen destituting of the boy, Abraham, our father. What we learn from Kafka's parable, if the teacher means for us to learn anything, concerns the failure of presentation. Ineffaceable, the lesion surfaces, as in "A Country Doctor," in the struggle over presentation. There is always a smudge of dirt where anointment occurs. As much a sign of the missed appointment as of a missed anointment—the appointment is made dependent in Kafka on having missed the point—the calling of Abraham disarranges hierarchy, subverts class expectation (why should the poorest student inherit the prize?), so that the good student is always tainted by the worst student who can come around, according to the order of a new curve, and be commended as the most prizeworthy. Yet the text at no point effects a dialectics or a genealogical switch as it swings over the breakage of singularity. The bad student does not turn into the good one according to a logic of secret negotiations with a higher power. He wins the divine lottery, but as a loser.

A lot depends in the parable on Kafka's use of *gleichzeitig*, on the simultaneous wish of the teacher to present reward and punishment. How can simultaneity be instituted and observed? Even God cannot practice simultaneity and must call out Abraham's name twice, if it is indeed Abraham's name that is being called—the question mark around which the parable rotates. We have a hard time imagining the voice that summons as a stammering one, resembling the syncopated speech of Moses. The voice of God has been reported to be clear, though not always, and there is some probability that somewhere voice can be cracked, split, even in His case. Kafka does not say whether the voice summoning Abraham was disarticulating or hoarse, whether on the contrary it rang out with unparalleled acuity. In a sense, it doesn't matter. God was not heard on the first try. God Almighty for the most part must submit His calls to the laws of temporization, which in order to be heard have to be repeated to begin with. Not to speak of what could have been *meant* when the call was made. Intention, when the name is called, remains rigorously unreadable. The best student may be Abraham—yes, maybe, but this story, the old one, we are told, has lost all interest. Neither God nor the teacher can have access to the intention that motivates the calling of the name since both are limited by the one name, by the oneness of a name that strictly defies spontaneous serialization. However mastered the intention, it does not in the end allow one to know which or who was called, for even in the utterance of the one name He can always conceive of another Abraham ("Ich könnte mir einen anderen Abraham denken,—"). As for the name, it cannot be reduced to the same or difference.

To the extent that it remains impossible to call out two names at once, the intention must be split, as with the cut that binds Judeo-slash-Christianity.

• • •

.... Assuming that Abraham did not sacrifice the child Isaac (though according to one midrash the son was executed),[20] the question remains of how and whether Isaac survived the near-death experience—how he survived a psychotic father, that is, everybody's primal father, Kafka's, yours and mine, even, or *especially,* when they are in sync with the Law, practicing the ineluctable *mainmise.*

Isaac, for his part, became a figure of traumatic repetition, he dug holes in the earth where his father had done the digging before him, puncturing mother earth, producing holes already marked by Abraham. The son reproduces holes, digging and emptying, as if responsible for a dumb show whose interpretation Hamlet subsequently imposed on Western consciousness. What Isaac was "getting at" we still do not know or cannot tolerate knowing. In any case, he turned out to be a bit of a loser, if he was anything at all in the end, the almost sacrificed son. It cannot be said with certitude that he survived, or that anyone survives that which we are calling childhood. One supposes that the child Isaac would have been better served had his destiny not been summed up in the Dostoevskyan freeze-flash of the nearly executed. Deprived of a martyr's grandeur, relieved of his stake in establishing an unprecedented contract between God and man—he had been a wager, he was dealt out—Isaac was condemned to live in the trauma zone of childhood's empty repetition, digging for a truth trove that was never to be found. The serial digger displaces the dagger, punctuating earth with the unreadable hieroglyphs of another story, that of another, untold Abraham. There could have been, there must be, yet another Abraham.[21]

• • •

As for the child, Isaac: The biggest bluff, for all that, may have occurred when the delusion was implanted, the hope nurtured of a chosen people. Isaac, he was and was not called. More radically uncertain than persecution (when you know they're after you, you're already dead meat, you *are* the ram caught in the bushes) is being cheated by the call. Too stupid to know if your name was called, you are ridiculous. You are ready to go up for the sacrifice, but in the last moment you are benched. They don't need you. An animal will serve the purpose, your purpose. This call, it told you that you were the one, the chosen. You set yourself up to receive it, you were set up. It was no longer recognizable whether the call meant to serve as punishment or reward. Your father took the call. You inherited it, with all the expected static; you inherited his burden, which you thought you could lighten. You followed your father in mute complicity, split between the father and God. As you were walking, as he was preparing to give you up, you could not tell, you simply could not decide whether this call which expelled you from your house was a blessing or a curse.

Notes

1. I discuss the relation of idiocy and its correlates to philosophy more fully in *Stupidity* (Urbana and Chicago: University of Illinois Press, 2001).

2. *The Inhuman: Reflections on Time* (Stanford, CA: Stanford University Press, 1991).

3. "Mainmise" in Jean-François Lyotard and Eberhard Gruber, *The Hyphen: Between Judaism and Christianity* (trans. Pascale-Anne Brault and Michael Naas, Amherst, NY: Humanity Books, 1999). It may be useful to consider the translator's note: "*Mainmise*— from the French *main* and *mettre*: 1. A term from feudal jurisprudence referring to the action of taking hold of or seizing someone because of infidelity or lack of devotion to the feudal lord. 2. The action of laying a hand upon or striking someone. 3. The freeing of slaves by their lords" (Emile Littré, *Dictionnaire de la langue française,* edited by Encylcopaedia Britannica, Inc., Chicago: 1978). The *Pluridictionnaire de Larousse* adds that *mainmise* can also refer to the action of laying a hand on and having an exclusive influence over something or someone—as in a state's *mainmise* over certain businesses (Paris: Librairie Larousse, 1975).

4. In this regard a careful reading of *L'expérience de la liberté* (Paris: Galilée, 1988) would complicate the trajectories we are pursuing. Freedom is linked to the singular experience of existence, an experience that does not obey the logic of *fact* that would be opposable to the law.

5. This becomes one of the fixed points of the ethics of psychoanalysis. See Jacques Lacan, *Le séminaire: L'éthique de la psychanalyse Livre VII* (Paris: Editions du Seuil, 1986).

6. For more addiction, see *Crack Wars: Literature, Addiction, Mania* (Lincoln and London: University of Nebraska Press, 1992).

7. Martin Heidegger, *Sein und Zeit* (Tübingen: Max Niemeyer, 1979). See also Christopher Fynsk, *Heidegger, Thought, and Historicity* (Ithaca: Cornell University Press, 1986).

8. *Peregrinations: Law, Form, Event* (New York: Columbia University Press, 1988).

9. My last conversation with Lyotard concerned depletion, his and mine, that is, my chronic fatigue and the preparations he was making to teach a course at Emory University the following semester on fatigue.

10. One of the chapters in *Peregrinations* bears the title "Clouds." Lyotard links cloud formations to thought.

11. There is a sense in which freedom wins out: "But modern emancipation did at least open up an horizon. An horizon, let's say, of freedom. Of a freeing of freedom. Yet as this freedom 'wins out' over itself, as it extends its *mancipium,* its grip, as we approach what I tried to designate, and very poorly, by the name postmodernity, this horizon (historicity) in turn disappears. And it is as if a paganism without any Olympus or Pantheon, without *prudentia,* fear, grace or debt, a *desperate* paganism, were being reconstituted in the name of something that is in no way testamentary, that is neither a law nor a faith but a fortuitous cosmological rule: development" (9).

12. George Steiner, *Comment taire?* (Geneva: Editions Cavaliers Seuls, 1986). The title homonymically combines "How to Keep Silent" with "Commentary."

13. Jacques Derrida, *The Gift of Death* (trans. David Wills, Chicago: The University of Chicago Press, 1995), 58.

14. Trans. Walter Lowrie. Princeton, N.J.: Princeton University Press, 1981, 35.

15. Franz Kafka, "Abraham," in *Parables and Paradoxes* (New York: Schocken, 1958).

16. "Abraham," *Parables,* 40.

17. While the Bible does not make Abraham clean his room before he can go out, it turns out that Kierkegaard does. "It was early in the morning, and everything in Abraham's house was ready for the journey" in the "Exordium," *Fear and Trembling/ Repetition* (ed. and trans. Howard V. Hong and Edna H. Hong, Princeton: Princeton University Press, 1983), 14.

18. For Freud and his analysis of the *"geschenkt,"* see his *Jokes and Their Relation to the Unconscious* (*Standard Edition of the Works of Sigmund Freud,* 8:166). On the connectedness of the gift and laughter, see Jean-Luc Nancy's essay "Laughter, Presence" in his *Birth to Presence* (trans. Brian Holmes et al., Stanford, CA: Stanford University Press, 1993): "Laughter is thus neither a presence nor an absence. It is the offering of a presence in its own disappearance. It is not given but offered." (383).

19. See also Kafka's parable "Die Prüfung (The Test)" in *Parables and Paradoxes:* "Bleib," sagte er, "das war ja nur eine Prüfung. Wer die Fragen nicht beantwortet, hat die Prüfung bestanden" (180).

20. In *The Last Trial: On the Legends and Lore of the Command to Abraham to Offer Isaac as a Sacrifice: The Akedah* (trans. Judah Goldin, Woodstock, Vt.: Jewish Lights Publishing, 1993), Shalom Spiegel describes the way in which the rabbinic tradition has engaged the puzzle of Abraham descending—to all intents and purposes *alone*—from Mount Moriah. ("So Abraham returned to the young men," Genesis 22:19.) Spiegel shows how significant was the interpretation that considered Isaac to have been wounded or indeed killed by Abraham, an interpretation that began to emerge in early rabbinic commentaries. By the twelfth century, Abraham Ibn Ezra saw a need to defend the verse

against this interpretation: "'And Abraham returned'—And Isaac is not mentioned. . . . But he who asserts that Abraham slew Isaac and abandoned him, and that afterwards Isaac came to life again, is speaking contrary to writ" (8).

21. Take still another Abraham, one who stages a collusion between the imaginary and real fathers—the depriving and castrating ones, the father, according to Lacan, elevated to the rank of Great Fucker ("if we are sufficiently cruel to ourselves to incorporate the father, it is perhaps because we have a lot to reproach this father with. . . . It is this imaginary father [the one associated with the experience of privation] and not the real one which is the basis of the providential image of God. And the function of the superego in the end, from its final point of view, is hatred for God, the reproach that God has handled things so badly"). Finally: "What is in question is the moment when the subject quite simply perceives that his father is an idiot or a thief, as the case may be, or quite simply a weakling or, routinely, an old fogey, as in Freud's case." Or Abraham. In *The Seminar of Jacques Lacan. Book VII: The Ethics of Psychoanalysis 1959–1960* (ed. Jacques-Alain Miller, trans. Dennis Porter, New York and London: W. W. Norton, 1986), 307–8.

Toward a Narcoanalysis

This work does not accord with literary criticism in the traditional sense. Yet it is devoted to the understanding of a literary work. It could be said to reside within the precincts of philosophical endeavor. Indeed, it tries to understand an object that splits existence into incommensurable articulations. This object resists the revelation of its truth to the point of retaining the status of absolute otherness. Nonetheless, it has given rise to laws and moral pronouncements. This fact, in itself, is not alarming. The problem is signaled elsewhere, in the exhaustion of language. Where might one go today, to what source can one turn, in order to activate a just constativity? We no longer see in philosophy the ultimate possibilities for knowing the limits of human experience.[1] And yet we began this study by citing Nietzsche. There were two reasons for this selection. In the first place, Nietzsche was the philosopher to think with his body, to "dance," which is a nice way of saying also to convulse, even to retch. And then, Nietzsche was the one to put out the call for a supramoral imperative.[2] This summons in itself will urge us on—for we are dealing in a way with the youngest vice, still very immature, still often misjudged and taken for something else, still hardly aware of itself . . .

What follows, then, is essentially a work on *Madame Bovary,* and nothing more. If it were another type of work—in the genre of philosophical essay, psychoanalytic interpretation, or political analysis—it would be expected to make certain kinds of assertions which obey a whole grammar of procedure and certitudes. The prestige and historical recommendation of those methods of inquiry would have secured the project within a tolerably reliable frame. However, it is too soon to say with certainty that one has fully understood how to conduct the study of addiction and, in particular, how it may bear upon drugs. To understand in such a way would be to stop reading, to close the book, as it were, or even to throw the book at someone.

I cannot say that I am prepared to take sides on this exceedingly difficult issue, particularly when the sides have been drawn with such conceptual awkwardness. Clearly, it is as preposterous to be "for" drugs as it is to take up a position "against" drugs. Provisionally they may be comprehended as master objects of considerable libidinal investment, whose essence still remains to be determined. As it happens, literature is on drugs and about drugs—and here I retain the license to open the semantic range of this term (which does not even amount to concept). I shall come back to the many fluctuations of meaning and usage in the course of my argument. For the present, "drugs" can be understood to involve materially (1) products of a natural origin, often known in antiquity; (2) products evolved from modern pharmaceutical chemistry; and (3) parapharmacological substances, or products prepared by and for the addict.[3] This says nothing as yet for the symbolic values of drugs, their rootedness in ritual and the sacred, their promise of exteriority, the technological extension of supernatural structures, or the spaces carved out in the imaginary by the introduction of a chemical prosthesis.

Under the impacted signifier of drugs, America is fighting a war against a number of felt intrusions. They have to do mostly with the drift and contagion of a foreign substance, or of what is revealed as foreign (even if it should be homegrown). Like any good parasite, drugs travel both inside and outside of the boundaries of a narcissistically defended politics. They double for the values with which they are at odds, thus haunting and reproducing the capital market, creating visionary expansions, producing a lexicon of body control and a private property of self—all of which awaits review.

Drugs resist conceptual arrest. No one has thought to define them in their essence, which is not to say "they" do not exist. On the contrary. Everywhere dispensed, in one form or another, their strength lies in their virtual and fugitive patterns. They do not close forces with an external enemy (the easy way out) but have a secret communications network with the internalized demon. Something is beaming out signals, calling drugs home.[4]

The complex identity of this substance, which is never as such a substance, has given rise to the inscription of a shameful history. This is not the place to trace its intricate contours, for it is an open history whose approach routes are still blocked; nonetheless, the necessity of pursuing such an endeavor still stands. On some level of thinking's probity it is either entirely self-canceling or far too *easy* to treat drugs. Precisely because they are everywhere and can be made to do, or undo, or promise, anything. They participate in the analysis of the broken word, or a history of warfare: methedrine, or methyl-amphetamine, synthesized in Germany, had a determining effect in Hitler's Blitzkrieg; heroin comes from *heroisch,*[5] and Göring never went anywhere without his supply; Dr. Hubertus Strughold, father of space medicine, conducted mescaline experiments at Dachau—indeed, it would be difficult to dissociate drugs from a history of modern warfare and genocide. One could begin perhaps in the contiguous neighborhood of the ethnocide of the American Indian by alcohol or strategic viral infection, and then one could never end . . .

The contagious spread of the entity described as drugs is discursively manifest. Drugs cannot be placed securely within the frontiers of traditional disciplines: anthropology, biology, chemistry, politics, medicine, or law, could not, solely on the strength of their respective epistemologies, claim to contain or counteract them. While everywhere dealt with, drugs act as a radically nomadic parasite let loose from the will of language.

While they resist *presentation,* drugs are still too readily appropriable. One problem dragging down thought is that the drug wars might scan well with the present atmosphere of consensual reading. It is actually becoming impolite to enter areas of conflict.[6] Anyone who has not been prudent in thinking through this fragile zone where non-knowledge dominates knowledge has in any case been burned.

I refer in particular to the professional history of Sigmund Freud who, for the sake of some unplumbable purpose, staked his early career entirely on cocaine and on the essays devoted to cocaine. As a result of *Über Coca*—this text and the subsequent defense, "Remarks on Craving for and Fear of Cocaine," are not included in the *Standard Edition of the Complete Psychological Works*—Freud was publicly reprimanded and privately assailed. Why he willfully ignored the underside of cocaine usage researched by Dr. Louis Lewin, shall have to maintain its status as enigma. His altogether favorable disposition toward cocaine (he recommended it for combating fatigue, against aging, as a local anaesthetic) earned him the published reproof of the famous Berlin psychiatrist, Albrecht Erlenmeyer.[7] Such attacks upon his scientific integrity for promoting the cause of cocaine might have cost a lesser ego its destiny. The personal aspect of disaster brought about by this impassioned research concerned his intimate friend, Von Fleischl, who was the first morphine addict to be treated by cocaine: our first European cocaine addict. Freud attended his friend through a night of paranoid terror, where he witnessed the felt invasion and devouring of Von Fleischl by endless insects and tireless demons. At great cost to himself, his friends, and his father (who was treated with cocaine by his son's prescription), Freud may have discovered something about the toxic drive that could not obtain immediate clearance. In his own work, the cocaine drama broke the ground for the study of hysterical neurosis.

If anything, Freud serves here as a warning system. He never, it seems to me, shook the trouble that cocaine advocacy earned him. This is not the place to analyze that fatal encounter, nor certainly would it be appropriate to concoct foolish moralizations as if one already understood what addiction is all about. There are good and bad addictions, and anything can serve the function of a drug. "Drugs," in any case, make us face the gaping chasms of *Beyond the Pleasure Principle*, where death drive and desire round up their victims.

In his more restrained estimations, Freud has characterized the addict as evoking the charm of cats and birds of prey with their inaccessibility, their apparent libidinal autonomy.[8] This is not very far from his description, in another context, of women. (The place where the addict meets the feminine in a desperate attempt at social renarcissization is carefully marked in *Madame Bovary*.) Narcissistic withdrawal equally introduces a scandalous figure into the society of humans by removing the addicted subject from the sphere of human connectibility. But perhaps the hint of libidinal autonomy, or what Félix Guattari describes as "the second degree of solitude," furnishes the most menacing among social attributes.[9] Jacques Lacan appears to confirm the conviction that drug addiction belongs to the domain of a post-analytical era reserved perhaps for schizoanalysis and the like; indeed, he sees the addict as constituting a hopeless subject of psychoanalysis: "Addiction (*la taxicomanie*) opens a field where no single word of the subject is reliable, and where he escapes analysis altogether."[10] This is giving up quickly. William Burroughs shares quite the same opinion from the other side of experience: "Morphine addiction is a metabolic illness brought about by the use of morphine. In my opinion psychological treatment is not only useless it is contraindicated."[11] A collusion on the parts of Lacan and Burroughs does not mean, however, that the psychotreatability of the addict is wholly out of the question, or that psychoanalysis would offer a useless or archaic access code for unlocking the whole problem. For, to the extent that addiction was at one point within the jurisdiction of *jouissance*—indeed, we are dealing with an epidemic of misfired *jouissance*—the major pusher, the one who gave the orders to shoot up, was surely the superego. In order to urge this point with some sustainment of clarity we shall have to enter the clinic of phantasms that Flaubert chose to call *Madame Bovary*.

The modern history of the attempt to stabilize a definition of drugs comprises long, dense, and contradictory moments (Queen Victoria waged war twice, for instance, in order to ensure the free commerce of opium).[12] The legal history of drugs compels analyses of the means by which drugs have been enlisted to erode the American criminal justice system. Airports now establish the clearest rhetorical space for reading the consequences of what Justice Brennan had once projected as the "unanalyzed exercise of judicial will."[13] State control towers have effected the merger between air and drug traffic, instituting the airport as a premonitory law-free zone where the subject's orifices are kept open to investigation. No probable cause is necessary here. *Droit de la drogue,* a significant French study of the problem, clarifies the prohibitionist spell under which America continues to conduct its interventions.[14] The study does not fail to analyze the effects of the xenophobic, racist, and economic calculations that have commanded moral, legal, and military discourses. Its theoretical propositions derive from constructions concerning the freedom of the legal subject and his right to be protected from the condition of enslavement that drugs are said unavoidably to produce. It is a matter of determining at what point the object takes possession of the subject. We shall leave these terms to flood their undeconstructed history.

I can make no pretense to possessing legal competence more elaborate than that of any literate person. I would suggest only that one consider the degree to which the literary object has itself been treated juridically as a drug. In one case it fell to the favor of the literary work to be handled as a medicinal substance, possibly indeed by an "unconscious" legal manipulation. This is the case of James Joyce's *Ulysses,* where the work's fate was considerably advantaged by its classification as emetic function rather than as pornographic inducement. These were the terms upon which it was performatively granted entry rights into the U.S. Be that as it may, *Ulysses,* whether legally conceived as emetic formula or as aphrodisiac philtre, was in the first place distilled down to its essence as a drug.

Naked Lunch evinces a similar collapse of the boundary between obscenity and drugs. In *Attorney General* v. *A. Book Named "Naked Lunch,"* the court finds the following:

> The Supreme Court of the United States has held that, to justify a holding of obscenity, "three elements must coalesce: it must be established that (a) the dominant theme of the material taken as a whole appeals to a prurient interest in sex; (b) the material is patently offensive because it affronts contemporary community standards . . . and (c) the material is *utterly* without redeeming social value [emphasis supplied]; *A Book Named "Johns Cleland's Memoirs of a Woman of Pleasure"* v. *Attorney General of Mass.* 383 U.S. 413, 418–421. . . . As to whether [*Naked Lunch*] has any redeeming social value, the record contains many reviews and articles in literary and other publications discussing seriously this controversial book portraying the hallucinations of a drug addict. Thus it appears that a substantial and intelligent group in the community believes the book to be of some literary significance.[15]

The slippage from obscenity to the representation of hallucination—in other words, the representation of representation—cannot fail to raise questions about the veilings that both literature and drugs cast. This order of questioning had already penetrated to the case of *Madame Bovary,* where it was held that the curtain of non-representation (the carriage scene) exploded hallucinatory rage in the open space of the socius. The menace of literature in these cases consists in its pointing to what is not there in any ordinary sense of ontological unveiling. The court is not wrong to institute the proximity of hallucination and obscenity as neighboring territorialities, since both put in question the power of literature to veil its insight or to limit its exposure. Literature is most exposed when it stops representing, that is, when it ceases veiling itself with the excess that we commonly call *meaning.*

The question comes down to the way literature dresses up the wound of its non-being when it goes out into the world. On this point, the cases of *Madame Bovary* and *Naked Lunch* are only to a certain degree different (it is all a matter of dosage), but the matter of representation continues to be the same: the court keeps a close watch on creatures of the simulacrum.

There can be no doubt about it. *Naked Lunch* gets out of trouble only when the social veil of literary review has been thrown over it. Literature has to be seen wearing something external to itself, it cannot simply circulate its non-being, and almost any article will do. This would affirm at least one value of the book review as that legal force which covers up the work.

§

Well, then. It is not so much a question of scientific knowledge. Nor certainly can it be a question of confidence in writing. There are certain things that force your hand. You find yourself incontrovertibly obligated: something occurs prior to owing, and more fundamental still than that of which any trace of empirical guilt can give an account. This relation—to whom? to what?—is no more and no less than your liability—what you owe before you think, understand, or give; that is, what you owe from the very fact that you exist, before you can properly owe. You do not have to *do* anything about your liability, and most finitudes don't. Still, it copilots your every move, planning your every flight, and it remains the place shadowed by the infinite singularity of your finitude.

The obligation that can force your hand resembles something of a historical compulsion: you are compelled to respond to a situation which has never as such been addressed to you, where you can do no more than run into an identificatory impasse. Nonetheless, you find yourself rising to the demand, as if the weight of justice depended upon your inconsequential advance.

It did not seem advantageous to put at risk the peculiar idiom of this work by installing ethical tonalities that may in the end correspond only weakly to its critical punch (Flaubert: "The worth of a book can be judged by the strength of the punches it gives and the length of time it takes you to recover from them.").[16] The task of producing an introduction made me hesitate, the way a translator hesitates over the prospects of a sacrificial economy that will nevertheless dominate the entire work. Might as well face it: Some hesitations are rigorous. They own up to the fact that no decision is strictly possible without the experience of the undecidable. To the extent that one may no longer be simply guided—by Truth, by light or logos—decisions have to be made. Yet I wanted neither to protect Emma B. from what was about to happen (she had to remain exposed) nor to pervert her further. I certainly did not want to create a disposable limit, an explanatory phase that, at lift off, could easily fall behind. This would have come too close to repeating a structure of dejection with which drugs have been associated—a structure where there is neither introjection nor even incorporation, but which posits the body as the no-return of disposability: the trash-body, pivoted on its own excrementality. Doubling for the remainder, however, this moment in my argument would occupy the terrifying position of quasi-transcendence because it can be made to determine the value of the inside from which it is ejected. And yet, one is liable, and one has to find a way of thinking this liability as if one were concluding an affirmative contract with an endlessly demanding alterity.

More so perhaps than any other "substance," whether real or imagined, drugs thematize the dissociation of autonomy and responsibility that has marked our epoch since Kant. Despite the indeterminacy and heterogeneity that characterize these phenomena, drugs are crucially related to the question of freedom. Kant himself devotes pages of the *Anthropology* to contemplating the values of civic strength as they are affected by intoxicating foods (under which he comprehended mushrooms, wild rosemary, acanthus, Peruvian chicha, the South Sea Island's ava, and opium). The questions attending drugs disclose only a moment in the history of addiction. As such, drugs have accrued a meager hermeneutics in proportion to a considerable mobilization of force.

No one has so much as defined drugs, and this is in part because they are non-theorizable. Still, they have globalized a massive instance of destructive *jouissance,* they assert desire's mutation within a post-analytic phrasing, or put another way, drugs name the exposition of our modernity to the incompletion of *jouissance.* Perhaps the quality of these stakes explains in part why they have become the elusive objects of planetary warfare at the very moment when "democracy" is on the rebound. The intersecting cut between freedom, drugs and the addicted condition (what we are symptomatologizing as "Being-on-drugs") deserves an interminable analysis whose heavily barred doors can be no more than cracked open by a solitary research.

Narcotic desire's implications for freedom did not entirely escape Kant's gaze (hence the need for prescriptions in general). But it was not until Thomas De Quincey that drugs were pushed toward a philosophy of decision. The *Confessions of an English Opium Eater* can be shown to perturb an entire ontology by having drugs participate in a movement of unveiling that is capable of discovering no prior or more fundamental ground. Unveiling and unclouding, opium, on De Quincey's account, brings the higher faculties into a kind of legal order, an absolute legislative harmony. If it perturbs ontology this is in order to institute something else. The ontological revision which it undertakes would not be subject to the regime of *alèthia,* or rather, the clarity which opium urges is not dependent upon a prior unveiling. Where the warring parts of the *Confessions* refuse to suture, one detects the incredible scars of decision. Always a recovering addict, Kant's subject was not particularly pathological in the pursuit of his habits; De Quincey's addict has been exposed to another limit of experience, to the promise of exteriority. Offering a discreet if spectacular way out, an atopical place of exit, drugs forced *decision* upon the subject.

Self-dissolving and regathering, the subject became linked to the possibility of a new autonomy, and opium illuminated in this case (Baudelaire, though under De Quincey's influence, was to use it differently) an individual who finally could not identify with his ownmost autonomy but found himself instead subjected to heroic humiliation in the regions of the sublime. Opium became the transparency upon which one could review the internal conflict of freedom, the cleave of subjectivity where it encounters the abyss of destructive *jouissance.*

The ever-dividing self was transported on something other than the sacred, though the effects of revelation were not unrelated. Decisions would have to be met, one had to become a master strategist in the ceaseless war against pain. The most striking aspect of De Quincey's decision resides in the fact that it resists regulation by a telos of knowledge. To this end his elaboration has uncovered for us a critical structure of decision to the extent that it has been tinctured by non-knowledge, based largely upon a state of anarchivization.[17] This leaves any future thinking of drugs, if this should be possible, in the decidedly fragile position of system abandonment. There is no system that can presently hold or take "drugs" for long. Instituted on the basis of moral or political evaluations, the concept of drugs cannot be comprehended under any dependent, scientific system.

These observations do not mean to imply that a certain type of narcotic supplement has been in the least rejected by metaphysics. To a great degree, it is all more or less a question of dosage (as Nietzsche said of history). Precisely due to the promise of exteriority which they are thought to extend, drugs have been redeemed by the conditions of transcendency and revelation with which they are not uncommonly associated. But qualities such as these are problematic because they tend to maintain drugs on "this side" of a thinking of experience. Sacralized or satanized, when our politics and theories prove still to be under God's thumb, they install themselves as codependents; ever recycling the transcendental trace of freedom, they have been the undaunted suppliers of a metaphysical craving.

There can be no doubt about it. What is required is a genuine ethics of decision. But this in turn calls for a still higher form of drug.

§

Madame Bovary I daresay is about bad drugs. Equally, it is about thinking we have properly understood them. But if the novel matches its reputation for rendering its epoch—our modernity—intelligible, then we would do well to recall that *epoch* also means interruption, arrest, suspension and, above all, suspension of judgment.[18] *Madame Bovary* travels the razor's edge of understanding/reading protocols. In this context understanding is given as something that happens when you are no longer reading. It is not the open-ended Nietzschean echo, "Have I been understood?" but rather the "I understand" that means you have ceased suspending judgment over a chasm of the real. Out of this collapse of judgment no genuine decision can be allowed to emerge. Madame Bovary understood too much; she understood what things were supposed to be like and suffered a series of ethical injuries for this certitude. Her understanding made her legislate closure at every step of the way. She was her own police force, finally turning herself in to the authorities. She understood when the time had come to end it all, whereupon she executed a brutal coincidence of panic and decision. She was no brooding Hamlet, whose tendency to read and re-read and to write down what he heard had granted him the temporal slack he needed to bring the whole house down. No doubt, Hamlet ends up sending himself the poisoned point by return mail and, like Emma, finally commits himself to a writing of suicide. But if they share the same poison, and even the banquets of the uneaten, one should not mix these up too readily, for *Madame Bovary* opens herself to an altogether different history of intelligibility, in fact, to another suicide pact, cosigned by a world that no longer limits its rotting to a singular locality of the unjust. This is not to say that Hamlet and his phantom

136

have been dealt with definitively, but they have been left in suspension by an interrogating openness, a kind of ontological question or futural transmission running interference with the most serene channels of forgetfulness. Emma Bovary, she has been understood. And the material proliferation of critical works surrounding the novel does not refute this statement. On the contrary: No one has claimed to be puzzled by this enigma—she has been the clearing space, the translating machine through which an epoch renders itself intelligible, if not quite above itself.

§

Hamlet, De Quincey, Emma Bovary, Balzac, Baudelaire, William Burroughs, Artaud (and scores of others) urged upon us a thinking of human nourishment. If they were not quite vegetarians, they tried to nourish themselves without properly eating. Whether injecting themselves or smoking cigarettes or merely kissing someone, they rerouted the hunting grounds of the cannibalistic libido. In a certain manner of conscious monitoring, they refused to eat—and yet they were always only devouring, or drinking up the toxic spill of the Other. Drugs make us ask what it means to consume anything, anything at all. This is a philosophical question, to the extent that philosophy has always diagnosed health, that is, being-itself or the state of non-alienation, by means of its medico-ontological scanners.[19] Where does the experience of eating begin? What of the remains? Are drugs in some way linked to the management of remains? How has the body been drawn into the disposal systems of our technological age?

It is perhaps not surprising that every utterance linked to drugs has something to say about what is appropriable. In his introduction, William Burroughs writes, "The title means exactly what the words say: NAKED Lunch—a frozen moment when everyone sees what is on the end of every fork."[20] Prior to this frozen moment, Baudelaire, the first worthy reader of *Madame Bovary* according to Flaubert, remarked: "In order to digest natural as well as artificial happiness, it is first necessary to have the courage to swallow; and those who would most deserve happiness are precisely the ones upon whom cheerfulness, as conceived by mortals, has always had an emetic effect (*l'effet d'un vomitif*)."[21]

The possibility of an altogether other health, pointing as it does to the great vomiter, Nietzsche, has to do with the properly *improper* character of the body. We seem to be dealing with forces of inscription that relieve the body of itself while resisting its sublation into ideality, spirit, or consciousness. The *purification* of the body described by Baudelaire paradoxically maintains the body in its material, corruptible state of dis-integrity. As that which can swallow and throw up—naturally or artificially—the body rigorously engages the dynamics

137

of becoming, surpassing itself without reducing itself to a passageway. These observations in fact model age-old concerns whose subscription to thought has been renewed by the way drugs negotiate the paracomestible substance.

§

Why should I begin my study of *Madame Bovary* in the mode of fiction? To fill a prescription; namely, that the provisions of the simulacrum be doubled. It is a method similar to the one I used three centuries ago for editing *The Sorrows of Young Werther.* There was another, more timely motive, which I did not discover until reading a passage from Gilles Deleuze in *Difference and Repetition:*

> On the one hand a book of philosophy ought to be a very particular kind of crime story, and on the other hand it should resemble science fiction. By crime story (*roman policier*) we mean that concepts should intervene, driven by a zone of presence, in order to resolve a local situation.[22]

This places our inquiry on the outer precincts of the detective genre, in the tradition of Sherlock Holmes, who was reputed, alas, to suffer from cocaine addiction.

Notes

1. Emmanuel Levinas, *Sur Maurice Blanchot* (Paris: fata morgana, 1975), p. 9.

2. Cf. in particular Jean-Luc Nancy, "'Our Probity!'": On Truth in the Moral Sense in Nietzsche," trans. Peter Connor, in *Looking After Nietzsche*, ed. Laurence A. Rickels (Albany: State University of New York Press, 1990).

3. Cf. Pierre Deniker, "Intérêt scientifique et dangers sociaux des hallucinogènes (1969)," in *Sigmund Freud et la drogue* (Paris: Editions du Rocher, 1987), p. 93.

4. The technologies of drugs and the medias are housed by a supernatural trait. Levinas writes in *Sur Maurice Blanchot*, p. 30: "Le discrédit qui frappe le surnaturel dans la pensée et les moeurs de l'Occident n'atteint pas le mystère de l'inspiration."

5. In fact, heroin was first produced in 1874 at St. Mary's Hospital in London. It was reinvented or "discovered" in Germany in the 1890s and marketed by Bayer under the trade name "heroin," which derives from *heroisch* (cf. Virginia Berridge and Griffith Edwards, *Opium and the People* [New Haven and London: Yale University Press, 1987], p. xx).

6. On the side of rigor, Jacques Derrida has offered a more restrained, judicious reading of the rhetoric of drugs in general. See "Rhétorique de la drogue," in *L'Esprit des drogues,*

p. 209: "Today, here and now, in my private-public life, and in the fixed situation of 'our' society, I feel rather more inclined toward an ethos, shall we say, that, according to the dominant codes, would be understood as repressive or prohibitory, at least in the case of 'classified' drugs. . . . But to justify the ethos which aligns me with an apparently 'repressive' attitude (in the case of 'classified' drugs) I would not, in the final analysis, rely upon any current discourses or axiomatics."

7. Louis Albrand, "Freud et le panégyrique de la cocaïne," in *Sigmund Freud et la drogue*, p. 39.

8. See Pierre Sipriot, "Psychanalyse, drogue: le malentendu," in *Sigmund Freud et la drogue*, p. 16.

9. Félix Guattari, "Une Révolution Moléculaire," in *L'Esprit des drogues*, p. 18.

10. Jacques Lacan, *Écrits* (Paris: Seuil, 1966), p. 534.

11. William Burroughs, "Letter from a Master Addict to Dangerous Drugs," in *British Journal of Addiction* 53, no. 2 (1953).

12. Involved in the Indian opium trade with China, Britain fought two "opium wars" against China, in 1839–42 and again in 1856–58.

13. *New Jersey v. T.L.O.*, 469 U.S. 325 (1985). See also discussion under "Warrantless Arrests and Searches" in Steven Emanuel and Steven Knowles, *Criminal Procedure* (New York: Emanuel Law Outlines, 1988), pp. 115ff.

14. Francis Caballero, *Droit de la drogue* (Paris: Dalloz, 1989).

15. William Burroughs, *Naked Lunch* (New York: Grove Press, 1959), p. viii. The book was adjudged obscene in the Superior Court of New York, G.L. c. 272, §§ 28C, 28E, 28F (each inserted by St. 1945, c. 278, §I).

16. Cited in Steegmuller, *Flaubert*, p. 283.

17. I refer to Jacques Derrida's usage of "anarchivization" in his contribution to the colloquium "Lacan avec les philosophes," organized by René Major and Philippe Lacoue-Labarthe, Paris, May 1990.

18. Jonathan Culler, "The Uses of *Madame Bovary*" in *Flaubert and Postmodernism*, ed. Naomi Schor and Henry E. Majewski (Lincoln: University of Nebraska Press, 1984), p. 4: "Madame Bovary has been used and will continue to be used to 'construct the intelligibility of our time.'" See also the introduction to the "substantially new translation" of *Madame Bovary* by Paul de Man (New York: W. W. Norton & Co., 1965), and also Harry Levin, "*Madame Bovary*: The Cathedral and the Hospital," in *The Gates of Horn: A Study of Five French Realists* (New York: Oxford University Press, 1963), p. 250: "Madame Bovary, c'est nous."

19. Cf. Philippe Lacoue-Labarthe, "History and Mimesis," trans. Eduardo Cadava, in *Looking After Nietzsche*.

20. "Deposition: Testimony concerning a Sickness," in Burroughs, *Naked Lunch,* p. xxxvii.

21. Baudelaire, *Les Paradis artificiels,* 193: "Quels mondes intérieurs! Etait-ce donc là la panacée, le *pharmakon népenthès* pour toutes les douleurs humaines?"

22. Gilles Deleuze, *Différence et répétition* (Paris: Presses Universitaires de France, 1968).

Deviant Payback

THE AIMS OF VALERIE SOLANAS

In 1968 Jacques Derrida brought out his pathbreaking essay "The Ends of Man" and Valerie Solanas began earnestly distributing *SCUM Manifesto.*[1] In June of that year she gunned down Andy Warhol as he was speaking on the telephone. These events may seem miles apart on the cultural shock charts, yet they are linked in ways that urge us to reflect on their ineluctable contiguities. Both Derrida and Solanas are interested in the aims and finality of the concept "man." Admittedly, that may be where their improbable rendezvous ends, somewhere on an existential corner of 1968, situated among the assassinations of Martin Luther King Jr., Fred Hampton, and Bobby Kennedy, at the moment they shared the beat of a feverishly agitated zeitgeist. This was the moment in any case when "man," getting a political pounding, was up against the philosophical wall and steadily losing ground. Derrida, conceptually fitted for the job, was concerned with the excess of man, which Solanas, we could say, enacted. Where he exposed the Greek ideal of *anthropos,* she went for the jugular of referential man, busting through layers of philosophical history to put out her own "ends of man," her own limit case of the classical unity of man. [. . .]

Solanas, part of whose pain grows out of a disturbed relationship to higher education, matches prints with those who situate the father as primal enemy (Freud et al.), paternity as fiction (Derrida et al.), gender as part of a performative effort (Butler et al.), capital flow as a traumatic historical outbreak (Goethe, Marx, Deleuze, et al.), and so on and so forth. She even installs a theory of *unworking* that matches up with some of Nancy's appropriations of Bataille that track the implications of *désoeuvrement.* Though she notoriously packs style in the mode of derangement, loading up on anger and furious rounds of righteousness, Solanas also carries theoretical issues to their assigned limits. This was not necessarily her intention or wish—to score theoretical points—but alongside her stubborn destitution and injured denunciations, Valerie manages to pick off the crucial themes associated with the dominion of phallogocentrism. [. . .]

It would be unwarranted, no doubt, to turn Valerie Solanas into a blindingly lucid catalogue of contemporary theoretical thought; at the same time, however, it would be ignorant to disavow what made her language, her appeal, her compulsive effacement, burdened confusion, and Hegelian struggle for recognition possible. Whether Solanas knowingly climbed into the think tank with the rest of them is immaterial. She borrowed the language and flashed the enduring complicities of urgent philosophical concerns. She was "inscribed" and as such took to the margins of major philosophemes or writers' blocs. She belongs with them, even if only as a limping straggler and wounded anomaly. The questions for us today might be, What made it possible for Valerie Solanas to shoot off the way she did?, Why is she rebounding and returning now, in arguably the most masculinist-imperialist phase of the American world take-over?, and, Where do we locate her—how and when does she arrive?

Despite communitarian insinuations I might have made, at least on the level of philosophical complicities or networks, Valerie Solanas was a loner. There is something poignantly American about the way she handled the self-acknowl-edged loser life with which she was saddled. One thinks of the petitions and plaints of the solitary ranters for whom missives and missiles collapse into an indissociable, deadly mission. Lacking the elegance or cultural legitimacy of a subcommandante Marcos, a Weatherman, or a proponent of the civil rights movement, the so-called Unabomber, David Koresh, and Solanas are more vagabond, unmoored, and alone with their inscriptions, offering a spare cluster of more deinstitutionalized and depopulated "revolutionaries." In the case of Valerie Solanas, her fringe existence was part of the package deal of untimely impacts, aspects of which derive from Stonewall (1969) and other American inventions of resistance. Valerie was not meant to have disciples or spawn a new breed of revolutionaries. She offered the uniquely American dead-end-one-warrior-revolution spinning on its own determined axis. She had no followers. She arrives too late or too early on every scene. Who needed a runaway Hothead Paisan, the comic strip lesbian avenger, in the summer of '68? Who cared about her target practice and rage against Great Art when King and Bobby and Malcolm X were being slaughtered—or for that matter, when women for the first time were protesting the Miss America Pageant in Atlantic City? [. . .]

[W]hen Valerie Solanas was sentenced in the summer of 1969 to three years in jail, the news was reported deep in the remote pages of the *New York Times,* in an article that appeared adjacent to a notice addressed to city residents concerning a change in the summer garbage collection. The world was headlining other news. This may seem a sorry and sad fate for the woman declared by Norman Mailer to be "the Robespierre of feminism."[2] It was no less a disappointment for Mr. Warhol, who saw his near extinction miniaturized by world events. Seeing themselves thus reduced and compressed, both Andy and Valerie were in the dumps that summer. Still, the garbage pile is where we wanted to land: it is the place from which Solanas was signaling, culturally rummaging, the impossible place of an irremissable "litterature." After all, one meaning of "scum" throws us into garbage, and we do not want to lose a sense of the excremental site to which Solanas relentlessly points and from which she speaks. [. . .]

I feel compelled to address the delicate topic of an indefensible text, of an event that occurs in terms of its own chronic misfiring, but that nonetheless bears grave consequences, annulling itself while searing the random addressee, responding ineluctably to a primal sense of injury alienating and magnetizing at once. Her text does all that. It rants, it goes off deliriously, it finds its destination in a sensitive target area swollen with historical pain. With Valerie, something goes off, something happens, even though her words appear to have been fitted for so long with a silencer. The no place that she occupies—whether on the historical page or in the Factory, at home or on the streets—is the place from which Solanas delivers her wounding insights. Wounded and wounding, she comes out shooting, unsnapping all manner of discursive safety nets and cultural supports that have allowed violence to be absorbed. She has removed the patriarchal shock absorbers, taken away the soporifics that push women into poses of an accepting stupor. Dismantling symbolic security systems that keep up the patriarchy, Valerie Solanas pierces through to the real with a series of highly calibrated psychotic intensities. Before one becomes overly confident about arresting her outrageous development in terms of psychotic aberration, it is important to note that psychosis speaks, that it often catches fire from a spark in the real; it is fueled and fanned and remains unsettling because, as wounded utterance, it is not merely or solely demented. I am not persuaded that we have before us only a psychotic text. But it does rise out of the steady psychoticization of women, a threat under which most of us live and against whose coarse endurance we contribute enormous amounts of energy. Unless one is able to perform the Freudian *Spaltung*, protective self-splitting, many of the minoritized, evicted creatures spend ourselves staving off the pressures of social psychoticization. But even in the land of social derangement Valerie Solanas got to travel the blind alleys and side streets of grand feminist mappings. It is not as though language and lit show no tolerance for a girl's derangement. On the contrary, some types of accepted derangement are hard-won. We have fought for every inch of clinical corroboration and for the symptomal housing projects that shelter our anguish. Certain diseases become a woman. Strengthening her stature in unexplored domains of suffering, they encourage

143

her daredevil collapses, linguistic feints. Valerie, however—poor Valerie refuses the prestige and license of hysteria or any of the neighboring neurotic dialects that might be understood in feminist precincts. She is no Dora, no Anna O., no Marquise von O . . ., she bears none of the finely crafted, delicate, brilliant flush of symptoms with which, thanks to the work of outstanding feminist theorists, a new form of dissidence and social disruption could be tried. Our Valerie, by contrast, was a psycho. Butch-dykey angry, poor, and fucked up: who could ask for more? [. . .]

One of the questions that the name Valerie Solanas continues to raise, at least for me, concerns those who have an acute sense of injustice. They drag around at the end, stuporous, drained, shivering in near autistic spheres of solitude. Their language shivers still. I think of Nietzsche, slumped over. I see the others, the "men," the "women," whatever they are or thought they were. On some nights, Valerie's weariness washes over me. I hear her typing out in the apartment above mine: "The shit you have to go through in this world just to survive."

PS—In college, Valerie Solanas majored in psych.

Notes

1. Jacques Derrida, *Margins of Philosophy* (trans. Alan Bass, Chicago: University of Chicago Press, 1982). In their introduction to the voluminous tome *Les fins de l'homme: A partir de travail de Jacques Derrida* (Paris: Éditions Galilée, 1981), 13, philosophers Jean-Luc Nancy and Philippe Lacoue-Labarthe write that the destination or *Bestimmung* of man is no longer merely "a question among others on the subject of man: it is rather man himself who has become a question. For this fundamental reason . . . the thinking of man becomes that of finitude—or, more rigorously, the ontotheology of the Subject sees itself shaken up by an analysis of finitude."

2. See Dana Heller's "Shooting Solanas: Radical Feminist History and the Technology of Failure" (*Feminist Studies* 27.1, Spring 2001), where she discusses Mailer's call to "encourage the psychopath within oneself, to explore that domain of experience where security is boredom and therefore sickness."

Preface to *Dictations*

The ubiquity of Goethe's name in the works I was studying at the time, led me, at the merciful end of graduate school, to read most of what he had written. Despite the pious thoroughness of Germanist scholars, Goethe opened the vertiginous experience of a suspended transcendence of the work. It was not that his single writings lacked beauty or rigor, but they in themselves could not account for the grandeur accorded to "Goethe" in the most prestigious texts of our modernity. I was not yet prepared to believe that, like the Wizard of Oz, Goethe was tied in the end to a rather unremarkable instance of empiricalness, a poverty, an ascesis. This would have meant that the mystified munchkins, Germanists, had never dared to wonder what was concealed behind the special effects of this awesome signifier—one that, like the phallus, might be effectually powerful yet empty. But it was not as though "Goethe" could be located within the limits of any single control room or even pinned to a discoverable repertoire of effects. The effort of tracking "Goethe" produced no doubt my first experience with the elusive, if not atopical, nature of essential writing.

Perhaps not until Nietzsche or Kierkegaard were the boundaries of what constitutes writing so consistently displaced as with Goethe. The traditional containments and institutional bodyguards which seemed to accompany "Goethe" into the late twentieth century fall away as soon as one encounters the genuine interlocution for which this name calls. It is a name that exposes us to the necessity of remapping that which distinguishes a life from a work, while it also reminds us to detach the concept of author from the remote regions in which his signature continues to make an effect. Indeed, the effects of Goethe's signature were so powerful that he continued to sign on the texts which any simple logic of chronicity could never comprehend. How is it that Goethe came to cosign psychoanalysis? How did his signature reverse and stimulate textual economies to the extent that he could name his debt to Freud prior to the empirical or historical occurrence of psychoanalysis proper? This work tries to deal with the noncanonic excess of Goethe's signature. His signatory powers tend to be invoked in works that name their struggle for survival. And yet, the source of the appeals to Goethe is not limited to what we traditionally have understood by works. The crucial intervention of "Goethe" in the dreams, the insomnia, at the deathbeds, and on the pages of Bettina, Eckermann, Heine, Nietzsche, Freud, Benjamin and Blanchot, started the program that has coded this work. To the degree that his name is consistently called upon to mark the relationship of a text to the possibility of its own survival, "Goethe," as an instance of limitless singularity, discloses the testamentary structure of every work.

The exceptional place that Goethe has occupied in the history of Western literature and philosophy is matched only by the static of subterranean channels which his phantom was rumored to inhabit. This work tries to address the more unconscious levels of diffusion through which his text continues to be disseminated. The first part of the book maps the traumatic yet *structuring* relationship between Freud and Goethe. Freud claims that Goethe produced in him the originary impulse that led him to found psychoanalysis. Freud's relationship to Goethe is not based on a concept of a reassuring genetic model, but points rather to a secret text that names Freud's terminal illness. On one level, then, this work asks about the relationship between a work and the articulation of a pathology: to what extent is aetiology inscribed in the textual corpus and, conversely: can the materiality we understand as a body be pathologized by writing? In this regard, I was preoccupied with the most basic problems of life-and-works, which involve reformatting autobiography as allothanatography, or writing's relationship to death. To the extent that every text poses itself as a demand for survival, the subtle textual pathos linking Freud, Goethe and Eckermann, became the exemplary site of dislocated boundaries which had hitherto assured easy transit between a life and its work within a relatively limited causality. An essentially mobile site, Goethe's oeuvre exposed itself to the complementary space of nondiscursive formations. The nonsubstantial drift wafting some of the writing in part motivated by usage of weather systems, which announce the sudden shifts and vaporous, or ghostly, accumulations by which one might try to gauge the "Goethe-effect." Goethe's "Theory of Weather" (which has been credited with having laid the groundwork for the intricate network of contemporary weather stations) disclosed a phantomic region of inquiry in which immateriality, probability, and divinatory skills are set in rapport with futurity. Goethe was then, for me, the pressure zone where discursive relations become associated with nondiscursive milieux.

The attempt to trace the outer limits of relations between texts and their authors required a type of experimentation that no doubt does violence to thought. It is, however, difficult to imagine how any reader of Goethe would fail to join the vital protest, continually reasserted in his writing, against established principles—though there is a history of that failure. But the notion of failure is by no means extraneous to Goethe's work, and belongs to the domain of experimentation that it insists upon. To begin with, I tried to test "Goethe" against the assumptions bequeathed to us moderns by his legacy. I do not wish to deny the *interested* historicity (e.g., my relation to the abiding disaster of German mystifications) which determined the contours of this field test—in other words, I have never entertained any illusions concerning the objective nature of scholarship, no matter how tedious or dusty it can appear to be. What were the evaluations and masks that supported Goethe's unquestioned greatness? In the first place, the transmission systems wired to the Goethe-effect led me to locate in Goethe's oeuvre a place that was utterly foreign to what we think we understand by "Goethe." That which seals the totality of Goethe, presenting him as the figure of unsurpassed monumental writing, is a man who was said to be his lip syncher par excellence: Johannes Peter Eckermann. When Nietzsche says that the *Conversations with Goethe* represents the "best German book," he is referring to Eckermann's work. But traditional certitudes concerning signature, ownership, authorship, original and copy, are henceforth shattered by the community of Goethe and Eckermann.

Eckermann was for me the figure of the ethical relationship from which I drew a lesson on responsible passivity. Staking his life on the fine lines distinguishing writing from passivity, Eckermann receded into the exigency of text as testimony. The exemplary struggle with parricidal writing, the way in which he submitted to the test of alterity and the allegory of an impossible survival, persuaded me that Eckermann was the hero, without heroics, of haunted writing. Eckermann not only became the shelter for Goethe's oeuvre—and for the work that Goethe was unable to finish or recognize as his own—but he had been already, prior to meeting Goethe, a repository for another's suffering. Eckermann was from the start a transistorized ventriloquy system, housing a resident phantom or alien body for which he himself doubled in Goethe's oeuvre. I fell for Eckermann because evicted, shunned, persecuted, he was also the noblest sensibility, ever on the way to language and already serving time—the *Goethezeit*—in the manner of a schizonoiac, captivated by that which captivated him, on the run but only according to the secret velocities of a stationary mobility. Nietzsche recognized Eckermann, but that's about it. He was an embarrassing leftover and crucial supplement to Goethe's oeuvre; he instituted a thinking of the parasitical relationship and existed, if he *existed*, in the shadowed areas of self-abnegation. But, largely forgotten, Eckermann marks the place of an absence, capable of presenting little more than a discourse of effacement. He left very few clues or traces, only enough to open his case. In a subtle scene of ethical allegory, Eckermann taught Goethe the universal law of nature. The fundamental structure of our being-for-the-other is that of adoptive parent. By nature's determination (an oddly nonbiological yet all the more "natural" relation to the other), we are exhorted to feed a Stranger, even if the Stranger will, out of gratitude or ingratitude—it can no longer be discerned, and, in any case, no longer returns to sender—swallow the adoptive parent. The encounter with the other, if it is to be ethical and "natural," is posed by Eckermann as a relation to the always abandoned other. But in order genuinely to become an ethical act, the "I" must surrender itself to the probability of being swallowed alive. The sacrificial moment offers no return, no dividend of a specular narcissism, and nothing on the order of recognition from the other whom one has adopted without appropriation. Upon hearing the ethical allegory, Goethe, in his customary manner, complicates matters a bit by supplanting the notion of sacrifice with the *desire* to be devoured by the other, and thus unfolds a phantasm whose principal figure, the legendary pelican, is shown to offer its body for devoration. While this allegory serves to elucidate the almost Bataillean qualities of the encounter between Goethe and Eckermann, it also points to the thirdness that they conceived between themselves and subjected to consistent morphing.

In addition to reading the *Conversations,* its genesis and hidden history, I explore the way in which Conversation quilts a story of being-with (*Mitsein*). How, indeed, are we brought together by the threads of Conversation? What does this type of relating enable and how is it in turn disclosive of possibilities for community and even for questions of diplomacy? Conversations by no means establish two equal partners but imply that no equalizing will ever be sufficient or appropriate to the encounter. A relation to alterity on the other side of mathematic equation, Conversation necessarily resists appropriation or any subsumption of the other by the tyranny of the Same. The fundamental dissymmetry governing Conversation, the distance at the origin and the rule of non-requital—these are so many markers of the condition of separation that keeps it going. Conversation, in a sense, allows withdrawal, all the while enjoining that which withdraws to keep and develop its own incomparable nearness. Conversation is not that which fuses you to me; but the experience of Conversation induces, once again, the vertigo of expropriation. It is not only the case that I am not identical to myself when I begin to converse with you, but more severely, perhaps: you are no longer the one I have interiorized or memorized. Breaking the secret contract that sealed you within me, you, in Conversation, are no longer you, or the you at least of whom I have preserved an image. No longer the selfsame, you only correspond to yourself when I respond to you. Something else occurs between us, and I cannot say it is altogether you, it's not you and me but something else still. Conversing with you I no longer see you, I am not even looking for you: I am oriented toward you, generously. This is the non-violent transitivity of my inclination toward you. And so the conversations initiated by Eckermann closely resemble what Emmanuel Levinas designates as face or, indeed, as Conversation. "The way in which the other presents himself, *exceeding the idea of the other in me,* we here name face."[1] Breaking away from the frozen image you had deposited with me, you give me a sense of your infinity. Levinas continues:

> For the presence before a face, my orientation toward the Other, can lose the avidity proper to the gaze only by turning into generosity, incapable of approaching the other with empty hands. This relationship established over things henceforth possibly common, that is, susceptible of being said, is the relationship of conversation. . . . To approach the Other in conversation is to welcome his expression, in which at each instant he overflows the idea a thought would carry away from it. It is therefore to *receive* from the Other beyond the capacity of the I, which means exactly: to have an idea of infinity. But this also means: to be taught. The relation with the Other, or Conversation, is a non-allergic relation, an ethical relation; but inasmuch as it is welcomed this conversation is a teaching [enseignement]. Teaching is not reducible to maieutics; it comes from the exterior and brings me more than I can contain. In its non-violent transitivity the very epiphany of the face is produced.[2]

A teaching, Conversation is not reducible to a moment in Bildung or even to anything we think we understand by education (*educere,* the drawing forth on which learning is premised). That is to say, there is always the matter of a surplus that comes from an elsewhere and that can no more be assimilated by me, than it can domesticate itself in me. A teaching that may part ways with Heidegger's motif of our being able to learn only what we already understand—when does learning take place? what do we already understand?—the Conversation belongs, as ethical relation, to the effort of thinking the infinite, the transcendent, the Stranger. None of this amounts to thinking an object.

Always marking the separation of what it enjoins, Conversation also holds a possibility, as Eckermann has shown, for extending a welcoming sign to the departed. Once we are so related and drawn to what withdraws, we incline ourselves in fateful submission to a power which comes from far away and for which writing is an offering. Conversation tells us, among other things, that writing never occurs simply by our own initiative; rather, it sends us. Whether

149

one understands oneself to be lifted by inspiration or dashed by melancholia, quietly moved, controlled by muses or possessed by demons, one has responded to remoter regions of being in that circumstance of nearly transcendental passivity that I am calling "Dictations."

A translation of *Dichtung,* "Dictations" implies that writing always comes from elsewhere, at the behest of another, and is, at best, a short-hand transcription of the demand of this Other whose original distance is never altogether surmounted. In a more recent work, Derrida has commented on this figure of dictations, locating it in the dissymetrical experience of the other which eventuates when one is given over to the other, to the extent, indeed, of being the prey of the other—an experience of quasi-possession "which dictates and compels a certain writing, perhaps all writing, even the most masterful. . . ."[3] The supplement of tyranny exerted by the notion of dictations suggests that, even where there is generosity, it is somehow compelled; it is the command performance issued by some unknown force that we can only welcome.

No matter how isolating, untimely or recondite, the obsession with writing inevitably involves a call to the Other, be the addressee figured as a neighboring companion, "the future," or even some unheard-of tracking instrument that could capture the secret signals of your text. If the teaching that is associated with Conversation does not simply coincide with a maieutics, a Socratic method for helping someone bring forth or remember latent ideas and memories, then something occurs that can be assigned neither to one nor the other member of a couple who, in being related by writing, function merely as provisional, transitory and evanescent points of subjectivation. The type of relationship that ties into writing involves an experience of common but assymetrical deterritorialization. The idiom of deterritorialization, introduced by Deleuze, belongs here principally because what happened (to us) between Eckermann and Goethe very nearly approximates the relations that *Dialogues* meticulously charts. For his part, Deleuze develops an understanding of Conversation that conditions a commonality in which the "we" does not work *together* but between the two. Writing between themselves they are writing a deux, each witnessing the other in his solitude—whether this should be hallucinated as a contemporaneous activity (one is never contemporaneous with the other and, in any case, writing never admits strict contemporaneity), or already posthumous, writing a deux, then, "is already a way of stopping being an author."[4] The evolution of a between zone, with which this work tries to negotiate in the cases of Freud and Goethe and of Eckermann and Goethe, makes it necessary to consider not only what happens between Goethe and his mutating text. This place, which is a place of testimony, remains essentially atopical, however, as it does not take place in one or two of the terms but tries to articulate what there is between, in the dynamic between that sets relations into provisional positions.

The multiplicity that Goethe named and Eckermann and Freud both adopted, involves as well a type of micropolitics, the implications of which I have tried to trace. What are the internal hierarchies, the axiomatic oppressions, the incredible violence and the ever-amended peace treaties which dominate such a relation to writing? What is the price of the unlimited finitude which Goethe sought to inscribe? In a sense, Conversation disrupts the possibility of a simple history because it dispenses with a personal or universal narrative in favor of what could happen to us between ourselves when we expose ourselves to this space, which belongs to neither the one nor the other. It is no doubt useful in this context to think of the way Deleuze motions Conversation away from its sedated place as universal or personal history toward his now familiar topos of becoming. "Becomings belong to geography, they are orientations, directions, entries and exits."[5] Supplanting the phenomena of imitation or assimilation, becomings are characteristic of "a double capture, of non-parallel evolution, of nuptials between two reigns."[6] Now, the concept of nuptials is favored by Deleuze because, always against nature, they "are the opposite of a couple. There are no longer binary machines: question-answer, masculine-feminine, man-animal, etc. This could be what a conversation is—simply the outline of a becoming."[7] While his delimitation of the couple may be somewhat too rigid, too "automatic" and perhaps, at the same time, not malicious enough, it is certainly the case that Goethe's couples mirror this type of nonnatural nuptials, serenely busting the binary hum of question-answer, masculine-feminine, and so forth, while setting the place for an altogether different history of what occurs between-us. Somewhat uncannily, Deleuze's example for becoming with regard to Conversation calls in the birds—recalling what, in the case study of Eckermann, I have tried to bring out as a metapsychological fact. From Mozart to Eckermann, Freud and Hitchcock, birds signal the uncanny space that travels between us when we converse. "It is like Mozart's birds: in this music there is a bird-becoming, but caught in a music-becoming of the bird, the two forming a single becoming, a single bloc, an a-parallel evolution—not an exchange, but 'a confidence with no possible interlocutor,' as a commentator on Mozart says; in short, a conversation."[8] Yet, in Eckermann's avian rhetoric the flight of becoming is never so smooth as to ensure that Conversation will not metamorphose into phantasms of exchange, not even in the unfolding in the *Conversations* of the project of single becoming. But "projects" is too great a word for becomings, which are basically imperceptible; these becomings are seen by Deleuze to be "acts which can only be contained in a life and expressed in a style"—is he not (nearly) lifting a passage of initiation from the *Conversations* when he writes this?[9] Well, lifting will be a recurrent theme in the pages to follow, though little will come down to whatever it is we fear when we say "plagiarism." Even where Eckermann was known to be Goethe's photocopier, there will always be something nonreappropriable about this encounter, something entirely alien to anything one or the other could have said about it; but, if this encounter took place anywhere beyond Eckermann's shocking captivity in a small room with forty birds (with some who produced song [*Gesang*, poetry] and others who were predators and all of them, with Eckermann, in common captivity), it would be precisely at the untranslatable border between life and style. Such border disputes occupy much of the work that keeps "life" and "style" at perpetual odds even as they go to the encounter with one another.

Eckermann will have witnessed the great poet in his solitude, but this does not explain what made it necessary for Goethe eventually to need Eckermann on his side, on *this* side of the life-and-works. They were tight, thick as thieves; it can even be said (I moreover appear to do so) that Eckermann finished off Goethe's natural progeny, his only son, August von Goethe. "This is the encounter, the becoming, the theft and the nuptials, this 'between-two' of solitudes."[10] I don't know for sure what makes any encounter possible, given your abyssal solitude. Perhaps it's about the more narcissistic solitude of a gang member. "(W)hen it comes down to it, you are all alone, and yet you are like a conspiracy of criminals. You are no longer an author, you are a production studio, you have never been more populated. Being a 'gang'—gangs live through the worst dangers; forming judges, courts, schools, families and conjugalities again. But what is good in a gang, in principle, is that each goes about his own business while encountering others, each brings in his loot and a becoming is sketched out—a bloc starts moving—which no longer belongs to anyone, but is 'between' everyone . . ."[11]

. . . You'd be wrong to forget that there are also girl gangs. They are possibly less conspicuous to you, as is the likelihood that there is, in all writing, a woman-becoming. This was pathologized most accurately by Flaubert, when he invested himself in *Madame Bovary*. There is, then, "a woman-becoming in writing," as Deleuze says.[12] Such a politics of becoming is everywhere in evidence in the dislocations that characterize the encounter between Freud, Goethe, and Eckermann. A tremendously shrewd strategist (the way you get, sometimes, when you feel oppressed), Eckermann at one point diverted the course of patricidal writing by turning Goethe into the pregnant figure of an unwed mother who prefers to keep to herself the secret of paternity. This provisional chance of gender will enable Goethe to win the custody battle over the *Farbenlehre*—but here we are getting ahead of ourselves, and giving everything away. In any case, woman-becoming is less a question of passing than it concerns itself with marking our participation in the minority-becoming of writing. Every work orients its struggle for survival through the no man's land of extreme minoritization, even where it comes to be signed by the monumentality of "Goethe."

What connects the names that are archivized in this work? "All these thinkers are of a fragile constitution, and yet shot through with an insurmountable life. They proceed only through positive and affirmative force. They have a sort of cult life."[13] I regard Goethe as my attempt at a Great Health. One can also regard him as an early exemplar of the rock star, though it can be argued that Jean Jacques preceded him in institutioning such a cult life, and before him, heavy metal's Joan of Arc. But Goethe—he became the sign for Nietzsche as for Blanchot, from Eckermann or Emerson to Rorty, in fact, for the possibility of affirming life and bypassing the ressentimental traps that cut us off from our own lifelines. Viewed in light of monumental history or canonic work, insurpassable origin of world literature (*Weltliteratur*), Goethe was however also a killer-text, inducing anxiety and suicide according to programs that were both in and out of his control. The novelty of the criteria which these effects institute requires one to read beyond the limits of authorized commentary and exegetic canniness. Yet, I would not hesitate to say that Goethe dictated every word.

Goethe, the great undead, opened up for me the ethics of haunting. What I mean by this can in part be understood in terms of the secret inducements in response to which we subject ourselves to phenomena evaluated as "great"—to freedom, to God, to work or love. What is it that holds sway over us like an unconditional prescription? What commands us to obey some hidden yet imperative force that may or may not make sense, or that may be discoverable outside of us, inside, beyond our grasp, ahead of us or in the past? The distance between us and that which commands our moves—or their opposite, our immobility—approaches us: it is a distance that closes in on you at times, it announces a proximity closer than any intimacy or familiarity you have ever known. At times it speaks to you, guiding you without manifesting itself as an identifiable or subjectivable someone. It could be the closeness of something that has been lost, obscured and forgotten, leaving you to be haunted by a sense of loss, without substance. Nonetheless, what haunts is also a haunt—something that doubles for a place, a familiar place. Haunting belongs to the family of *Heim;* it in fact has never been properly evicted from the home, as Jean-Luc Nancy has demonstrated.[14] The proximity of a command or imperative could well be the *Unheimlichkeit* that haunts our thinking, because in its remoteness there is something very close, and it is disquieting only to the extent that it is close: "They're back!" Whatever is to be called home, to a familiar dwelling, is related to *ethos*. The questions, as the spirits, that have been raised by the hauntings which have invaded us are not merely a strange fixation of film makers and obsessional neurotics. The relation to a past that, never behind us, is hounding and calling up to us, on good days friendly and populated, implicates nothing less than an ethics. This ethics—provisional, restless, untried—has little to do with the ethics you'll find in your philosophy books or in the works of a science or a discipline; nor will it appear as a moral sentiment. Nonetheless, it is an ethics of the haunted. Haunted: this means that thought is not thinking beyond its time but in its time. Haunted writing writes on this limit, which is that of our time. Thinking, Nancy writes, means "exposing oneself to that which comes with time, in this time. In the time of being-haunted, there can and should not be any other thought or ethics—if that's what it is—other than that of haunting."[15] Where Nancy is commenting upon the excessive nature of the categorical imperative, haunted writing focuses the remote control effects of Goethe's name, which has little to do with a thematizable occurrence, and even less with presence. What haunts existence, now, in our time, is linked to the "domestic" dimension that can never be domesticated. This is the definition of hauntedness, whether we are speaking of the categorical imperative or of Goethean command systems: it does not belong to the economy which it haunts. Hauntedness allows for visitations without making itself at home. Nonetheless, I am talking about a visit, which is to say: a relation has been opened to another text which manifests itself without presence yet with infinite nearness. Henceforth, one is on assignment, somnambulizing, taking dictation from a text of the Other.

Notes

1. Emmanuel Levinas, *Totality and Infinity: An Essay on Exteriority* (Pittsburgh: Duquesne University Press, 1969), p. 50.
2. Ibid., 50–51.
3. Jacques Derrida, "Rhetorique de la drogue," in *L'Esprit des drogues: La dependance hors la loi?*, ed. Jean-Michel, Herviev (Paris: Autrement Revue, 1989), p. 210.
4. Gilles Deleuze, *Dialogues*, trans. Hugh Tomlinson and Barbara Habberjam (New York: Columbia University Press: 1987), p. 8.
5. Ibid., 2.

6. Ibid., 10.

7. Ibid., 2.

8. Ibid., 3.

9. Ibid., 14.

10. Ibid., 9.

11. Ibid.

12. Ibid., 43.

13. Ibid., 6.

14. Jean-Luc Nancy, "Le Kategoriein de L'exces" in *L'Imperatif categorique* (Paris: Flammarion, 1983), pp. 10–11.

15. Ibid., p. 11.

Part Three
Psyche–Soma

The Finite Body

Q. *In your essay "The* Sujet Suppositaire,*" you suggest that "a question regarding the transmission of sexual marks as a condition of knowledge can be posed under the name 'Oedipedagogy.'" Rumor has it that you have also taught a graduate seminar called Oedipedagogy. Would you unpack that term for us and tell us a bit about the seminar?*

A. What I mean by "Oedipedagogy," briefly, is the way pedagogy is linked to desire but also to the structures of parricidal writing or overcoming your teachers. This intentional dimension abides in the teaching relation where all sorts of aberrant transferential or counter-transferential structures can be observed. At the same time, you never entirely overcome the teachers that you are killing. This situation is something I try to read with and against the grain of something like the anxiety of influence, upping the amps on parricidal engagement or on such tropes as jealousy and appropriative rage. In the introduction to *Stupidity,* I speak of graduate students packing heat. When you publish something, you're putting yourself before this tribunal that is going to judge and evaluate what you've done. And there were so many graduate students, especially at Berkeley, who were intensely competitive and jealous of one another or of me. Some were loving and wonderful; but, obviously, the site of learning and teaching is a highly charged at-mosphere, and I wanted to bring to the fore the impos-sibility of teaching *while* I was teaching and also to scan the virginal space of the student body that lets itself be filled by the professorial phallus. Of course, these were quite controversial ways of considering our profession, but they're also canonical discursive formations around the fact of learning that I don't want to exclude.

In the seminar, I wanted to explore the more phantasmatic dimensions of acts of teaching, beginning with Socrates and his affairs of the heart and the phallus. We read Lacan on transference, Derrida's *Carte Postale*, and *Frankenstein*, which is an allegory of teaching and learning, self-education, and the relationship of the master to the creator. (At one point the monster says, "You may be my creator, but I am your master.") We also read Blanchot on the difference between a teacher and a master teacher, which is very compelling. In the Rat Man, especially, the parameters of the relationship between the analyst and the analysand were very interesting to explore. And with all the difficulty and disjunction of translation, I wanted to see what could be retained of that relationship in the scene of teaching: What are the differences among Lacan as analyst, as teacher, as writer? What's the relationship between Plato and Socrates, as analyzed by Derrida in *Carte Postale?* What's the relation between the mentor and student— between Heidegger and Arendt, Goethe and Eckermann, Batman and Robin? We also looked at the new laws legislating against sexual combinations in the classroom or in the university. When they first were proposed, Foucault, who was at the time at Berkeley, said it was absurd to try to legislate desire out of the scene of teaching. But what interested me especially was the hidden phantasm of sodomy as the groundless ground of the

transmission of knowledge, and how its ghostly echoes
still sit in on sem(e/i)nars—the etymological roots of
seminar, seminal works, and other offshoots of the seed
of knowledge. . . . .

Q. *Pedagogy-pedarasty?*

A. *Voilà.* The relationship reversed, or arse upwards, so to
speak. Plato and Socrates, for example, as read by Derrida. And certainly in the case of Freud's Rat Man, the
obsessional neurotic, where the Rat Man is exemplarily
coached by Freud. The Rat Man was unable to name his
symptom or disease, so Freud, filling precisely the space
of learning, decides to guess in order to help him. In
German, the word is *erraten,* for guess, so that's the first
"rat" insertion: he is going to *rat him out.* Freud says the
Rat Man, trying to explain, stammers, "and then . . . and
then . . . and then," which is followed by ellipses and a
dash, and then Freud writes, "Into his anus, I helped
him out." This, for me, became the paradigm of learning: let me help you out: "—Into his anus, I helped him
out." There's this kind of moment of violence, of sticking
it to you that true teaching has to enact. Of course, I
am symbolizing highly here; no one should think we're
solely pursuing a dildological pedagogy. But the question is where teaching arrives. When? Is it a trauma? Is
learning a trauma, as Werner Hamacher once suggested? If so, does it come to us at night? When does
the promissory note that you give to each class (you are
promising that they will have understood) come due?
Will they understand five years from now? In a dream?
In the space of the so-called unconscious?

From "Confessions of an Anacoluthon" (276–78).

A Note on the Failure
of Man's Custodianship

Never felt to be a natural catastrophe, AIDS has from the start carried the traits of a *historical* event. If AIDS had been comprehensible only in terms of natural calamity, it would not have called for a critique: you cannot throw a critique at an earthquake, nor can you really complain about the pounding waves of the ocean, not even if you were inclined to view it through Bataille's pineal eye, as the earth's continual jerking off. But catastrophe, folded in by traits of historical if not conventional markings, calls for a critique; it demands a *reading*.

I started writing about the catastrophe at a time, now difficult to imagine, when the acronym AIDS was not acknowledged by the Reagan White House to exist, either in official or common language usage. The collapse of rumor and disease control was considerable; it was thought, in the obscure ages of the Reagan presidency, that to allow the word to circulate freely would in itself encourage the referential effects of naming to spread. There is nothing very new about language policies that try radically to abbreviate the itinerary of the rumor thought to be co-originary with the spreading velocities of disease. Defoe's *Journal of the Plague Year* would supply one among numerous examples of the way language is seen to be, as they now say, a virus. Ever since the original Reagan ban on the word (however repressed or forgotten this initial "response" may be), a politics of containment and border patrol has dominated the way this culture looks at AIDS. On a level of far lesser consequence, AIDS had not yet acquired the status of an object worthy of scholarly solicitude. Looking back, we can understand why there was such resistance (evidenced by the political and linguistic behavior of straights and gays alike) to admitting the epidemic into the rarefied atmosphere of academic inquiry: AIDS *infected* the academy, dissolving boundaries that traditionally set the disciplines off from one another, if only to secure their sense of self-knowledge. It is small wonder that conservative literary critics, and those generally concerned by questions of history and reference, initially deplored the inclusion of this "outside" referent, which by its very existence challenged the purity of institutional divisions. When it did come about, the study of AIDS encouraged the emergence of new, marginal, and "deviant" areas of inquiry in the humanities: gender studies, gay studies, queer theory, mutant French theory, and even computer-based cyberpunk speculations.

My need to write about AIDS was originally motivated by a number of considerations, each felt by me to be as urgent as the next. My close friend, Marc Paszamant, was among the earliest victims that AIDS had claimed; an entire community was soon to follow. I was anxious over the ways in which the event of acquired immunodeficiency syndrome was being consistently put under erasure. The syndrome appeared to intensify the culpabilization of minorities and the social margin. Finally, those who were called upon to investigate the seemingly originary pathogenesis were being guided by uninterrogated metaphysical assumptions concerning its constitution. The first of the assumptions understood AIDS to derive from one cause, and this cause was reduced to a virus; secondly, the methodologies used to interpret the syndrome involved codes of research that depended upon the old news of a hidden matrix of signification and an absent center of meaning from which the truth was assumed to be pulsing in secrecy. Finally, those who had the funding and authority to study AIDS gave little consideration to the likelihood that the mutation of this virus—if it was a matter principally of virology—owes its existence to a multiplicity of factors, which locate it in our age of technological dominion, social inequity, and inwardly turned violence. The resistance to admitting the multifactoral aggregate which is responsible for AIDS, and the collective impulse to "isolate" a single cause, seemed to lack a judicious construal of derivation. The sustained fabrication of autoimmune laboratories in our polity seemed worthy of consideration as well; that is, the protocols by which the United States was beginning systematically to turn weaker forces into contained spaces of internally discharged violence (of which the drug wars or, more locally, South Central Los Angeles are indisputable signs).

A genealogist—or anyone, for that matter, including the scientific "community," who knows something about the way science legitimates its procedures—must readily grant the possibility that the phenomenon submitted to study is routinely framed by theoretical assumptions, the reliability of which may be only partial. While we in the West are no longer restricted, in principle, in our thoughts by the divine monopoly that dominated medieval medicine (when doctors and theologians were one, and the plague, for example, was seen to originate in those carriers that were recognized, after much research, as Jews), I find it curious that AIDS, for all the discontinuities and anomalies it reflects, nonetheless leaves untouched the tradition by which epidemics come to be associated with minorities including, nowadays, the greater part of the so-called Third World. In fact, the culpabilization of minorities was "grounded" once and for all in the twentieth century in the way we have permitted ourselves to think about the uncontrolled proliferation of AIDS. In one of his works, I can't remember which, Heidegger said that an error in thinking could mess us up for hundreds of years to come. I suspect that our inability to read AIDS constitutes such an error in an already overdrawn historical account. If this remark may seem excessive, it is so only to the degree that excess is constitutive of thinking; however, given the gravity of the subject, I consider these observations to be an exercise in understatement. In any case, I try to demonstrate in "Support Our Tropes" (p. 38) how the inability to read AIDS has spread to the body politic, where the Persian Gulf War, as the phantasm of a safe and bloodless intervention, becomes the symptom par excellence for the uncontrolled translation of the syndrome into other bodies which feel the need to achieve, in a world historical operating theater for example, HIV-negative test results. But the failure to read AIDS is not reducible to a simple power failure or strategy of avoidance—it is bequeathed to us by the Western logos.

In the trajectory that my own work has tried to follow, therefore, the appearance of AIDS constitutes a crucial figure in the technological disclosure, while it also disarticulates any claim to subjective recuperation.[1] As it underscores the essential relationship between testing and technology, AIDS, for us, has made clear the notion that no technology exists that will not be tested; additionally, however, AIDS has shed light on the way our modernity has technologized the subject into a testable entity under state control. An effect of technology, AIDS is part of the radical destructuring of social bonds that will have been the legacy of the twentieth century. It is a bit of a platitude to observe that every epidemic is a product of its time; but the cofactors that have produced the destruction of internal self-defense capabilities still need to be studied in a mood of Nietzschean defiance toward the metaphysico-scientific establishment. For surely AIDS is in concert with the homologous aggression that is widely carried out against the weak within the ensemble of political, cultural, and medical procedures. It is not farfetched to observe that these procedures, today, take comparable measures to destroy any living, menacing reactivity, and thus have to be considered precisely in terms of the disconcerting reciprocity of their ensemble.

If AIDS appears to us as an event within history, or even as *historial* event, this means that it cannot be seen, as a misfortune, to come from elsewhere: it comes from man. Situated within the limits of a history gone bad, revealing its infirmity, AIDS for us does not come from God. But because it is not (yet) curable, it is perceived as a kind of self-destruction of a society abandoned to its own immanence.[2] The renewed experience of God's mute complicity of historical withdrawal ("God" is to be understood here as a promissory transcendence capable of forgiving debts and healing), explains in part why AIDS is a peculiarly *human* symptom, functioning as the locus of a suicidal impulse that increasingly determines our species. AIDS is the affair of man at the end of the millennium; it is "about" man's self-annihilating toxic drive and his scorn for the figure of humanity as it has been disclosed until now. A sign of the failure of man's custodianship, AIDS is the end of the credit line humanity thought it could have with some form of transcendence.

While AIDS displays historical qualities, it should not be temporally confused with absolute emergence. "The brutal appearance of an epidemic, within a set of multifactoral conditions that have evolved gradually, depends upon a quantitative threshold of emergence," cautions Michel Bounan in his critically important work *Le Temps du sida.*[3] In effect, this epidemic should not be viewed as sudden, epochal appearance, but as culmination in the history of a debilitating milieu of forces, the effects of which underscore the turning of a humanity rigorously set against itself. Dr. Bounan has written a treatise deploring life-despising medicine, or, in equally Nietzschean terms (though he does not himself articulate these terms), his scientific invective against the current state of AIDS research discloses the *medicalization of ressentiment* in our time. Indeed, it would be necessary to see the extent to which resentful medicine (for example, those branches of modern medicine that are servile to the dictatorship of pharmaceutical companies) is coresponsible, together with those effects of capital and technology to which we owe the degradation of the environment, for the increase in infectious and tumoral disease. The manifest inability to question the entire apparatus of theoretical presuppositions under which research has been conducted (cancer remains incomprehensible, AIDS confounds them absolutely), leads one to wonder whether this paralysis is not symptomatic of the paranoid condition typified in all epochs anticipating the end of civilization.

Medical science has been reluctant to ask the critical question: What are the multifactoral conditions for the possibility of this epidemic? The motivation behind the failure to ask is no doubt related to the narcissistically defended boundaries that scientific research has lacked the courage to cross. Though dominated by a logic of invasion and intervention, medical science halts its investigations on this side of a diagnostic ethics. Still bound by laws of causality and isolationist views of the phenomena to be studied, medicine is equally beholden to the idiom of limited polemological approach. There is probably nothing outrageous about mapping the body as an intensive conflictual site

THE FAILURE OF MAN'S CUSTODIANSHIP

where war is continually being waged, for example, by one cell or another. And yet the strategies of attack that have been charted appear (despite high tech manipulation) to rely until now upon the premises of resentful medicine for their insight.

Still pre-Nietzschean in the strategic mapping of disease, medical science unfailingly favors "conquering" symptoms by means of violent interventions. According to Bounan, medical science should seek to diminish pathogenic aggressions rather than adding to them; it should intensify defensive reaction rather than suppress it; and it should let disease follow its course rather than "vanquishing" it—for the paradigms of absolute defeat are moored in phantasms of militaristic conquest. Diseases are not provoked *by* a pathogenic environment that would be merely destructive, but *against* it by a patient who is defending herself. These immunopathological actions directed *against* the pathogenic environment constitute efforts to *conserve* life. Illnesses are the "natural de-fense" of the living, and not a message from the dead, which is in effect the only object of biological research. (Bounan demonstrates how biology, a misnomer, can interpret only what is dead and can never come to furnish, therefore, an understanding of the living.) Science has to ask itself what life is—a question, if not increasingly politicized, then at least problematized by technologies of reproduction and life extension—and what is foreign to life. The immunitary apparatus, the natural terminator of foreign formations, has itself become for-eign. Modern medicine's principal pride consists of the antimicrobial war it has waged, which focuses on foreign productions. This war has mandated that vaccinations be globally deployed, an action that has contributed to massive resections affecting the living totality of *reactional coherency;* these interven-tions are coresponsible for ulterior pathologies. Is it a mere coincidence that the African AIDS epidemic followed a program of massive vaccination? Did not the introduction of vaccination in Africa, despite all good intentions, contrib-ute to the destruction of the reactional coherency of indigenous communities, serving only to weaken their resolve to defend themselves within and outside their political bodies? In short, what sort of aggression does mass inoculation imply, what kinds of shots are being administered to "pacify" the West's other? "A disease appears when an ensemble of 'homologous' aggressions, simultane-ously physical and climatic, alimentary and toxic, microbial and emotional, self-induce a defensive mechanism, reaching a lesional threshold."[4] Whether or not Western medicine was forcing upon Africans an internalization of *Ge-stell* (technological posure or framing), by injection, it is no exaggeration to say that Africa was *invaded* medically, just as doctors on the equally "moral" side are assisting, via injection, in the administration of capital punishment in

America—an absolute perversion of their responsibilities. On the one hand, medicine is answerable for its reluctance to *read* the decisive cuts it has made in understanding theoretical assumptions which support uninterrogated research habits; on the other hand, it must be made responsible for the effectivity, whether consciously or unconsciously conceived, of its own interventions. If diagnosis were truly to become what it is, it would have to respond to the reactional, if not revolutionary, exigency of discovery in relation to ever mutating conditions.

The censorship exercised by the medical community and the punitive measures taken by the National Institutes of Health against virologist Peter Duesberg is a case in point. When he proposed the theory that HIV is unrelated to AIDS, arguing that AZT (one of the few government-approved AIDS prevention and treatment drugs) constitutes a powerful poison which itself causes the body's immune system to collapse and can instigate full-blown AIDS, Duesberg was defunded—a fact which interests me only to the extent that it serves as an example of the insistence upon strict viral causality and the corresponding reluctance to explore the homologous aggressions to which AIDS must be linked. Just as etiological, lesional, or psychiatric treatments can be justly regarded as dubious interventions, so the "precise cause" of a disease is to be understood as a trap.[5] It cannot be denied that a genuine treatment of AIDS would require us to risk overturning those pathological ideologies and metaphysical deceits which continue to dominate the world to this day. On the rise, suicide, anguish, poverty, and epidemics sign off the immanence of the one on one, humanity against itself—a humanity steadily abandoned by the promise of future or exteriority and barely able to read its multifactoral histories.

Notes

1. In "Ce qu'on aura pu dire du sida: Quelques propos dans le désordre," *Poésie* 58 (Dec. 1991), Alexander García-Düttmann demonstrates how AIDS has restructured the possibilities for self-disclosure in the autobiographical narrative and the "confessional" texts of Jean-Paul Aron (*Mon Sida*), Pierre Bachelier (*Moi et mon sida*), Renaud Camus (*Tricks*), Susan Sontag (*AIDS and Its Metaphors*), and others. A major question that García-Düttmann proposes for analysis concerns the relationship of deconstruction to AIDS, beginning with an interpretation of Heidegger and the subject of illness: "La maladie occupe-t-elle une place dans la méditation sur l'histoire et l'historialité . . . Quelque soit l'angle depuis lequel on considère ses symptoms, la maladie reste toujours un phénomène existentiel, et cela à même titre que la mort. Or il s'agit peut-être de

comprendre que la maladie affecte le *Dasein* lui-même, qu'elle touche au *Dasein* en entier, ou que le pouvoir-être-entier (*Ganzeinkönnen*) qui caractérise le *Dasein* ne se laisse penser sans penser la maladie" (10).

2. Jean-Luc Nancy, in his "Entretien sur le mal," *Apertura* 5 (1991): 29, argues that we now exist in absolute malignancy, which is to say that we no longer experience malignancy [*le mal:* "evil" and "illness"] as misfortune [*malheur*]—that is, as an irreparable rupture which still makes sense—nor as infirmity [*maladie*]—that is, a reparable rupture, because "classical thought reasons on the basis of the disappearance or the cancellation of death." The malignancy (or evil) in which the history of malignancy appears to culminate is neither reparable nor does it any longer make sense; it is linked to the question of technology, which designates an immanence without transcendence. *Le mal* can also consist in the positive possibility of existence which occurs (as in Schelling) when freedom is free to unleash within itself forces against itself. See Nancy, *L'Expérience de la liberté* (Paris: Galilée, 1988), 164. On the relationship between infirmity and racial markings, see the works of Sander Gilman, especially *Inscribing the Other* (Lincoln: University of Nebraska Press, 1991).

3. Michel Bounan, *Le Temps du sida* (Paris: Éditions Allia, 1990), 59.

4. Ibid., 85.

5. Ibid., 77.

The Disappearance
and Returns of the Idiot

"Believe me, I said it without thinking,"
  he explained, at last,
  wondering.

"Never stay up on the barren heights of cleverness,
  but come down into the green valleys of silliness."
  —Ludwig Wittgenstein

Nietzsche, the first modern philosopher to put his body on the line, to write for and with it, prescribing distinct regimens and monitoring cultural habits, if not addictions, shares with Dostoevsky a certain acceptance of that which has been abjected, excreted by the major cultural codifications of corporeal enactment. Both writers perpetually return to the sheer facticity of bodily existence but not so much as a mute actuality anticipating meaning by way of a transcendent consciousness—there is some of that in Dostoevsky, but it gets constantly subverted and remains merely a temptation—more as a kind of unassimilable scandal. The difference between them, to say it in abbreviated form, is that Nietzsche dances with joy while Dostoevsky swoons in horror—a question of temperament or even of the temperature, of climate, no doubt, to which both were acutely sensitive. In any event, both thinkers bring forth the body as a massive disruption of inherited meaning and, in the case of *The Idiot*, as an always imminent disorientation of sense. The body is in the world and pins down the vague locality of world, but when brought into view, it threatens the solidity of the world. As with television, when things get very local, there is something uncanny and incomprehensible about materiality: it gets delocalized. The close-up of the body that these thinkers invite breaks with traditional modalities of understanding, which is why, in the one case, we are said explicitly to be dealing with idiocy.

Idiocy materializes itself in a kind of negative corporeal stylization, yet it points to the generality of a human predicament: Idiocy has something to do with the nearly existential fact of being stuck with a body or, to put it differently, with the fact that the body has claims upon us. It is not only the case that we are largely but necessarily stupid about our bodies—whether or not they are seen to have functioned in so many ways as some signifying practice or are routinely submitted to a profusion of info tags—but that the body exists as if to mark the dumb impassiveness of our being. There is nothing to know and little to understand—maybe how to feed it, when to fast, how to soothe, moisturize, let go, heal; mostly, though, there is no epistemological stronghold, no scientific comfort or medical absolute by which to grasp your body once and for all, as if it were ever merely itself once and for all: one can only bear witness and offer testimony.[1] This is why writing is so often bound up with illness and why the writer and invalid are often secretly one, like their inversion in Clark Kent and Superman (Prince Myshkin, the invalid, the reporter and magical writing pad, tells stories and endlessly receives narratives from the society of compulsive interlocutors; moreover, he flies high, pitched forward by his epiphanies and crack-ups). All cultural phantasms of bodily mutations aside, the body never stays put long enough to form self-identity. That is why our ancestors used to fast-forward and just lose it, *Trauerspiel*-style, in favor of more ethereal forms and nebulous promises.

But before we inspect how Dostoevsky unfolds these ordeals by taking on the prodigious case of idiocy, let us recall that the body deposited in this novel, as drafted by the kenotic tradition, is variously insulted and humiliated; it is that which is subjected to injury, but an injury capable of language and disclosure. Dostoevsky consistently focused the suffering among the humiliated, insulted, and injured.[2] And idiocy offered a delicate conflagration of soma and psyche, where it became confounding to speak with confidence about health or illness, strength or weakness, as if these were mere opposites. Idiocy allowed access to the insulted body, the enfeebled mind—though for Dostoevsky these qualities are set in flux, reversing their values according to momentary displacements. As for the Prince, he sees himself as ill and experiences this state of illness as a kind of materiality to which he is strapped. Despite his saintly innocence, he is forced to revert to his body, to situate it as reference. At every step of the way, illness, even in its condition of latency, forces his hand.

Illness, if that is what it is, exhorts the body to reveal something of itself. But is there an *object* of the revelations provoked by illness? Is anything learned or understood? Or is not illness the stealth master, the teacher whose lesson is unremittingly opaque yet purposeful? The body takes time. In any case, illness prompts a temporal warp, a lengthening of days and shortening of hours, a future telescoping into sweat beads. There is so much time, yet this time you are clocked by the quickening sense of finitude. You're in a pinch. This is when you ask, How much time do I have?

Your body, localized to its place of pathology, reminds you how it used to make itself invisible, a point or pulsation in the unconscious. When it was on your side, it carried you by leaving itself behind. Maybe you had cut your finger or banged your knee. A spider bite. Little things that would signal, as if by metonymy, "Honey, I'm home, I am your home." Now your body prevails in a reproachful sort of way, and there is nothing for you to know (there are charts and medical histories, comparative analyses, information and data, prognoses and projections, all cognitive stammers in the face of illness). You become its amnesiac witness, capable of momentary attestations, observing and monitoring, unsure of ever recovering from these irruptions of total contingency. You understand yourself as dead meat, repeating the ancient cry of abandonment and knowing that this time, this time it's for real, you have been forsaken. Forget about getting past this. Though there are little, altogether secular resurrections: your fever goes down, a little energy suddenly rises, you can eat or walk or pee alone, and it is not clear why this is happening to you right now, I mean, that you're not yet dead. Still, something has happened to you. One morning you wake up like Gregor Samsa, can't get out of bed. Or you've been throwing up all night. Something has happened. You took a fall, fell ill; KO'd, you were thrown, cast out of the heavenly body that certified innocence in the form of health. You are sick as a dog. Everything stops. There are times when this suspension of being can be affirmed. Like when Gregor dances on the ceiling: he doesn't have to go to work! You get to stay home and regress. Read, watch television, hallucinate. Still, though, there's something very wrong, like culpability without a known cause. You're in trouble, unbalanced. The inventions and inflections of the future vanish. But something is released as well. The store of toxicity spills, sometimes in slow motion, and something like time starts cleansing. Your body—your body is *fighting for you.*

It's a fight, sometimes, without teleology; it can be a losing battle or a healing without cure, one big healing crisis. It's war, and one small part of yourself is standing up for you, standing up to you. Maybe for the first time.

Illness: essentially related to the experience of injustice, it is your *Geworfenheit,* your dharma. Something beyond or within you has put you down, smashed you firmly against a wall of indifference, pressuring you with your own capacity for suffering. It was uncalled for, illness, yet there may be something you did, you think, to bring it on. An accompaniment to your finitude, illness visits you at will and does what it wants to your body, biting organs and stinging surfaces you didn't know you had. To underscore this point, Dostoevsky made sure that the Prince would endure, so to speak, the intensity of injustice by determining that his experience of illness would not be obscured by social injustice. This is why Dostoevsky throws money and station at him. The martyring of the Prince is related to a destruction tendered irreparable because there is no way to separate the destruction of mind from a body in desperation: hence the Prince suffers a sacred illness. It is not the body that, though entrusted to us, is as such sacred but the illness, which disorders sense and even convention, that appears to maintain that auratic quality of ongoing sacrifice, its sacredness.

Illness offers its own system of subverting social norms, independent of subjectivity or volition: "I can't marry any one. I am an invalid." Framed by panic, illness gives access to the devotional mode of surrender, abandoning to itself something other than the self, the will. Whereas Nietzsche thematized a going under that was pivoted on a promise of recuperation, Dostoevsky parses illness for a rhythm of remission, a promise offered only for provisional reprieve. But there is no phase of attestable overcoming, for the disease, experienced in the mode of a silent chronicity, is always with the Idiot, even where it refrains from proposing signs and symptoms or ceases to substitute itself for perception and mime consciousness. Another kind of mediation, illness, indeed, brings with it an alternative system of ecstasy and meaning. Under paradoxical sway, classical tropes of harmony and balance are shown to be sustained only in the distortions produced by the pained body, beside itself, pitching toward massive collapse. The measured chill of absolute endangerment. As one Dostoevsky scholar puts it, "this beatific vision of harmony can only be experienced by a half-witted epileptic who knows it to be an aberration of his disease."[3]

In *The Idiot* there are two infirm bodies. They are labeled explicitly by the graphosomatology of the text as ill, as dying. Of course no one is excused from the exigencies of this becoming (the limits of health are not always very clear, one cannot be found not to be dying, and anyway, illness is an inescapable condition of being), but two bodies—those of Prince Myshkin and of the young nihilist Ippolit—are presented without ambiguity under the name of illness. Ippolit, the consumptive, in the process of dying, is tied to his process by confessions and the incessant composition of last wills and angry testaments. The Prince endures an illness that stays the execution but offers premonitions of death episodically. He walks about, ever in anticipation of an attack, all along in the inexact assurance of punctual recovery. When restoration appears to present a possibility, he is undercut and then, suddenly, reestablished again. It is not known how much time he has. No question of a cure, though there are reprieves, sudden and exhausting. Idiocy and epilepsy reinforce each other in the novel, as if to emphasize the impossible separation of domains, notably, where the body ends; extending toward a limit, disfiguring this limit, their conjunction makes us ask, How could a proper phenomenology of mind be traced that would not ditch the body? (If it were proper, it would have to be improper.) While the introduction of epilepsy brings definition to the parameters of infirmity with which Dostoevsky is working, such a medicalization of idiocy does not clear away the questions that he persistently raises. In fact, epilepsy itself, what Shakespeare in *Julius Caesar* called "falling sickness," brings one big question mark to the table of any speculative diagnostics.

Even though Dostoevsky "had" epilepsy, it remains unclear what he had or what we have at hand when we think we are discussing the condition so named. It has a heritage backed up by literature, seconded by philosophy, and claimed by mythology. A thorough modern cultural anthropology studying the place of the purported disease would include the fact that epilepsy is the only somatic illness to which Freud devoted some pages in the postneurological phases of his career. Located between psyche and soma, between the theory of trauma (which focuses the history of the subject) and the theory of fantasy (which refers to transference and countertransference), epilepsy is not just another somatic illness. In distinction to other types of somatic aggravations, epilepsy is inscribed in the history of thought without being restricted merely to the history of medical thought.[4] The only illness to have its own mythological figure, it may provide the ur-phenomenon of all subsequent forms of madness and visionary excess. Hercules, the herald of epilepsy, has mutated and manifested historically in the Buddha, Alexander the Great, Julius Caesar, Napoléon, Lord Byron, Pascal, Van Gogh, and others to whom we shall no doubt return (epileptics are said to fear returns, *revenants*). For now, let us follow Dostoevsky in postponing a discussion of pathogenic specificity until the general tour of the more global effects of illness has been accomplished.

The sick bodies of Ippolit and Myshkin mark the disruption around which the text is organized. This may be one reason why the text comes off as so disorganized, barring the historical contingencies of its *Entstehung,* the conditions of its emergence (under great duress, the author dashed off the serial installments in exchange for payment, his beloved infant daughter had died, and he, inconsolable, suffering, was exiled for the most part to Germanic precincts). Everyone is susceptible to the ailing bodies, almost unaccountably attracted to them as if they could be, in the first place, psychically infectious. No one stands forth as the body of health, for there are gradations of illness and entire taxonomies of foolishness—the novel suffers fools of many kinds and supports drunkards, maniacs, the pathologically resentful, the envious, a rapist, a crowd of cheaters, classic neurotics, subjects of delusional rantings and criminal intent, not to speak of, worst of all, what constitutes for the narrator the blatantly ordinary. On several occasions Nastasya Filippovna is labeled by the Idiot himself as a lunatic. The supporting cast of troubled figures, while received by the novel for the most part with compassion and capable of emanating a nearly magical radiance, functions only to stoke the sacred intensity of the Idiot's illness.

The idiot body, presented as eccentric and awkward, convulsive and worn, in some instances as a battered body, is particularly susceptible to attack. It is not always clear where the attack comes from, for it is hard to locate the force that hits him—it can come from above, from inside, from the alter ego and spiritual brother, Rogozhin (though presenting an alter ego to the nearly egoless Myshkin would involve another problem), from the weather or the unconscious or, even more precisely, from the *drive,* that is, neither from the conscious nor the unconscious. Attacks of the sort he suffers, bouts of illness (Dostoevsky does not make it easy to divide up the territory of illness—is it a continuity folded back by occasional recession, or is it closer to a punctuality, a return, an interference or interruption of another state?), aggravate the problem of presenting the body—the weight of the unpresentable—at all. The sick body presses the issue of this impossible presentation to the fore. It is not merely mired in passivity, though each day it awaits its fate, wondering if a vague spell of dizziness does not portend the beginning of another episode, the event of another destruction. The difficulty lies in predicting the daily histories of a sick body, the varying intensities of its constitution (the day of the ill is divided into about four parts, the afternoon fever, the evening reprieve, nocturnal sweats—this changes with different types of illness, the signified, I mean, but the day divides up in much the same way no matter what you've got—and the liver works the late-night shift, rousing you at two or three in the morning, no matter who you are). In the life of the sick the primary relationship is to this alternate being, at once indwelling and eventuating from without.

When the Idiot says he cannot marry, it is because he is bound by another contract to his illness, whose distinct personality he serves. By nature imperious, illness demands devoted appeasement, understanding, the endless manipulations of care. You lie with your illness—something that seems foolish to have to say: it takes you, in many cases, to bed. But there are some forms of illness that do not show, do not lay you low or keep you supine, decumbent. Shadowed by a passive transitivity, you walk around in them, you're an idiot, ever on the verge of having an attack. He says he cannot marry, but he is betrothed to two women; toward the end he has prepared for the wedding with Nastasya Filippovna. But this offers no contradiction: the sick often find someone who is even sicker to take care of, and this is the case with the Prince. He offers his hand to

Nastasya, it is noted, out of a feminist impulse—she has been scorned by men, denounced as a lost woman, sexually mishandled—but with unaffected fervor because she is, to his mind, a sick child, a lunatic, delirious and deranged. He also takes care of Ippolit, whose terminal condition prompts, throughout the novel, dramatic anxiety.

The Forbidden Body

Despite the pressure it exerts on reading minutely the signs or symptoms that accrue to the sick body, the labor of understanding abandons all semiology or phenomenology. It encounters a limit, mute and stupid, that cannot be grasped even in terms of a negative knowledge. There is yet another dimension of the stupid to which infirmity subjects us, one that remains indifferent to those registers of stupidity still affected by the fading empire of cognition. Without knowing, the body is not, as such, ignorant either. A literality that is no longer legible, this body at once withholds itself and produces resistant signs of itself. Perhaps this offers one reason why literature, which delights in radically ambiguous conjunctions, always points to the incorporation of such a body. If the body of the king is the thing, purloined or missing in action, the Prince's body drags along, in need of treatment. And it is no wonder that literature treats this body where philosophy might sack it with the rest of the provisional hostages of the concept.

According to Jean-Luc Nancy, literature has always tried to produce the body, which philosophy suppresses. In fact, this relation enacts an allegory of their link, for "one could say that literature and philosophy have never stopped wanting to relate to and/or oppose one another as body to soul or spirit." Moreover, "one is tempted to say that if there has never been any body in philosophy—other than the signifier and signified—in literature, on the contrary, there is nothing but bodies."[5] Nancy provisionally divides the body according to a discursive custody suit of sorts, where literature gets to carry bodies to house and form them. Still, we can't just go around thinking that these bodies are easily reclaimable or anchored in reference. Nor can we think that we can ignore the body, the way people commonly step over the homeless bodies on their streets. Any discussion of the body risks engaging a "double bind, a psychosis." Failure is necessarily given at the outset: "And a double failure is given: a failure to produce a discourse on the body, also the failure not to produce discourse on it" (190). One might venture, though, that the sick body, in a kind of frenzied state of belated, compensatory awakening, demands a reading or at least occasions interpretive and diagnostic strategies that often culminate in an excess of discourse. This excess itself, an attempt to construct knowledge around the symptomizing body, opens up the space of necessary obscurity by which our bodies come to us: "This non-knowledge is not negative knowledge or the negation of knowledge; it is simply the absence of knowledge, the absence of the very relation of knowledge, whatever its content" (199). Nancy continues, holding the body as uninscribable, as that which exscribes everything, starting with itself:

> The body does not know; but it is not ignorant either. Quite simply, it is elsewhere. It is from elsewhere, another place, another regime, another register, which is not even that of an "obscure" knowledge, or a "pre-conceptual" knowledge, or a "global," "immanent," or "immediate" knowledge. The philosophical objection to what philosophy calls "body" presupposes the determination of something like an authority of "immediate knowledge"—a contradiction in terms, which inevitably becomes "mediated" (as "sensation," "perception," synaesthesia, and as immense reconstitutions of a presupposed "representation"). But what if one could presuppose nothing of the kind? What if the body was simply there, given, abandoned, without presupposition, simply posited, weighed, weighty? (199–200)

Ever elsewhere when it comes to cognitive scanners, the body evades the regimens of knowledge that would claim to grasp, sectionize, or conceptualize it. Somewhat surprisingly, the site of nonknowledge that the body traverses, and of which it is a part, is related by Nancy to thought, to acts or contracts of thinking, for the body thinks in a sense, beyond giving or making sense (which would belong under the auspices of knowledge); conversely, thought embodies: "If one agrees to say, and if it is fitting to say, that thought does not belong to the order of knowledge either, then it might no longer be impossible to say that the body thinks and also, consequently, that thought is itself a body" (201). Linked to the thought of thinking, responding with an almost unreadable acquiescence to the question "What is called thinking?" this inert presence, detached from the knowledge that would seek to contain it, has let go of "a treasury of sense to which only those united with God have access" (191). Thought, which Heidegger unhitched from philosophical operations, weighs in as body, and, more perplexingly still, to the extent that it is possible that the body thinks, the thinking body throws itself against the prevailing winds of the Western philosophical tradition.

If, in Dostoevsky's work, the body commended by illness still bears a memory trace of the sacred, it nonetheless encounters its finitude, and the finitude of all bodies, in the haunting limit drawn by Holbein. "With the death of God, we have lost this glorious body, this sublime body: this real symbol of his sovereign majesty, this microcosm of his immense work, and finally this visibility of the invisible, this *mimesis* of the inimitable" (191). Putting to rest the glorious body, Holbein's "Christ Taken Down . . ." concludes a double act of reversal. Figuring Christ's body without the lift or iconicity of intended transcendence, Nancy says: "'God is dead' means: God no longer has a body" (191). Henceforth bodies, bereft of trickle-down symbolicity, will have to be pumped up, prosthetically amplified, steroid-enhanced, "built" and buffed, bionically ensured, drugged or "medicated," cloned, remade—henceforth, the technobody or replicant will be made to substitute for the lost body of the divine trait—that body which could still be sacrificed. In *The Idiot,* Dostoevsky sees the apocalypse, or at least he has Lebedyev reinscribe it, in terms of technological dominion, citing the spread of the railroad and the distribution of connectors installed by new technologies as instigators of the unsacrificeable.

The novel opens with the three principals—Myshkin, Rogozhin, and Lebedyev—being carried by train into Saint Petersburg station. It starts, therefore, according to tracks laid out in the later parts of the novel, in the apocalyptic tenor—or vehicle—of a technological momentum. Later on machinery itself is cast by Ippolit as a dumb beast, the *bêtise* that is part of an inexorable movement of world-historical dumbness. The novel's first chapter roars into the station, a mythological terminus bound from the start to determine the fate of the Idiot.

What emerges from the train is the last body, a sputter or remnant of the lost, glorious body. It is a body in transit, making the transition from the sublime body to what is pictured by Holbein as the decreation of world—the unnameable end of the body, even if this should be consecrated in our memories as an endless end that only keeps on ending. Nancy phrases it thus: "The dead, rotten body is this thing that no longer has any name in any language, as we learn from Tertullian and Bossuet; and the unnamed God has vanished together with this unnameable thing. It might very well be that with this body, all bodies have been lost, that any notion, any truth, any representation of bodies has been lost" (191). Having displaced the lost body, the inglorious corpse implicates the mediations that historically have touched all bodies and kept them, if not safe, then at least representable. In Dostoevsky, infirmity effects something of a return of the glorious body as the memory and phantom of what can no longer be.

To the extent that Myshkin's illness still binds him to the sacred, his serves as a body, perhaps the last, still capable of being sacrificed. The residue of sacrificeability is due in part to the fact that this body retains and persists in making sense. An expression of unbearable singularity, the illness continues to produce sense if only as a hallucinatory byproduct of its disordering interventions. Nonetheless, there is provisional sense, epiphany—there is the inflection of divine disclosure, though without a proper object. There is nothing to disclose but the exposition itself to another regimen or register of being. Outside the realm to which the severity of illness opens, there is only the exhaustion of the body and the congealed sense of the body. To keep this body sacrificeable, Dostoevsky has had to protect it from the emptying of sense induced by the evacuation of the sacred, staving off that depletion of purpose congruent with the degradations of poverty, hunger, deportation, torture, deprivation, ugliness, horror: "Such are the sacrificed bodies, but sacrificed to nothing" (195).

There may be no truth of this body other than that which speaks to the nothingness of its sacrifice, no Empedoclean remnant out of which to piece together some final sense, not even the announcement of an approaching Fortinbras, who would bring up futuricity by means of order and commemoration. "'Sacrifice,'" says Nancy, "designates a body's passage to a limit where it becomes the body of a community, the spirit of a communion of which it is the effectiveness, the material symbol, the absolute relationship to itself of sense pervading blood, of blood making sense. But sacrifice is no more" (176). The historicity of the wound involves its despiritualization, and the body recedes, taking on the status of the forbidden body. "There was a spirituality of Christ's wounds. But since then, a wound is just a wound—and the body is nothing but a wound. . . . The body is but a wound. None of our wounds, in a sense, is new, regardless of the economic, military, police, psychological techniques that inflict them. But from now on, the wound is just a sign of itself, signifying nothing other than this suffering, a forbidden body deprived of its body" (196).[6]

An embodiment of a pure tautology, an emptiness, the forbidden body offers the experience of an inert presence with little or no ontological consistency. The community, having surrendered the meaningful body, becomes the site of a private ward of contingency, the unattested sacrifice. Illness at once grounds the body here on earth, marking its subjection to time and destruction in time, but it also suspends, while reestablishing, the very corporeal contingency under whose rule it operates. Illness calls for the emergence of another body—a multiplicity of bodies—for a healing and for another understanding. It plays the phantasmatic body against the real body. Complicit with the demand for another understanding, Christianity, from one perspective, offered the promise of performative acts of healing. The teaching of the Incarnation, saying that God was also meant to inhabit a body, underscored how we are fated to inhabit our bodies. Instigator to the many legendary scenes of spontaneous healing, Christianity, one major recovery program, insistently addressed the failing body, whether in discursive rites or by means of constructions such as Lourdes—the offering of allegories of woundedness that it dressed with emergency supplies of meaning. In a text that was commissioned by his doctor for a roundtable discussion, Nancy writes about the fate of pain, marking it off from suffering and the tradition that appropriates these terms. Pain, according to the title of the improvised text, is strictly unjustifiable ("La douleur existe, elle est injustifiable").[7] That is, the moment one attempts to justify or make sense of it, one has reappropriated pain to its Christian history; one has returned or restored it to meaning.

However, pain abhors meaning; it grotesquely etches meaning's interruption and self-sameness. Pain is unjustifiable. Without a doubt it is unjustifiable that pain be unjustifiable. Anyone who tries to present a case for its justification is a Stoic or Christian or worse. One could be a Hegelian, getting by on the "work, patience, and pain of the concept."[8] Whereas suffering and distress tend to subsist on themselves or expand their scope by morose delectation or masochistic surplus, pain, in contrast, acts as its own repellent, rejecting itself while refusing any justification, assumption or sublimation. "Pain is perhaps nothing but this refusal of itself."[9] Allowing for little secondary benefit (to speak with Freud), pain is its own destitution, which no amount of dialectization or ideological recuperation could justify. When pain persists without remedy and nothing else exists besides its pointed compression, its tightening, a kind of paradoxical if instantaneous flash goes off, a momentary insight occurs: something like a pure attestation of being becomes possible, a kind of "I'm not well, I'm in trouble, therefore I am."[10] It is not that "I am" in the sense of a sudden retrieval of self; I am no more than the piercing pain that is tearing me apart, and in such a way that I am no longer a self, this madness of pain.[11] Nancy, who is very French on this point, offers that this split-second flash is like the double or reverse of the bang of *jouissance*. Pain and *jouissance* (which can be seen as a pain that "succeeds") share the extremity of such a radiating flash, pulsing from that place where being, utterly exposed, is external to itself, posed outside any self (*soi*) as pure explosive flashing, ripped, thrown. This extremity does not take place except within the split between pain and the extreme point of pleasure. Which is to say that in a sense it cannot ever take place or that it is "impossible," as Lacan says of *jouissance*.

Nancy by no means endeavors to efface the irrefutable urgency of pain, of which he has had his share. Instead he concludes his intervention by stating that the it's-not-happening experience you get with pain *is* reality.[12] He ends his remarks by allowing that the recognition of the certitude, the reality of which he writes, does not amount to a justification: "C'est une attestation." When the punishing thrashes of pain come down on you, you are at a loss for words, the fiction of agency collapses; even so, you are preparing your testimony. If one can do no more than testify, attest to that which cannot take place, it is also because the solidity of empirical ground slips away from under pain, leaving it to grope in the dark, fumbling for language, when it seeks description through the intercession of "as if." It's as if my head were splitting open. Or, doubling the stakes of abstraction, I feel as though I'm going to die. But pain is destructive of language's capacity to name.[13] Unshareable, it bores through language. Virginia Woolf once said that we know how to describe great torrents and we capture tempests, but we cannot convey the essence of a headache (my paraphrase). This goes for the dancing invalid in Kleist's story as well as for a throbbing toothache in Dostoevsky's *Underground Man*. Pertinently elusive of referential content, the language that seeks to get a handle on pain becomes dependent on a speculative grammar for its expression; rather than offering confirmation of the empiricalness that we thought we had recourse to, it radiates through metaphoricity; pain exists—unjustifiably—to disfigure, leaping about abrasively in figural language, searing your sacred idiot body.

Myshkin arrives at the station with a clean bill of health. Well, almost: he has been released from the doctor's custody. It is as if he were meant to cross the moment of a reprieve drawn by the fragile span between a clinical discharge and a final collapse. To the extent that he is presented as partially healed (but still an "idiot"), resurrected and exposed to the community, subjected to mockery, derision, and love, as emanating a sacred quality, he returns to Russia as the figure of a renewal but also as an undead God, conditionally resurrected. He occupies the purposive space evacuated by the living, eternal God, though he does not quite yet serve as the reminder that God is dead—maybe that God is capable of dying. He arrives as a last recapitulation of the divine in the form of sacred simplicity and a body that still sacrifices while forbidding itself to the other.

If he at once fascinates and horrifies, this is due in part to the way Myshkin embodies what is deficient in the Other. Incessantly returning to the Other its own lack, he reflects a certain abhorrence of the sacred. The idiot body is absorbed by the community to the point of marking its own exclusion, ever poised as a foreign body within the ambivalently receptive milieu that welcomes him. Because he has been away for so long, Prince Myshkin speaks Russian with a foreign accent; he is native and foreign at once, an inclusion that is meant to be excluded, familiar and aberrant, both dear and bizarre, the intimate figure of idiocy. The very woundedness by which he is bound protects him: this body, in need of a healing that cannot be ensured, actually saves the Prince from a brutal execution at the hands of a jealous Rogozhin. As he is about to be assassinated in a dark stairwell, an epileptic seizure erupts and takes over the scene, supervening upon the intention of murder, frightening away the killer.

The Seizure

Elusive yet inescapable, the body presents itself as pure surplus of objectivity, something moreover, that cannot be reached by the very knowledge it invites. Whether infirm or sound—the difference dwindles—our body doubles for trauma, or, rather, it *acts* as a traumatic place that causes a series of failures. The way we locate it elicits the thought of trauma inasmuch as the body appears to occupy the empty place of the real. It recalls the Lacanian engagement with the real to the extent that the body presents itself as an entity that does not exist, or barely exists, except perhaps in failure or exaggeration, in beauty or mortification.[14] Some of these assertions become evident in the experience itself of the epileptic fit, when consciousness is extinguished by the force of surplus intensity—

> *Then suddenly something seemed torn asunder before him; his soul was flooded with intense inner light. The moment lasted perhaps half a second, yet he clearly and consciously remembered the beginning, the first sound of the fearful scream which broke of itself from his breast and which he could not have checked by any effort. Then his consciousness was instantly extinguished and complete darkness followed.*
>
> *It was an epileptic fit, the first he had had for a long time. It is well known that epileptic fits come on quite suddenly. At the moment the face is horribly distorted, especially the eyes. The whole body and the features of the face work with convulsive jerks and contortions. A terrible, indescribable scream that is unlike anything else breaks from the sufferer. In that scream everything human seems obliterated and it is impossible, or very difficult, for an observer to realize and admit that it is the man himself screaming. It seems indeed as though it were someone else screaming from within that man. . . . The sight of a man in an epileptic fit fills many people with positive and unbearable horror, in which there is a certain element of the uncanny. (227)*

Whereas other passages describe a state of extraordinary emotiveness in the form of ecstatic self-departure—the incomparable *pleasure* offered by the seizure makes you want to trade in everything for one such moment of desubjectivizing rapture, an illuminated, coruscating giddiness—this episode brings up the experience of severance, the blaze of an intense inner light followed by the extinction of consciousness. The Prince, losing presence in this passage to the fit, is placed at an increasing remove, and so Dostoevsky has the narrator name the condition ("It was an epileptic fit") and track its manifestation. But even the external, diagnostic gaze collapses at the limits of language, contorting into the "indescribable scream" issued by the suffering body and shared by narrative reduction. In excess of signification, an impossible metonymy of the convulsing body, the scream, indescribable, "is unlike anything else" and breaks from the body. In the scream everything human is obliterated and the subject is delocalized, "as though it were someone else screaming from within the man." Split, divided, bereft of properly human properties, the seized subject produces a medused effect, terrorizing and petrifying the other, even if he is Rogozhin and about to murder you.

"Myshkin, worn out, depressed, and physically shattered—"

In a more Freudian light (though what could be more Freudian than the simultaneity of assassination attempts, somaticopsychic collapse, and the close proximity of your best friend?), this scene could be viewed as the *Entstellung*, or truthful distortion, representing the severe ambivalence that the Idiot, the seriously ill subject, tends to elicit. The scene says as much about itself (the "sight of a man in an epileptic fit fills many people with positive and unbearable horror") but deflects its own insight toward the more material contours of the episode. Still, it stages the murderous rage inscribed by Myshkin's alter ego and soulmate at the scene of extreme illness. The distortion lies in the narrative decision to linearize and condense the story, showing that Rogozhin desists from committing the intended murder when horrified by the fit. The murderer is seized by terror; the seizure makes him disappear from the murder scene. Whether the seizure is responsive to violence directed toward the subject or is at the root of the other's rage remains unsaid. Yet somehow the sick body invites social rage, the other side of brotherly love: it incites the absolute hostility that supplants hospital(ity). In fact, though, a number of characters in the novel respond to the Prince's condition with a spontaneous violence that is then shown to be repressed or eventually sublimated to charity and love.

How can the scene of the seizure be read? One exhaustive clinical study depicts the epileptic fit as a repetition of the infant's terror when first faced with the parental death wish—as a response to the threat of infanticide visited upon baby.[15] On the other hand, Ferenczi had seen the epileptic seizure as an enactment of a wish to return to the womb, and Freud, when it was his turn to consider the enigma of epilepsy, rather than allow a purely neuropathic status to stand, had somewhat surprisingly kept it close to the mode of hysteria he identified as conversion hysteria; more recently, in *Dostoïevski et Flaubert*, Marie-Thérèse Sutterman locates epilepsy in the sadomasochistic phantasms that feature the self as murdered child. In view of her indications, the scene composed by Dostoevsky could be seen to represent a *metaleptic fit*, for Myshkin, in fetal position, subverts the murder, having produced the fit that in fact reenacts a prior murder scene. I offer these considerations as a kind of sneak preview, for there remain in this story a number of sadomasochistic contracts yet to be drawn.

Aglaya Epanchina is not the least consequential of the attending figures who, although ostensibly attached to the Prince by love, are in any case at once horrified and fascinated by his debility and respond to him with a consistent capacity for sadistic vengeance. Aglaya's sadistic repertory commences with the many instances of poking fun at him and by her demands that while in social view he be stilled, silenced, rendered stationary and invisible. Moreover, she at times prompts his faltering incapacitation to the extent that she programs failure, "foreseeing" with anxiety that at a party he is meant to break a prized vase and deliver rants in place of conversation. To announce a premonition to the hysterically suggestible Myshkin, to predict, is, as his beloved well knows, to dictate its execution. At every level, from the ingratiating nurse, Lebedyev, to the case of Ippolit, Dostoevsky indicates how illness summons forth exploitation, codependency, malevolence, how it draws blood and excites social violence. Repugnant and uncanny, the Idiot, in a kind of Bataillean reversal (being at bottom unmistakably Christian), provokes . . . love. Everyone loves the Idiot, who becomes a global symptom within an ambivalent economy governed largely by disgust. The idiot evokes horror, but this circumstance does not stop the community from loving him. On the contrary. There exists a barely discernible distinction between love and disgust in the novel. One could say of every couple equally that they are drawn to each other by irrepressible hatred or unavoidable love, that desire is fueled by disgust, run on aversion—Dostoevsky makes these affective determinations reversible in a manner that retains the accent on ambivalent intensity. The undecidable limit between hatred and love, contempt and reverence dominates the community of every couple: Rogozhin and Myshkin, Aglaya and Myshkin, Nastasya and Myshkin, Lebedyev and himself, the general and his wife, Kolya and the general, and just about everyone else who comes together.

Let us return momentarily to the scene of Myshkin's seizure, which undecidably suspends/provokes Rogozhin's murderous rage. The crisis and its ghostly suspension perform a doubling within the novel that earns it the narrative quality of "uncanny." The horror attending the convulsed body, its scream of abandonment coming from elsewhere, unlocatably, reinscribes the scene in Rogozhin's house before Holbein's *Christ Taken from the Cross.* Anna Grigoryevna has used the same diction in her diaries to describe her husband's turn of mind when he first saw Holbein's tableau in Basel and the cast of his feature when he went into seizures: she delineates "an expression of terror."[16] A concentration of terrors is, in her view, established by these events, which somehow mirror each other, causing a fright, an apocalyptic strain of anxiety. Epilepsy is notoriously prodded and harassed by certain representations and recurring memories; the epileptic must avoid these triggers. A kind of daredevil masochism incites Dostoevsky to return to condemned scenes or moods of representation, however. Forbidden by his doctors to represent to himself the scenes of the fit, Dostoevsky delves into them, repeating and reworking the event of the seizure. For the epileptic, a partial recall of the forbidden experience in itself runs the risk, as do flashing lights or intense imaging, or provoking another fit. So when Dostoevsky refuses to forget but instead describes Myshkin's panic, reviving terror and aura, when he flashes back to the dead Christ and reaches down into the abyss in order to come up with this scene, he has his hand on at least three triggers. The murder, the love of Christ, the horror before his mutilated body, in sum, the general vocabulary of unsupported suffering, are dispatched to Myshkin, where it is no longer known whether he "had hurt himself, or whether there had been some crime" (227).

Persistently recalling the cry that seemed to come from someone else, the novel continues to proffer two bodies, as if to underscore the double bind that any body language necessarily engages. Whereas Faust had reported that two souls inhabit his body, *The Idiot* speaks to us of two bodies, which, in part hallucinated and internalized, replicate themselves in a determined drama of unsettled malaise. Faust rid himself of his ailing body with drugs dealt by Mephistopheles, the witches' brew. It was only after switching body types that Faust started tripping beyond the bounds of traditional cultures of knowledge, exceeding the limits of the human intelligence quotient. Myshkin stays body-bound and busted, constrained by an experience of corporeality that, though finally earthly and ordinary, in itself proves capable of producing double takes and self-departing splits. In a sense there are nothing but body doubles, reflecting one another as if to mark the failure of integrating the traumatic singularity of what is given to us as our ownmost body. Thus there are two sick bodies, those of Myshkin and Ippolit; Myshkin is split between two women, Nastasya and Aglaya, and there is an articulated split between the blood brothers Rogozhin and Myshkin. The proliferation of doubles continues, having originated in the double body of God, which appears to lose its transcendence until, as if compressed in the end of the novel, there remains one corpse watched over by Myshkin and his negative mirror, Rogozhin. By the end of the novel spirit has evacuated the scene, leaving behind the abandoned body, which is to say, the inglorious corpse. This body, now reduced to the smell of preservatives, is covered by a medicalized trace called America: "'Do you notice the smell?' . . . 'I covered her with American cloth—good American cloth—and put a sheet on top of that, and I put four uncorked bottles of Zhdanor's disinfectant there. They are there now'" (591).

Notes

1. I realize that such assertions concerning our stupid bodies may sound nonprogressive, particularly in the face of such movements as Positive Action, Positive Choices, and the marks of similar tags of empowerment that issue from the hope that we know what we're doing, that we can take charge and act up and affirm our bodies, our selves, that we can now stop being victims and relinquish passivity. One need only read Mark Doty's elegiac memoir to be reminded of our unshelteredness in the face of the hopelessly stupid language of health care and all the AIDS acronyms (AZT, ARC, DDI, HIV, etc., etc.), signs of the severely impoverished, technologized idiom of the late twentieth century. Part of the memoir addresses the ruses of knowledge as concerns the afflicted body, in this case subjected to "viral activity"—an expression systematically used by doctors when they do not know what to call or how to describe, much less heal, the enigmatic symptom. Anyone who claims to know the body, who responds solely with prescription and denies the factum of stupidity when it comes to bodies in their unbearable singularities, anyone suspending suspense—from torturer to healer—has become entangled in a political dilemma of significant ethical proportions. "There is no relief in long illness, which suspends us in not-knowing. Every case of AIDS is unique, each person has AIDS in his or her own way. We couldn't know what was coming, we could only hold our breaths as it began, slowly, it seemed then—though so swift now, in retrospect's compression—to make itself known" (*Heaven's Coast: A Memoir* [New York: HarperCollins, 1996], 204). While the course of the disease will have made something ("itself") known, there was never a present attestable by Doty in which such knowledge was at hand.

In a catalog of recent paintings by Titina Maselli (Galleria Giulia, April 15, 1998), Alexander Garcia Düttmann, whose philosophical reflection on AIDS is well known (*At Odds with AIDS* [Stanford, Calif.: Stanford University Press, 1996]), comments on a poem by Tom Carey that begins, "'I watch my body like I watch someone else's pet / It lives in my peripheral vision / Poor dumb thing, it can't see, speak or hear / it grunts, blows, and weeps.'" Even, or especially, the so-called healthy body, not entirely there, trails stupidly behind, as in Dennis Cooper's *Frisk* (New York: Grove Press, 1991): "Usually I don't notice my body. It's just there, working steadily. I wash it, feed it, jerk it off, wipe its ass, and that's all. Even during sex I don't use my body that much. I'm more interested in other guys'. Mine just sort of follows my head and hands, like a trailer" (50).

2. Dostoevsky's relationship to the intensities of such suffering prompts further reflection. On the masochistic stirrings of the humiliated, see, for instance, his depiction of the character of little Nellie in *The Insulted and Injured*. Having been "ill-treated," she is "'purposely trying to aggravate her wound by this mysterious behavior, this mistrustfulness of us all; as though she enjoyed her own pain, by this *egoism of suffering*, if I may so express it. This aggravation of suffering and this revelling in it I could understand; it is the enjoyment of many of the insulted and injured, oppressed by destiny and smarting under the sense of injustice'" (quoted in Frank, *Bounds of Reason*, 323).

3. Alex de Jonge, *Dostoevsky and the Age of Intensity* (New York: St. Martin's, 1975), 142.

4. The place of epilepsy in poetry and the history of thought is elaborated in Marie-Thérèse Sutterman, *Dostoïevski et Flaubert: Écritures de l'épilepsie* (Paris: Presses Universitaires de France, 1993). For an outstanding analysis of epilepsy and temporality, see Kimura Bin's *Écrits de psychopathologie phénoménologique* (Paris: Presses Universitaires de France, 1992), which is based on the existential analysis (*Daseinsanalyse*) of Ludwig Binswanger. Epilepsy, of which Bin writes that "personne ne sait ce qu'il en est au juste" (no one know exactly what it is [58])—it remains an enigma—is understood here as that which most closely approaches death in life, the *morbus sacer* that brings the subject to the most extreme disorder and destructuration. The epileptic episode is located by Bin as the originary anxiety (*Urangst*) that determines all other crises of anxiety. He analyzes the perturbation of temporality introduced by the epileptic episode, what he calls the reduction of temporality "au présent instantané ponctuel" (to the indivisible, instantaneous present [92]). In the chapter "Le Temps et l'angoisse," Bin focuses on the ethical constitution of the afflicted, who display an exasperated sense of obligation, a heightened consciousness of duty in relation to others. See also Ludwig Binswanger, *Über Ideenflucht* (Zürich: Orell Füssli, 1933); H. Tellenbach, "Zur Phänomenologie der Verschränkung von Anfallsleiden und Wesensänderung beim Epileptiker," *Jarbuch der Psychologie, Psychotherapie, und medizinischer Anthropologie* 14.57 (1966); and V. E. von Gesattel, "Störungen des Werdens und des Zeiterlebens im Rahmen psychiatrischer Erkrankungen," in *Prolegomena einer medizinischen Anthropologie* (Berlin: Springer Verlag, 1954).

5. Jean-Luc Nancy, *Birth to Presence*, trans. Brian Holmes et al. (Stanford, Calif.: Stanford University Press, 1993), 193 (subsequent citations occur parenthetically in the text).

6. It would be tempting to imagine Nancy invoking the nostalgic trophies of an original wound, after which there would be only serial replication or the buildup of a hysterical

mimesis—endless counts of wounding that could never coincide with the originary spirituality of those lacerating Christ's body. At times Nancy's propositions appear to betray a tendency to share with Bataille a longing for past states and histories that are capable of relaying us back to an epoch when blood flowed with purpose and meant something—when, as in the case of Hegel, war (to cite one example) was still wageable because it was productive of sense. However, Nancy disdains the nostalgic inflections to which a number of Bataille's interpretations have pointed. Unless I am mistaken in this assumption, it is not part of Nancy's insight or intention in this text to make Christ's body the referent, though it becomes somewhat difficult to deny that such a movement or tendency is afoot.

What can be original about a wound, especially if it is susceptible to hysterical mimicry? The seriousness of Nancy's interventions has always involved the retrieval of lost continuities and their syncopic returns. In other words, Nancy reads the opaque historicity of woundedness from a consideration of Western thrownness—what he has called elsewhere "our history"—and, as always, his work rigorously capitulates to the ambiguities on which Western thought continues to be based. If we were engaged in military strategy or metaphor, capitulation might not be a good thing. Here it indicates acceptance, the marked passivity of a vigilance that demands a certain number of inclusions and remembrances without reestablishing the values they have held or continue to hold in a forgetful and metaphysically laden world. It is useful to bear in mind that there are different kinds of wounds involving archetypes of wounds that won't heal: Prometheus, Philoctetes, the Fisher King, and the sudden wounding of Kafka's "Country Doctor." Derrida discusses the referent to "Corpus" from yet another point of view in *Le toucher, Jean-Luc Nancy* (Paris: Galilée, 2000).

7. Jean-Luc Nancy, "La douleur existe, elle est injustifiable," *Revue d'éthique et de théologie morale* 95 (Dec. 1995): 91–96 (all English translations are mine).

8. Ibid., 95: "le travail, la patience, et la douleur du concept."

9. Ibid.: "La douleur n'est peut-être rien d'autre que ce refus de soi."

10. Ibid.: "une sorte de j'ai mal, donc je suis."

11. Ibid.: "et de telle façon que je ne suis plus 'moi,' mais ce mal même, cette folie."

12. Ibid., 96: "Mais ce ne-pas-avoir-lieu est aussi bien la certitude même, et la réalité."

13. Elaine Scarry writes in *The Body in Pain: The Making and Unmaking of the World* (New York: Oxford University Press, 1985): "Physical pain does not simply resist language but actively destroys it, bringing about in immediate reversion to a state anterior to language, to the sounds and cries a human being makes before language is learned" (4). Consider also her discussion of analogical verification and the resistance to language, the unshareability of pain (5–20). For a compelling reflection on the quality of language and illness, see Susan Sontag, *"Illness as Metaphor" and "AIDS and Its Metaphors"* (New York: Doubleday, 1990).

14. See Slavoj Žižek, *The Metastases of Enjoyment: Six Essays on Woman and Causality* (London: Verso, 1994), 171ff.

15. See Sutterman, *Dostoïevski et Flaubert.*

16. "This painting, by Hans Holbein, depicts Jesus Christ after his inhuman agony, after his body has been taken down the Cross and begun to decay. His swollen face is covered with bloody wounds, and it is terrible to behold.

"The painting had a crushing impact on Fyodor Mikhailovich. He stood before it as if stunned. And I did not have the strength to look at it—it was too painful for me, particularly in my sickly condition—and I went into other rooms. When I came back after fifteen or twenty minutes, I found him still riveted to the same spot in front of the painting. His agitated face had a kind of dread in it, something I had noticed more than once during the first moments of an epileptic seizure.

"Quietly I took my husband by the arm, led him into another room and sat him down on a bench, expecting the attack from one minute to the next. Luckily this did not happen" (Anna Dostoevsky, *Dostoevsky: Reminiscences,* trans. and ed. Beatrice Stillman [New York: Liveright, 1975], 133–34).

The Philosophical Code

DENNIS COOPER'S PACIFIC RIM

In an era that understands the reduction of subjectivity to a thumbprint or a medical record, not to speak of a police profile, Dennis Cooper captures the subworld that has slithered by metaphysics and that could not be accounted for by traditional notions of beauty and identity. Clearly marked by events that bind us—but also pressed by the silent chronicity of illness, stupor, kiddie porn, the global takeover of signification—his works achieve a level of pertinence that give them a cult vitality, an uncommon literary vigor. Still, the thematic registers of the work consistently reduce the energy that Cooper's texts release, in a sense neutralizing representation and voice, calming the nervous disclosure of which his language proves capable. No monumental overhaul or prophetic prideful- ness lines the works that exhibit an existential bareness while exposing the intimate regions of what was once known as a subject. Cooper does not erase the subject, but holds it in custody, suspending a history of reappropriations and justifications, allowing a steady technologization or leveling of meaning to determine its mutant contours. Such tactical switches become complicated when the purported object of contemplation appears to be desire—a network of relays and effects that commonly depend upon a subject open to invasion. But in Cooper the subject is, from the get-go, radically expropriated, divested of all sorts of capacities to act upon the world or read its dense mappings and respond to its demands. This is perhaps where I come in, for the strategies of expropriation are not limited to the circumscribed characters of Cooper's works but sting those who attempt to approach them, feel called by them, or are somehow needed in the lonely districts of his unrelenting insight. Still, in a Heideggerian sense, the world as unitary concept no longer exists since Coo- per, even though his areas of intense scrutiny continue to rely upon bouts of worldliness. He is implacably of this world, on the side of being that knows no escape or getaway plan. Unless you count the drugs and their transcendental- izing effects, the over-the-top breakthroughs that his works at once posit and shoot down along with the quivering bodies that knock themselves out, one after the other. He situates the shattered, frayed, floated aspect of existence, though without pathos, without a project for regathering the splintered imago of a put-together world or establishing a remembered working title under which things are supposed to make sense. Not a trace of nostalgia for the fuller living arrangements of other novels, no word of rescinding what throws his texts against aberrant constellations of semi-sober behaviors. The world, to the extent that it still "worlds," mounts his texts yawningly, eating whole sentences or phrasal regimes on which we have come to depend for some sense of solidity. Dennis, for his part, meticulously opens new dossiers of the unsaid, venturing a stuttering kind of relatedness that slips beyond any conceptual grasp, cataloguing its dismal ecstasies, at once indifferent and invested, roused and limp, a discarded vegetable. He is plastered to the language of this world, smoking entire neighborhoods of metaphysical thought. Though he runs with Kafka, Genet, Duras, and Bataille—he pounds the literary pavement differently, exhausted yet running on a fascistic form of empty, as he might say— one is left little choice but to trail him around, scope out the orifices of little boys to whom one shouldn't get attached because . . . Ok, ok, so what am I doing working this side of the literary street? I'll tell you.

When I visit with a text, I look for signs of welcome or an authorization code that would let me step in. Sometimes I circumvent the customary yet hidden systems of politesse or legal niceties, which is when I simply break in and enter. But I prefer not to get hauled away or eventually entangled in custody battles—engaging those textual skirmishes that begin, "Who invited *you*?" I prefer the polite way so that we can all pretend I belong where I don't belong. The encounter with a given text by no means occurs matter-of-factly, without apprehension or, as I make my way through, without skid marks or serious bruising. When Kafka offered that he wanted his works to read or arrive like an axe in a frozen sea—well, that's what happens to me, I think, if I can see myself starting out as the frozen sea, glacialized, severe, resistant. Or at least shivering and receptive in an obstinate sort of way. In any case, I take a hit, even when I'm invited nicely or well defended, like Venus in Furs.

But invitations are queer speech acts, making you feel responsible and obligated, forcing abrupt turnovers that switch the invitation into an injunction, merciless and cold. If not by invitation, I am called at least to a work's precincts or respond to a summons, a citation summoning me. The summoning call comes through according to all sorts of delayed call forwarding systems, muffled and transferred to my reception desk in ways I can't always seem to trace. All I know is that I am being compelled: I am held under the sway of an imperative that I can neither understand nor shake.

Dennis Cooper's work calls and compels me in this way. It orders me around according to prescriptive moves that I can barely fathom. In one sense I am called to the scene of reading by a resolutely French space and dossier that his writing opens up. If one had to issue identity papers to his text, one might be tempted to conclude that there is nothing more American than the corporeal scanners, the permutations of slacker ethos, and the pallid landscape of Cooper's precise suburban explorations. You would be wrong. Besides the fact that desire is made in France—I stand by this statement: desire inevitably arrives at our shores as a French import that needs to be translated into American idioms and practices—it is the case that Cooper's works are explicitly tagged by French markings: nearly every work opens—is cracked open like an ass—with a French citation. The stench in any event is decidedly French. Thus we are led into or met at crucial junctures of the works by Rimbaud, Genet, and Bresson, and more recently, the sublime Blanchot heads up the work. This lineup, perhaps, saves a place for my intervention, indicating where I can come in, slated, on the line to French theory. To put it in condensed form, "French theory" is a way of not having to decide between literature and philosophy; it offers a site that circumscribes the undecided limit between literature and philosophy. Though it may come as a surprise, Cooper's work, it seems to me, signals a philosophical urgency and points to a subterranean corpus designated expressly by so-called French theory. Admittedly, nothing could seem further from the truth. But Cooper is far from the truth, thankfully, though his tropology is engaged by the dominant tendencies of our modernity. Thematically his work travels through the devastated landscape of love, mortality, consciousness, representation, identity, and so forth. I can offer here only an indication of where I would be going with this corpus had I been given free rein and more time.

I would take recourse to French theory to designate a particular modality of thinking about literature (in my world French theory includes German texts and philosophemes, such as Heidegger's appropriation of poetry or Kant's phobic evasions of the literary in his writing) because Cooper engages three aspects of literary questioning that I find compelling and that exceed the thematic thrills of which he is an acknowledged master. In the first place, his writing is a reflection on writing. (I suspect that this dimension of his work is not what drew in his devoted fans: "Oh, Dennis Cooper, he has reinscribed acts of writing!") His allegories of writing are developed on several levels, which for a literary theorist are driving points. Incidentally, by the end of this micro-intervention, I hope to have proved to you that you are drawn to this work because of the way it reinscribes writing: rimming and writing are closely connected, and even the most debilitated, stuttering subject is a writer in Cooper's book. One need only think of Ziggy and his 'zine, "I Apologize: A Magazine for the Sexually Abused," his manner of submitting simultaneously to his magazine and a sadistic father, upping the ante of Kafka's "Penal Colony," where the writing machine mutilates the body. The writing machine, the torture, are administered, both in Kafka and Kooper (if I may), by the Father-Commandant.

Cooper's works are so-to-speak self-reflexive to the extent that they supply running commentaries on types of writing, from the epistolary to the snuff film, in which the boundary between what is real or fictive is decisively abandoned. The drama of reading is included in the thematic unfolding of the work. Thus the character Dennis's friends in *Frisk* cannot determine whether his letters document events of the fantasy or are charged with miming reference and exploiting the real—whether, indeed, it is all a matter of event or sheer literary invention.[1] It bears noting that every serious literary work produces this constitutive confusion. In the idiom of speech act theory, every work of literature asks itself whether it is constative or performative, whether it is in the process of describing or inventing effects of the real, or scrambling the master codes that allow for such distinctions. This is why Cooper's work feels dangerous and gives you the sense that it could be busted at any moment, or get you busted, and land in court like *Madame Bovary* or *Ulysses*—those works that got snagged for exceeding the sanctioned pornographic code. If Cooper's work were merely pornographic it would not feel dangerous or be looking for trouble. I have studied the legal briefs around works that get censored. In the case of *Ulysses,* the judge has had to decide, he declares, between the emetic and pornographic qualities of the work. (This litmus test breaks down in the face of Cooper's writing.) In the case of *Madame Bovary,* they threw the book at the book on the basis of a nonrepresentational moment—when you don't know what's going on. The novel points to an interiority that refuses narration, shutting out mimetic or referential authority. *Madame Bovary* was officially cited for the scene in which the carriage, sealed and tomblike, rocks around the town square for several hours. One does not know what is going on inside and can only surmise what Emma and Léon are up to. This sealing off of the enamored protagonists represents a moment when the novel desists from telling, offering only the traumatic pricks of a socially unsymbolizable wound.

As in the case of Schlegel's novel, an eighteenth-century scandal that infuriated the greatest philosophers, Cooper's novel gets into trouble by installing two incompatible codes—that of philosophical speculation (albeit covertly transmuted, discreet and in drag, philosophically in drag, disfigured but still traceable) and pornographic description. His descriptive technique often resembles what Deleuze, writing on Sade and Sacher-Masoch, prefers to see as *pornology* rather than pornography, since Cooper's writings carry a pocket of reflection, an allegorical avenue that offers a crawling commentary beneath the text's explicit facet. It is a language not satisfied with mimetic pretense, no matter how close it gets to the bone of naturalist description. The truly scandalous marks of texts such as those of Schlegel, Sade, and Sacher-Masoch reside in their compulsion to provide theoretical sidebars and philosophical disquisitions—often, as Deleuze points out, cruel and cold, toned by apathy or distance. If Sade had been a mere pornographer, he would not have been locked up; if Schlegel had separated out his philosophical obsession from his sexual diction, he would not have been the persistent target zone of thinkers including Hegel, Kierkegaard, Dilthey, and Schmitt. Just as Sartre could not abide Bataille's philosophical raids in his most graphic exposures, Schlegel and Sade courted trouble for their politics of contamination, folding in philosophical speculation on the subject of their foldouts. Hence the need for überpsychoanalyst Jacques Lacan to come in and put Kant and Sade on the same couch.

Cooper's relation to philosophy travels a different yet equally trackable route. Inclusive of what he expels, Cooper bounces philosophical gravity off his corpus with insistent irony. Ziggy, recruiting Nietzsche to his cause, says at one point, "Nietzsche, right? Whatever. Drugged brains are so easily exhausted. *Whatever.*"[2] If I had the presence of mind to do so, I would unpack this amazing utterance and follow the many trajectories that it implies. Fatigue does not figure in classical pornographic texts, where no one gets tired or, as Lacan points out, where bodies aren't hurt or made to fall ill after endless sessions of pounding. The pornographized body maintains its unshakeable integrity, staying intact regardless of the degree of intrusive pitches and relentless sieges. The body barely burps. Only Masoch has the masochistic torturess sneeze all the time, but that's another story. Cooper, by contrast, stokes corporeal anxiety, exposing its fragile finitude at every bend. Its susceptibility to exhaustion is one means by which he passes the body through the lockup of metaphysical pornography, which at once asserts the freshness of the finite body but does not let it wither or fade. Even in its desecration it remains theologized, always awake to the entreaties of others. The noiseless negotiators with metaphysics let things fade and wither, expire of exhaustion. That is why, if time allowed, I would want to read with you the theme of exhaustion in Nietzsche and also in Blanchot, whom Cooper cites at the beginning of *Period.*[3]

Blanchot opens his important book *The Infinite Conversation* (which I would be tempted to translate as *Infinite Maintenance,* from *L'entretien infini*) with two weary men, fogged by fatigue, contemplating the exhaustion of language and the faded promise of guiding philosophemes. Fatigue deserves its own history, if something like fatigue were locatable or in any serious way readable. Or, to put it in a more familiar way, the history of consciousness might be reconsidered in light of fatigue and the persistent wearing down of mind by weather or drugs or disappointment or grief and other nebulae, other barely appropriable formations of mental eclipse that also belong to our histories without quite showing up. I remember one Saturday morning sitting around the table when Levinas asked the children he was working with, "If God is what He is, why does He need a day of rest? God cannot be susceptible to fatigue, can He?" They were translating passages of the Old Testament. Levinas's response to the stumped silence of the gathered children was that God was setting an example of which He was not a part: God's children need to rest, are prone to fatigue. But let us return to the sentence, "Nietzsche, right? Whatever. Drugged brains are so easily exhausted. *Whatever"*—a series of sentences to which we are sentenced.

Naming Nietzsche, it opens the dossier on the culture of narcotica that Nietzsche had said we have yet to read and write about. "Who will write the history of narcotica?" Nietzsche asks at one point, indicating that our so-called high culture depends upon drugs and persists in masking chronic dependency. Drugs not only belong to a repressed thinking of culture but point to a nanotechnology installed in the human body, which is set up with receptors to receive the chemical prosthesis. Why is the body prepared for drugs? The enigmatic technology of drugs sends signals all along Cooper's work, transforming the way we think about consciousness and marking a region of being that Cooper relentlessly explores: the *whateverness* of being.

By having the protagonist utter, "Nietzsche, right? Whatever. Drugged brains are so easily exhausted. *Whatever,*" Cooper at once introduces and subdues the philosophical code, marking and effacing—in other words, writing philosophy, writing that is opening and bracketing, tracing and erasing the mark. I would want more time to make this stick, to review the entire corpus with an eye to the double entry of its philosophical registry. Let's just say that the names are there and that we are still searching for the access code. There is a stealth channel set up to catch furtive philosophical channels. Behind closed doors these novels jack off to philosophy, vibrating to philosophical representation.

Moreover—and these questions are all connected—the question of *readability* emerges at several critical junctures in Cooper's work. The anguish over questions of unreadability is evinced all over the place. The texts turn in on themselves by allegorical or explicit means as they point up the blurs and blanks that constitute their relation to meaning and their effort to produce effects of sense. It is not as though they get out of the dilemma of unreadability, clearing the runway for unperturbed lucidity: they are always jammed, pulled off the purported union of sign and meaning, questioning the referential ground on which they crawl. Unreadability governs the scene of reading even when one of the characters thinks he has understood or found the provisional roadmap, the treasured other. Let me move on, though, and leave the elaboration of these aperçues for another occasion. I can only ask that you open a credit account for me, grant me credit so that I can build on what has not scrupulously been demonstrated or proven. You need to trust me on the philosophical track before you install the laugh track or repeat, "Nietzsche, right? *Whatever*." Other, equally important things are going on here.

First, Cooper's works, particularly in the instance of *Try,* tend to ironize the predicament of anyone who would seek to consolidate an identity politics. They express a lack of conviction over stable sexual identities or even so-called preferences. Straight–gay boundaries are frequently rescinded (Ziggy has sex with Nicole but is in sexless love with the heroin addict Calhoun, who is, if one can say so, straight, though all determinations of this sort—gay, straight, bi, tranny, etc.—get reshuffled and annulled by the whateverness of being). This is where unreadability returns, together with the distinctly Blanchotian motif of weariness, in the fatigue of identity: "Roger and Cricked looked tired and unreadable, especially him/her, whose makeup smeared face and tangled hair are more Heavy Metal than girl now" (*Try* 163). Cooper executes entire bodies of theoretical work when he jumps channels on sexual determination or flips on sexuated entities and perturbs the presumed readability of private histories—if the notion of history can even be recruited to establish some solidity of character and story. Let me finish this part of my broadcast segment by pointing to the way Cooper tends to conflate the beloved ass in his works with the production of meaning, and, irreversibly, with the act itself of writing.

There are times when a more experienced teacher takes to the pen and writes to a wary disciple. Much in the manner that Rilke wrote a letter to a young poet, Roger writes a letter to disciple, son, stoner editor Ziggy. The contents of said letter describe what could be called a rhetoric of rimming. The didactic dispatch construes the ass as a site of mapping. It organizes the signifier by displacing the phantasm of the phallus:

> *My Dear Ziggy, [. . . .] I choose friends selectively, and bed partners even more selectively still. To me teenaged boys of the sort I have indicated are an example of human beings at their most fiercely alive, most . . . evolved, let me say [. . . .] As for what I like to do with them, rimming's the technical term for it. "Eating ass" is a lowlier synonym. Do you know that many, many gay men are more interested in asses than they are in big cocks, despite all the hype to the contrary? [. . .] I love to spend quality time with a beautiful teenaged boy's ass, massag-*

ing, mapping, recording its factual data, putting my tongue in the hole (this is a common gay sex act). . . . Then the letter apologizes for being so crass for about half a page. Ziggy skims. (*Try* 19)

If one imagined Hans Georg Gadamer having something to say about this business, one would be inclined to see, in the manner outlined in *Truth and Method*, that Ziggy's response to the letter corresponds ideally to its latent demand: refusing to be penetrated, the ass-letter allows itself only to be skimmed. It is as if Roger were producing a manifesto for another type of reading, one that repeats and notarizes the surface relation to a possible reading.

The disquisition on the ass continues later in the novel, making room for itself: "Ahem. What *is* the source of my interest in asses? (This gets better. Wait.). . . An ass is the most vague in meaning and structurally flexible," he writes.

> What is an ass if not the world's best designed, most inviting blank space, on the one hand, and, on the other, a grungy peephole into humans' ordinariness, to put it mildly?
>
> L.A. was entirely smogged over that morning . . . (*Try* 100)

I am interested in a double trajectory that is being established: one that reads and maps the ass as a place of writing, a space of considerable indeterminacy yet open, as it were, to (critical) approach—a page, a blank space inviting intervention, marking, the stylus, the hand, the tongue probe (not to mention the way it reasserts the excremental structure of all writing). Yet, at the moment one might have been led to expect the glorification of the ass, instead of a displaced glory hole, we are given a peephole. Into what? Into ordinariness. Roger is attracted, if that is the word, to ordinariness, bypassing the idealizations on which his *apologia* appeared to be escalating. The ass offers a figure for sheer vacancy, a blank yet ordinary space yielding a dumb body, evacuated, so to speak, by the promise of transcendence. Life unfolds in its idiomatic dumb-ass terms, stuck between trauma and meaning. The ass is the space of signification to the extent that it resists signification, hovers between singularity and generality: it is recessive and quasi-absent when compared with face and genitalia, which threaten with excess. For Roger the face and genitals are too present, and do not allow for the withdrawal, the Heideggerian *Entzug*, that writing exacts. All I can say now, as time presses, is that, in what we think or are led to believe is the greatest pornographic moment, a rhetorical switch occurs: the act of penetration is reassigned, though without a colloquial hitch, to designate a problem of cognition. The ass proffered, Roger desists from penetrating but shifts the registers of language from its literal to figural dimensions, precisely, to penetrate the "givens of people I crave" (100). Roger's language swerves, passing over the ass in order to name the desire to grasp, mark, write, capture the "givens" of people he says he craves—givens that are never simply given and which continue to withdraw, erase, as he incessantly resumes the project of devouring the blank space of voracious indeterminacy. The ass in a certain sense designates an originary scene of writing, a wounding—a traumatic imago that guides the narrative unfolding of other novels by Cooper. Submitted to rimming rituals, it offers itself up as something that cannot be assimilated or internalized like a phallus yet is ever mourned as the lost, beloved object, unyielding because it rebuffs symbolization. In Rousseau the ass-whacking routinely known as "spanking" slaps together the first inscribed pages in memory—the child is written upon. In Cooper, the ass, already a metonymic displacement of cock and face, circumscribes a trauma zone that gets marked by intrusive phenomena, unsettling flashbacks, and the instant replay that inhabit the work at hand. Read in its entirety, the corpus engages a theory of mourning—more exactly, of failed mourning and breached introjections that could be said to disclose the pathology we call America:

> I would hazard a guess that this little fixation involves an avoidance of more resolute body parts, namely the face and genitalia, both of which, while fascinating, present too much personality, thereby reinforcing my failure to penetrate the givens of people I crave. For, of the body's main features, an ass is the most vague in meaning and structurally flexible. . . . L.A. was extremely smogged over that morning, so I was denied the adrenaline rush of floating into its endless and bleached teenaged-boy-peppered grid. I deplaned, crossed the airport, caught the car rental's agency minibus. Avis. After a torpid half hour of waiting in line, and superficially friendly blah-blah with an I.Q.-less employee, I shot away cramped in a red Honda Civic. An hour later, it and I whirred into the scrubby, arid San Gabriel Valley, whose flat neighborhoods were inexpensive enough for my brainless, job-flitting assholish ex-boyfriend. (*Try* 100–101)

Attributes of the ass revert to L.A.—vague, polluted, disruptive of a spermatic economy. L.A. denies the rush, the phallic heave of a desire that might know its aims. That is why the landscape of liminal loss—boundaries are snuffed out, objects turned to their vague interiors, unfixable—allows itself to be punctuated by sheer dumbness, the facticity of life without cognitive bolsters. The I.Q.-less employee, the flat neighborhoods, the brainless ex all conspire to maintain the weight of our dumbass existence. The ecstatic temporality of phallic desire would, by contrast, lift the smog of lassitude, being capable of turning out the rush of a certain kind of brilliance or existential sparkle. For Roger, try as he might, "lust wrests the power away from my intellect" (100). Unlike the brilliant schemers and instructors of Sade's enlightened universe, Cooper's ruminators frequently shore up on the dim, depleted banks of desire. Thus his characters tend to be keenly aware of the aporias of intelligence, enumerating the way we score intelligence and drugs. *Guide* clues us in to cognitive drug raids by these means:

> LSD can make anyone brilliant—temporarily, at least—but there's a catch, i.e., it also renders one freakish, inarticulate, an idiot savant uncomprehendingly jailed within the crude rights and wrongs of the world's "sane" majority. Opiates, on the other hand, tend to instigate a flirtation with death which . . . makes one's flirtation with dying inherently profound, since "profound" and "unknowable" are synonymous, right? (8)[4]

Like Walter Benjamin, Cooper plumbs surprising depths of unknowability along the lines of drug schedules. Drugs—or what I have elsewhere called "hallucinogenres"—blur the boundaries between intelligence and idiocy, between what is knowable and unintelligible, yet often give the impression of grandiose insight. Something is lost in these transactions on the level of understanding, grinding down the certainty that one has understood desire and the sum of privations on which it is postulated. Intelligence can be feigned, artificially manipulated to show up as a kind of sacred stupidity. Or stupidity could be the way things are run nowadays, without shame or apology, without bothering to accommodate the rumored showdown with intelligence. In any case, Roger's attraction to ordinariness, and the work of mourning that his disquisition on ass and meaning implies, redraws the map on which aggression builds its arsenal. Phallic prongs are dulled, faces blurred to a ground level of bald stupefaction. By no means diminished, aggression finds different, less pointed outlets. Things have become pointless. In a Nietzschean sense, there is good and bad pointlessness—the measured scales of liberation and continued suppression. All sorts of unanticipated occurrences can creep up when everything has become pointless, when the gods and worldly telos have receded. The ordinary ass thrones on the metaphysical recession. When Roger writes of the ass that it "is the most vague in meaning," he gives focus to that which withdraws, veils, and refuses itself. Feminized, it is organized around an abyssal center, a hole, that, for Roger at least, marks the defunct matrix of signification. The writer Roger positions asses (they start out as split and double, even as they fold into an abjected center) as the serialized marks of displaced and deferred presence, as the nonpresence calling up desire. Whether giving or taking, asses remain inert, resisting when they appear to give or open up. They determine the excitability of a nonpresence that causes Roger to write and assert the excremental nature of all writing. At the same time, they turn things around, averting thought from the emblazoned logos, the centered pride of phallic discursivity and derivation. There is no weapon that purposefully duplicates the ass. Withholding face and phallus, the ass doesn't even invite a proper mourning or a syndromic anxiety, such as the complex that Freud designated as castration anxiety. In terms of presence, light, and logos, the ass is already lost to figuration, a flattened face of metaphysics. Much of Cooper's work leverages the flattening of landscape and desire, the dulling and dimming of mind. His world is exercised on a kind of fringe mourning, whimpering or grieving over that which is not entirely absent, never having given enough to merit a full-on work of mourning, if such a thing were possible.

Uh, my intention, as confided to Dennis, was to talk about the registers of stupor that inhabit his texts. I wanted to explore the minutely filtered residue of traumatic events in Cooper's novels, the way they are circuited through different qualities of stupefaction, ranging from drug and sex and America-induced mindlessness to the sheer stupidity of Being—its whateverness or failed "consciousness." I have managed to correspond only minimally to my intention. Everywhere in Dennis's oeuvre you find the trace of irreducible stupidity—from the I.Q.-less employee to the lover who appears mentally retarded when looking up from one's ass, to the asinine lyrics of Slayer's Heavy Metal Onslaught, the idiot addictions, and dumb corpses. The surrender of the body, abandoned to its fate and solitude, has little to do with cognition or revelation but expires with a dull existential thud. Or it shakes itself off, the body, and gets over itself excrementally: "shaking piss off their dicks" (*Guide* 8).

Stupidity, sex, and trauma need to be shelved for now, Dennis. I feel I owe you more than I have been able to say about the magnificent, withholding asses that bare themselves to your writing. I also wanted to work with the poems and the photographs. When I first encountered you, I was voracious. Then, interruption—plane tickets, subletting, change-of-address ordinariness that nearly overwhelmed me. The question that I wanted to address emerged from the relentless rigor with which you pursue a consciousness that is blocked and debilitated by what the author ("you," I suppose) calls at several junctures STUPIDITY. As for me, I am still working on stupidity, the fading of cognition, the taboo signifier in philosophical works, the question and politics of stupidity, so I was particularly attracted to the way Dennis Cooper ("you," I continue to suppose) pumps up the paraconcept of stupidity (it is neither a concept as such nor a pathology nor even a moral default, yet participates in decreating world)—I was interested in the way he ("you") map(s) stupidity in the territories your novels claim. Throughout the work we encounter aporias of intelligence, intricated relations to dumb bodies we trail around, a diminished consciousness or fake intelligence carried like a fake ID. Intelligence, like identitarian closure, tends to crumble. Many of the tracks on stupidity, be they effects of rock lyrics, drugs, or metaphysics, revert to Dennis's uncompromising hermeneutics of the body. In your work we consistently get a portrayal of the body without transcendence, sheer corpse, mangled and mutilated, which has yet to be rescued by the promise of release. I think that when I pick this up and rework it, I want to write on the becoming-corpse in your oeuvre, the sputtering epiphanies that occur in the undead moments of threadbare existence, the minute detachments that you trace and convolute in your incomparable way—it seems more like a . . . whatever, liminal, abyssal probe of destructive, um, *jouissance.*

Notes

Ronell gave this lecture at a major exhibition of Cooper's works in New York University's Fales Library on March 2, 2002. The exhibition was entitled "Beautiful: The Writings of Dennis Cooper."

1. *Frisk.* New York: Grove Press, 1991.

2. *Try.* New York: Grove Press, 1994, 105.

3. *Period.* New York: Grove Press, 2000.

4. *Guide.* New York: Grove Press, 1997.

Part Four
Danke! et Adieu

On Hookups and Breakups

Q. *In the "Activist Supplement," you suggest that "the opposition between passive and active proffers a deluded equation. Take a look around you," you write, "haven't we, as a culture, been too active, too action-filled?" And you note that a "true ethics of community . . . would have to locate a passivity beyond passivity, a space of repose and reflection that would let the other come." This is not the typical view of community, which is usually posited as a product to be built and which therefore requires the active subject building. Would you elaborate on this ethic of community?*

A. I made these remarks on community in the context of the Gulf War with its attendant overestimation of virtual reality. This thought comes from the works of Heidegger, Freud, and Levinas—and, obviously, from Derrida as well. As Heidegger and Freud in their own ways posted, there has been too much action. When Heidegger went off track, it was under the aegis of "acting." The qualities that I am trying to describe are difficult to abbreviate, and I do not want to invite misunderstanding. The action hero, as we know—and there is no quarreling with this valorizing of the action hero—is not the thoughtful subject, though action and thought, activity and passivity, should not be easily opposed. It is much more complicated than that. Thinking is assimilable to acting. Rather than presuming and making predictable what could happen in a community, giving assigned places and determinations, if one opened up a space of radical passivity, one might see what comes, what arrives. Rousseau, for example, called for a mode of being that is in recession—he calls it the *far niente,* the nondoing that opens you up to a disclosive dimension of being. From there, one might be able to hear the call; or, the call might be put out in a way that is entirely surprising, perhaps unrecognizable and perhaps irreducible to codified meaning. Something would occur on the level of absolute and unconditional hospitality to being, to the other. These are the kinds of considerations that have prompted me. Rather than think we know in advance what community is, or what we are building, as if it were ours to build, we might allow it to come. To allow and allow and allow is the experiment that I would want to conduct.

From "Confessions of an Anacoluthon" (268–69).

The Sacred Alien

**HEIDEGGER'S READING OF
HÖLDERLIN'S "ANDENKEN"**

> "Hölderlin's Dichtung ist für uns ein Schicksal."
> "Hölderlin's poetry is a destiny for us."
> —Martin Heidegger

"Geh aber nun und grüsse" (Yet, go now and greet). I would like to devote my-self tonight to a moment in the unprecedented testimony of Hölderlin's late thought—to that moment in which Hölderlin named the modern experience of mourning. While Heidegger's later work and many Heideggerian discourses ap-pear to be characterized by a similar tonality of mourning, Hölderlin's thought of finitude is often more joyous and affirmative, or, in terms posed by Jean-Luc Nancy, Hölderlin appears to affirm a more abandoned experience of dispos-session than Heidegger's texts allow.[1]

"Wo aber sind die Freunde?" (Yet, where are my friends?) In order to approach this question, I seek the alien in Hölderlin, the figure of the stranger or, indeed, the refugee, whether in transit or detained. Some of what follows is drawn out of a passage in Hannah Arendt's reading of Kant. I cannot dwell on this frame but would like to indicate some of its salient aspects. Arendt's thought on Kant and cosmopolitanism pivots on the hesitant allure of the stranger—on the pos-sibility, that is, for welcoming the stranger. We hesitate to confer love upon the stranger and yet the stranger, the alien, is what calls for love and incomparable ethical responsiveness. In the milieu of the stranger, Arendt asks what it is to love. Citing Augustine's "Amo: volo ut is," she asserts that to love is in effect to say "I want you to be."[2] Because of the sheer arbitrariness of being, because of the fact that "we have not made ourselves," we "stand in need of confirmation. We are strangers; we stand in need of being welcome."[3] It is difficult to overlook the fact that "we" has become the stranger. I will try to resist the assimilation of "we" to the strangers—Heidegger performs a similar operation on Hölderlin's sacred alien but with a different foreign policy than that of Arendt. As some of my work continues to be marked by current (or recurrent) events, I choose

to cite "the sacred alien" in order to level the word of Hölderlin against the accelerating velocities of hostility that are directed against foreign bodies in this country. It may seem odd to state that Hölderlin has already responded to mainstream desecrations of the alien, but it is so. There is always yet another arrow—"einen anderen Pfeil," to quote one of his greatest commentators, Peter Szondi—to draw from the corpus of Hölderlin's poetry, another address or unmarked destiny.

In the twentieth century, a subtle shift occurred in terms of which we locate the ethics and values of responsibility. Arendt's unpublished lectures point to the subtle and almost subterranean shift in ethical investiture, to the movement away from the concept of the citizen and toward the *refugee* as the figure that carries the demand for clear ethical responsiveness. Since Arendt, it is no longer the citizen, the one assumed to occupy the secured interior zones of a polity, who generates the affect and discourse of care, concern, responsibility, and rights; rather, the refugee—the foreign and shifting body with no home base—has become the exemplary locus for any possible cosmopolitan ethics. If one understands this frame and the shift it portends, one will see why I am bound to pose it in relation to Heidegger's anxiety around Hölderlin's sacred aliens, including the dark-skinned women who appear in "Andenken." In a sense, the figure of the refugee emerging in Arendt rereads Heidegger and discloses an empirical scarring, a thematic irritation or bafflement that occurs in his commentaries on Hölderlin's poesy.[4] Arendt affirms the fact that we are strangers who stand in need of being welcome: "Volo ut is."

This evening I will focus on a moment in Heidegger's reading of Hölderlin's poem "Remembrance," a moment that opens the dialogue between poetry and thought, proffering a Greeting. When the poet and thinker greet one another, they momentarily enter an imparted domain that exposes them to time, history, and being. Heidegger seizes upon Hölderlin with relentless adherence to his own project but avoids the regions of Hölderlinian questioning that would undermine his appropriation. This is one reason I am interested in exploring the reading Heidegger and Hölderlin share of the nonappropriative Greeting. For the Greeting establishes a relationality between texts and historicity; it has everything to do with the relation of history to the poetic act. The Greeting reflects the double movement of approach and withdrawal that issues in a passage tracking the very movement in history that defines the conditions of historical existence. The Greeting, in a strictly Hölderlinian sense, can be understood as a saying that originates the relation between man and the divine, marking a co-belonging set in the very task of holding the separation between gods and man. In other, perhaps more contemporary words, it offers a trace of a relation to an ungraspable alterity, a sign of—or from—the sacred. The sacred in Hölderlin is part of the "intense intimacy" of the infinite belonging of gods, mortals, earth, and sky. The temporality of "Andenken" is paradoxical because remembrance, as Heidegger has pointed out, implies forgetting. The poet has named the *Ungleiche,* the absolutely dissimilar, whose task is to hold together the separation between man and gods. As demigod, the dissimilar does not assume merely a mediating role, though Hölderlin scholarship has frequently ascribed to the figure a mediating function. The absolute dissimilar cannot neutralize the poetic function to the point of mediation as such or effect the merger of the sacred with terrestrial destinies. The poet, attuned and alert, is himself not a vessel but a fragile being exposed to the danger zones of historicity and language in such a way as to maintain dissimilarity while holding together the intense intimacy of infinite belonging.

I should perhaps indicate, before proceeding directly to Heidegger's thought on "Andenken" and questioning some of its premises, that my own reading is considerably inflected by Levinas's reading of Paul Celan, and in particular by the letter to Hans Bender in which Celan writes that the poem is like a handshake[5]—offering "this presence," as Levinas says, "of the Infinite in a finite act."[6] In a larger work on politesse, from which Hölderlin's topos of the Greeting is extracted, I trace the fine points—indeed, the vanishing points—of the language and gestural syntax of politesse in the works of Marx, Althusser, Kant, Arendt, Levinas, and Celan, among others. It was Carl Schmitt who designated politesse as a place of theoretical excess between internal policing and foreign policy: close to the two derivatives of the *polis* (politics that point to an *outside* and police that fixes an *inside*) comes the third angle, that of politesse. The point of this work-in-progress is to produce a reflection on justice. To put it all too briefly, but with a Levinasian twist, justice, exercised through institutions, which are inevitable, must always be held in check by the initial interpersonal relationship. The priority of the other is presupposed in all human relationships. If it were not that, Levinas points out in *Ethics and Infinity,* "we would not even say, before an open door, 'After you, Sir.' It is an original 'After you, Sir!' that I have tried to describe."[7] Thought begins with the possibility of conceiving a freedom external to my own.

Another way in which my concern about politesse is tuned by Levinas's work occurs where it marks its own sense of fragility and finity. He consistently offers an allegory of politesse where, to borrow from Heidegger, thinking and thanking are part of the same experience of declension. Levinas has written that in the work the thesis, for him, is not posed but imprudently and defenselessly exposed.[8] Rather than flexing a thetic muscle that would buff up under the light of truth, Levinas offers a discourse vulnerable to its own sense of exposure, frailty, and uncertainty. "This weakness," he writes, "is necessary." In fact, if he seems sure of anything, it is that "There must be this weakness, the relaxing of virility."[9] The destitution and de-situation of the subject is the condition from which politesse begins its course.

By now we have virtually attained to the Greeting. When Hölderlin names the Greeting in "Remembrance," he tells us something about the poetic act and what it means to "live poetically on the earth."[10] Both Hölderlin and Heidegger define art as a fundamental event for Dasein. Art is necessary to the production of something like world. The topos of the Greeting in "Remembrance" addresses the issue of the work's being. In its withdrawal the work sets forth the fact of its being. As Christopher Fynsk observes in *Heidegger: Thought and Historicity*, the artist's "that it be" answers to and is a repetition of a more original saying that happens in the work.[11] Moreover, "Dass es sei" is the only apparent trace of the artist's intention, though the artist is only answering to a more original speaking that occurs in the work. To whom is the work addressed? In Heidegger's "Origin of the Work of Art," as in his commentary on Hölderlin's poetry, the work is shown to address some alterity and not posed by man for man.[12] I cannot now focus on the paradox delineating the way in which the work demands and requires its setting up, nor on the measure to which the artist answers by shaping and first opening the work—this paradox of creation would require a close reading of "The Origin of the Art Work" as well as other crucial texts by and on Heidegger and Hölderlin. For now let us bear in mind that, although it addresses some alterity and is not posed by man for man, the work, like being, nonetheless places a call to man and is therefore not without man. Dasein's project consists essentially in preparing a response. The response is what allows the call to occur. How does the motif of the call bear upon the Greeting?

THE GREETING. *"Geh aber nun und grüsse"* (Yet, go now and greet). The Greeting first establishes a distance so that proximity can occur. To acquaint ourselves with the Greeting—in other words, to be greeted by it, and welcomed—I am approaching a text that I can greet only from a distance and, no doubt, against its entrenched grain. To read a text is not necessarily to endorse it, as one endorses a candidate running for political office. Once in a while reading a text is tantamount to submitting it to a blunting level of interference such that one rarely wants to read, in the space of published thinking, what one truly loves, which is to say, what one truly relinquishes. At any event, and despite everything, I am going to move us through a work officially dated 1943. Paul

Celan has taught us what a date means, and Derrida has shown us that a poem that marks its date cannot be absolutized: the date gives "an idiom" to be commemorated in an untranslatable but firm manner.[13] The structure of a date as both singular and repeatable casts it into a domain of self-estrangement. We will try not to lose sight of the ghostly structure of those dates responsible for appearances and torments that may or may not forego thematization. So, I take us to a work written in 1943. Hölderlin, as designated driver of historical instauration and "poet of poets," was, as Lacoue-Labarthe notes, set up by Heidegger—his very exemplariness amounts to his being posed as *pharmakos*, ultimately, a scapegoat of the philosopher's project. Let us therefore anticipate what follows with our alert "little rabbit ears," as Heidegger says, which never listen quite without fear.[14]

Something of a dramatic pause attends the opening of Heidegger's reading of the poem "Andenken." The lectures on Hölderlin, edited by Curd Ochwadt, were delivered in Freiburg in the *Wintersemester* of 1941–42. This may send chills down your historical spine. Yet these are the lectures in which Heidegger is said to have had his encrypted *Auseinandersetzung* with National Socialism, repugning its vulgarity and biologism—its crude racisms—and noting the failure of the movement to fulfill what in 1934 he had seen as its exceptional promise.[15] By now, Heidegger had gotten over himself and was turning his thought to a tragic notion of history. He had originally announced that he would hold a seminar entitled "Nietzsches Metaphysik." Instead, Heidegger devoted the course to reading a moment in Hölderlin. The approach to Hölderlin's poem, given in one-hour lecture segments and amounting to sixty-seven handwritten pages, is slow, motivated, one might say, by a kind of tentative disavowal and caution that sets a halting rhythm. Fynsk argues that this commentary in fact is less violently appropriative of Hölderlin than Heidegger's other readings.[16] Heidegger's commentary on Hölderlin's tropes of greeting, sending, celebration, and commemoration begins, in this version, by postponing the encounter with the poem. The preliminary lectures, intended to prepare his students for hearing the word of poetry ("Vorbereitung des Hörens auf das Wort der Dichtung"), begins with a lecture that names "What the Lecture Does Not Want" ("Was die Vorlesung nicht will"), referring mainly to literary historical scholarship and willful interpretations of poetry. The encounter with the poetic word is preceded by this prescriptive utterance: one ought to resist being awed by the beauty of Hölderlin's hymn. Faced with the sheer beauty of the hymn, we are astounded; we are prone to dissolve with awe, for the awe and "beauty" of the poem are undeniable. But if we were to remain in this mood, then, despite appearances, we would not be awestruck, and not even struck by the poem:

we would have missed the encounter with it. In fact the astonishment would mean that we took the poem for an object, one created by a poet. We would stay within the confines of the history of poetic production. We would admire a product, a possession, and be pleased by a "cultural" achievement. In other words, while the sense of awe inspired by the poem's beauty might be heartfelt ("echt"), we would not have allowed ourselves to be *greeted* by the poem—that is to say, met or truly struck by it.

What we commonly call a critical approach to a work, or a close reading—or whatever it is we think we are doing when we welcome a word to our lives and are welcomed by a word—subtends the question of the Greeting. Whether reassured or devastated by a word, which can hit us, says Kafka, like the axe in a frozen sea, we have been met by the poetic Greeting. Heidegger starts unfolding the senses of the Greeting through his encounter with Hölderlin—less violent than before, as said—in part to underscore the poetic instauration of interlocution. The urge to merge desisted, poet and thinker expropriate one another: they never experience a fusional encounter but maintain the Differing for which Hölderlin's poet—assuming the position of the *Ungleiche*—is a figure. They do little more than greet each other. The possibility of Greeting opens us up to one another, but this still has to be learned. Hölderlin's poem moves us by the exceptional encounter that takes place, and continues to take place, under the sway of the Greeting. The repeatability of the Greeting is inbuilt to its singular occurrence—something we have yet to grasp—for Hölderlin's thinking of the Greeting is also a work of mourning: it is part of his saying of partedness (*Abgeschiedenheit*), or the infinite separation that holds us together. But we have not been properly greeted yet.

For our encounter with the poetic word to be what it is, it must not succumb to the experience of ravishment or even transport, though these are very closely linked to the essential possibilities of the Greeting. In fact, Hölderlin shows how we are initially blown away by this moment that affirms itself, if groundlessly ("Der Nordost wehet / Der liebste unter den Winden / Mir" [The Nor'easterly blows / The most beloved of winds / For me]). We have to hold still and risk nonrecognition. The poem should resemble nothing, nothing grand or classifiable, nothing secured. To recognize in the poem the markings of a great work is not to let oneself be greeted by its word but to grasp its perceived importance—that is, to grasp it (conceptually), to account for its status as a beautiful object that one can proudly classify as canonical or as belonging safely to one's heritage. Such reception gives a sense of mastery over the object. For Heidegger this arch traced by standing "over" the object indicates error. We have to watch ourselves and refrain from lording "over" the poem, talking above or even about it ("Denn

schon ertappen wir uns wieder dabei, das wir 'über' das Gedicht reden").[17] The
supplement of mastery that going "over" a poem indicates suggests not only that
we are on top of the material in our little bureaucratic-academic way, whether
or not we waver or wonder or repeat how unique this work is, but further that
we have blocked the poem from speaking to us. In other words, by getting on
top of the material, we have not let it speak its word—we have not let ourselves
be greeted by the poetic word. If we allow ourselves to be greeted by the poem
rather than *over*whelming it with our "knowledge" and facility for reformatting poetry according to cultural or philological codes, then we are faced with
the enigma from which the poem cannot be wrested by our acquired habits
of mastery. Mastery is itself not a content but a habit. A disposition altogether
different from that of knowing is required if we are to let the poetic word speak
to us in the form of the Greeting. The poem ends with the famous line, "Was
bleibet aber, stiften die Dichter," announcing the remains for which poets are
responsible. Heidegger duly notes that the poem concerns itself with founding, with grounding futurity—yet, oddly, not with recalling the past. How can
a poem dedicated to "Remembrance" point to the future, to that which is to
remain, and not to tropes of impermanence or to the past?

Between the first line ("Der Nordost wehet") and the final line ("Was bleibet
aber, stiften die Dichter"), between strong gusts and the founding gesture of
poets, something happens, something links the wind to futurity and the poetic
word. The blowing wind that opens "Remembrance" announces an arrival
and a departing that swirls into a future. Everything is filled with the coming
that arrives from the future. This wind flows through the poem thematically
as a promising wind for ships, which is to say, it is annunciation, reassurance,
and a gift. Opened and carried by the wind, the poem does not decrease to
the opposition between inside and outside, content and form; nor does it, as
wind-poem, present an argument *over* or about a theme that it can dominate.
It brings promise of a word, the most exceptional promise ("Der liebste unter
den Winden / Mir"), which, in order to sustain itself as what it is, *is* not but
scatters like a promise sent into a future that will have come from another
current, another past, another weather system or tempestive time that is not
necessarily "mine."

The wind has opened the poem. "Geh aber nun und grüsse" ("But go now
and greet") names the injunction, the wish, the hope addressed to the wind.
Heidegger asks if this moment does not threaten to turn the poem around, for
that which exposed the poem to its possibility, the wind, is told now to "go and
greet," to go away. The *Nordost* is cast forth; the poet stays behind. The Greeting
means that the poet is thinking back to a prior sojourn. He is overcome with

the past. Departure and renunciation are somehow bound up with the Greeting. Do we know what parting (*Verabschiedung*) is? Do we know what the wind's blowing is, if we are not simply referring to registerable wind patterns or velocities? *Das Wehen:* a coming that goes and that, in going, comes. Parting is not a mere leave-taking and empty staying behind. Parting is also not a mere going away and disappearing. The poet remains in the rustling wind, to the extent that he goes with its going. This going-with should no longer be seen in terms of a voyage. Nonetheless, the poet stays with the wind. Accompaniment now shapes the Greeting. As the gusting wind is alternately a coming and a going, so is the Greeting a staying behind that nonetheless flutters away, becoming a going-with.

"Geh aber nun und grüsse" (Yet, go now and greet). The parting is of a peculiar sort. For the staying behind of the poet under his sky and in his beloved wind is at once a going-with to other skies—for heaven, says Heidegger, is named differently according to different places. The going-with is, however, a Greeting. But let us back up and get some basic questions down. How often do we greet others with the best intentions? What is more common than a greeting? What is there to think about?

We could be satisfied with the way we greet or fail to greet if only the secret of "Andenken" were not embedded in this "Geh aber nun und grüsse," which also tells the secret of an inappropriable remainder. "Andenken" requires of us an "anders Denken," another kind of thinking. That is why this time, unlike other times, we must know what it means to greet. For Heidegger the Greeting uttered in the poem has everything to do with grounding and historicity; he goes so far as to manipulate the Greeting into a welcoming of his own work. Let us consider the inclinations of the Greeting more closely.

What happens between or among the greeted? To the extent that the greeter ever necessarily says anything about himself, he says only that he wants nothing for himself, turning everything toward the one to be greeted; everything in the Greeting is offered to the greeted as a sort of promise. The genuine Greeting amounts to a kind of "promising correspondence," a reciprocal promise that aims to correspond to the most essential level of the other. It is through such acknowledgment—the greeted one, in Heidegger, is acknowledged in the nobility of his essence—that the other is given leave to be what it, she, he is. The Greeting is a letting-be of things and of human beings. Greeting indicates that something like a will is at play, a will of belonging to the greeted, though not in the sense of *Anbiederung*—cowed submissiveness—or even calculated counting on one another. To greet does not engage an economy or offer a deal on the order of, say, You can count on me; I can count on you. The simplest yet at the same time most intimate Greeting is the one through which the greeted is first and newly returned to his essence, as though each time initiality were to emerge, discovered from the word go, for the first time. Only if we think through the Greeting so essentially can we sense the way Hölderlin lets the Greeting occur through the *Nordost* and its "going." His saying—what is said and how it is said—is defined by the fact that it is a Greeting. Yet this Greeting is itself keyed by a more fundamental attunement that still remains hidden to us.

"Geh aber nun und grüsse" (Yet, go now and greet). Only by means of the Greeting does the greeted being stand revealed to its own splendor. If that which is to be greeted evokes splendor, this is only so because the Greeting elevates the addressee to this reality. The Greeting reaches into a domain in which "truth" and "poesy" ("'Wahrheit' und 'Dichtung'")—that is, the real and fictional—are no longer to be distinguished from one another, because poetry, according to Heidegger, lets the authentic truth of what is true emerge. Everything in the poem—the landscape, the tropes, figures, images—is in the end inflected by the Greeting.

"Geh aber nun und grüsse" (Yet, go now and greet). Only through the Greeting has that which is greeted become ("erst seiend geworden").[18] It now stands in the splendor of the poetic word, stands and appears so that the poet can henceforth contemplate this being, although he is distant and this distance is decisive: "Noch denket das mir wohl . . ." The poet's staying behind is crucial. Staying behind is not meant to mark the isolation or even desolation of the poetic act. Embodying the suchness of the Greeting, remaining behind radiates an intimacy that must come from its own source. Neither passive nor active, remaining behind indicates a way of going back, a returning to the source.

"Geh aber nun und grüsse" (Yet, go now and greet). The Nor'easterly is co-missioned by the poet to deliver the Greeting. One of the secrets of "Andenken" involves its relation to memory. Greeting stirs memory and its peculiar temporal climate. Brought to a thoughtful halt, the one who is greeted inclines toward the greeter. Though disposed to the greeter, your thoughts, leaving the present, incline not so much toward a person as toward what was. At the same time thinking-toward takes you in the other direction: one thinks toward a past, a what-has-been-between-you. Not in order to pose a present in which to while but to invite the present of making-present. Tapping the past in order to spring futurity, Heidegger may be thinking of Nietzsche's view of the friend as the future. However, the relation of the greeter to the greeted does not amount to a politics of friendship. Something more bare and essential appears to be at stake. A history of friendship is not out of the question, though history cannot be presupposed by the Greeting but must be made. If we allow to the remembered one, the greeted,

the entire essence which is his or her due, and in no way disturb or invade her "space," then we experience how the remembered one upon returning does not at all stop at the present in order to jolt the past back into presence. The one thus remembered swings over our present and suddenly stands in the future, which comes at us and is still somehow not fulfilled—an undiscovered treasure that had been reckoned as something belonging to the past.

Gestures of contemplating and remembrance—thinking *about* something or someone—do not merely shade into the past. Remembrance is more secretive in its thinking. It breezes in, coming and going, carrying and delivering events that are related to poetry and thinking, to breath, inspiration, and even "spirit." The Greeting of the poet discloses an aspect of thinking ("Das Grüssen des Dichters ist ein 'Denken'")—it announces a "thinking" secured by quotation marks.[19] The poet's Greeting consists in a thinking-toward, and here Heidegger recasts the originariness of the relation: it is in the relation related by the Greeting that Dasein opens itself up to a trace of alterity. The pinch put on "*Denken*" could be squeezing thinking's alterity, as if poetry could not in good faith be accorded the rights of thinking. Or perhaps by collating the Greeting and "Thinking," Heidegger aims at restricting the destination of the gesture, clamping down on a type of alterity to be greeted—though Heidegger would not limit the range or declension of thinking's purported addressee. He would probably not go as far as Derrida, who reaches for a trace beyond the human, in the animal, but Heidegger does not restrict the scope of alterity made available by the Greeting.[20] The poet is responsible for finding the way for Dasein's embrace of alterity. Greeting is the poet's most essential mode of being. Still, the Greeting does not originate with the poet as a flex of agency or spark of will. The one who transfers the Greeting must be responding to something, to a movement already inclined toward the poet-receptor.

For Hölderlin the Greeting arrives at a special time, or, we could say, the Greeting delivers and *confers* the special time, the time of holiday, a sacred sense of timing, "an Feiertage." The poem turns the clock as if to provoke the appearance of alterity. Time gets opened up to a historical standstill, a temporal clip, engaging a gesture that also brings about a mark of gender and race. The Greeting breaks open the famous lines, "An Feiertagen gehen / Die Braunen Frauen daselbst / Auf seidnen Boden" (On holidays / Dark-skinned women walk / On silken grounds). Calendrial time suspended, dark-skinned women appear to the poet, gently giving ground to the holiday. The ground is padded, silkened by the brown women, whose tread plants texture and text on poetic ground. It is not clear to me that commentators have associated the women of color with sheer poeticity, "silkened ground." If anything, the women seem to have served as a means for men to get on each others' backs, or they provide a transit by which to get back to the figure of man. Enigmatic and unseizable, Hölderlin's rainbow coalition of purportedly human figures has faded into familiar aspects and grammars of man. Theodor Adorno observes that in this passage Heidegger colonizes the other.[21] Heidegger's rhetoric seems, however, less sure than that of a colonizer, I would submit: it is even more perturbed and perturbing than Adorno allows, more frazzled than Adorno has let himself imagine. Heidegger backs up to ask first, "And why women?" Why are women named in this initializing occurrence of the Greeting? Besides the dark-skinned women, the poem also hosts the woman associated with Bordeaux ("die Garonne"), the French influence marking "Andenken."

To explain the sudden incursion of the foreign feminine, Heidegger needs to establish, before all else, the meaning of *holiday* in the work of Hölderlin. He's stalling. Short on time, he goes to time, changes the time, then changes his mind. Heidegger, in this version of his exegetic claims upon the poem, fumbles. A vocabulary of shame and disgust befalls the commentary, almost inexplicably. It has been noted that Heidegger pounds the institutional forms of litcrit without mercy. But one of the most peculiar articulations of his contempt for academic procedure is triggered by Hölderlin's line on brown women. Heidegger abruptly averts his gaze from this poem and, finding different contexts that must be brought into comparative perspective, pieces them together like body parts of a missing corpus: this diversion, this movement of critical thought gives him the space he needs to express his horror, or, at least, his commentary automatically swerves into a patch of protest (we are barred from going inside the man Heidegger, or from presupposing an interiority; maybe metaphysics is at the wheel, forcing this turn), spinning out a sudden lexicon of doubt, shame, guilt, and disgust—all of which is displaced onto the procedure he must critically engage: "Fragwürdig und fast beschämend sind diese Hinweise, weil sie der widerlichen Art folgen, 'Stellen' aus Dichtungen anzuführen . . . und sogar schuldhaft bleibt es, überhaupt mit 'Stellen' zu 'operieren'" (These references are questionable and almost shameful, because they pursue the repulsive manner of pointing out "passages" from poetry . . . and to "operate" with "passages" indeed remains guilt-laden).[22]

I understand that Heidegger does not like to resemble a scholar. I have these crises myself. Nietzsche certainly led the way into scholar bashing, which he occasionally, in very determined ways, backs off from. However, Heidegger's accent gets heavy: locked into an identificatory impasse, he is grossed out, ashamed ("almost" ashamed), guilt-ridden, and fraught with doubt when it comes to comparing different moments of Hölderlin's oeuvre. It does seem a bit hyperbolic to get all worked up in order to conclude that we now know what is meant in the hymn by "holiday" and "women" (the conclusion being—and here Heidegger resonates with early Madonna—that "holidays" are "days of celebration," "'Feiertage' sind 'Tage des Feierns'").[23] But are "women" and "holidays" the same kind of existents? The comparative literature internal to Hölderlin scholarship begins with a citation from "Germanien" ("O nenne Tochter du der heiligen Erd'! / Einmal die Mutter . . ." [O daughter of the sacred Earth name / once the Mother]). These are moments conjoining women and festivity, instigating a purposeful enmeshing that appears to bring something like shame to Heidegger. It is almost as though the comparativity that Heidegger indulges were to double for the contamination of bringing-together inherent in the *Brautfest* (wedding), the downside of which invites implicit impurity. The *Brautfest* opens the field to the sacred yet tolerates the conjoining sanctioned by a wedding of incalculable alterities. Heidegger claims that he has been driven by urgency ("notgedrungen," "das Nötigste")[24] to throw together pieces of Hölderlin's oeuvre in order to arrive at only the most provisional sense of what to do with the brown women on whom he has had to "operate." The operation that evolves from such an effusion of disgust, revealing a kind of compulsive ontology of shaming, dissimulates yet another snag, another unavowable espousal.

In another passage where *Not* (urgent distress) signals, Heidegger refers to the "war to which we Germans are subjected in a sense of utmost *Not*."[25] In the edition of Heidegger's text that has now become standard, one of his original dedications has been dropped—one meant to commemorate the fallen soldiers of World War I in Verdun, 1916. However, another dedication was retained, if only in muted form. This involves a reference to "14 December a quarter of a century ago when Norbert v. Hellingrath fell in Verdun as artillery observer of the first line."[26] Heidegger interrupts the initial exposition of the Greeting ostensibly to touch upon Hölderlin's madness. The detour clears the way for bringing in von Hellingrath's lecture on "Hölderlins Wahnsinn," as well as a letter that Rilke wrote to Hellingrath's grandmother and finally a poem written by Stefan George to commemorate the young "Norbert." After this curious caesura, Heidegger takes up the broken thread of his reading by stating summarily that no "biographical-psychological material can help us to comment on poems, because biography, to the contrary, first acquires it meaning and determination from the work."[27] Thus Heidegger sutures the disrupted greeting to Hellingrath. His disposal of biographical materials gives every appearance of referring, however, to Hölderlin, although Heidegger used the thematic residue of Hölderlin's madness to sanction an excursus on the fallen soldier of Verdun.

After the secret encounter, which has allowed him to pass his intimate greeting to the other commentator-soldier, Heidegger returns to the flow of poetic Greeting. He reorients his commentary through the corridors of Hölderlin's wind-language, bringing tidings of an unreappropriable other. Nearing this other, the poem at the same time prompts the ambiguity of going or letting-go. The Greeting is a staying behind but also a going-along.

No news, no announcements come from the other; the Greeting just travels to the impossible place of the other, a place that cannot be stabilized insofar as the Greeting, to carry out its temporal tasks, rides the wind and depends upon the wind's velocity not to arrive but to come and go without touching down or finding ground. We have been moved along by the force of Heidegger's argument, yet the women have been left hanging in the air.

"*Geh aber nun und grüsse*" (Yet, go now and greet). When the figure of the brown women comes out of nowhere, Heidegger reverts to defensive forms of scholarship. He must perform an "operation"; he is repulsed by and almost ashamed of the way he is reading his way around these women. He parachutes in a heroic, historical soldier-commentator, as if to secure some philosophical ground. He has said, or wondered: And why shouldn't women be named in this poetic description of the land and its people? That's what makes the whole poem "lyrical" and strengthens the poem's impression on the "reader." Then he says that the poem is not to be merely enjoyed by whomever accidentally comes upon it and seeks to be satisfied by it, as if it were a sensual delight; what needs to be elucidated is the meaning of holiday for Hölderlin. Enticing its readers, the poem itself risks being feminized—a hymn could at any moment turn into a her, offering sensual delight and easy *jouissance*. It could make the reader forget time, which is why Heidegger zooms in as law, interrupting the abyssal enjoyment to which the poem entices, reinstituting the domain of Father Time in the suspensive form of holiday. Clocked in and becoming-history, the brown women, after a number of detours, come to serve as reclaimed otherness, recovered from the origin—the Mediterranean (French) women are retrofitted to Greek women and finally, homecoming, metonymized to Greece. The holiday is a wedding of the gods and mortals, of the present and its origin, in which the Differing must abide. But the entire network of relations and non-relations depends upon the Greeting, on its address.

At this point in his commentary, Heidegger begins to work some of his most famous passages. He asks about the conditions enabling the delivery of the Greeting. Where does the Greeting come from; how does it land and take off from the poetic site? What if the poet can say the Greeting only to the extent that he himself had encountered a more originary Greeting? The verse with the brown women offers the completion and perfection (*Vollendung*) of the Greeting that enigmatically turns back on itself because it names a prior Greeting. Only when we grasp the fact that, when Greeting, the poet is thinking of what (or who) is Greeted can we begin to understand the "remembrance" poem. The exceptional reception of the Greeting occurs with time. Holiday means not only the negativity carving out the interruption of work, but it implies a pause, a rupture with work, which allows one to pause for thought, to ask, to look around, to await something else: it indicates the wakeful presentiment of wonder—the wonder, namely, that there is a world around us that worlds, a world that is being and not nothing; that things *are* and we are in their midst, that we are and yet we hardly know who we are and we hardly know that we hardly know. Holiday understood in this way as inward pause (*Innehalten*) brings us to the threshold where these things gather and thus to the neighborhood of the questionable. The inhabitual, what we do not inhabit habitually—where we do not live and work—does not mean here an aberration, the sensational state of exception or the never-before-seen. To the contrary, the inhabitual is what is always there as the simplest and ownmost of beings (I am following Heidegger closely here in order to convey his drift as accurately as possible: "Das Ungewöhnliche ist das ständig Wesende, Einfache und Eigene des Seinden").[28] Normalcy harbors the unexpected: it is solely in the habitual, says Heidegger, that the inhabitual can appear within its clearest contours. To celebrate is to become free of the habitual: when celebrating, one honors the becoming of the inhabitual. To celebrate is to listen to what the poets call the "gentler law." Hölderlin bends the law here, allowing a feminine drift and deviation.[29]

The inhabitual is nestled within the habitual. The calendar, which appears to assure routine and regularity, is actually a holiday calendar (*Fest-Kalender*). Holidays are regularly returning and sequential occurrences within the historically notable course of weeks, months, and other times of year. For Hölderlin, claims Heidegger, the holiday is not an occurrence in the context and ground of history, but "das Fest" itself provides the ground and essence of history.[30] Once we begin to understand this level of historical enactment, we will be in the decisive domain of Hölderlin's poesy. Holiday and history—the essence of history—stand revealed in the celebration that enjoins us to think the relation to our true commencement—that is to say, to the beginning logged in by Greece. Another fragment however tells us that Greece was laid to waste, at once exalted and devastated: "Versäumet und erbärmlich gieng / Das Griechenland, das schönste, zu Grunde."[31] If anything, Greece as beginning also revs up the engine of tragic finitude. When the memory of Greece returns in Hölderlin as the ground of commemorative celebration, it does so in the form and on the grounds of this *zu Grunde,* marking, I believe, the beginning as the experience not so much of ground as of going aground, in strict terms of finitude, setting the destitute ending/perfection of that which we try to appropriate as our alien grounding, or what Hölderlin understands as the "sacred alien." This is not necessarily the way the wind blows in Heidegger's commentary, but I am following a dominant, if unbridled, current in his reading. Celebration is where the tensional coming together of unlikes (*"alles Einander-Entgegenkommende in seiner Entgegnung"*) tunes the unsounded voice of the original Greeting, establishing the immemorial passage through which humans and gods first assume the standing of the Greeted.[32] Only as those greeted by genuine festiveness, and only as such, can they—the gods and mortals—reciprocally, greet one another, sparking something like divine enthusiasm. The festiveness that the celebration encourages constitutes the original Greeting, which Hölderlin in "Wie wenn am Feiertage . . ." calls the sacred (*das Heilige*). Celebration as *wedding celebration* conveys the event of an original celebration.

This original Greeting contains the hidden essence of history. That is why Heidegger reads the original Greeting as *the* event, *the* beginning. He understands the Greeting in terms of the coming of the sacred: only through this Greeting can the tensional coming together of mortals and gods originate. Two moments might be isolated so that we get a clearer sense of the Greeting's genesis and endurance. In the first instance, the sacred greets, opening the possibility for the gods and mortals to be greeted. Still, a moment in Greeting must ensure that henceforth gods and mortals, as those embraced by the sacred, can continue to greet; in other words, the Greeting must be *repeated* so that it can hold and can moreover affirm the gesture of holding on to one another. Holding, also a gesture of helping, is distress. Heidegger does not say that holding and helping come out of distress or serve as signal and symptom of distress but that they *are* distress. The basis for holding-one-another is provided by Hölderlin's Titanic hymn:

> Denn keiner trägt das Leben allein.
> (For no one can bear life alone.)

Holding-on in this way, while never set to take hold forever or intended to deflate the Differing, nonetheless modifies the sense of the Greeting as pure letting-go. Letting-go is still a way of holding. It maintains a fateful holding whose destination somehow involves the brown women. Despite it all, the form of enunciation that emerges with celebration takes a melancholic turn, bringing together while keeping apart the distress that comes from the Greeting.

Heidegger underscores the necessity of guaranteeing the iterability of the original Greeting, without which there would be no possibility of history. Maybe "iterability" evokes too much of a Derridean count not yet accommodated by Heidegger's commentary; among other issues that could be taken up, Heidegger does not emphasize a split or disseminative spill at the origin. Still, the Greeting prompts complications that release some of the Heideggerian knots by which it might seem unduly tied. While Heidegger has been rightly taken to task for insisting on and at times exalting instauration, ground, and the peculiar privileges of German destiny, it is possible, I hope, to see how the Greeting comes from the (future and past) experience of running aground, posing an eloquent resistance to any project of fusional gathering or cited mission. The Greeting has to be sanctioned calendrially, as a return and anniversary commemorating a date. Thus Heidegger exposes the need for a return of the holiday, which has in the meantime disappeared. Historically contained by calendrial time, the holiday leads him to situate remembrance as mourning. Penciled in as loss and return, remembrance no longer stands opposed to joyous festivity: the celebration, the festivity of the festive, is more originary than the most joyous ravishment and more original than mourning or the greatest affliction. The festive lays the ground for joy and sorrow, which is why it establishes an original intimacy, the co-belonging, of both joy and sorrow. The one expresses itself through the other, and both together are presented as festive commemoration. On joy and sorrow expressing each other, Heidegger says, rather suddenly: let us calmly confess that we know very little about all that. He retains only the sense that the sacred (*das Heilige*)—the festive grounded by the celebration—stands above (*über*) humans and the gods.[33] Humans and gods need one another: "Denn keiner trägt das Leben allein." Now we are getting closer (says Heidegger) to solving the riddle of whom the Greeting—"Geh aber nun und grüsse"—actually targets. It speaks to the celebration that has been, invoking the tensional coming-together "that has been" of the gods and mortals of a Greece "that has been." But can a has-been greet?[34]

To some extent, the Greeting can only reach that which is still real. When served, the Greeting goes after a living destination. Yet Hölderlin levels his salutation at the past. Is not the past the no-longer-real? The poetic launch accomplishes something different. It advances a kind of Greeting that actually brings into being that which seems no longer to be. The Greeting does not exhaust itself in the sending forth and away of "salutations" but actually thrives on bringing back, on conducting a kind of retrieval of the greeted. To the degree that the Greeting hauls out the lost or forgotten past, it proves capable of an outstanding exercise of bringing back—an original resurrection.

Still, does that which "has been" simply revert to the past? One could hardly expect that Mr. Heidegger would let such a shallow notion of the past slide. Accordingly, he asks: Is not that which has been distinguished from the merely past and ephemeral by the fact that, *having-been*, it at the same time essences?[35] Heidegger detects a remote activity of essencing at play: that which has been is the still-essencing, if at a distance. Hölderlin has discovered and named the remote "essencing" in a figure that greatly resists lexical or exegetical comprehension. The name of the distancing of this distance through its presencing is given, Heidegger avers, in the line "die braunen Frauen daselbst."[36] The poet shoulders in this line a double burden of estrangement, for not only does he turn up the unanticipated bustle of race and gender, but he drops into a sudden platitude. Even if his language usage should seem prosaic, adds Heidegger (referring largely to *dasselbst*), it should be noted that Hölderlin around this time did not shy away from reproducing distinctly unpoetic and, therefore, within poetry, alienating language. Heidegger thus doubles his anxiety about the brown women and displaces it onto a discernible backslide of poetic regression. Hölderlin imperturbably swerves into common usage and brings on the women of color. That which seems furthest away signals through the nearest at hand, by means of a commonplace. Strictly out of place poetically, the most common idiom proves capable of retrieving the remotest past. What may have seemed vulgar and vulgate is in the end sublimated by Heidegger into a trace of our historical origins. Recuperated, the completion of the Greeting falls on the women. ("Die zweite Strophe des Gedichtes "Andenken" nennt in der Vollendung des Grüsses die Frauen"). Holiday has opened up an access route to the origin. The women are named, repeats Heidegger, because the poet's thought vacates the habitual and turns toward the holiday. If the Greeting finds its essence in letting the greeted be what it is, then Hölderlin is greeting that which has been as the has-been in its essence.[37]

Geh aber nun . . . (Yet, go now . . .). The figure of the brown women, whether on Heidegger's watch or singularized by Carl Jung, indicates an early archetype, a primal and matricial source in whose lap Western metaphysics starts stirring. In both cases the brown women, multiplied and dispersed by the poet, are gathered up into a single site, a condensation, taking up the functions of a Subject. What invites notice in terms of Heidegger's dossier is the way his tactical maneuvers around the brown ladies in the end conflates type with essence.[38] In more Freudian terms—which neither Heidegger nor Jung would or could appreciate—a glitch appears to have occurred in the implicit mimetology that Heidegger pursues; an identificatory hiatus appears to have been insinuated, momentarily blocking the festivities, thus putting at risk the integrity of the poetic word: for a split poetic second the women turn into an enemy of the poetic community of "Remembrance," threatening its frame. The radical variance in figure and signified that occurred required an "operation" that would bring the brown women home, settle them as and in the home, if not in the house of being: Make them the absolute origin, the furthest and nearest at once, keep them close and at a distance, clean up their act, put a watch on Hölderlin's poetic acting out. Let it happen off the clock, according to the tapping of a more essential metronome. Converting the unruly girls into a controlled limit of the Western cartographies, Heidegger designs a closure or reappropriation that, despite it all, locks them into a schema of subjectivity. At once promoted and subjected, they get thrown on a grid of "the archē-te-leological domination of the Subject." Through this determined gesture, "the modern epoch . . . has refastened itself to the Greek origin and finality of the West, that is to say, has tried to reassert itself as the subject of its history, and as the history of the subject."[39]

• • •

Initially, the poem may have trumped him. Disturbed by an unreadable tread in "Andenken," Heidegger covers for Hölderlin's unsettling use of the brown women. The poet's language usage had slackened, opening borders. To meet the challenge, Heidegger allowed himself to regress from thinker to philosopher, a title he had tried to outrun. His tack of bringing home that which remains inassimilably alien seems familiar—so familiar, in fact, that it naturalizes the foreign in ways that have exhausted metaphyics and me. Consternated, possibly even panicked, Martin produces a characteristically philosophical move of reappropriation, aptly wiping out traces of rough-edged remainders. Here's the deal, as I understand it, even though he eventually covered his tracks: the outsider gets quickly promoted to insider; the alien exclusion, mastered and contained, now serves to hold the fort of *Ursprung* and origin, resuming the offices of the Subject. In his political writings, Lacoue-Labarthe identifies the greatest "political stake" of our day as the "question . . . of re-appropriation: Is not re-appropriation—in which one has dreamt of an end to alienation—itself the condition of possibility for totalitarianism?"[40] Since 1806, philosophy has gone after the alien, stopping refugees of the cogito, with the dubious enticement of nonalienation. In the language of psychoanalysis—but this gets snagged on different registers of meaning—philosophy is capable of offering its runaways, at moments of disturbing estrangement, the illusion and comfort of noncastration. This drug takes the edge off. But poetry isn't buying and stays in the rift.

In the end the poem itself leads us to its only question. The poem's language, restless and succinct, casts about for allies, interlocutors, or guardians in the form of friendship. The agitated search put out for the missing friend links "Andenken" with the "Hymn of the Titans" and *Hyperion:* "Wo aber sind die Freunde?" (Yet, where are my friends?) This cry places the question of the finite essence of friendship at the center of remembrance: "But where are my friends?" Linked to the possible of friendship, conversation is valued as good (*Wohl ist ein Gespräch gut*)—but it can never be coerced or in any way compelled. It must be given, says Heidegger.[41] Even the preparation for a *Gespräch* is always a gift (*Schenkung*) for which the poet can only plead. The "plea" submitted by the poetic word does not beg for a gift that would supplant the celebration and relieve us of the attendant preparations. The poem does not imitate a plea bargain or provide a shortcut to the sacred precincts of friendship. The poet's plea, a beseeching petition, asks for a kind of destinal granting. Supplicating for a bestowal to follow the hours of celebrating, the "Hymn of the Titans" corresponds to "Remembrance:" "Indessen, gieb in Feierstunden / Und dass ich ruhen möge, der Todten / Zu denken. Viele sind gestorben. . . . / Ich aber bin allein." (Please, give in the hours of holiday / And so that I may rest, the dead / To my thoughts. Many have died. . . . / But I am alone.)[42] This solitary place, more solitary than death, is the same one from which in "Andenken" the poet asks the poem's sole question—as if this question alone could reach the true longing of remembrance. "Wo aber sind die Freunde?" (Yet, where are my friends?) The friends are not "there," which is to say, they have not come to the place from which the poet is greeting. They are scattered, gone—or not yet in existence. Asking after absent friends, the poet asks about the nature of *future* friendship. Primed by absence and the solitary echo, the poet breaches the narcissistic returns of friendship, keeping the friend necessarily remote, insubstantial and out of political reach. In this way Hölderlin's plea, structurally unanswered—affirmatively defunct—indicates a deliteralization of Heidegger's projects around the time of the Rectoral Address: to the extent that the Greeting spans absence and involves an endless commemorative retrieval of the friend, the political instauration never comes to be—at least, it never settles on a site that could be considered locatable or in any way decisive. The sole question raised by "Andenken" illuminates only the poet's bereaved singularization. Friendship seems less to correspond to Heidegger's understanding of interlocution and friendship or even to the Graeco-Roman and political model of friendship (based on reciprocity) than to fall on the asymmetry and infinity of nonreciprocity and nonrequital of which Derrida writes in *Politics of Friendship*.[43] If the poet accomplishes the mediated instauration in history of a communal form of human existence (*Menschentum*), then this may well occur solely in the manner of the ungrounded grounding and the donation out of excess that Heidegger, in "The Origin of the Work of Art," identifies as modalities of a poetic "founding of truth."[44] Still, the unrequited question argues for an even more fragile establishment of community, pointing instead to what is abiding—an utterance that invites being to reveal itself as open and empty. To the extent that the Greeting can be understood as the trope for the poetic word, then its foundational capacities remain, in Hölderlin, ever precarious and questioning.

Bound to the impossible task of commemorative retrieval, "Andenken" persistently reorients the discussion concerning a decisive locality and the placing of the political, blowing apart the premises upon which one could build a substantial work or project of asserted nonalienation and secured returns—a political project mirroring the narcissistic totality of a state. The Greeting, terribly close to a "hail" and its evil twin, "*heil,*" cannot prevent aberrant variations but seeks to establish in Hölderlin's work a lacerable communication with the passing or the parted without zoning a place for settlement. Greeted and greeting, the poet stands on responsive alert, clear about the limits of poetic dwelling on earth. The spark of finitude illuminates the momentary passage of the Greeting's destinal velocity. Since the day before Greece perished, plenitude has belonged to the tracts of fictioning. States of security, windswept, reveal the nature of illusion. There will be no gathering home, even if the poet has projected a homeward turning.

Notes

Ronell originally gave this lecture as a job talk at New York University in 1996 and revised it for this collection. An essay based on the revised version was published in *PMLA* 120, no. 1 (2005): 16–32, as "On the Misery of Theory without Poetry: Heidegger's Reading of Hölderlin's 'Andenken.'"

The title of Hölderlin's poem, "Andenken," is usually translated as "Remembrance."

1. See in particular *Le sens du monde* (Paris: Galilée, 1993).

2. *Lectures on Kant's Political Philosophy* (ed. Ronald Beiner, Chicago and London: University of Chicago Press, 1982), 14.

3. Ibid., 16.

4. I'm drawing on the following two editions of Heidegger's commentary: *Erläuterungen zu Hölderlins Dichtung,* vol. 4 of *Gesamtausgabe* (Frankfurt am Main: Klostermann, 1982), and *Hölderlins Hymne "Andenken,"* vol. 52 of *Gesamtausgabe,* part 2: Volesungen 1923–1944 (Frankfurt am Main: Klostermann, 1982).

5. "Paul Celan: From Being to the Other," *Proper Names* (trans. Michael B. Smith, Stanford, Ca.: Stanford University Press, 1996), 40–46.

6. *Ethics and Infinity: Conversations with Philippe Nemo* (trans. Richard A. Cohen, Pittsburgh: Duquesne University Press, 1982), 92.

7. *Ethics and Infinity,* 89.

8. *Otherwise than Being: Or Beyond Essence* (trans. Alphonso Lingis, Pittsburgh: Duquesne University Press, 2000), 184.

9. Ibid., 185.

10. Friedrich Hölderlin, *Sämtliche Werke,* Grosse Stuttgarter Ausgabe (Stuttgart: Kohlhammer, 1985), Band 4, 246.

11. Ithaca: Cornell University Press, 1986.

12. "Der Ursprung des Kunstwerkes," in *Holzwege, Gesamtausgabe* 5 (Frankfurt am Main: Klostermann, 1977), 66, translated by Albert Hofstadter as "The Origin of the Work of Art" in *Basic Writings* (ed. David Farrell Krell, London: Routledge, 1993), 203.

13. See *Schibboleth* (Paris: Galilée, 1992).

14. *Erläuterungen,* 108.

15. Philippe Lacoue-Labarthe, "L'oblitération," *Le sujet de la philosophie: Typographies I* (Paris: Aubier Flammarion, 1979), 147–48.

16. Ibid. The next several paragraphs, to the extent that they include relevant German passages, follow Heidegger's argument closely for both heuristic and pedagogical reasons.

17. Ibid., 24.

18. Ibid., 26.

19. Ibid., 92.

20. Derrida's lectures at NYU in 2000 and 2002 aimed at the animal other and philosophy's stuttering intolerance around extreme alterity. His 2004 lectures envisage "The Sovereign and the Beast."

21. *Jargon der Eigentlichkeit,* vol. 6 of *Gesammelte Schriften* (Frankfurt am Main: Suhrkamp, 1974), 148–52.

22. *Hölderlins Hymne,* 61. Importantly, the passages inspired by and surrounding the brown women disappear in other published and reedited versions of Heidegger's commentary. However, even in the most whited-out pages that remain, the exegetic language hems and haws, showing signs of alternating anxiety and indifference. Hölderlin's brown women reappear in Rilke's poem "Aschanti," where they are contrasted to the "helle" people—the bright, white folks—or, in some instances, I would suppose, the people from hell.

23. *Erläuterungen,* 52.

24. *Hölderlins Hymne,* 45.

25. Ibid., 32. Again, these passages do not appear in all editions of the "Andenken" commentaries. Someone removed them.

26. Ibid., 45, also suppressed in subsequent editions.

27. Ibid., 46.

28. Ibid., 129.

29. Heidegger himself frequently bends the law to invite a feminine inclusion. He does so when smuggling in the figure of the teaching mother, in *What Is Called Thinking?*, who sets the scene for the nonpolemical comportment of true thinking (48) and when changing "Das Gedaechtnis" into *"die* Gedaechtnis" in his lectures on memory and the feminine. See also the first lecture of *What Is Called Thinking?* (ed. Ruth Nanda Anshen, New York: Harper & Row, 1968).

30. *Erläuterungen,* 75–77.

31. Ibid., 131.

32. Ibid., 103.

33. Ibid., 121.

34. Ibid., 81.

35. Ibid.

36. Ibid.

37. Ibid., 84.

38. Lacoue-Labarthe's work is devoted in large part to the crucial significance of type in philosophy. See *Typographies: Mimesis, Philosophy, Politics* (ed. Christopher Fynsk, Cambridge, Mass.: Harvard University Press, 1989).

39. For a full treatment of this maneuver and its philosophical implications, see Philippe Lacoue-Labarthe and Jean-Luc Nancy, *Retreating the Political* (ed. Simon Sparks, London and New York: Routledge, 1997), 117.

40. "'Political' Seminar," in *Retreating the Political,* 103.

41. *Erläuterungen,* 128.

42. Ibid.

43. Trans. George Collins (London: Verso, 1997). I have tried to pursue this logic of friendship in "Kathy Goes to Hell: The Scandal of Kathy Acker's Death," forthcoming in *Lust for Life* (New York and London: Verso).

44. "Origin," 199.

On Friendship; Or, Kathy Goes to Hell

13

(The question of friendship brings me to this point. I will be reading the split, especially the split that is figured on many of her book covers—the torn photograph, where she is already figured as the morcellated body. Shortly after she passed away, I began teaching a seminar on friendship and the gift—on the value of nonreciprocity. We were guided by a number of texts and considerations, but especially by recent works of Jacques Derrida. A starting point, offered by Emmanuel Lévinas, posits the amorous couple as a figure of injustice, always excluding a third. Bearing this observation in mind, we sought to explore friendship as a crucial modeling of justice. As for me, on the subject of friendship, I have a thing about gathering my friends around me, having them meet or somehow, in a calculable way, cross one another's paths—or pathologies, depending on what configuration of encounter seems more improbable. It's the perv in me, or the hysteric, who likes to stir up trouble. Or maybe the desire to hook up friends is more ordinary than all that. It doesn't always have to be science fiction, risking the wrong blend and watching the uncontrollable spill of consequences. Anyway, a few months ago at the airport I introduced Acker to Jacques Derrida. He wasn't greatly familiar with her works, though he knows what she represents for me. I showed him pictures of Kathy and me, one on Kathy's motorcycle. I'm modeling my Japanese look, she's staring sternly at the camera. Derrida likes to get to the airport early, very early. So we normally sit in the Air France terminal and I bring my show-and-tell. Gil was there, too. I don't like going home alone after Derrida takes off. It's dark and the world seems dangerous again, unfathomed like childhood. This time I am determined to present some of my thoughts about Kathy's work, read from some marked passages, give him a couple of her books for the flight and an early draft of this talk. If you are reading between the lines, and you don't have to be doing so, you can tell that friendship, as I practice it, often involves triangulation and the drama of departure—a straightforward history of flights. Well, straightforward only to a point. I am not always sitting in the airport in anticipation of a heart-

thudding separation. Or maybe I am, but it's not always played out so literally, with airport soundtracks and interiors.

Kathy and I sat through all sorts of technological stopovers, we moved through peculiar intersections and shared a highly invested though by no means exclusive relationship to Europe—mostly, to the more subversive power surges of French and German texts—though, due to a childhood trauma, I was not as big on London as she was, and I haven't yet done Haiti, except to the extent that I "do" anything, namely, through literature and music. To get back to my course on friendship, the first sustained meeting place of Acker and Derrida under my command, I'll sketch the key concerns and trajectories of the arranged rendezvous in what follows. Getting Kathy to go along with me was not so easy. I faced some dilemmas that I should point out at the outset: Kathy Acker and I are not the same; yet, as her friend, I found myself tempted to reduce her to sameness, to love her as a part of me. This reduction implicates me in unjust acts, eliciting as it does a sense of violation: is it possible to remember and engage a friend without the calculation of sameness, without this reserve of narcissistic appropriation? These reflections represent some of the questions that have haunted this piece of writing.

Our title mimes and recites the title of a work for which Acker didn't much care, Kathy Goes to Haiti. *Nonetheless, I invoke it here because "Kathy Goes . . ." recalls that traveling for Acker was linked to reading. To me, she's still going, still reading.*)

.01 The Citation

When I first met Acker, it was as if *memory,* mother of the Muses, had been engaged in advance. I had already read her, begun the process of introjection according to a private transferential bureaucracy of self. There was something ass backwards about our encounter, which occurred as a kind of material extension of a friendship already begun—a constellated relationship already capable of its idiomatic quarrels and turns, complicities and rushes. As in any number of transferential engagements, Kathy preceded herself in my life and already occupied an internal territory of considerable consequence. In a sense, I recognized her at once. To my astonishment, she claimed to know me, too. We found each other immediately—a quirk for which Derrida reprimands Lacanian psychoanalysis, when it claims to find what was always there or "meant to be," relying on a kind of metaphysical latency. At the moment of our encounter we said that we felt destined to each other—in need, in any case, of the complementarity that our writing invited and indicated. We had been writing to one another, in correspondence. Still, she allowed space for the utter strangeness that we each were able to hold; I might have wanted to efface those edges at times but she held steady, keeping her stubborn alterity intact. There was proximity without takeover, invasion with little violation (it would be foolish to deny any trace of violation, because Kathy Acker rearranged you on a molecular level, she was that powerful).

For Bataille, friendship is part of the sovereign operation and is linked to reading. It seems necessary and appropriate to begin with a citation from Kathy Acker's corpus. In fact, it would seem to me indecent if I were to refrain from resurrecting a passage from *her* work at this fragile point of entry. In rhetoric, citation is called "apostrophe." It is a way of calling to the other and in this place can function as an address to Kathy, from Kathy, to you, through me. As apostrophe, citation opens up as well on what Derrida sees as the possibility of a postmortem discourse: it is always the case (no matter what, but especially here) that citation is linked to memory, to acts of bringing back, recalling. When we cite and recite, when we quote the other, we are calling to the irreplaceable one for whom there is no substitute. Acker has written on the subject of memory and in memory of the subject, *In Memorium to Identity:* "'They teach you stupid things in universities and universities are no good for anybody.' I was angry, though I didn't know why." There is something about the institution of learning that has angered Acker—something that is associated for her with a studied curriculum of stupidity. The site for gathering a certain type of cognitive circumscription, the university was for Acker a destination troubled with the double projectile of desire and repugnance, interest and disdain. She'd send me her CV when she wanted in. She taught at a number of institutions, gladly accepting the invitation of Laurence Rickels to come teach, for instance, at University of California at Santa Barbara. At the same time, the university was a dead letter box—not as such bad news for a writer who trafficked in dead letters and parasited the canonic corpus but, still, somehow too numbing, even for her. For all its dumb and numb lethargy, the university issued a menace to her exercise of linguistic promiscuity, threatening at every turn to revoke her poetic license; it put her in a libidinal straitjacket, calmed her roguish stories—wait a minute, I may be mixing us up here and talking about myself. Nothing calmed Kathy Acker, not even the massive institutional tranquilizers which she desired. She remained unsheltered, teaching more or less as an adjunct, bereft of the benefits that would have pulled her out of her medical crisis. I will never get over the fact that Acker had to suffer the refusal of medical benefits. Like many Americans, she was uninsured. No one or no institution should get away with the degradation that was visited upon her, determining her fate. We know that Kathy took out no insurance policies to safeguard thinking or writing, to protect herself against countless intellectual calamities. But that is a wholly other matter . . .

.02 Split Ends

When Amy Scholder invited me to speak about Kathy Acker, I was very pleased but I was split. I am tempted to say right now, at this early stage of my reflections on Acker, "end of story:" "I was split," story of my life, Amy invited me, I was split; I split. [I get anxious. It's been a long time. I miss her. I expect her at any moment to pull me away from the pain of melancholic piety. My first paper on her after Kathy's demise was in Vermont, at the behest of writer Bob Buckeye. The stumped sense of loss made me freeze.] If I were Kathy Acker—and in a sense, I am, representing her, I am bringing her here with me—if I were her, I would disseminate in the page the way she does in *Blood and Guts in High School* with her Persian lexicon, the word "split"—I was split would proliferate anagrammatically, turning on and against itself, unstoppably splitting with no origin or end, instituting a kind of "spliterature," splitting us up, me and Kathy, though not without memorializing the fact of a singular encounter. We were each in her own right the split subject of which French psychoanalysist Jacques Lacan writes, though our splits were arguably more dramatically transparent than those of the sorry signifiers which he had exposed. We were the sorriest signifiers we had ever known. More on that later.

.03 The Trouble with Kathy

But I did not want to begin by risking or invoking the vertiginous splits that characterized the friendship I enjoyed with Kathy Acker. In fact, we were split only on one major issue—it was our *différend,* if I may cite Lyotard's important term, which means a dispute or difference that cannot be resolved by the cognitive or linguistic resources we have at hand. The concept of *différend* responds to a situation that leaves us stranded at a site that offers no legal recourse, knows no appeal, indicating rather a rupture in the presentation of testimony. It is admittedly a bit grandiose of me to say that Kathy and I had a *différend*—it was at the very least an untouchable pulse of disturbance in the intellectual harmony we shared: she did not approve of my recourse, however critical, to Heidegger, and I did not think that Heidegger was a matter of approval. He (meaning his work) was an event, an irreversible event, not something you could turn your tattooed back on or choose not to read. In any case, Kathy and I were split on the issue of Heidegger; this constituted our *différend,* which neither of us could properly litigate, on which neither of us would budge. I would never have presumed to pull her off Bataille or Rimbaud or some of the other Frenchies she was stuck on. Of course I, too, like my theory with a French accent and in this domain I do not like to split hairs or heirs between the French or Germans . . . But the signifier "split" has carried me off center, I got carried away at the very beginning of an homage to a beloved and irreplaceable friend. I was pushed around by language and got carried off the aim I tried to establish. Language does that to you, pushes you around, I mean, undermining your cognitive grasp of things or the intentional meaning you had hoped to secure. I was not intending to reveal to you that Kathy and I had a disagreement, that we were split on an issue or two. Something from another zone intervened when I wrote that I was pleased to be writing about her but that I was also split about it. I was split for other reasons and according to altogether different registers of anxiety.

Kathy and I were friends. We spent days and evenings together, years together, in San Francisco and Berkeley, where she and I taught, performed, stirred up trouble, complained, ate, and wrote. We both left the Bay Area at the same time, fed up, tired, narcissistically depleted. We both fell ill at the same time. And according to this logic, I feel we should have both disappeared at the same time. A Deleuzian friend of mine once said, following the Jonestown mass suicides, that there exists a strong desire in us for a synchronicity of death, a wish that we all die at the same moment so that, on the one hand, no one will be left alone, weeping, in a state of inconsolable solitude or, on the other hand, that no one would have to think that the world would go on after her own very shocking and altogether inexcusable demise. Ego would like that, if everyone would disappear together: "ashes, ashes, we all fall down." I am not sitting here to bring you down to my level of torment, however. On the contrary; a poetic sensibility teaches celebration at these moments of radical incomprehensibility.

.04 Kathy's Community

Kathy Acker created community wherever she went, insistently. Not the Christian or politically suspect kind. Her implementation of community was something she took from Bataille: she insisted on community without relying on transcendence—a community without communion, without fascistic bonding rituals or strangulating close ties. This was a community without illusions about itself; it erupted ecstatically, multiplied addresses, instigated trouble, defied all sorts of instances of social degradation, and didn't even believe in itself or its momentary manifestations. Her community was self-annulling. Yet, it remained rigorous. She practiced the installations of community that were un-folded in the singular works of Bataille, Maurice Blanchot, and Jean-Luc Nancy, who wrote *La communauté désoeuvrée* (*The Inoperative Community*), which thematizes, among other things, a kind of literary communism—something that strongly informs Acker's works. (Nowadays Giorgio Agamben builds on this work and configures community as Kathy would have acknowledged.) The notion of literary communism "belongs" to Nancy, if property attribution makes a great deal of sense in this context. Kathy shared literature and imparted it freely. Her adherence to an ever fracturing community was reflected in the work to which she appended her name. She practiced literary depropriation, renouncing property, the proper—any claim to her ownmost inventiveness, "originality"—propriety. It was a package deal of social transgression. She gave up the mystical foundations of authorship, the capital claims, looting and van-dalizing legally protected stores of knowledge. The difference between Kathy and other authors was that she was caught on tape—or, rather, she kept turning herself in to the authorities with that defiant narcissism of a proud trouble-maker, a punk criminal. Her bud Burroughs used to say, "steal everything in sight." And she did. Most authors conceal such evidence of a hijacked corpus or they transvaluate theft back into property, with proper holdings, sanctioned attributions, and ideologies of "influence."

As for me, I have partially incorporated her voice. I have found myself in-teriorizing Kathy according to altogether surprising exigencies—it has been surprising to receive her dictations. Like a true neurotic, I have installed sound systems through which Kathy booms words. Though fairly regular, she remains unpredictable: sometimes I am talking to the dean on behalf of my depart-ment and the word "cunt" comes up, midsentence, in Kathy tonalities ("we're requesting additional funding for a visiting CUNT professor"); and I find my-self saying "fucked up" where she might have offered that locution, though I haven't mastered her intonation—my ways of saying such things still line up with Scorsese and Brooklyn, I'm afraid. But what does get said, coming from within me and from beyond me, from Kathy, is "byee!"—her consistent way of saying goodbye.

About our friendship, of which there is so much residue, so much that still awaits reflection and comprehension, though without comprehensiveness—I shall never catch up with our friendship—about our friendship, there was something old-fashioned and inappropriable, new, at the same time. There were literary discussions, support for one another's work. Calls to say we had read something that the other had published, we were blown away, we were thinking about x, y, or z that had been asserted. This seemed to me old-fashioned; we could have been eighteenth-century correspondents, corresponding to one another, responding, responsible. She energized what the German poets of that era called *Ge-spräch*, emphasizing the "co" in correspond or, more literally, in conversation. In this sense, she was reliable, to be counted on. But she was also rigorously perverse in a way that I found exhilarating, getting us thrown out of restaurants on Sunday afternoons, pissing off people, uncompromising, punching a hole in any manifestation of family values. This woman, Kathy, practiced zero tolerance for the insolence of valuations derived from family, religion, or state. The load of crap she had to fend off, even from well-meaning lefties, sometimes strained her more private hegemonies. She was always getting in a fight with someone.

It has been hard on me, responding to a nearly prescriptive invitation, to speak about or for Kathy Acker. What struck me as particularly difficult was the necessity of including myself in a narrative. The requirement of constructing such a narrative filled me with dread, as if I were attracting bad luck. Who am I to eulogize Kathy Acker—and then, how could I not, is it not a duty, a responsibility of friendship? I was double bound to her by the rules of friendship and the law of finitude. In much of my work I had concerned myself with the duties of the survivor, be it Johann Peter Eckermann, who took dictation from Goethe even after the great poet's death, or Alexander Graham Bell, who connected up with his departed brother, fatefully heading for the electrician Watson's bench. Yet, when, philosophically speaking, is one *not* paying duties or energetic taxes to the departing other? Is there any discernible duty-free zone in friendship? (There ought to be—but "ought" belongs to prescriptive registers, is duty-bound.) The friend leaves you . . . with a number of pressing questions, a number of pressure points susceptible to unceasing pain. When did Kathy start leaving me? Did she have leave to take leave? Permission and leave permeated our sustained encounter. It is hard to stop thinking about when it started ending between us. And has this rapport to her essential finitude begun only after her death, or does not every friendship figure the death, the mortality of the friend? Isn't friendship somehow based on this knowledge—the prescient knowledge that you must go, that one of us must go?

.05 Who Is She?

Split between two poles that do not form a polarity, I am caught. Reflecting on Kathy Acker, on assignment, makes me examine the disjunction between *narcissism* (where I claim the friend is a part of me) and *alterity* (I cannot appropriate the friend to myself or exercise a narcissistic reappropriation of sorts, operate a reduction of the friend to the same or to the friend as other). The paradoxes and aporias posed by this disjunctive crevice are manifold. Sometimes I am seduced by the possibility of giving in to proximity—I have pulled Kathy in, close to me, and I want to accomplish the fusion of you and me. But then I remember Nietzsche's lessons, the call to maintain or keep a relentless distance within a good friendship. To keep it separate, as we did for the most part in life. What Nietzsche emphasizes—this becomes important for Bataille but also for a liberationist politics—is a domestic policy of *disidentification,* the necessity of separation in order to make friendship and community possible. Hence the non-Christian communion, the pulling apart that he sees in terms of an infinite wrenching. (In another idiom, on a decidedly rhetorical register, such energized separateness could be read as belonging to the frugal gains of irony and allegory: yielding a politics of allegory, that is, of noncoincidence, it institutes a covenant of the severed. The Nietzschean severance policy is opposable to political tendencies toward unification that assert a mystified oneness, as in Heidegger's usage of the *Volk.* Nietzsche versus Heidegger, but that's another story. (Kathy and I shared many Germanic tropes, philosophemes, and itineraries. We especially shared Nietzsche.) Nietzsche argues for the necessity of the dissociated, singularized, *vereinsamt* (isolated, alone), for that which is constituted by monadic alterities. So he asserts the necessity of resisting what I have been calling the fascistic fusion, the oneness that characterizes totalitarianism and attempts at totalization. As indicated, the exorbitance of individuation goes against the grain of the Heideggerian gathering, grinding down the instances of gathering in which the *Volk* congeals into a politics of one and sameness. Instead, we have *laceration,* the cuts and break-off points that punctuate communication—much of which is handled in Nancy's reading of Bataille, where he draws up a plan for a community without communion, shifting the grounds of the desired erasure of difference. A nonsubstantial policy, laceration offers a political *Liebestod* averted. No one gets mashed up in the political machine as a work, as a substantial project that swallows you whole.

Good friendship, then, for Nietzsche requires that we affirm the break and enact the split-off points.[1] Friendship, if it is to be marked up as "good" in the noble Nietzschean sense, is not the narcissistic glom-on, though God knows he practiced it with Wagner: "Ich bin Du, Du bist Ich," as Tristan and Isolde say to one another, one as other or rather, one and the same. "Good friendship" supposes disproportion. It demands a strong measure of rupture in reciprocity or equality, as well as the interruption of all fusion or confusion between you and me. Borne of disproportion, it is evidenced, claims Nietzsche, when you respect the other more than yourself. This cast of friendship commands that one abstain prudently from all confusion; wisdom asks that one surrender the wish fulfillment of merger between the singularities of you and me. Why dwell on Nietzsche's concept of a good friendship? The good friendship, borne of disidentification, enables you to *see* your friend. When you identify with your friend, you don't see her, you are blinded by him; empathy has replaced understanding. Understanding, on the other hand, presupposes differences and distance, pivoting on the Nietzschean tact of *Dis-tanz*. When distance is bridged you cannot see each other; instead, you are thrown off by this narcissistic extension that the other, as appropriated by your identification, has become.

Essentially a gift, friendship dissolves the economy of give and take yet retains an ethical strain. Friendship at once obligates you but also absolves you of all obligations. A friendship made or kept out of duty would not qualify as a good friendship. Thus the logic of the gift elaborated in Derrida's several works on the topic reorients our more common understanding of friendship, calling it back to the aneconomic terms of nonreciprocity, dissymmetry, or disproportion.[2] The political consequences of such a rupture in reciprocity, particularly in regard to democratic formations, are considerable. Nietzsche puts us on a search for a justice that would break with sheer equivalence—something that Levinas explores in altogether different tonalities and philosophical circumstances. What would be a concept of equality, an equity, which would no longer be calculated according to our systems of equivalence? Or a political structure that would inscribe a movement beyond proportion or appropriation, exceeding thereby all love of the proper? Traditionally, friendship has modeled politics, which is why they are often anamorphic of one another, mirroring and distorting, calling the other to order, working without respite on justice and the possibility of being a good friend—perhaps offering a little more in the life of political tryouts than the merely "good enough" friend, a portion with which familial formations must be satisfied. If justice cannot be served in the precincts of friendship, why bother magnifying the scope to more politically assigned domains? But the politics of friendship involves all sorts of recesses and temporal complications, implicating structures and paraconcepts from which an overhaul of political theories may benefit. The friend, in one sense, has not yet arrived, even after her departure. Perhaps the same can be said for democracy or the historical experience of justice.

Friendship, according to Derrida, opens up the experience of time. The apprehension of survival constellates time and a relation to lived life as that which already exceeds the living; hence, the languages that underscore survival (*sur-vie, über-leben*). Derrida locates in surviving the origin and essence of friendship. Not empirical or chronologically clocked but fundamental, the structure of surviving means that one of you will be left behind, responsible and responsive to the intemporal, irretrievably mute other. The itinerary can get complicated, as in the case of Eckermann, who played dead after Goethe's departure and let the poet dictate to him in the long night of their refused separation. Or, again, there was the cable that Aleck Bell threw to his dead brother, beginning a massive history of telecommunications which, no matter how currently dispiritualized, continues to offer the promise of reaching out and touching the absent other. Disavowed and forgotten, there is a survival guide coiled into every phone call, every attempted connection.[3] These slightly aberrant structures and histories themselves respond to a call more prior and essential. There is something about loving the friend that is, from the start, pitched on the grieved act of loving, which is to say, when you become friends, when you fall for the friend, you already acknowledge the finitude that defines the friend. As Derrida offers, the anguished apprehension of mourning haunts and plunges you, the loving friend, before mourning, into mourning.

Exemplary friendship embraces, in a resolutely unrequited way, an unwearied capacity for loving generously without being loved back. Marking the limit of possibility—the friend need not be there—this structure recapitulates in fact the Aristotelian values according to which acts and states of *loving* are preferred to the condition of *being-loved,* which depends for its vigor on a mere potentiality. Being loved by your friends just pins you to passivity. For Aristotle, loving, on the contrary, constitutes an act. To the extent that loving is moved by a kind of disclosive energy, it puts itself out there, shows up for the other, even where the other proves to be a rigorous no-show. Among other things, loving has to be declared and known, and thus involves an element of risk for the one who loves and who, abandoning any guarantee of reciprocity, braves the consequences when naming that love.

.06 The End, My Only Friend, the End

Every encounter with the friend has also borne this attestation: I do not survive the friend; in fact, the friend who encounters me in my mortality already bears my death, which is thus expropriated in advance. Such an attestation appears to go against the grain of Heideggerian claims made on behalf of the absolute aloneness of one's death, which, in its fortified ownness, no other Dasein can take up for you. Heidegger's essential insight cannot be refuted. Yet even he, in *Being and Time,* had installed the ghostly voice of a friend in such a way as to mortally shake up the absolute aloneness of which he wrote. Friendship enacts a scene, however displaced or repressed, of the friend's disappearance—or, through the friend, it scores a secret knowledge of one's own demise. Friendship maintains a holding pattern over the separating distance, taking place, in the first—and last—place, without proximity. Such is the lesson handed down to us from the Aristotelian model of loving the dead, loving without reciprocity, to Nietzsche's assertion of disproportion and distance in friendship. Reading the transmissions filtered through Aristotle and distributed by Nietzsche, Derrida installs the temporal qualities of survival that inform the possibility of friendship from the start. There have been different ways to state these experiences of friendship and the quasi-betrayals built into the very structure of loving the friend. For Nietzsche, friendship unfolds without the bolstering guarantors of proximity or presence but is kept among a population of solitudes; favorable intimacy abides in a community of those who love in separation, at a distance and in withdrawal.

Acker dedicates a section of her book *My Mother: Demonology* "(to B, who's dead)." She limits her inscription to the letter "B," but we can hear it homonymically as a cipher for Being, as stating "to be or not to be, who's in any case dead." The section is titled "My Dream Showed Me that I Don't Belong among Respectable People."[4] Kathy, writing to the dead, dedicating to the dead, making friends, conversing with the departed. In another section, she avows her loyalty to reading, a figure, for her, of true amity—but not in order to become intelligent, she warns:

> "*Right after I saw him, I wrote . . . in my secret notebook. . . . I'll travel and travel by reading. I won't read in order to become more intelligent. . . . I knew from the first moment I was that I hated them, the hypocrites." As soon as I had written this down I knew that I was dreadfully and magnificently alone.*[5]

• • •

Ugh! Another way to have approached Kathy would have been to delineate her theory of prophesy. Much of what Kathy had to say was prophetic, hence her particular brand of irony. In *My Mother: Demonology* she opens a section called "Dreaming Politics" with these questions: "Where does Bush's power stop? Where does an authoritarian leader's power stop? Tell me, Mommy, where and how will Bush's power stop?"[6] She saw the terrifying lineage, the future history of spilt blood.

. . . Oh, the history of blood. I forgot to say that the book's cover is bright red. Yes, red. Here's another red thread that I would have wanted to follow (I cannot stop reading Kathy, finding it impossible to let go, to end). The narrator states that she loves the color red. Her unconscious turns up in red. Under the opening section, "Into That Belly of Hell Whose Name Is the United States," she opens the novel with the subtitle "My Mother:" "I'm in love with red. I dream in red."[7] Further along, she affirms that "red gave me the authority to be other than red. . . . In me dead blood blushed crimson into the insides of roses and became a living color that's unnameable."[8] Ok, I finally know how I should have begun to speak about Kathy. Now that I have reflected on her romanced red, it becomes clearer to me. To do some justice to Kathy's thought, I should have begun with the utterance, signaled under a somewhat representational drawing, "my red cunt ugh." It's so obvious to me now. This is where she locates an origin and matrix. Now, when it has become too late, I understand where my mistress would have wanted me to start, where I might have begun on the path of a worthy homage. Oh, Kathy! It's all in this endless little phrase. The repugnance and desire, the unreadable "ugh" that blossoms forth from the red cunt, that which we presume to have read. You wanted me to begin by reading the red "ugh," at once asignificatory and polysemic, but in the first place barely linguistic: a heave, a groan, a punctuation, a way of marking your beautiful, unmystifiable cunt. Ugh! Now it dawns on me, the way you pull away from your own boldness, you avert your gaze with a grunt—is it guttural or soft, maybe hoarse? I am trying to hear you—in this nearly visceral moment, your sigh and your sign, the way you pull away, the distress held in an autocritical sputter. How you were and weren't re(a)d.

Notes

Ronell delivered this keynote address at "Lust for Life: The Writings of Kathy Acker," a symposium held at New York University, November 7, 2002. An essay version of this talk, "Kathy Goes to Hell: The Scandal of Kathy Acker's Death," was published in *Lust for Life: On the Writings of Kathy Acker,* Amy Scholder, Carla Harryman, and Avital Ronell, eds. (New York: Verso, 2006), 12–34.

1. More about breaking up and Nietzschean modalities of self-testing in *The Test Drive* (Urbana: University of Illinois Press, 2004).

2. See Derrida's discussion of Nietzsche and friendship in *Politics of Friendship* (trans. George Collins, London and New York: Verso, 1997).

3. The umbilicus of the forgotten phone call—what Nietzsche calls the telephone to the beyond—is one of the traces I put on the genealogy of technology in *The Telephone Book: Schizophrenia, Technology, Electric Speech* (Lincoln and London: University of Nebraska Press, 1989).

4. *My Mother: Demonology, a novel* (New York: Pantheon Books, 1993), 153.

5. Ibid., 17.

6. Ibid., 174.

7. Ibid., 7.

8. Ibid., 14.

Loving Your Enemy

(Shortly after this lecture was delivered, the planet was beset with different levels of natural catastrophe, much of which was concentrated in the United States. Every day newspapers carried stories of horrific climatic aberration—a whirlwind of floods, earthquakes, uncontrollable fires, and hurricanes were visited upon the land. According to a psychoanalytical legend of the global unconscious, disasters of this order emerge when one fails to honor the dead enemy. —AR)

I give up; I surrender. I yield without hesitation to the incomprehensibility of what is taking us down at this time. In the epoch and text of Hegel war *meant* something. It was productive of sense: the future was counted in, and depended on the way the Weltgeist waged its wounding temperament. The enemy figured as the negated other. War in Hegel served as a pregnancy test for historical becoming; on some pages, bearing the dignity of a solemn signifier, war spoke to us with worldly gravity. Delivering difference and future, it was sheltered by metaphysics and encouraged by the creation of value. In the past several years I have argued that we no longer know how to wage war or balance the books of some of its more remorselessly sacrificial economies. The notion of a just war is, as Hannah Arendt observes, a fairly recent invention. For all sorts of reasons tied to the breakdown of our metaphysical inheritance, war can no longer be justified, however. And despite God's reappearance at the head of so many armies and insurgencies, the transcendental guarantor has by all counts gone AWOL. Transcendental wannabes show up where the names of God have deserted man. Hence the regressive hue of current aggressions, played out on repeat, running through immemorial desertscapes.

War itself has become a rogue state in terms of the meaning and renewal it aims historically to yield, the sense it promises to make or break. For war also offers the express delivery of rupture and recognition, the emergence of a new order. It promises world, or a restoration at least of the confidence owed to the notion of world. These considerations are being stated too quickly, I know, mainly because I have worked similar assertions elsewhere, largely in

terms of the conjunction of God and technology and the new teletopies of
aggression that presented themselves when I was tracking the cartography of
the maternal empire. Elsewhere I have tried to raise deceptively simple questions about recent maternal incursions into the scenography and rhetoric of
armed conflict: what it means that mothers go to war or that the United States
puts together the mother of all bombs, the MOAB, or that those on bombing
missions watch porno videos before they strike. I have been alert, moreover,
to feminine registration codes and the maternal trace in the technological
revealing from Heidegger to the Bushies.

Today's assignment is a bit different; it's also a tough one due in part to the
pervasive and elusive qualities of the topic, at once obsolesced according to
essential protocols of reading, yet somehow inerasable. Now we are asked to
speak about the return of an archaic, truly primitive construal of enmity, which
strikes me as being phallogocentric to the bone. *The enemy.* Let me start up
the engine, slowly, the enemy engine. To be frank with you, I didn't know that
facing the enemy was in my job description. Just as friendship has been shown
to leave out women, based historically on entrenched notions of fraternity,
brotherhood, and other essentially masculinist tropes, I must wonder what I,
of all putatively sexuated beings, am doing here speaking with the enemy: my
enmity. On the other hand, I am uniquely qualified for the job. I remember
that Hegel considered women to be the enemy—not only the irony, but the
enemy—of the community. Who could ever forget such a slight, such a truth,
smack in the middle of being? This still burns me up. But I will hold fire. In
terms of a more literary backdrop one thinks of the proud machismo of enmity exhibited by Wyndam Lewis and Ezra Pound as they flexed some poetic
muscle; turning to cinema one thinks of the sustained fiendship of Kinski and
Herzog or other foaming warrior poses that have been binding men since Cain
and Abel. Proximity tightens the hug of enmity, rolling back to the pulses of
brotherly love: absolute hostility is reserved only for a brother, which puts in
place an unavowable synonymy of opposing forces, repeating, as Derrida writes,
a murderous tautology of tremendous biblical and Greek consequence.

I am trying to get traction on some of these enemy narratives. I can't keep
from wondering, Who targeted me for keynoting the enemy line? What motivates me especially for the task of establishing the stakes of a colloquium that
interrogates the thought and figuring power of enmity? I've been a tough cookie,
often vulnerable to the subtlest forms of institutional assault, sometimes not
so subtle, sometimes not so vulnerable, more times than not nearly shredded
by hostility felt or sensed or, to stand by Melanie Klein, I have stood up to aggressions projected from an early paranoid or depressive position when the

241

breast or, truthfully, the bottle, attacked me. I was ready for action on day one, when I saw what I was in for. I was a survivor already in the womb, prenatally, born combat-ready. Standing my ground and running maneuvers before I could crawl, I was a war baby. I can't be certain that my colleagues took these qualifications into account when inviting my contribution at the head of the class of enemy arbiters. We're certainly not friends, my colleagues and I, but that's no doubt an indiscretion and in any case another story. I mean, that's pretty close to a question raised by Husserl somewhere in his relation to the exemplary disciple, Eugen Fink. Can colleagues or disciples or students or analysands or even so-called peers (though I go for Levinasian asymmetry as concerns relations) be or become or *make* friends? And if not, does that forcibly relegate them to enemy territory? Well, according to Freudian records, at least on symbolic grooves, someone is always gratefully sitting in parricide position, ready for your demission or retirement. Every research assistant is all about Eve, but that doesn't turn him into an enemy combatant. Or does it? How many Eves have I taken out in my career so far? But that, too, is another story. I'd like to gain on the enemy differently.

I have been working a lot on Nietzsche lately, looking at the way he's still making trouble and running into highly controlled dead ends. Perhaps, I thought, I've been invited to assist in and to embody the resurrection of the Nietzschean fool, the living fool who cries out, "My enemies, there is no enemy!" The living fool is placed next to the dying sage in Nietzsche, the one who cries out, "Oh, my friends, there is no friend," an utterance that Jacques Derrida famously restarts and reads in his work on friendship.[1] It is certainly a temptation and a trap to come here and proclaim, "Enemies, there is no enemy," to play the living fool and refute while addressing, apostrophizing, the enemy. Still, I've turned in my dunce cap for this one (maybe), so let me try another access code and consider a different lead-in.

Even though the enemy, according to major war theorists and strategists, practitioners and promoters of war—the ace polemologists—should not elicit affect, I'm going to follow my so-called heart on this one, go to where it hurts, to where the enemy is hurting and hounding me, to where my enemy truly persecutes me. Because *the enemy is mine,* there is little doubt about it when you think of all the stories and divine marketing strategies and sheer commandments that require us to hold the enemy, and let's face it, since it's in our faces, to *love* the enemy. I have to move cautiously on this mined field, where the enemy, as I say, is mine. This is a tough one, because the enemy is also often its own enemy, as a concept I mean; it's always undermining itself, repelling its own advances, even where political theorists and dubious presidents are trying to stabilize the enemy position as a fixed one. If you know anything about me, you know what I'm up to: I am going to try to attack the problem of an *ethics of enmity*. But first let me back off and try again, I got off to a false start; I'll need to renew my tactics, find another password or access code.

OK, where the enemy hits me, is persecuting me—that's a pretty large range. I'm going to narrow it down and ride in, or write in, on the words of Theodor Däubler, "*Der Feind ist unser eigene Frage als Gestalt*"—the enemy position is our own question as figure. The enemy position, the posited enemy, is our own question. As a figure. Daübler's statement notably involves a rhetorical move, but also cuts to the quick, playing the figural against the blasted literality of the enemy. "The enemy as my own question:" I think I can handle this (maybe); at least this perspective sees the enemy as originating in a daunting close up, and not as an alien invader or external disruptor of otherwise mendaciously smooth relations. That feels right, if only because this makes the enemy unavoidable for the thinker. The enemy is coextensive with questioning. In French the question, *la question,* also means "torture." The enemy resides or takes shape as my own torture chamber to the extent that the question marks me. That's what I think Däubler is saying. The very practice or act or recessive posture of thinking summons the enemy, calling on us further to reflect on what it is that gets said and done when we conjure the enemy. One cannot bypass, eliminate, or easily sublimate the enemy, this ownmost questioning, a question that by the way injures me, putting me unavoidably in harm's way; it is a wound within myself. Facing down the question, I am in the field of aggression, traumatism, war.

The enemy acts on me in the form of the question—the enemy responds to the call of my question, externalizing and giving form to it. And if I do not have a question or have not encountered the night of thinking but can only make war and irritate and nettle the body politic with uninterrogated certitudes about evil and the looming enemy, the enemy is still my question, prior to questioning.

Interestingly, the title of this conference switched a number of times between "The Enemy" and "Enmity," effecting a slippage that marks an internal disturbance in its conception. It's a tough one: posted as such, "The Enemy" is admittedly problematic, presupposing firm boundaries that set off the purported inside from an outside, as though one could get THE enemy in one's sights which, for political reasons according to Carl Schmitt, one nevertheless needs to do: politically it is imperative that one fix the enemy, if only to secure the state. Push this logic a lockstep further and you'll see that security depends on the enemy. What we do know and see today is that the production of the enemy is a way of presenting opposition, binaries, a way of locating, othering, and expelling inassimilable alterities, as religious fundamentalism everywhere today tries desperately to do: in a world where walls were crumbling, sides were lifted and political topographies shifted, there was a sudden violent return of a primitive vocabulary that is trying to reinstall good/evil, friend/foe, ours/ theirs, readable borders, and other regressive binaries. The binary machine has accelerated to the point that we now stand opposed to our allies; foreclosive moves have been made on enemy signifiers so that even the French fry (and its edible allegories) is toast. Ever since hamburgers and frankfurters became the national craving after WWII, we have been eating our enemy.

• • •

Trolling after the enemy, I keep on running into friends. This is one dead end that I want to resurrect with you, obsessively and again, as if returning to a crime scene—maybe to scour the place where a brother has been killed, a friend disposed of, a student has turned. Maybe it's just that whenever I am searching for the enemy, a friend pops up. How did that happen? My return to a designated scene, admittedly obsessive, may not be arbitrary but is programmed by the very concept of enmity, primed by the rapid turnover of friendship into enmity within a cycle that can be stabilized only by provisional maneuvers. My confusion has already been documented by Aristotle. It could be, as Aristotle suggests, that your best friend has stopped calling you, is showing distance, starts disappearing: this is enough, states the philosopher, to start up the engine of enmity. In Aristotle, then, the friend's distance, silence, abandonment makes him enemy territory. Let's continue on this road of ambivalence—that is where I am most comfortable, where the one converts into the other and you're split, exposed to a double exigency. You cannot always or precisely tell the difference between friend and enemy, hence the necessary suspension of "*THE* ENEMY." Or, do you remember when Osama bin Laden was our friend and when the other one, Saddam Hussein, was an ally? I cannot go into this conversion theory now to the extent that I did in an essay devoted to the Gulf War, whose title was "Support our Tropes," but did you notice that there are always two fathers, two enemies, as in Lacan following Freud following Goethe following the biblical split between God and the Devil, each of which posit the partnership of imaginary and real fathers in the target zone of rageful intention? Did you also notice that W.'s record-breaking overtaking of his father in the killing of Iraqis constitutes a double gesture, as much a binding homage as a castrating strategy so that when he plays golf with his father nowadays while the wars wage, he feminizes him, pokes holes and fun at him, and calls him "Betsy" when the elder Bush misses a hole?

244

So your friend stops calling, or you are Blake writing a poem, exhorting your beloved friend with these words: "Do be my enemy." Yes, you are Blake and you appeal to the friend, saying, "Do be my enemy for friendship's sake." I supplicate your enmity. More intense, present, permanently on duty and more alive, the enemy is my best friend. Or you are Freud and you ponder the formerly loved relative who turns into a demon and becomes malignant. You role-play into Lacan, checking out the resistance to "love thy neighbor as thyself," proofing the fundamental evil that dwells within the neighbor, the unfathomable aggressivity from which I flee, where I turn against . . . me. There's more. The internal enemy of state, the family—I mean the Mafia—holds its enemies close and plants a kiss on the lips when you're toast. In all these instances, the enemy is the closest, the most familiar, the most familial, the ownmost filiation. Enmity is located within the very intimacy of friendship. As Derrida writes in *The Politics of Friendship*, enmity did not rise up to get you one bad day into the relationship—it did not come after the friend to oppose or negate him, but is already there. An inerasable and fast-going commutability destabilizes the friend/enemy opposition.

In the interest of full disclosure I should state, however belatedly, that a lot of my presentation prepared for this evening went through the shredder. On assignment, I started writing before the continuous war on Iraq re-erupted and suspended my hopes of patiently considering the possibility of presenting an ethics of enmity. My focus had been, or was intended to be, on Nietzsche's declared enemy and the figure of the noble traitor in his works—in other words, on why Nietzsche considered Brutus unsurpassable: the most intimate, the most loyal, the greatest adversary. Nietzsche of course jammed on the adversary in the form of the *versus* when signing off: Dionysus *versus* the Crucified can serve as an example of this tendency.

Brutus was the man, the exemplary turncoat, the noble traitor and worthy enemy. Hamlet, says the philosopher, is trivial compared to Brutus, and Shakespeare himself prostrated himself before Brutus as before no other of his characters. Nietzsche's proof? Shakespeare cleverly conceals his pathological adoration of Brutus by naming the play . . . *Julius Caesar*. The battle of names has everything to do with enmity in Nietzsche but, as said, it went to the shredder, along with Nietzsche's enactment of ethical enmity when he dumps Wagner—a historial event, according to Heidegger, affecting us all. All gone. This is how far the destruction of our civil liberties is going: the war invades my body and strip-searches my work, diverts your energies, and dumbs us down. I am not trivializing the murderous range of the missives and missiles that we are all on one existent and corporeal level dodging with more or less success, depending on how much you can take or where you can take it, but locating its effects even in the most minute or indifferent preparations of my homework. It is not as if war does not target our inner core. Which brings up another moment gone up in flames: truly tracking the topos of the inner enemy, I have let fizzle the formation of the superego and the pervasive problem of misrecognition, in other words, what it means to love your enemy within the ambivalence mapped out by Freud and Lacan, especially in terms of the latter's *Ethics of Psychoanalysis*. The ambivalence of love and hatred painstakingly explored by psychoanalysis is crucial to a careful elaboration of the idea of enmity. (The German resistance to psychoanalysis belongs here, a largely continued and highly guarded resistance.) To return to the stakes of loving your enemy, a thinking of love and the love of thinking belong to the question of enmity: Lacan points out that love is like military service—something we might explore, I submit, in terms of the famous gap strategically placed in the *Marquise von O. . .*, which scrambles the master codes that have allowed us to distinguish between the despised enemy and beloved friend, between good and evil, angel and devil, devastation and fecundity. All such polarities collapse in Kleist's story, which tries to account for the invasive assault of an unspeakable enemy. Kleist's story, and the other one that held Kafka in thrall, the other story, which tells of the making of a terrorist and the collapse of two towers, *Michael Kohlhaas,* develop what I call a *militerary* strategy, a strategy that probes and unsettles conceptual border zones that admit to this day a rhetoric of sheer enmity. Kleist's moves might even take down the war machines installed by Schmitt, who separates out, he thinks, war from crime and murder—dropping out homicide and genocide. Literature begs to differ. From Antigone, who got backed into a cave, to Ahab or to Acker's *Pussy King of the Pirates* and Padilla's *Shadow without a Name,* literature sets up the enemy as a deeply disturbing structural condition, rarely conceding the enemy as a surpassable moment in civic identity and other provisional offshoots of enmity. I am preparing to make a hostile move and let literature start a rumble with philosophy.

Philosophy, for its part, shows up and tries to cordon things off, keep them clean, manageable. The enemy is parachuted in mostly in order to ensure state boundaries. Sucking up to state power, philosophy—I should say, mostly metaphysics—holds the enemy in strict custody. In Plato's *Republic,* philosophy endeavors to protect the purity of the distinction between *stasis* and *polemos.* The purity of *polemos* or the enemy remains unattainable, however: no politics has ever been adequate to its concept. I'm of course more interested in the scrambling device or the torsion that makes it difficult to tell who the friend and the enemy are. In Schmitt, politics prescribes that you know who the friend and the enemy are, and that you be equipped to know how to identify them. Even if war and politics have no essence, are not determined by a ruling *eidos*—and we do not know how to pin down the essential whatness of war or politics or hatred or love—you have to know your enemy. But even in Schmitt, the enemy remains elusive, sometimes picked off as a foreigner, sometimes as a homegrown fellow citizen. For Schmitt, the figure of the enemy secures the condition of the political as such. Losing the enemy would mean losing the political. The fact that I can kill the other binds the mortal aspect of friendship and enmity to finitude: the other as mortal (friend or enemy) is exposed to being killed, possibly by me. The "real possibility of the enemy being killed" is crucial according to Schmitt, as it identifies politics as such. Thus losing the enemy doesn't at all guarantee peace, reconciliation, or any sort of progress report on the species, but depoliticizes and Mad Maxes out the whole territory of relations: losing the enemy risks unleashing unprecedented violence, creating the evil of a malice that knows neither measure nor ground, provoking the incommensurable release of monstrous forms of unreadable aggression. The enemy poses as a safe place for relation and nation building. Importantly, the antithesis of friendship for Schmitt in the political sphere is, however, not enmity but *hostility.* Political enmity should admit of no passion, no affect: the political enemy should not inevitably be inimical; he would not necessarily hold me in enmity. Pathological enmity laced with hostility voids the account: in this regard the U.S. has not known in recent times how to be or find the enemy.

Clearly, a lot more needs to be said on these matters and their distinct qualities—and the function of the keynote is to sound the motifs as well as the intervallic tonalities, even the lost causes, of a major theme. Let me inch toward a possible ethics of enmity, tying in what presses upon us today without relinquishing the responsibility that we share to the unrelenting demands of thought, no matter how difficult, distant, dispiriting, or untimely. We cannot allow ourselves to follow the way of regression, dulled by the ease of forgetfulness or mere thematic compliance. This is part of the ethical urgency that I wish to consider with you tonight. It has to do with the promise of epitaph, with the becoming-epitaph that is due to the enemy—a discourse that calls up the dead. I feel, I hear, I sense that we have received a summons to appear before a court of the dead.

There is the matter of the dead enemy that has been forgotten. In fact the title of my presentation should have been "The Dead Enemy" or "Loving the Dead . . . Enemy." If there has been any discussion at all about the way this nation treats the enemy it has been restricted to the captured, living enemy. I do not recall hearing one word about our relation to the dead enemy. How in fact can the dead be the enemy?—something that Schmitt does not consider: the invasive haunt of the enemy. I will proceed by way of Freud's exhortation to us under the title "Treating the Enemy," by which he means the dead enemy. Let me now relinquish my narcissistic pump to become your research assistant. The fortuitous juncture of the theme of enmity and our world historical distress, at this time, makes me sense the need to do the legwork for what I hope you will take on and relay, commit to thought. I quote Freud at length:

> We may be inclined to suppose that savage and half-savage races are guilty of uninhibited and ruthless cruelty towards their enemies. We shall be greatly interested to learn, then, that even in their case the killing of a man is governed by a number of observances which are included among the usages of taboo. These observances fall easily into four groups. They demand (1) the appeasement of the slain enemy, (2) restrictions upon the slayer, (3) acts of expiation and purification by him, and (4) certain ceremonial observances. . . .
>
> [I]n the island of Timor when a warlike expedition has returned in triumph bringing the heads of the vanquished foe . . . sacrifices are offered to appease the souls of the men whose heads have been taken. "The people think that some misfortune would befall the victor were such offerings omitted. Moreover, a part of the ceremony consists of a dance accompanied by song, in which the death of the slain man is lamented and his forgiveness is entreated. 'Be not angry,' they say, 'because your head is here with us; had we been less lucky, our heads might now have been exposed in your village. We have offered the sacrifice to appease you. Your spirit may now rest and leave us in peace. Why were you our enemy? Would it not have been better that we should remain friends? Then your blood would not have been spilt and your head would not have been cut off.'" . . .
>
> Other peoples have found a means for changing their former enemies after their death into guardians, friends, and benefactors. This method lies in treating their severed heads with affection, as some of the savage races of Borneo boast of doing. When the Sea Dyaks of Sarawak bring home a head from a successful head-hunting expedition, for months after its arrival it is treated with the greatest consideration and addressed with all the names of endearment of which their language is capable. The most dainty morsels of food are thrust into its mouth, delicacies of all kinds and even cigars. The head is repeatedly implored to hate its former friends and to love its new hosts since it has now become one of them. . . .
>
> In several of the savage tribes of North America observers have been struck by the mourning over enemies who have been killed and scalped. When a Choctaw had killed an enemy, he went into mourning for a month during

which he was subjected to severe restrictions; and the Dakotas had similar practices. When the Osages, reports a witness, have mourned over their own dead, "they will mourn for the foe just as if he was a friend." . . .

In Timor . . . the leader of the expedition is forbidden "to return to his own house. A special hut is prepared for him, in which he has to reside for two months, undergoing bodily and spiritual purification. During this time he may not go to his wife nor feed himself; the food must be put into his mouth by another person." . . . . In Logea, an island in the neighbourhood of New Guinea, "men who have killed or assisted in killing enemies shut themselves up for about a week in their houses. They must avoid all intercourse with their wives and friends, and they may not touch food with their hands. They may eat vegetable food only, which is brought to them cooked in special pots. The intention of these restrictions is to guard the men against the smell of the blood of the slain; for it is believed that if they smelt the blood they would fall ill and die." . . .

"Among the Natchez of North America young braves who had taken their first scalps were obliged to observe certain rules of abstinence for six months. They might not sleep with their wives nor eat flesh; their only food was fish and hasty-pudding. . . . When a Choctaw had killed an enemy and taken his scalp, he went into mourning for a month, during which he might not comb his hair, and if his head itched he might not scratch it except with a little stick which he wore fastened to his wrist for the purpose."[2]

According to Freud, "the conclusion that we must draw from all these obser-vances is that the impulses which they express towards an enemy are not solely hostile ones. They are also manifestations of remorse, of admiration for the enemy, and of a throbbing bad conscience for having killed him. It is difficult to resist the notion that, long before a table of laws was handed down by any god, these savages were in possession of a living commandment: 'Thou shalt not kill,' a violation of which would not go unpunished."[3]

• • •

I cannot *not* leave you with an allegorical trace, an instance of ethical enmity, most of which was fed, as said, to the shredder, for I feel compelled to read the remains, to replay the torment of an exemplary enmity. Please put on your al-legorical ears. I need to return to a historical and dominant scene of disastrous embrace—to the moment, still eternally returning, when Nietzsche stood up to the Christianized Wagner, boldly declared enmity, and tunneled through the refusal to mourn that characterizes so many instances of lived enmity. This is a clash of some consequence, pitting philosophy against art, and Nietzsche against himself, because Wagner was and remained, as he indicates, not merely indwelling—a part of him—but also a temptation and a drug, an unquittable desire, which is maybe why when he was irreversibly sinking Nietzsche played on his mother's piano the strains to *Tristan and Isolde* over and over and over again. I am going to fast-forward and link up the points that would gather up an ethics of enmity because, despite it all, Nietzsche, most untimely, most unseemly, most shrill and polite of them all, ranted out a quiet ethics, a low-voiced canon of attack.

The Nietzschean attack displays a peculiar learning curve. Attack for Nietzsche is more often than not an indication of gratitude. When Nietzsche takes on Wagner he loads up on gratitude. In fact, his attack is backed by thankfulness, which, in a sense, has forced his hand. Ever on Wagner's side, Nietzsche feels obligated to take him apart. This is part of the transferential duty. One's thankfulness goes to the ability to mourn—more or less, assuming "true" mourning to be possible. When letting go occurs or arrives or has happened without arriving, thanks are given to mark an almost historical ability to split off from a powerful, a once-necessary convergence of forces that held you to the tyranny of promise. It is important to climb into the think tank with him in order to have a sense of what Nietzsche is aiming for here, and how he orchestrates the offensive.

Nietzsche, most thankful and most ballistic of philosophers, obeys a restraining order. As unique and shattering as it was and in some ways continues to be, his assault on philosophy, of which he was the last stand, was raised traditionally, directed by a certain relation to truth-telling.

When attacking, Nietzsche sizes up the adversary to make sure that the enemy has more fire power, superior forces, than he himself can show for. He guns for wildly popular genealogical winners, the successful cultural looters: Wagner, Christianity, the Germans, and other shortlisted culprits, without end. He will not take on a loser, the destitute or minoritized nebbish. (By the way, when he threatened to shoot all anti-Semites Nietzsche was locked up.) In his writing, where he stands his ground, Nietzsche mostly attacks only those causes that are victorious. His statement: I attack only when I stand alone. He firms up the adversarial stance. Nietzsche does not go for the jugular of a person or human being, however—he does not go after aloneness or impoverishment, or even after the singularity of his opponents. He pounces where they begin to generalize and dominate, where they bloat up as an idea or harden as a cultural icon. In contrast to the sprawling tendencies of the other, Nietzsche refrains from rhetorically seducing or conscripting recruits to serve his cause, which remains unsupported by any generality or guaranteed backup. "I attack only when I stand alone" *and:* "I never attack persons." This sums up my Nietzschean code of ethics for attack.

Still, when he says, "I never attack persons," you may be inclined to suppose Wagner to be a person. Not so, not always or only so. He moves in on Wagner deliberately, preparing to rush a particular stage of history and its undocumented events. Nietzsche's several postscripts to the *Case of Wagner,* his conclusive inability to finish with finishing off Wagner, are meant to serve as reminders that, despite his abiding love for Wagner, he is bound by duty to attack *his case.* Nietzsche loved Wagner to death. The interlinguistic pun earns some surplus value as well: *der Fall Wagner* brings to mind that *casus* is related to falling, even to decadence. Nietzsche, who fell hard, loved Wagner—this point needs to be hammered home; he *had* to give him up ("To turn my back on Wagner was for me a fate. To like anything at all after that, a triumph").[4] Nietzsche loved Wagner, and that is what interests me: what led him to break the friendship of ten years was not intersubjective, but ethical. It was not a whim, a mood, an episode, a sense of harm, or an account of the other's wrongdoing or evil that instantiated the break and brought on the enmity—the parting almost had nothing to do with Mr. Richard Wagner, for what do we care about Herr Wagner and his messy little opinions, his tyrannical grammars? The parting shots were destined for something else and, in any event, boomeranged on poor Friedrich Nietzsche.

Interestingly, the charges that Nietzsche pressed against his teacher and friend have not been dropped or seriously refuted in the philosophical follow-ups that we have at our disposal. Heidegger retains Nietzsche's principal griefs against Wagner. This breach cannot be shortened to narrate only a private squabble but reaches beyond its apparent contingency to inflect the way we think about and live the relation to history and the future.

If he embraced and affirmed enmity, this is because Nietzsche knew friendship, he understood and nurtured it, articulated it, lived it, which is why his politics of *fiendship* is so poignant. Loving the enemy means that the case of Wagner did not come from or happen to someone for whom friendship was foreign or remote. Friendship was not a contingency for Nietzsche and his work, something that you could take or leave, blow off or restrict, like limiting the phone calls you make or deciding to go out only two evenings a week. The end was written into friendship as its ownmost possibility and its finite ground.

For Nietzsche enmity would be, and was, an engagement, a commitment—a vow that does not restrict itself to the acknowledgement of a fact but which firmly invokes a responsibility, submitting itself to the test of the eternal return. Another way of seeing this is that Nietzsche proceeds without benefit of

Christianity or a dialectical apparatus that would at once sublate and exalt the end. Dialectics reabsorbs what it separates and cuts; what it holds onto changes its character, accommodating the severance as part of its unfolding. Nietzsche stares the severance in the face, takes it straight, so to speak, without transforming Wagner into something more "tasteful" or dialectically assimilable, without redeeming him. Nietzsche, the great vomiter, can't even throw him up (the reverse of dialectics). The loss stays with him. The multiplication of texts around him tells us that Wagner is here to stay, if only as the pressure point of loss. Nietzsche cannot simply write off this loss but continues henceforth to count the losses ("Other musicians don't *count* compared to Wagner"). Driving him into his own abysses, Nietzsche somehow still holds on to Wagner. The friendship has to be surrendered on historical demand: only weakness and a flagging integrity would vote to keep it. Nietzsche recognized that friendship was not itself a stable substance but split into so many hetero- and homogeneities, occupied by a multitude of personae and subpersonalities, a gift that life offers, one that is dealt significant blows and revised itineraries by time.

In the case of his Wagner, friendship was often a mimetic hideaway for the philosopher who fancied himself a musical composer. If the temptation to merge hadn't been so great, Nietzsche would not have had to devise an enemy and install a fissuring machine to get himself out of the mess. Nietzsche stayed with the departed friend, hung on to him as he spun away. It was not easy to lose Wagner or to indulge the loss. It seems that the circuitry of mourning as we have studied it since and thanks to Freud is interrupted by the cancelled friendship. Nietzsche had a hand in calling Wagner off and everywhere suggests that he has lost the rights to the melancholic sheltering by which he guarded the other one whom he kept close, his father's phantom (sometimes he hallucinated his father crouching behind him as he wrote). Calling off the friendship, graduating early (or too late) from the apprenticeship, Nietzsche creates the disturbingly arid circumstances of the other's deathless death, which inhibits friendly or stark phantomizations and introduces another site on the fringe of mourning, where one is called upon to liquidate the transference. (What I had to wipe out here is a different topology of mourning that enmity implies and that would have returned us directly to the site of the dead enemy.) Dissolving the Wagner account while maintaining the debt, Nietzsche embarks on what Goethe famously called, with regard to the suffering Werther, "a long insomnia." The enemy belongs to a transferential apparatus, keeps you awake at night. (Our leaders emphasize nowadays that they haven't lost a wink of sleep—it's a compulsive wink, a wink of disavowal, denying loss: I haven't lost anything, not even a night of sleep, they repeat.) Nietzsche—he, for his part, stays up together with Werther, you, and me: it's the long insomnia, says Goethe.

When enmity supplants friendship mourning takes another turn, mourning invades differently, according to another law, in this case, as when Nietzsche takes a prisoner, detaining him indefinitely. No reality testing controls the sensibility of one who has had to call off the friendship. The lost friend still travels the surface of a world that is meant to wound or trouble the decision that continues to be negotiated in some back room of last hope, even where the decision to shed the already introjected image has been announced and partially enacted. The writing on internal walls indicates that an alternate history always threatens to break through, weaken the resolve, or force a recount. The friendship taken off the agenda, Nietzsche refines the experience of enmity. With Wagner he made it a clean break to the extent that it can never be done with but compels residue and return. It is a clean break only in the transvaluated sense: Nietzsche is not so naïve as to think that he could walk away under the protection of erasure. Keeping the break clean means staying in touch with the history and pain from which you've bolted, particularly where it outlives your own particularity. It means that something vital goes down with the other and will return to bite our collective asses.

• • •

Ronell delivered this keynote address at NYU's Conference on the Enemy, in May 2003. All notes have been added by the editor.

1. Jacques Derrida, *The Politics of Friendship* (trans. George Collins, London and New York: Verso, 1997).

2. Sigmund Freud, *Totem and Taboo* (trans. James Strachey, Standard Edition, New York and London: Norton, 1950), 46–52. In each case, Freud is citing J. G. Frazer's four-volume *Totemism and Exogamy*.

3. Ibid., 49.

4. Friedrich Nietzsche, *The Case of Wagner* in *The Birth of Tragedy, and The Case of Wagner* (trans. Walter Kaufmann, New York: Vintage Books, 1967), 155.

Part Five

The Fading Empire of Cognition

Q. Stupidity *traces the question or problem of a kind of transcendental stupidity. Would you tell us a bit about this project?*

A. It was Deleuze who named the future necessity of reading stupidity, and a transcendental stupidity, asking, What are the conditions for the possibility of stupidity? He said that philosophy hasn't been able to think stupidity. First of all, because philosophy has been hijacked by epistemological considerations of error; error has derailed the thought of stupidity. As he says, literature has always brought the question of stupidity to the door of philosophy, who slammed that door shut, finding the "theme" (it is a paraconcept) somehow unworthy. Deleuze suggests that philosophy is haunted by stupidity, which, nonetheless, it won't consider. There is something about stupidity that is violently resisted by philosophy. That is where I come in: where something has been marginalized, minoritized, evicted, persecuted, left out of the picture, and of course *feminized.* Certainly, an impetus for reading stupidity is promoted by a kind of post-feminist passion, protesting the way women have been called "stupid bitches" and noting what this indictment might involve, how stupidity became an accusatory force, a devastating demolition of the other. Minorities are considered stupid, women are considered stupid, and so forth. . . . . Stupidity is a very slippery signifier and often turns into its other. It is not the opposing other of thought; it is sometimes, literally, the figure of sheer reflection, proffering something like pure thought. But what interested me above all was located in the poetic act, the passivity of the poet in the extreme inclination toward surrender, the near stupor that characterizes the poetic disposition—the structure of exposure, something that poetry knows about, the extreme and secret experiences of stupidity. In this work, what I am doing, essentially, is appealing to the debilitated subject, the stupid idiot—the puerile, slow-burn destruction of ethical being, which, to my mind, can never be grounded in certitude or education or prescriptive *obéissance*. There is something about placing the question of responsibility close to the extinction of consciousness that interests me. Against the background of the ethical anxiety that has been expressed in recent years, my question tries to invoke a parallel track that is thematized in so many ways, reverting to the platitudes of dumbing down, the dumb and dumber and dumbest. What does a generalized dimwittedness, a diminished sensibility, imply for ethics?

In addition to addressing this kind of transcendental stupidity, which, of course, one needs to ponder and reflect on, I also consider other questions: for instance, Who are the secret beneficiaries of stupidity's hegemony? and, What are the somatizations that occur in stupidity? For Marx, for instance, stupidity is third in terms of what determines historical world power. In other words, the world is motored by economy, violence, and then stupidity. . . . I am also very interested in the idiot body and in our relation to our bodies when they are ill, when they collapse. How do we heal them? What do we know? Why is it that the scanners, charts, and medicalizations of the body tend to disappoint us? The rapport to the body is already something mechanical and stupid. I focus on the monthly period, which is a kind of "stupid" repetition to which women are routinely subjected.

From "Confessions of an Anacoluthon" (261–62).

Slow Learner

"Life is tough,
  but it's tougher
  when you're stupid."
—John Wayne

The temptation is to wage war on stupidity as if it were a vanquishable object—as if we still knew how to wage war or circumscribe an object in a manner that would be productive of meaning or give rise to futurity. One could not easily imagine circumstances in which an agency of state or government, even a U.S. government, would declare war on stupidity in the manner it has engaged a large-scale war on drugs. Though part of a politically suspect roundup, the presumed object of the drug wars offered a hint, at least, of materiality. Stupidity exceeds and undercuts materiality, runs loose, wins a few rounds, recedes, gets carried home in the clutch of denial—and returns. Essentially linked to the inexhaustible, stupidity is also that which fatigues knowledge and wears down history. From Schiller's exasperated concession that even the gods cannot combat stupidity, to Hannah Arendt's frustrated effort, in a letter to Karl Jaspers, to determine the exact status and level of Adolf Eichmann's *Dummheit,* to current psychoanalytical descriptions of the dumb interiors of the despotic mind (heir to the idiot-king of which Lacan has written), stupidity has evinced a mute resistance to political urgency, an instance of an unaccountable ethical hiatus.[1] In fact, stupidity, purveyor of self-assured assertiveness, mutes just about everything that would seek to disturb its impervious hierarchies.

Neither a pathology nor an index as such of moral default, stupidity is nonetheless linked to the most dangerous failures of human endeavor. I hesitate to say here what stupidity is because, eluding descriptive analysis, it switches and regroups, turns around and even fascinates, as it fascinated Flaubert's Saint Antoine.[2] While stupidity is "what is there," it cannot be simply located or evenly scored. Not since Nietzsche pulled the switch and got the powerful forces of alternative valences going. Typically for the genealogist, stupidity, in the end, is extolled for promoting life and growth. To the extent that morality teaches hatred of too great a freedom, it implants the need for limited horizons and immediate tasks, teaching the narrowing of perspectives "and thus in a certain sense stupidity, as a condition of life and growth." Not without consequence, Nietzsche distributes the tyranny and discipline of stupidity equally among slave morality, Christian values, and scholarship. Narrowing perspective and limiting freedom, these forces of historical moment—tyrannical and arbitrary in the way they have regulated human affairs—are viewed by Nietzsche as instances of "this rigorous and grandiose stupidity [that] has educated the spirit." Stupidity, in Nietzsche's estimation, does not lack rigor but, on the contrary, is responsible for discipline and breeding, for education ("the indispensable means for spiritual discipline and breeding").[3] Benevolent and disdainful at once, Nietzsche reserves a place for stupidity that, after all is said and done, puts it on the side of life, of discipline and education. However devalued and Christian, grandiose or enslaved, stupidity belongs among the powerfully determining forces with which it enjoys shared custody of our destiny.

Because it generates so many startling contradictions, stupidity, for philosophy or for the end of philosophy, acquires a status that needs to be claimed, if not entirely understood. What does stupidity have to do with thought or the affiliated branches of knowledge or scholarship? Where does it belong on the map of dogmatic philosophy, which continues to divide the territories of thought into empirical and transcendental sectors? Nietzsche does not say where to locate it, how to read it, or whether or not stupidity properly belongs where philosophy reigns. Raising it, he more or less forgets stupidity, like an umbrella. But then he remembers; it comes back to him when he affirms the protective values of deception and self-doubting: "One of the subtlest ways of deceiving, for as long as possible, at any rate of successfully posing as more stupid than one is—which in everyday life is often as desirable as an umbrella—is called enthusiasm."[4] Part of the grammar of shrewd behavior, connected to the everyday and self-protecting, stupidity opens up against the sky, receiving or bouncing off itself the intrusive rains of transcendence. Implied by enthusiasm, it allows one to have a nice everyday day—on the surface of things. In any case, stupidity now belongs to the famous repertoire of Nietzschean poses, to the domain of fictions and will to power.

I am going to defer the matter of situating stupidity since, anyway, everyone else at some level of understanding has situated and filed a report on it, which is to say, for the most part, let it go.[5] Whether abandoned or put to work, its fate was the same: the case was closed on stupidity, as if either way it had been adequately dealt with. At this point in its career, hesitation and deferral seem to be the most dispassionate ways to approach stupidity. The more we defer it, the more the knowledge we think we have about knowledge weakens (as long as I don't *know* what stupidity is, what I know about knowing remains uncertain, even forbidding). All we know at this juncture is that stupidity does not allow itself to be opposed to knowledge in any simple way, nor is it the other of thought. It does not stand in the way of wisdom, for the disguise of the wise is to avow unknowing. At this time I can say only that the question of stupidity is not satisfied with the discovery of the negative limit of knowledge; it consists, rather, in the absence of a relation to knowing. In a Nietzschean sense, this absence of relation (which is also a relation, Blanchot's "rapport sans rapport") invites at least two different types of evaluation that, inexhaustible and contradictory, can be seen in terms derived from war. There are those who seek to wage war on stupidity or feel attacked and besieged by it, and—assuming there exists an alternative to war, a space in which the combat zone is neutralized, turned into a lawn or a beach, no sharks, no holes in the ozone—there would be the other of war, the peculiar experience of an exorbitant peace treaty, a kind of relinquishment that resolves itself into passivity.

We go first to the poets, and then to war.

It would be comforting, no doubt, to suppose that these destinations present two different beats, following Hölderlin's suggestion that poetry indicates the most innocent of exertions. But we have been taught early on, by Homer and by Hölderlin himself, that going to the poet often involves going to war. Whether reading polemological maps, devising strategies of attack or retreat, surveilling a hostile territory, practicing poses of surrender, or getting iced by a particular turn of phrase or wind, the poetic and war efforts appear often to overlap.

What links the two efforts in terms of syntax of doing or a shared rhetorical energy involves, above all, the issues of surrender and retreat, modalities of being that yield to necessary attenuation—a humbling bow to finitude, a humbling, we could say, that implies courage as it confronts the narrowing recession of limits. The war cry enfolds the poetic solitude of the *schreiben/Schrei* (inscribing/cry)—the energy of historical inscription that dissolves into combat fatigue, into sheer stupefaction, effecting a brush with urgent nullity. The poets know from stupidity, the essential dulling or weakening that forms the precondition of utterance. This is perhaps why Hölderlin's poems "Dichtermut" and "Blödigkeit"—fated to link the trope of courage with that of stupefaction, the crucial dull-mindedness of the poet—co-emerged, one giving birth to the other.[6]

"Dichtermut" (the poet's courage) has been widely considered the blueprint for the poem on which my discussion centers. It is bound by a mysterious contract to what Hölderlin calls "Blödigkeit." Yet however enigmatic may be the connection asserted in these poems between poetic valor and sheer intimidation of mind—a facet of stupidity—the disturbing drift of the poems, each an anamorph of the other, is in fact not unique to Hölderlin. The severest of poets ventured, as if prompted by some transcendental obligation, into a consecrated domain where language meets its unmaking in stupidity, idiocy, imbecility, and other cognates of nonknowing. One poet's highly contested encounter with idiocy, the perplexingly sustained thought where utterance is reduced to repetitive hoots and stammers, will especially concern us, though Wordsworth need not have been the only poet with whom to hold a conversation on the recession of being, the nothingness to which poetry is responsible. There could have been—there is—Rilke's "Lied des Idioten" (Song of the Idiot), where nothing happens ("Wie gut. / Es kann nichts geschehn." [How good. / Nothing can happen.]) or Hart Crane's "The Idiot" or Richard Wright's haiku #579 that asserts "the idiot boy / Has dignity." There are moreover—"at the black earth, at the earth mute"—"The Idiots" of Joseph Conrad, "who are forgotten by time, and live untouched by years till death gathers them."[7] And signals from elsewhere still, some of which we pick up—for instance, those from the pages of a massively conceived struggle between idiocy and stupidity in the work of Dostoevsky, where a citational war front erupts between Flaubert and Gogol. The failure of cognition is the province of literary language, though it is difficult to speak of failure where nothing has been promised, tested, or essayed; yet, poetic language remains sheer promise and, in the way shown by Hölderlin, capable of hearing the alien unsaid.

We can no longer say in Heideggerian tonalities that when Nietzsche fought with Wagner (or so-and-so said this or that) it was a historial event. Yet we can still intimate the gravity of an emergence, no matter how complicated, when Hölderlin welds "Blödigkeit" to "Dichtermut." Relinquishing the codified mythemes of heroic poses, "Blödigkeit" finally divulges the blunted, bludgeoned being of the poet that goes to meet its task, stands up to its calling. To all appearances a deflation, this is another flex of muscle, an internal restraining order holding back the values associated with the intelligence of doing, the bright grasp of what is there. Poetic courage consists in embracing the terrible lassitude of mind's enfeeblement, the ability to endure the near facticity of feeblemindedness. The readings and translations that have accrued to Hölderlin's ode "Blödigkeit" have tended to efface the embarrassing openness with which the poet names stupidity, even if it could be recuperated as Hölderlin's way of transposing for modernity Pindarian awe, the Greek sense of being awe- and dumbstruck. In Walter Benjamin's exalted reading, which Gershom Scholem judged "too metaphysical" and Benjamin himself left unpublished, the disturbing moment in the semantic chain is elided so that Benjamin can claim without undue heuristic anxiety that "Blödigkeit" represents the overcoming of "Dichtermut."[8] Still, the power of the unread title has a hold on his commentary, which practices a syntax of extraordinary subordination, a cultivation of the passive voice "to a degree unheard of even in bad academic writing."[9] This mortification, this utter exhaustion of the passive enacts the reading that Benjamin and others have avoided, which could be called the dispossession that entitles as it enfeebles the writer, disengaging and defaulting the knowing subject who enters into contact with the poetic word. The passive voice registers a secret agreement with the title of an inexplicable passivity it has sought to elude.

The tradition of diverting the title from its disturbing implications has been honored recently by Bart Philipsen, Michael Jennings, and Stanley Corngold, who give grounds for valorizing the term *timidity* (in one of his translations, Michael Hamburger opts for "diffidence.")[10] Corngold, to his credit, pauses over the decision, noting that "Benjamin does not pay equal attention to the troublesome word *Blödigkeit,* which while unquestionably meaning 'timidity,' also, like *Blödheit,* suggests short-sightedness and, in certain contexts, stupidity. Even if this unsavory connotation is set aside, there is still the relativizing effect that this title exercises on the full poetic affirmation that Benjamin finds in the poem."[11] Eventually the poem must overcome dialectically its title, which then dives out of sight. We should not be surprised to note that such a maneuver, which sets aside the unsavory trace of stupidity, even when named by Hölderlin as an essential mark of poetic existence, replicates an entire series of gestures performed by critics and philosophers who are invested in making recognizably sanctioned sense of the poet's claims.[12]

The need for redirecting or forgetting stupidity's course is not hard to decipher because, beyond its unsavory aspect, stupidity, as Musil has demonstrated exhaustively, at least initially produces itself when approached. We could say with Hölderlin that it is in the nature of stupidity to stump—to enfeeble and intimidate—but also to release. In this regard, "Blödigkeit" cannot be seen as opposable to "Dichtermut" but as decisively inflecting the reading of poetic courage, perhaps offering another way of naming the sacred task to which the poet has been assigned. Bringing forth stupidity as a crucial poetic sign, Hölderlin continues to receive his orders from Rousseau, whose reliance on "simplicity" and "lethargy" as an exemplary "self-forgetting that opens the self to another sort of being" he bears out.[13] The special resonance of *Blödigkeit* as that which encourages releasement is thus linked to Rousseau, for whom sloth (*paresse*) "and even a certain 'stupidity' are the preconditions of a rapport with being."[14]

The poetic bearing is staked in Hölderlin's revisions. An exhortation, the poem, much like "Dichtermut," invites the poetic spirit to venture out into time and world, to let itself be held "at the turning of time" by the god of heaven. Even those who pass away in their sleep are "Drawn erect on golden / Leading strings, like children." Whereas the poem stating the poet's courage begins, "Are not all the living related to you?" the later version, "Blödigkeit," opens by asking, "Are not many of the living known [or, rather, "familiar" (*bekannt*)] to you?"[15] A question of relation or proximity and knowledge, the initiatory call situates the poetic disposition with regard to the living. The poet—or, more exactly, the poem—is subordinated to the passage of time. Subdued by that which has a leash on his child spirit, the poet is restrained by golden strings. The restraining order of "Blödigkeit," resolves Benjamin, has become the authentic disposition of the poet ("die eigentliche Haltung des Dichters").[16] The poet's bearing places him in the midst of life, among the living. But this emplacement denucleates the poet, who has nothing left, no core, no boundary other than formless being, utter passivity ("das reglose Dasein, die völlige Passivität" [2(1): 125]). Such self-emptying, according to Benjamin, is the essence of courage: being capable of complete surrender. "Capable" perhaps continues to hold onto an element of cognition. The poet yields entirely, giving in to sheer relatedness ("als sich ganz hinzugeben der Beziehung" [2(1): 125]). Relatedness begins and ends with the poet—or, rather, the poem. For in this extreme inclination of surrender, the poet and poem are no longer separate ("Dichter und Gesang sind im Kosmos des Gedichts nicht unterschieden" [2(1): 125]). The poet (poem) is nothing more than the boundary set against life, pure indifference, the untouchable center of all relations. The poet is not a figure but the principle of figuration. Coming out from under "Blödigkeit," the poet is a suspension, a caesura, a dead and dumb center without a core. Poetic courage consists in taking the step toward this exposition, that of pure exposure ("only step / Naked into life" [1:22]).

If the poet needs to be coaxed in the direction of the living and is shown to be tempted by temporality to the extent that it ensures passage and passing, this in part is due to the fact that the inaugural recession marked by the poem as it exhorts, invites, pushes toward the living, begins in nonlife. The extreme passivity, the near stupor characteristic of the poetic disposition, situates it dangerously close to the side of depletion and even death, which is why the poet has to be roused and jump-started with the deceptive promise: "Then just wander forth defenseless / Through life and have no care!" ("Timidity" 1:22).[17] Poetic spirit is invited to enter life without defense or care, nakedly, to a warlike beat, following an order issued from another topos of self: *Drum!* In the second version, the poet, split in two, self-addresses the spirit or genius (*Genius*) who subsists in *Blödigkeit*. The poet ventures forth undefended, brave, like Wordsworth's Idiot Boy, whose adventure takes him through an unnarratable safety zone where, inexplicably immunized and protected, he has encountered the greatest danger.

The gesture of traversing peril and running a risk—a risk that does not know and cannot tell where it's going—points in these poems not to a morph of the action hero, quick and present to the task, sure of aim, but to the depleted being, held back by fear or indifference (we are never sure which), a being from the start stupefied, nonpresent—"not all there." No one has been able to account for that which is missing, not there, in poetic origination, but the poets have in their way avowed the secret experience of stupidity, the innate experience of writing (henceforth not simply innate since stupidity names a structure of exposure), and have left it concealed in the open space of a title, a mantelpiece, like a purloined letter. When Rilke titled his poem "Das Lied des Idioten," he made the uncomfortable particular of idiocy a matter of poeticity, as if each song, each poem were the song of an idiot, in this case one signed by Rilke, who sang "The Song of the Idiot." What has been blithely called the poetic act is retracted, drained. The idiot does not act in a recognizably willful way: stifled and disfigured, he forecasts inaudible acts of sheer, mute poeticity.

Of course, literature has found other ways of divulging its secret without necessarily headlining idiot relations and stupid remainders. Henry James, writer of secrecy, has a good deal to say about stupidity but even more about intelligence. In an essay on Maurice Blanchot and James, Pierre Alferi writes of the incommunicable secret of intelligence in the novels of James and, in particular, of the figure of the idiot Gilbert Long, in *The Sacred Fount,* whose unexplained surge of intelligence lays everyone to waste.[18] There is a kind of hydraulic system at work here, for Long receives only to the degree that May Server is completely drained of intelligence, leaving the shell of a zombie where she once flourished. Stupidity vampirizes; it can zap your girlfriend, finish off your lover, blunt your teacher. "He was stupid, in fact, and in that character had no business at Newmarch; but he had also, no doubt, his system, which he applied without discernment."[19] In James, sovereign intelligence serves to promote life. A supreme form of life, it quickens the beat of temporality and, when socially converted, accelerates time, permanently metamorphosing wit and repartee, improvising rhythmically on the infinite conversation. Intelligence, quick and alert, ever productive of acts of presence and associated with presence of mind, does not, in James's work, allow itself to be confounded with presence. By virtue of the theme and performance of subtlety, intelligence presents itself in the modality of a particular absence, that of reserve. Even as it accelerates the collective critical sensibility, reserve puts on the brakes. Avoiding revelation, it punctuates texts in which occur events whose causes cannot be known. Reserve holds up the other side of nonknowing, simulating a sense of depth or reticence. Stupidity, on the other hand, tends to sever with the illusion of depth and the marked withdrawal, staying with the shallow imprint. Unreserved, stupidity exposes while intelligence hides.

If stupidity were that simple—if stupidity were that stupid—it would not have traded depths for the pits and acted as such a terror for Roland Barthes or Robert Musil or preschoolers. (The little ones receive their first interdictory instruction when told that they mustn't call anyone "stupid"—the ur-curse, the renunciation of which primes socialization in this culture.) It is not always at odds with intelligence but can operate a purposeful exchange with its traits, as in the case of Gilbert Long or of any number of high scorers on the standardized tests of social communion. Intelligence itself depends on a withholding pattern that in some cases matches the irremediable reluctance of the stupid. For its part, stupidity can body-snatch intelligence, disguise itself, or, indeed, participate in the formation of certain types of intelligence with which it tends to be confused. For the writer, the problem of stupidity occupies a place of deliberate latency; ever on the prowl for your moment of greatest vulnerability, it prepares another sneak attack. Unless you really know what you're doing—and then it's in your face, all over you, in fact, showing no pity. It seizes your autobiographical effort, taking the place of your "I," henceforth enfeebled, dominated by shame. Thus Barthes, delicate and watchful, writes of himself when he's on himself in the third person: "It is curious that an author, having to speak about himself, is so obsessed by Stupidity, as though it were the inner thing he most feared: threatening, ever ready to burst out, to assert its right to speak (why shouldn't I have the right to be stupid?); in short, *The Thing*." Attempting to exorcise it, Barthes, in his Lacanian phase of dreading the Thing, plays the fool: "He puts himself inside it. . . . In a sense this whole little book, in a devious and naive way, plays with stupidity—not the stupidity of others (that would be too easy), but that of the subject *who is about to write*. What first comes to mind is stupid."[20] If Barthes puts himself in the third person, then stupidity is the first person, what happens first, what has happened agelessly, at the time, which is all the time, when the subject is about to write, endeavoring symbolically to repair the lesion induced by the Thing.

Stupidity is so radically, pervasively inside ("threatening to burst out," Barthes "puts himself inside it"), that it is prior to the formation of the subject. Flaubert, the other subject ever about to write, recognized writing as "l'acte pur de bêtise," arguing that writing was always an immersion in stupidity. So what's new? We suffer from only one thing, Flaubert has decisively asserted, *la bêtise*—an insight and experience that Barthes repeats and repeats.[21] Stupidity, the indelible tag of modernity, is our symptom. Marking an original humiliation of the subject, stupidity resolves into the low-energy, everyday life trauma with which we live. It throws us. Following Barthes, it functions as the Thing to the extent that it wards off the symbolization that it also demands. Like life itself, stupidity, according to Flaubert, cannot be summed up or properly understood but resembles a natural object—a stone or a mountain. One cannot understand a stone or a mountain, or offer a critique or a twelve-step program to change their descriptions.[22]

Of the ending of *Candide*, Flaubert remarks: "That tranquil conclusion, stupidity 'like life itself' is for me the striking proof of Voltaire's genius. Neither melodrama not synthesis, neither tragedy nor success, the ending is calm and even mediocre. Tailing off, explicitly rejecting reflections on the final state of affairs, it asserts its own reality and stops there, 'stupid like life itself.'"[23] What kind of a life is this? It is life neither assessed by the delicate instruments of evaluation monitored by Nietzsche or James, equal to measuring the forces of vitality and future, nor simply a life force that Nietzsche would shake off as decadent. Positioned as caesura—the hesitation between life viewed as vitality or descent—it pinpoints stupidity as a foreign body that can be neither fully repelled nor successfully assimilated. Flaubert explores stupidity as a gratuitous if inerasable inscription that tags our bodies and is scratched on memorializing monuments. His striking example, recounted in his letters, of the superficiality and shallowness, the surface scripture of stupidity's Etch A Sketch tracings, involves the stubborn ubiquity of graffiti. Subway graffiti is (or was) one thing. Signing a subway surface does not operate the sublime in the same way as would the alien signature on an ancient monument. Flaubert's trip to the Orient was nearly derailed by this other experience of graffiti. What could be more stupid than the *bêtise sublime* of carving one's name in huge letters on Pompey's column? "The name itself—'Thompson'—is quite meaningless," writes Culler, "yet it stares one imperiously in the face, looms before one as a surface which one does not know how to deal with."[24] Flaubert complains: "It can be read a quarter of a league away. There is no way to see the column without seeing the name 'Thompson' and consequently without thinking of Thompson."[25] Well, how stupid is that? This Thompson fellow got Gustave Flaubert to think of him and to re-immortalize the name by pasting it onto his columns. "This idiot has become part of the monument and perpetuates himself with it?" (2:243), the monumental Flaubert writes. Flaubert sizes up the situation: "Not only that, he overwhelms it by the magnificence of his gigantic letters" (2:243). The industrial-size signature attests to the "serenity" of stupidity. Uninhibited by the grandeur of the desecration, Thompson, another kind of orientalist, changed the nature of the column: signed and delivered a blow by the history of vandalism, the violence of appropriation—delivered, that is, to history—it has now become a monument to stupidity.

The story calcifies. Flaubert himself is medused and petrified: he turns stupidity into stone ("Elle est de la nature du granit, dure et résistante" [2:243]). Stupidity has supplanted the monolith. In keeping with Flaubert's excremental politics (in his works and letters, beginning with the "Éloge de la constipation," he was alert to such bodily functions), "Thompson" is seen to have left a huge turd where a monument once stood. As remainder and hieroglyph, "Thompson" has left the column behind, transfigured, resistant, suffering only this sign of its defeat by stupidity. Parasitizing the Egyptians, this self-magnifying Thompson signs up the ageless monument for his own little tourist's sense of time and place and manages still, if inadvertently, to hitch a ride with the corpses of the pharoahs. It is not only that this Thompson nobody, bloated and self-important, felt that his name deserved to be brandished, mummified, sculpted upon the unreadable meaning of the column but that the gigantic lettering imposes itself with certitude, an early John Hancock of righteous insistence. In his letter of June 26, 1852, Flaubert was to write: "l'on meurt presque toujours dans l'incertitude de son propre nom, à moins d'être un sot" (1:442). Unless one is a complete jerk, one leaves this earth insecure over one's name: one remains stupid about its destination. Thompson, his name was secured 4–ever.

Now the story of Thompson's signature, of what happened when Mr. Thompson, on that day, passed into perpetuity, cannot be restricted in range or significance to the status of example or anecdote, a parable in which the column would be left standing. In a rigorous sense, Thompson did pull the column from a context it might have enjoyed without his appropriative signature. It is as though the signing, a synecdoche of stupidity, defacing the memorial, had unstoppable consequences. Henceforth the monument essentially attributes stupidity and, for Flaubert at least, will have always been its attribute: Thompson has effected a substantiation of the attribute, for there is no stupidity without monument. Flagging the ancient monument, he answered a call that was not put out. The naïve and insolent arrogance that consists in responding where no response is invited is an effect of monumental arrogance. Derrida writes parenthetically, as if to counterbalance the offending gesture with discretion: "(and for Flaubert, stupidity is always monumental, equal in size to a stone monument covered with inscriptions)."[26]

Acts of responding where no response is called for, whether by carving huge childlike letters into an Alexandrian column or, in the same neighborhood, answering the call of God as if you were the one being summoned (Kafka's

Abraham)—these are reflexes of stupidity. In such instances, responding to a call that was not made—but how, precisely, can we *know?*—demarcates in Flaubert the action zone of stupidity, announcing a type of disaffirming intervention. It consists of that which is uncalled for, the performance of a colossal blunder. This is where Kafka comes in, for he explores with relentless precision the predicament of the one who thinks the call was meant for him. Abraham, primal father, turns into a kind of Thompson who has imposed his name in an act of monumental error. Recalling Dostoevsky's treatment of a crucial facet of Christ, Kafka turns the figure of Abraham toward its ridiculous origins, one name on the pillar commemorating a shared past. These unforgettable names, associated with the greatest acts of submission and returning untraceable calls, have muscled their way into our historical memory. In the hands of Dostoevsky and Kafka, followers of Christ and Abraham become what Erasmus called "foolosophers."[27]

Anyone coming up against the pervasive power of stupidity risks being turned into a foolosopher; even, we think, the thinker's poet, the formidable *Dichter des Denkers,* Hölderlin, succumbed to such thoroughgoing abasement. Indeed, nearly anyone who has become fatefully entangled with the nonthought or paraconcept of quasi transcendental of the ur-signifier Stupidity has had to invent apotropaic rituals in order to hold off the megadeath promised by the unseizable term. Dangerous and obscene, ridiculous, laughable, attribute of power and monument, accomplice to abuse and cruelty, the pride of humiliation, stupidity is the name that spells out the ruination of any monument, just as the monument was ruined for Flaubert by "Thompson," where the name mourns the thing. In this version of the crumble, the temple was not destroyed by Sampson or even by the winds of God's wrath but by the stain of stupidity, the excremental trace imperturbably bequeathed to eternity. The monument falls to pieces under the weight of that stain. Flaubert concludes the unconcludable episode: "Stupidity is something unshakeable. Nothing attacks it without breaking itself against it. It is of the nature of granite, hard and resistant."[28]

The danger at hand, stated and restated by the texts under consideration, appears to consist in the fear of breaking apart, raising the threat of pulverization that befalls those who would attack the mighty forces of stupidity. This is why Barthes calls stupidity the Thing—the core recalcitration against which any writing breaks open. The Thing does not pull *Dasein* together but confronts it with the fear and fantasy of morcellation. Before its looming aggression even the toughest cookies crumble.

Strangely enough, in many of the texts devoted to the installation of the semantic chain generating stupidity, idiocy, imbecility, puerility, the ridiculous, and so on, there appears at the head of the line of fire the almost requisite figure of a German—the inexorable buffo of the whole dossier. Associated with study and strain, the German gets the lowest grades, earning the highest visibility in the world-historical chronicle of stupidity. Naturally, I will not fail to track this phenomenal deformation of spirit. After all, the work *Dummkopf* needs no subtitle. Flaubert, for instance, presses into literary service a German mathematician—the emblem of serious intellectual effort. In the first *Education sentimentale* we find "Shahutsnischbach . . . [who] was always working at mathematics, mathematics were consuming his life, he understood nothing about them. Never had M. Renaud had a more studious or stupid young man."[29]

And so we go to war.

Extreme yet ordinary, the forces of stupidity press forward a mirage of aggression, a front without limits. As part of his body of early works entitled *Rhapsodies,* the German Romantic writer Jean Paul wrote "Von der Dumheit," a short article that belongs thematically to the context decisively marked by Friedrich Schlegel's essay on unintelligibility but is inspired directly by the works of Pope and Erasmus.[30] This particular piece justifies its necessity by stating that the greatest minds have touched on the problem of stupidity, but they have done so in infuriatingly soft tones. Jean Paul's task, as he sees it, is to proceed brutally and take down stupidity's empire. The righteous tone that he strikes is justified by the claim that the stupid have been conducting covert operations to smash the forces of the smart. He declares war on them. While the situation is diagnosed by Jean Paul as one of war, the sides that are drawn up do not appear to be entirely stable. Nevertheless, taking aim, the author generates politicized battles around a rhetoric of warfare according to which the stupid are isolated as indefensible. If they take no prisoners, they take some pleasure. We are shown that the dummkopf's pleasure consists in attacking enlightened minds.[31] These attack-happy imbeciles pose a problem because greatness has been toppled not by greatness but by intellectual dwarfs. Such creatures, who never stand alone, move in group formation, stimulating one another to wage war against those who are smart.[32] Gathered into an insipid group, the stupid, a band of thugs, begin to resemble the armies of *ressentiment* raised later on by Nietzsche. The noble or the smart ones—the strong who turn out to be the most vulnerable—are felled by what amounts to the incessant mosquito-biting binges of the stupid.[33] Greatness should not scorn stupidity, writes Jean Paul, because although stupidity does not deploy the strength of elephants, like termites it secretly eats through the throne of loftiness until it crashes and crumbles. Was Olavides crushed by a second Olavides? No, by the Holy Inquisition.

Stupidity is an engagement, a condition of war to which those who are not stupid turn a blind eye: they fail to see the devastation wrought by the blind pilots of the stupid revolution, a permanent revolution. Interestingly, stupidity acquires definition in Jean Paul's work owing to its reactionary cast. It has been from the start a political problem hailing from Father. Incapable of renewal or overcoming, the stupid subject has low Oedipal energy: he has held onto the ideas, the relics and dogmas transmitted in his youth by his father. Unwilling to have surpassed and suppressed the father, the stupid one stays on the side of death: his head, limited and dead, reflects a heart equally dead, small.[34] Those who are allied with stupidity—that is, with the father, according to Jean Paul—fight with patriotic fervor for preserving the inherited legacy of their forefathers, deploying all possible weapons of malice and stupidity to ward off the enemies of ancestral rights. Thus every new discovery robs the stupid of their certainty, peace, and pride, destroying the edifice of their knowledge and arming (*wafnet*) with rage against the innovator. Their petty spirit is nourished by petty things, which means that large and great things threaten to defeat them. Jean Paul switches addresses to reach you: You may think you can destroy some spiderwebs of the past, but don't you know that there are certain beings that need and feed on these webs?

The dummkopf works only with the known. A mere adulator, a creature of mimesis, he has a passive, even dead, imagination. Everything gets handed down to him. Father has known best. Somehow alive even in death. Father continues to press down on you. Not a whimper of protest from you. Jean Paul thus identifies the gravity of stupidity as insipid reverence, as the submission of those who have not had to give up or separate from the father. In an acute sense Father lies buried in the imagination, which has been bowed by the burden of the dead. The dummkopf works with what is known because what is known, or what comes down to us as knowable, is already dead, DOA. He is himself dull, half-dead yet dangerous. Because the stupid dummy cannot grasp things vitally ("die Dinge nicht lebhaft sieht" [1:268]), he lacks understanding. Our insight into things depends upon the vitality and life upon which the basis of thinking is formed. The dead need to be thrown off our backs if understanding is to thrive.

Curiously, the stupid subject is for Jean Paul a reader, one who shows more interest in the thought of others than in generating his own thought.[35] The way he reads reflects the country-loving, father-hugging propensities of the stupid. What we may have here is a Goethe complex nearing in the background of the essay's war cry. Be that as it may, whether it's a matter of Goethe or your thesis advisor, you had better get over him (or her, although we are dealing mainly with the paternal fiction at this point). The dummkopf reader as sketched by

Jean Paul remains loyal to the text; he doesn't have the energy to supplement, warp, or distort. There is no appropriative drive in the slavish reader, just a deadly repetition compulsion that stiffens memory and blunts thought. If you are thinking that this dummkopf has not read about "difference and repetition," you are right. The only thing that the stupid have over the smart is mechanical memory.[36] They can memorize anything, as long as they don't have to produce their own thoughts or images. Whoever can't think for himself cannot think the other, cannot grasp what others think. For this reason, argues Jean Paul, he turns his memory into an "Archiv der Dumheit," the container of worthless items. The stupid mind preserves—retains—much, holds without remembering. It cannot claim an interiorizing memory or, we could say, accomplish a proper burial, a true mourning: it holds onto everything, neither letting go nor internalizing; the dummkopf cannot keep by negating and transforming. Everything is there, Jean Paul maintains, but only on the condition of following the laws of simultaneity ("Gesezze der Gleichzeitigkeit" [1:267])—a form of shallow presence. A superior mind notices less at one time, but a single thing recalls thousands of others.[37] The stupid are unable to make breaks or breakaways; they are hampered even on a rhetorical level, for they cannot run with grammatical leaps or metonymical discontinuity. They are incapable of referring allegorically or embracing deferral.

A faithful reader, the one whom Jean Paul designates as stupid and who offers only faithful renditions of the past, acts in the realm of hypocrisy, which is to say, within the restrictive parameters of sanctioned religion. The painfully stupid sensibility is a religious one that for Jean Paul is suffused with superstition and prejudice. In this essay he dodges a struggle with the more difficult implications of religion and its pronounced predilection for simplicity of mind—we find this struggle raging in Dostoevsky, for whom Christ was necessarily ridiculous, rigorously an idiot, an emanation of sacred stupidity—but stays on the boundary of an unambiguous battle, goaded on by "the image of the stupid Holy One" ("das Bild des dummen Heiligen" [1:274]). The rhapsodic Jean Paul is no fool for Christ, as many late Romantics would become (his later works, such as the famous "Speech of the Dead Christ from Heaven That There Is No God," agonizes over the abuses of Christianity in a manner preannouncing Dostoevsky).[38] Closer to Nietzsche in the way he cites Christianity in this text, he sees the stupid as having inherited the earth and showing all the signs of power: they have the positions, they hold the power while the refined and smart and thoughtful are piss poor.[39] The brotherhood of dunces has planted itself firmly in a pragmatic world that undermines the fragile nobility of intelligence. The pledges reward one another, promoting the causes of planetary mediocrity. Adding insult to injury, the order of the dunces has banished anyone who would be enlightened enough to become a rebel in the placid domains of asses.[40] Nietzsche's zoomorphs are beginning to show up on the radar.

There is one more thing, one more problem. The stupid cannot see themselves. No mirror yet has been invented in which they might reflect themselves. They ineluctably evade reflection. No catoptrics can mirror back to them, the shallowest, most surface-bound beings, the historical disaster that they portend. The declaration of war concludes with this polished shield, brandished by Jean Paul, in the figure of mirrors. The author soon gets lost in the impossible mirroring that his text projects, however. He registers a loss, acknowledging confusion, but pins it on the stupid: "One has been mistaken—the mirror has been there all along—first, give the stupid one eyes to look into it, that is make him smart!"[41] These words conclude the essay, folding it back on itself or disfiguring the intention that opened the case. (Another piece, "Übungen im Denken," works on the way the genius and dummkopf camouflage each other and ends abruptly, for fear on the part of the author that he may become the fool of which he writes: "Thus I must cease—to talk about the fool.")[42] Reflection turns into reflectors beaming out at the end of the essay. Jean Paul installs a catoptric, a device by which rays are concentrated by a series of concave mirrors and reflected in one beam so as to make it visible at a great distance. Whether a mirror of polished body, this speculum reflects by deflecting, pointing to itself from afar. When Jean Paul asks for eyes for the stupid he is beside the point of the catoptric, which in a displaced way he avows ("—Man irt sich—"[2:275]). The stupid could be made smart (Whom is the non-religious author addressing? beseeching?) with the donation of eyes. As for his own gaze, has it not been averted? Jean Paul is himself looking away, and not at himself—so, according to the beam logic, he may be in the spotlight, being mirrored, since his gaze is at no point secured as a self-reflective one.

More troubling than the fact that the catoptric cancels any type of self-reflection is the way it makes the essay end, as often does a certain genre of horror films, by collapsing the distance it was supposed to warrant and turning the narrated tide of events stealthily against the safe homecoming of the endangered hero. What does the end of the essay show, despite itself, but that the stupid—consider the language of opacity and shallowness by which they have been defined in their surface being—are a mirror reflecting us? In a kind of rhetorical ploy of bait and switch, the warrior Jean Paul becomes the specular target at the end of the war he was waging against an alleged other. The stupid are shown to have doubled inadvertently for him, effecting a ghostly nearness of opposing forces. It is perhaps no small irony that the writer Jean Paul was to originate the doppelgänger motif, introducing the uncanny element of doubling into our modern literary vocabulary.

The spectrum of impotence that travels in Jean Paul from the *Leser* to the laser of stupidity—from the figure of the reader to that of the catoptric—points to the beginning of another, possibly "alternative" ethics whose contours I trace. There is a space—more precisely still, a caesura—for which no account has been made, although its disruptive force has been acknowledged in various historical guises. Like Musil after him, Jean Paul felt that he was refining Enlightenment principles and responding in his way to the persistent question, Was ist Aufklärung? Stupidity, which cannot be examined apart from the subject accredited by the Enlightenment, poses a challenge to my sovereignty and autonomy. Where politics intersects with ethics the question emerges of where to draw the line, if there is one, of responsibility. To be what it is, responsibility must always be excessive, beyond bounds, viewed as strictly unaccomplished.[43] You are never responsible enough, and it is unclear whether, like Heidegger, whom I discuss in chapter 1, it suffices to say, "I made a stupid mistake," in order to adjudicate a lapse in responsible thinking. To explore the extreme limit of such responsibility, I have appealed to the debilitated subject—the stupid, idiotic, puerile, slow-burn destruction of ethical being that, to my mind, can never be grounded in certitude or education or lucidity or prescriptive obeisance. These issues are most compellingly addressed by the troubled writer Fyodor Dostoevsky, whose acute sense of answering for the other is frequently invoked by Emmanuel Levinas: "We are all responsible for everyone else—but I am more responsible than others."[44] Dostoevsky teaches us about the assumption of ethical liability by placing responsibility close to the extinction of consciousness, where it becomes necessary to ask: What can be assumed by the limited subject? The domain of the human, all too human, menacing enlightenment with dim-wittedness, punctures any hope of an original ethnicity that, in the case of *The Idiot,* Dostoevsky posits as well.

Like malice, cruelty, or banality, with which it is often allied or confused, stupidity has largely escaped the screening systems of philosophical inquiry. In *Difference and Repetition,* Gilles Deleuze argues for the necessity of confronting its troubling facticity by exploring the inert horizon of a transcendental stupidity.[45] For the most part, stupidity has been assimilated to error and derivative epistemological concerns. The reduction of stupidity to the figure of error has produced the hybrid character of its bland concept, which is expulsed from the inner domain of pure thought to which it nonetheless belongs. Stupidity, Deleuze writes, needs to be sought elsewhere, among figures other than those subsumable by error. In a certain manner some philosophers have not ceased to mark the necessity of such an undertaking. Philosophy has been asking around about stupidity; at least, a need has been expressed to enrich the concept of error by determinations of a different sort. The notion of superstition, important for Lucretius, Spinoza, and, in the eighteenth century, for Fontenelle, among others, pushed the envelope past what was established by dogmatic thought as a legitimate division between the empirical and the transcendental. The Stoics had been responsible for introducing the notion of *stultia* to designate simultaneously madness and stupidity. Even the Kantian idea of an inner illusion—internal to reason—departs radically from the extrinsic mechanism of error. Moreover, Deleuze reminisces, there is the matter of Hegelian alienation, which presupposes a profound readjustment in the relation of truth to falsity. Neither true nor false, and bound to an altogether other contract, stupidity has no place on the map drawn up by dogmatism—a map still used to get philosophers where they're going, no matter where they're coming from.

Error has served as the compass by which philosophers have driven their notions forward. The concept of error, however, cannot account for the unity of stupidity and cruelty or for the relation of the tyrant to the imbecile. According to Deleuze, that which has made us avoid making stupidity a transcendental problem is the continued belief in the *cogitatio*: "Stupidity can then be no more than an empirical determination, referring back to psychology or to the anecdotal—or worse, to polemic and insults—and to the especially atrocious pseudo-literary genre of the *sottisier*" (151).[46] But whose fault is this deportation of stupidity to miserable precincts of utterance? Is it not the fault in the first place, Deleuze asks, of philosophy, which has let itself be roped in by the concept of error, regardless of its arbitrary and finally insignificant nature? Even the worse, most degraded kind of literature catalogs idiotic blunders and plots all manner of imbecilic routes taken by its half-baked characters or self-complacent narrators; the best literature is haunted by the problem of stupidity and knows to bring it to the doorstep of philosophy, giving it cosmic, encyclopedic, gnoseological dimensions (Flaubert, Baudelaire, Bloy). It would suffice that philosophy accept literature's gift with the necessary modesty, understanding that stupidity is never that of another but the object of a properly transcendental question: "comment la bêtise (et non l'erreur) est-elle possible?" ([197]; "how is stupidity (not error) possible?" [151]). Cowardice, cruelty, baseness, and stupidity are not corporeal forms (though it will prove necessary to read bodies of nonknowledge in what follows), nor are they mere facts of society and character, but rather *the structures of thinking as such*. Reformulating the question of stupidity is another way of stating the interrogatory challenge, "Was heißt Denken?": What calls forth thinking, or why is it that we are still not thinking?

But there's something else as well that involves the thought of thinking as a doing or its miscarriage, and this becomes clear in times of acute political distress. To the still anxiety-laden question of how one could have responded lucidly to Nazism in the early 1930s, Robert Musil contributed a number of distinctive essays, including "Ruminations of a Slow-Witted Mind" and "On Stupidity." He intended to publish the first essay, written in 1933, in *Die neue Rundschau,* a major German intellectual journal he once edited. Although the details of its failure to appear in published form remain unclear, the article records Musil's attempt to understand what was taking place while sounding the alert for the community of intellectuals. His concerns in "Ruminations" explore the possible independence of the intellect with regard to politics and group formation. The problem is aggravated, in his view, because National Socialism "demands above all that the intellect completely assimilate and subordinate itself to the movement,"[47] thus interfering with every intellect's independence of politics. Musil emphasizes that unlike the French Revolution or the Marxist revolution, this German revolution was not heralded by noted writers and a literature that could be taken seriously.[48] According to Musil, one cannot understand the National Socialist revolution by "looking for its sources in German intellectual life." This revolution, claiming to have produced a new mind, was not one of the intellect; to the contrary, it manifested "the mind's struggle with mindlessness" and furnished an example of the intellect having to relinquish its powers. The sinister project for "the renewal of the German mind" led Musil to state, "Politics prescribing the law for the intellect: this is new."[49]

I am not so sure how new this is, nor do I share Musil's faith in the intellect or so-called intellectual, whose stability in Musil's works often depends on crushing the women that appear in the examples he provides. These casualties commonly occur with concepts based on the universal subject.[50] While his sideswipes on behalf of the intellect are of considerable significance in terms of maintaining the integrity of such an argument, they are not limited to Mr. Musil's private prejudices (for which I nonetheless get him). Be that as it may, Musil presents an unavoidable challenge to thinking the depressing conjunction of stupidity and politics—a conjunction that remains to this day irrefutable. One of the issues that will be confronted in the earlier sections of this book is Musil's assumption that the domain of the intellect can be severed from that of politics, which is to say that his work supposed the relation between politics and the intellect is not politicized. Warranted perhaps by the urgency of the situation, Musil's definition of politics is reined in to fix the narrowest sense of the political. Still, the argument relies on a series of exclusions and humanist strongholds that invite further reflection: it cannot be the case that the alarm sounded against the degradations of totalitarianism depends upon such regressive posturings as can only beleaguer the hope for a just politics. The point to bear in mind is that when politics finds itself in crisis, when it prompts ethical anxiety and goes off the scales of justice, it releases the cry (the *schreiben/Schrei, cri/écrit*): "Stupidity!"

In more recent and altogether different circumstances, Stanley Cavell makes this remark on the politics of stupidity and attendant delegitimations: "It is as if we and the world had a joint stake in keeping ourselves stupid, that is dumb, inarticulate. This poses . . . the specific difficulty of philosophy and calls upon its peculiar strength, to receive inspiration for taking thought from the very conditions that oppose thought, as if the will to thought were as imperative as the will to health and freedom."[51] The beginning of the paragraph broaches the possibility of a secret investment in stupidity, a joint stake that "we and the world" might share in terms of its institution. Echoing Adorno's concern about "planetarische Dummheit" in "Wishful Thinking"—Adorno gives the title in English[52]—Cavell's tentative observations clue us in to a question that awaits further reflection: Given the possible existence of a secret account, a joint stake, who are the secret beneficiaries of stupidity's hegemony? What, in more Freudian terms, can be construed as the secondary benefits of stupidity? Cavell shows rather more confidence in philosophy's strength to pull this one off than may be called for in this area of inquiry—an area that may not be as alien to the effective range of philosophy as the passage indicates: stupidity is not so stupid as to oppose thought (with which Cavell links philosophy). Inspired by the very thing that it repels, philosophy bootlegs thought from a territory foreign to its premises. It is driven by a will to appropriate what, in Cavell's view, ought to remain alien to thought. Yet if stupidity is seen to yield to thought, to surrender and annex itself to philosophy's strength, this peculiar circumstance must be derived from the way stupidity resists subsumption or substantialization into an entity that would be opposable to thought—or even, possibly, to health and freedom. (It is not clear, though the case has been mounted to prosecute such an idea, that health and freedom are the sworn enemies of stupidity.)

The expectation that philosophy can train thought to detach from stupidity has its source in the Enlightenment. The updated version, hounded by war and genocide, reinforced its basic trajectories, and the hope promised by the light of the eighteenth century saw a renewal. Enlightenment principles regenerated, as if the truth of a teaching had been momentarily eclipsed, darkened, indicative merely of a deviation that remained in essence corrigible. The ongoing concern with freedom, internationalism, and "the morality of the humane" that forms the core of Musil's response to the rise of National Socialism is reflected as well in crucial testimonials such as Primo Levi's *Survival in Auschwitz* and Jean Améry's *At the Mind's Limits* (the translated title shows another way of straining to the point where mind debilitates). Améry survived Gestapo torture and Auschwitz until his suicide on October 17, 1978, after he received the Hamburg Lessing Prize. An article reflecting many of Musil's principal commitments indicates in the title—"Enlightenment as Philosophia Perennis"—that Améry, like Musil and Levi, took recourse to the "light of classical Enlightenment[, which] was no optical illusion, no hallucination. Where it threatens to disappear, humane consciousness becomes clouded. Whoever repudiates the Enlightenment is renouncing the education of the human race."[53]

Améry's position on keeping intact Enlightenment values is unambiguous: he puts a ban on its repudiation; and he does not consider how modern forms of racism have been fashioned by the major proponents of Enlightenment motifs. Maybe there was nothing else to turn to; maybe Améry did not want to renounce one last hope after the violence was done. (The violence never ended, there was no "after," but that is another issue.) Certainly, no one could refuse the poignant appeal to the Enlightenment on which his writing is balanced; the authority of assertion neutralizes any critical policing of the effort made by Améry to recuperate something from the collapse of dignity. The melancholic gravity of his adherence to the Enlightenment subdues the impulse to question the defensibility of such an understanding. But the violence to which the world had succumbed is of understanding: understanding is itself at issue. There is a frontier beyond which the Enlightenment cannot go in order to lend its support or illuminate the poverty of being. This in part is why I take the route through the other German tradition, that which opens the dossier on unintelligibility and non-understanding. Cutting through another territory of thought, the tradition initiated by Schlegel's reflections on that which cannot be adapted to human understanding uncompromisingly searches out a language, marked by the crisis of permanent parabasis, that would be capable of answering to the punishing blows of an indecent, unassimilable historical injury.

Is Enlightenment strong enough to contain, repel, or calm the permanent insurrection of stupidity? At this point in our shared experience of history it may be time to contemplate getting off the thought drug, powerful and tempting as it is, that allows equivalences to be made between education and decency, humanism and justice. When Améry is provoked by the specter of delusion and must insist that Enlightenment is no hallucination, we are given to understand that the unpronounceable threat is upon him—there always exists the danger that Enlightenment remains related to hallucination, to favorable forms of comforting deception. In a Nietzschean sense one must compel oneself to confront every mask of good conscience to which commitments have been urgently made. On the other hand, one is enjoined to step up to that which has covered for massive acts of unjustifiable indecency. Often such acts have been consigned in the realm of politics to stupidity—a historical type of narcotic, as Marx observed, involving historical dumbing. Even if philosophy has managed to duck it, history requires us to deal with the dope.[54]

On another register of ethical anxiety, though not discontinuous with what has been said until now, stupidity sets the mood that afflicts anyone who presumes to write. To the extent that writing appears to be commandeered by some internal alterity that proves always to be too immature, rather loudmouthed, often saddled with a pronounced narcissistic disorder no matter how much it makes you want to hide and isolate; or, as part of the same debilitating structure, to the extent that the powerhouse inside you is actually too smart for the dumb positings of language, too mature even for superego's sniping, and way too cool to attempt to put the Saying into words; to the extent, moreover, that writing makes you encounter time and again the drama of the lost object never lost enough, summoning you once more to commit to pointless chase scenes and sizable regressions, all enacted before a sinister superegoical tribunal of teachers and colleagues and those who dumped you and mean-spirited graduate students trying to surpass you, packing heat (sometimes they're on break, but not all that often)—it abandons you for these and other reasons, more reasonable ones that momentarily elude me, to the experience of your own stupidity. There is the additional turn of the vise when it comes to publishing what you write, submitting to a judgment without end. The folly of publication combined with the sense of the utter dumbness that comes with putting yourself on the line—and, anyway, who cares; and Heidegger is still contemplating the line, so what line?—makes one always wander in the precincts of the uncertain justness of what has been said.

When preparing his essays for publication, Paul de Man suggested that he was beset by the guilty sense of watching a grade B movie.[55] The melancholy of reviewing one's own failure to overcome a ground level of stupidity (yours or theirs) in writing has been felt and expressed by any number of writers; sometimes that ethical feeling, should it occur in academic publishing, is miniaturized and displaced to the acknowledgments, where those thanked are said not to be responsible for the stupidity of the work to come, which the testamentary politics of friendship announces. This is at once a way of retracting the debt owed them—parceling oneself out among too many friends, one publicizes the deficiency of acknowledgment—and of allowing space, in their names, for the articulation of an essential default that the work produces and in which it originates. It is as if the Heideggerian conjunction of thanking and thinking produced the necessity of naming the perceptible slump of any project.

Thomas Pynchon is one who puts himself on the melancholic line of self-re-proval. Gathering his early writing into a commissioned volume, he relentlessly reviews the stupidity of the writer he was. The agony of avowal accompanies the whole introductory ritual of *Slow Learner.* "You may already know what a blow to the ego it can be to have to read over anything you wrote 20 years ago, even cancelled checks. My first reaction, rereading these stories, was *oh my God,* accompanied by physical symptoms we shouldn't dwell upon. My second thought was about some kind of a wall-to-wall rewrite." At last he accedes to a level of acceptance, a tranquility that will allow writing, and its extension into publishing, to take place. "I mean I can't very well just 86 this guy from my life."[56] Well, as far as I'm concerned a blow can be served to the old ego by something written twenty days ago. Even twenty minutes. It is a matter of unrelenting assault and battery on whatever in you thinks it can write and live to tell about it. Writing from Hölderlin to Pynchon, you to me, brings about a crushing blow that comes from someone or something (this is why there is something rather than nothing), addressed to you but exceeding your grasp. The matter of receiving the blow is already beyond your capacity to understand. You don't know under whose command you put yourself through it, whom you're addressing, or why it must be this way. In a Beckettian sense, there's not much else to do but dumbly go on, you can't go on, you must go on. The imperative doesn't interrupt the wave of stupidity but rides it, relying on stupidity to bring it home.

One aspect of the sickening state of affairs made clear by Pynchon concerns the somaticizations that occur in the closeup of stupidity. Pynchon is discreet enough not to dwell on them. I do. Meaning I'm not all that discreet about body's writhing habits or even so sure of the length of distance I have from the stupidity gaining on me. The hijacked body, fallen to the mute chronicity of illness, is one of the focuses of this mediation on stupidity. I survey the meeting grounds where psyche runs into soma, the surfaces on which the borrowed body impresses its pain, leaving an inappropriable text in its tracks. If the body writes—the sweat, the nausea, sudden highs, certain crashes, headache, stomach weirdness—and is written on, even "overwritten," as I argue, then it cannot simply be ignored in the drama of self-accusatory tracings. To write is to take a retest every day (even if, brooding, stuck, anguished, you are not empirically writing), to prepare a body, adjust your drive, check in (out of respect) with superego, put ego on sedation, unless you are a total memoir-writ-ing-I-know-myself-and-want-to-share-my-singularity idiot. As he reviews his writing, Pynchon admits to a puerility of attitude, his capacity for idiocy, and the problem of "adolescent values . . . able to creep in and wreck an otherwise sympathetic character" (9), which nonetheless allow for a certain fit with his time: "The best I can say for it now is that, for its time, it is probably authentic enough. . . . There had prevailed for a while a set of assumptions and distinctions, unvoiced and unquestioned, best captured years later in the '70s television character Archie Bunker" (11). The archedebunker of de Man's characterization will have exposed the stupid adherencies in American culture to what readers of an early story would see as "an unacceptable level of racist, sexist and proto-Fascist talk" (11). Stupidity is often fitting; it functions as the jointure of timeliness, marking the failure to produce incongruence or to respond to the Nietzschean call for untimeliness. It is that which arrives on time and in time, satisfying a kind of inverted harmony. In the texts under consideration I review how stupidity functions both to name racist, sexist, and proto-Fascist impulses and also to nail the presumed object of such discursive tendencies as "stupid." No longer merely a verbal sign, it has, in other words, perpetrated myths on the skid marks of erroneous attribution. Destructive and clear in its aim, stupidity as an act of naming commits barely traceable acts of ethnocide (this includes the targeting of ethnic groups whose members are seen as blindly intelligent or mechanically competent—the stupidly clever). Nowadays, even if it is no longer acceptable to pronounce oneself in overtly racist tones, one can reappropriate stupidity, load it up and point it, as do a number of public institutions, at the minoritized subject. Nothing keeps you down like the mark of stupidity. Nonetheless, it some areas of life, it is what lets you get by.

Pynchon, for his part, comes clean, to the extent that one can do so, and offers his apologies. Apologizing, he resists exculpating himself within the performative complacencies of an excuse. He reflects on how we have been kept divided and thus relatively poor and powerless. "This having been said, however, the narrative voice in this story here remains that of a smart-assed jerk who didn't know any better, and I apologize for it" (12). He gives himself away, denouncing the unrelenting puerility of his time, his undergraduate mood, his stances of knowing "more about the subject of entropy than I really do. Even the normally unhoodwinkable Donald Barthelme has suggested in a magazine interview that I had some kind of proprietary handle on it" (12). Pynchon persists, taking down with him those who indulged his stupidity, letting them, as in Barthelme's case, get blindsided by the self-denouncing moves: "But do not underestimate the shallowness of my understanding. . . . I was more concerned with committing on paper a variety of abuses, such as overwriting" (13, 15). He thus points to another facet of stupidity, raising the stakes in what may have appeared to rely on an economy of loss or measurable failure. In terms established by the self-examination of his writing, stupidity issues from an experiment in excess rather than from an experience of lack—one tries too hard, one overwrites; or, in Kant's example for stupidity, one overstudies. Blind overdoing—in Kant's idiom, "outdoing"—steps up the pace of stupidity's tack. Shooting ahead, these velocities point to the foreclosive speed of the overachiever, designating those who travel the fast track: they have created a situation in which the conventional connotations of *fast* derail and no longer support an equivalency with *smart*. Inevitably, coming around a sharp curve of logic, fast means slow. Hastening to finish, achieve, conclude, these overachievers prove that one can be fast and stupid. One can have been precocious, and then one looks back over the record of one's prematurity—and crashes with insight. Of his own procedural errors Pynchon writes, "If this sounds stupid, it is" (15).

Though assimilated to the notion of error and in principle corrigible, the surfeit of stupidity that Pynchon confronts, as if to release himself from the past, functions to mark a historical rapport that the reflecting subject engages with himself. Forward and backward looking, stupidity comes from a past that discloses itself in the discontinuities and breaks of an unfolding history where history has been diminished to the raw grappling—the solitary warfare—of a distressed subject. Very often one who names a stupid mistake or faces a reserve of dumbness, newly discovered, speaks from a place of some enlightenment, as if stupidity had compelled subjection to a strenuous process of overcoming. Hence the enlightenment accent on learning, no matter how slow going. Still, the structure of one's own stupidity is such that it continues to haunt and heckle, creeping up as the other work in progress and threatening from a vague presentiment of the future. No act of will or shedding of past embarrassment can guarantee that stupidity has been safely left behind—or, indeed, that it does not belong to the very core of your writing being. What you risk each and every time is the exposure that Hölderlin called *Blödigkeit*. As Pynchon sees it,

> *Everybody gets told to write about what they know. The trouble with many of us is that at earlier stages of life we think we know everything—or to put it more usefully, we are often unaware of the scope and structure of our ignorance. Ignorance is not just a blank space on a person's mental map. It has contours and coherence, and for all I know rules of operation as well. So as a corollary to writing about what we know, maybe we should add getting familiar with our ignorance, and the possibilities therein for ruining a good story. (15–16)*

A corollary to knowing, ignorance has its own story, a story that needs to be told, but one, perhaps, that can spell only ruin. Yet, as Pynchon somewhat paradoxically offers, ignorance is not just a blank space. While it draws a blank and is *about* blanking out, ignorance, at once perniciously coherent and seriously lacking in coherence—not in itself contemptible—downshifts from stupidity in the sense that you may still find the owner's manual somewhere or, for all he knows, some rules of operation. Ignorance holds out some hope, you can get to know it, maybe move on. I am not so sure about stupidity. It comes closer to Blanchot's sense of nullity—the crushingly useless, that which comes to nothing; the bright side of nullity is that the oeuvre, its essential possibility, originates in it: "The lesson is sad, as Dion always sez, but true" (13).

I have in the past had things to say about writing, the instability of its destination, the death of writing, which I mourn, remainders that I guard, contemplate, introject, and revisit according to a particular mortality timer. Writing has been different things for me, and I shall never really know how to name it, except by pet names and metonymy, by different experiences of nausea and mania—a friend has said that, for him, writing is the experience of mania whereas reading marks the time of mourning. If anything, writing is a non-place for me, where one can abandon oneself to abandonment—I, the infinitely abandoned (one of my "issues"). I am always on writing, especially when I am crashing, and stalled in the time of suspensive nothingness, the hiatus, the interruption, where nothing happens, and it is a hollow time, a time of recovery without recuperation. Writing and trauma: a conjunction to explore—particularly if trauma is seen as the impossibility of receiving experiential markings, as the very disruption of experience. It is not clear to me that writing can be an experience as such. In any case, I always arrive late to its encounter. Today, in order to respond to the interlocutive demand, I run after something someone has said to me—they felt stupid. So I trace out the problem and indeed the experience of stupidity. It is a very difficult topic, as it turns out, and it has called in from two concurrent zones. The first was my Tai Chi class in the fall, when I arrived in New York City. I was utterly dyslexic in reproducing the simplest gestures expected of me. My feeling of idiocy and shame before the Tai Chi master returned to me scenes of stupidity in school—and I suddenly remembered, after all these sedimenting years, how stupid I was as a child, certainly as a pupil. I could make compassionate excuses for myself, I suppose, and say I was an immigrant, didn't understand English, but I was also stupid in math, and I still don't exactly understand plain language, and when someone speaks to me, I can go into seizures of somatic compliance, get hives, hang up the phone too quickly, interrupt the other, not having understood very much at all.

The other motivation for a meditation on stupidity involves Gilles Deleuze. While I was resolutely not learning the Tai Chi vocabulary, Deleuze had ended his life. In the memories and papers that remained, Deleuze, it was reported, had called for a thinking of stupidity: no one had ever produced a discourse, he was remembered to have said, that interrogated the transcendental principles of stupidity. I received this call as an assignment—when I write I am always taking a call, I am summoned from elsewhere, truly from the dead, even if they are my contemporaries. Nietzsche and then Levinas have said that no one can be contemporaneous with the other, not really. So, in a sense, I took my cue from Deleuze. On a more banal register, I had just left Berkeley and I thought I should really think about what that experience had meant to me, maybe figure out why some of those folks and institutions had rated so unaccountably high on the national scoreboard for university learning. Anyway, to get back to him, Deleuze had left some puzzling traces, including what he wrote in his book on repetition, where he figures bêtise *(stupidity) as "l'indéterminé adéquat de la pensée" and the "genitalité de la pensée."*[57] *I've got to admit, that sounded kind of sexy.*

There was yet another call, on an internal call-waiting system. It was Beckett. I remembered having read an interview, a pretty famous one by now, in which he said that Joyce tended toward omniscience

285

and omnipotence as an artist, but I'm working with impotence, igno-rance. That's what he said; it really stuck with me, in fact, it signaled a stupendous breakthrough. At once simplifying and complicating the whole itinerary, it belonged together with the times he says, "I don't know why I told this story," or the avowal in "Texts for Noth-ing": "I don't try to understand, I'll never try to understand anymore, that's what you think, for the moment I'm here, always have been, always shall be, I won't be afraid of the big words anymore, they are not big."[58]

Notes

1. Friedrich Schiller, *Jungfrau von Orleans* (act 3, sc. 6), in *Werke Nationalausgabe,* ed. Julius Peterson and Hermann Schneider, 42 vols. (Weimar: Böhlau, 1942), 9:257; Hannah Arendt and Karl Jaspers, *Correspondence, 1926–1969,* ed. Lotte Kohler and Hans Saner, trans. Robert Kimber and Rita Kimber (New York: Harcourt Brace, 1992), 439; Alain Grosrichard, *The Sultan's Court: European Fantasies of the East,* trans. Liz Heron (London: Verso, 1998); Jacques Lacan, *The Seminar of Jacques Lacan,* bk. 7: *The Ethics of Psychoanalysis, 1959–1960,* ed. Jacques-Alain Miller, trans. Dennis Porter (New York: W. W. Norton, 1992). The same concern over the sheer stupidity of Eichmann's positions is voiced in Hannah Arendt and Mary McCarthy, *Between Friends,* ed. Carol Brightman (New York: Harcourt Brace, 1995), 296–98. One might additionally consider in this context the remarks made by Ernst Cassirer to open his political contemplation *The Myth of the State* (New Haven, Conn.: Yale University Press, 1946): "But in man's practical and social life the defeat of rational thought seems to be complete and irrevocable. . . . Imagination itself cannot account for all its incongruities and its fantastic and bizarre elements. It is rather the *Urdummheit* of man that is responsible for these absurdities and contradictions. Without this 'primeval stupidity' there would be no myth" (4).

2. "When Catoblépas, a black buffalo with the head of a pig that drags on the ground, addresses him, he [Saint Antoine] is sorely tempted: 'Sa stupidité m'attire'" (Jonathan Culler, *Flaubert: The Uses of Uncertainty* [Ithaca, N.Y.: Cornell University Press, 1985], 183).

3. Friedrich Nietzsche, *Beyond Good and Evil: Prelude to a Philosophy of the Future,* trans. Walter Kaufmann (New York: Random House, 1989), no. 188.

4. Ibid., no. 228.

5. Among the few who did not ignore its potential significance in modernity was Schopenhauer, for whom stupidity implied, together with vulgarity, a complete reversal of the will-understanding relation. In "On the Sublime and Naive in the Fine Sciences," Moses Mendelssohn devotes several paragraphs to a description of stupidity as embedded in facial features. The face imparts different levels of stupidity: "if the simplicity in the movements betrays thoughtlessness and lack of sensitivity, then it is called 'stupidity' and if it is accompanied by listlessness, then we have . . . *niais* (silliness)" (*Philosophical Writings,* trans. Daniel O. Dahlstrom [Cambridge: Cambridge University Press, 1997], 226–27).

6. Friedrich Hölderlin, *Sämtliche Werke: Frankfurter Ausgabe,* 20 vols., ed. D. E. Sattler (Frankfurt am Main: Verlag Roter Stern, 1975), 4:261, 336–40; 5:683–700.

7. Rainer Maria Rilke, "Das Lied des Idioten," in *Werke,* 4 vols., ed. Manfred Engel et al. (Frankfurt: Insel Verlag, 1996), 1:327; Richard Wright, haiku #579, in *Haiku: The*

Other World (New York: Arcade Publishing, 1998), 132; Joseph Conrad, *Tales of Unrest* (New York: Penguin Books, 1977), 57.

8. Walter Benjamin, "Zwei Gedichte von Friedrich Hölderlin. 'Dichtermut'—Blödigkeit," in *Gesammelte Schriften,* 7 vols., ed. Rolf Tiedemann and Hermann Schweppenhaüser (Frankfurt am Main: Suhrkamp Verlag, 1972), 2(1): 105–26 (for English-language translations see Benjamin, "Two Poems by Friedrich Hölderlin: 'The Poet's Courage' and 'Timidity,'" trans. Stanley Corngold, *Selected Writings,* 2 vols., ed. Michael Jennings [Cambridge, Mass.: Harvard University Press, 1996], 1:18–36); Gershom Scholem, *Walter Benjamin—die Geschichte einer Freundschaft* (Frankfurt am Main: Suhrkamp Verlag, 1975), 26.

9. On the avoidance of personal agency see Stanley Corngold, *Complex Pleasure: Forms of Feeling in German Literature* (Stanford, Calif.: Stanford University Press, 1998), 153.

10. Bart Philipsen, "Herz aus Glas—Hölderlin, Rousseau und das 'blöde' Subjeckt der Moderne," in *Bild-Sprache: Texte zwischen Dichten und Denken,* ed. L. Lamberechts and J. Nowé (Louvain: Presses Universitaires, 1990), 177–94; Michael Jennings, "Benjamin as a Reader of Hölderlin: The Origins of Benjamin's Theory of Literary Criticism," *German Quarterly Review* 56.4 (Nov. 1983): 544–62; Corngold, *Complex Pleasure,* 150–70; Friedrich Hölderlin, *Selected Verse,* trans. and ed. Michael Hamburger (London: Anvil Press Poetry, 1986), 238.

11. Corngold, *Complex Pleasure,* 162.

12. Wolfgang Pfeifer, in *Etymologisches Wörterbuch des Deutschen* (Berlin: Akademie-Verlag, 1989), s.v., *"blöd(e),"* dates the use of the term as "dumm, schwachsinnig [dumb, feeble-minded]" to the sixteenth century. It clearly carried this connotation—if not the outright denotative value—for Hölderlin.

13. Philipsen, "Herz aus Glas," 192 (my translation).

14. Corngold, *Complex Pleasure,* 168. Reverting to a position of relative safety, Corngold places *stupidity* in quotation marks.

15. Benjamin, "Two Poems," 1:22 (subsequent citations occur parenthetically in the text).

16. Benjamin, "Zwei Gedichte," 2(1): 125 (subsequent citations occur parenthetically in the text).

17. Hölderlin, *Sämtliche Werke:* "Drum! so wandle nur wehrlos / Fort durchs Leben, und sorge nicht!" ("Dichtermut," 4:261); or "Drum, mein Genius! tritt nur / Baar ins Leben, und sorge nicht!" ("Blödigkeit," 5:699).

18. Pierre Alferi, "Un Accent de vérité," *Revue des Sciences Humaines: Maurice Blanchot* 253.1 (1999): 153–71.

19. Henry James, *The Sacred Fount* (New York: New Directions, 1983), 17.

20. Roland Barthes, "Barthes to the Third Power," trans. Matthew Ward and Richard Howard, in *On Signs,* ed. Marshall Blonsky (Baltimore, Md.: Johns Hopkins University Press, 1985), 189.

21. Another text, "Images," repeats Barthes's obsessive anxiety over Stupidity: "In the arena of language, constructed like a football field, there are two extreme sites, two goals that can never be avoided: Stupidity on the one end, the Unreadable at the other. . . . Stupidity is not linked to error. Always triumphant (impossible to overcome), it derives its victory from an enigmatic power: it is 'Dasein' in all its naked splendor. Whence a terror and a fascination, that of a corpse. (Corpse of what? Perhaps of truth: truth as dead.) . . . Stupidity 'is there,' obtuse as death. Exorcism can only be a formal operation which confronts it 'en bloc,' from outside. . . . Here I am back at the same panic that Stupidity inspires: Is it me? Is it the other? Is it the other who is unreadable (or stupid)? Am I the one who is limited, inept, am I the one who doesn't understand?" (Roland Barthes, *The Rustle of Language,* trans. Richard Howard [Berkeley: University of California Press, 1989], 351–52.)

22. The resemblance of a rock to stupidity's hard place ends there, for the recourse taken by Flaubert to a natural object is a desperate one, designed mainly to offset the grasp of understanding and to allow stupidity to borrow from inorganic nature the attributes of its hardness. The imperturbable inertia characteristic of some forms of stupidity in fact unsettles any rhetorical resolution into an object. If Flaubert deploys an unreliable analogy to get a hold on the traits of stupidity, it is to show the limits of understanding: "One can understand facts about [a stone or a mountain] or problems that are posed when a human project or discourse operates on them, providing a focus, asking a question" (Culler, *Flaubert,* 175).

23. Gustave Flaubert, *Correspondance,* 9 vols. (Paris: Louis Conard, 1926–33), 2:398 (my translation, all such; subsequent citations occur parenthetically in the text).

24. Culler, *Flaubert,* 176.

25. Flaubert, *Correspondance,* 2:485: "A Alexandrie un certain Thompson, de Sunderland, a sur la colonne de Pompée écrit son nom en lettres de six pieds de haut. . . . Il n'y a pas moyen de voir la colonne sans voir le nom de Thompson, et par conséquent sans penser à Thompson."

26. Jacques Derrida, "An Idea of Flaubert: 'Plato's Letter,'" trans. Peter Starr, *Modern Language Notes* 99.4 (Sept. 1984): 758–59, translating Derrida, "Une idée de Flaubert: La lettre de Platon," *Revue d'Histoire Littéraire de la France* 4–5 (July-Oct. 1981): 666: "(et pour Flaubert la bêtise est toujours monumentale, de la taille du monument pierreux couvert d'inscription)."

27. Playing on the name of his close friend, Erasmus dedicated his *Moria* (as he usually called the work) to More—Thomas More, in whose house the work was written.

For a discussion of *morosophos*, see the translator's introduction in Desiderius Erasmus, *The Praise of Folly*, trans. Clarence H. Miller (New Haven, Conn.: Yale University Press, 1979), xiii.

28. Flaubert, *Correspondance*, 2:243: "La bêtise est quelque chose d'inébranable; rien ne l'attaque sans se briser contre elle. Elle est de la nature du granit, dure et résistante."

29. Quoted in Culler, *Flaubert*, 174.

30. Jean Paul, "Von der Dumheit," *Werke*, pt. 2, ed. Norbert Miller, 4 vols. (Munich: Carl Hanser Verlag, 1974), 1:266–75 (subsequent citations occur parenthetically in the text).

31. Ibid., 1:270: "Der Dumkopf ist meistens glücklich, wenn er den aufgeklärten Kopf angreift."

32. Ibid.: "Nie sind diese Geschöpfe allein. Sie . . . fülen ihre gegenseitige Anziehung am stärksten im Kriege gegen den Klugen."

33. Ibid.: "Der grosse Man verachtet die Mükkenstiche der kleinen Geister; er betrügt sich."

34. Ibid., 1:269: "Sein Ideensystem beschränkt sich auf eine kleine Anzal Begriffe, die tief in ihm haften, weil sie in seiner Jugend ihren Weg durch den Rükken namen, die er für heilig hält, weil sie die Reliquien von dem Geiste seines Vaters sind und einen Teil seiner Erbschaft ausmachen."

35. Ibid., 1:268: "Die Gedanken des andern interessieren ihn mehr als seine eigne."

36. Ibid., 1:267: "Das Gedächtnis ist die einzige Fähigkeit, die der Dumme vor dem klugen Tier voraushat."

37. Ibid.: "Ein besserer Kopf merkt weniger auf einmal aber eine einzige Sache erinnert ihn an tausend ähnliche."

38. See Jean Paul, "Siebenkäs," *Werke*, 2:7–565.

39. Jean Paul, "Von der Dumheit," 1:275: "Überall sind reiche und mächtige Dunsen gepflanzt."

40. Ibid.: "Der zum Orden der Dunsen gehört und verbant den Aufgeklärten als einen Rebel aus den friedlichen Reiche der Esel."

41. Ibid. (my translation): "—Man irt sich—der Spiegel ist längst da—gebt dem Dummen erst Augen zum hineinsehen, d.h. macht ihn klug!"

42. Also, Jean Paul, "Übungen im Denken," *Werke*, 1:95 (my translation): "Ich mus also aufhören—vom Narren zu reden."

43. Derrida's recent works have been devoted to the unfinished aspects of responsibility. See also Thomas Keenan, *Fables of Responsibility: Aberrations and Predicaments in Ethics and Politics* (Stanford, Calif.: Stanford University Press, 1997), and Drucilla Cornell, *The Philosophy of the Limit: Justice and Legal Interpretation* (New York: Routledge, 1992).

44. See Emmanuel Levinas, "Responsibility for the Other," *Ethics and Infinity: Conversations with Philippe Nemo*, trans. Richard A. Cohen (Pittsburgh: Duquesne University

Press, 1985), 93–101. Levinas's reading or responsibility points to powerful political events in his discussion of the massacres at Sabra and Chatila in 1982. See his "Ethics and Politics," trans. Jonathan Romney, in *The Levinas Reader*, ed. Seán Hand (Oxford: Blackwell, 1989), 289–97.

45. Gilles Deleuze, *Difference and Repetition*, trans. Paul Patton (New York: Columbia University Press, 1994); originally *Différence et Répétition* (Paris: Presses Universitaires de France, 1969) (subsequent citations occur parenthetically in the text).

46. Deleuze, *Différence et Répétition*, 196: "la bêtise ne peut plus être qu'une détermination empirique, renvoyant à la psychologie ou à l'anecdote—pire encore, à la polémique et aux injures—et aux sottisiers comme genre pseudo-littéraire particulièrement exécrable" (196).

47. Robert Musil, "The Ruminations of a Slow-Witted Mind," in *Precision and Soul: Essays and Addresses*, ed. and trans. Burton Pike and David S. Luft (Chicago: University of Chicago Press, 1978), 224.

48. See Arnold I. Davidson, "1933–1934: Thoughts on National Socialism," *Critical Inquiry* 17 (Autumn 1990): 35–45.

49. Musil, "Ruminations," 224.

50. Consider Jean-François Lyotard, "The Tomb of the Intellectual," *Political Writings*, trans. Bill Readings and Kevin Paul Geiman (Minneapolis: University of Minnesota Press, 1993). Lyotard's attack on intellectuals, Big Brother, and other experts generally concerns the presumption to authority in politics. "The responsibility of 'intellectuals' is inseparable from the (shared) idea of a universal subject" (3). In his introductory comments, Readings argues that the intellectual, exiled from the particular in order to reach the universal, is a citizen of the universe who speaks to everyone and to no one in particular. "The intellectual, as a modernist creature, rationalizes history by means of abstraction, constructing a grand narrative of the liberation of a subject as self-realization. The end of history is thus the liberation of mankind as essentially free from ignorance (Enlightenment), essentially capable of providing material needs in a free market (capitalism), or essentially laboring (Marxism). Actual events are merely the raw materials for a metadiscursive reflection upon the progress of this narrative of self-realization" (xxii). For a discussion of the crisis in the legitimation of knowledge after the "death" of the subject, after the failure of Enlightenment liberalism, see Chantal Mouffe, "Deconstruction, Pragmatism and the Politics of Democracy," in *Deconstruction and Pragmatism*, ed. Chantal Mouffe (New York: Routledge, 1996), i–x, and *The Return of the Political* (New York: Verso, 1993).

51. Stanley Cavell, *Pursuits of Happiness: The Hollywood Comedy of Remarriage* (Cambridge, Mass.: Harvard University Press, 1981), 42.

52. See Theodor W. Adorno, *Minima Moralia: Reflexionen aus dem beschädigten Leben* (Frankfurt am Main: Suhrkamp Verlag, 1993), 263.

53. Jean Améry, *Radical Humanism: Selected Essays,* trans. and ed. Sidney Rosenfeld and Stella F. Rosenfeld (Bloomington: Indiana University Press, 1984), 136. See also his *At the Mind's Limit: Contemplations by a Survivor on Auschwitz and Its Realities,* trans. Sidney Rosenfeld and Stella F. Rosenfeld (Bloomington: Indiana University Press, 1998). For a discussion of history and its relation to hallucination (to that which "does not belong to the domain of knowledge"), see Eduardo Cadava's reading of Bergson's *Matter and Memory in Words of Light: Theses on the Photography of History* (Princeton, N.J.: Princeton University Press, 1997), 95–97.

54. According to the *Oxford English Dictionary,* a dope is "a stupid person, a simpleton, a fool," and in U.S. slang, "a person under the influence of, or addicted to, some drug."

55. Paul de Man, *The Rhetoric of Romanticism* (New York: Columbia University Press, 1984,) viii: "Such massive evidence of the failure to make the various individuals coalesce is a somewhat melancholy spectacle." In the foreword to *Blindness and Insight: Essays in the Rhetoric of Contemporary Criticism,* 2d rev. ed. (Minneapolis: University of Minnesota Press, 1983), de Man sets up the melancholic practice of self-review in the mode of disavowal: "I am not given to retrospective self-examination and mercifully forget what I have written with the same alacrity I forget bad movies—although, as with bad movies, certain scenes or phrases return at times to embarrass and haunt me like a guilty conscience. When one imagines to have felt the exhilaration of renewal, one is certainly the last to know whether such a change actually took place or whether one is restating, in a slightly different mode, earlier and unresolved obsessions" (xii).

56. Thomas Pynchon, *Slow Learner* (New York: Little, Brown, 1984), 3 (subsequent citations occur parenthetically in the text).

57. Gilles Deleuze, *Différence et Répetition* (Paris: Presses Universitaires de France, 1969), 43–44.

58. Samuel Beckett, *Samuel Beckett: The Complete Short Prose, 1929–1989.* Ed. S. E. Gontarski (New York: Grove Press, 1995), 189.

The Experimental Disposition

NIETZSCHE'S DISCOVERY OF AMERICA
(OR, WHY THE PRESENT ADMINISTRATION
SEES EVERYTHING IN TERMS OF A TEST)

> Wasted a fair bit of patriotic young flesh
> in order to test some new technology.
> —William Gibson, *Neuromancer*

We do not always know how to calculate the importance of a work. In some cases, there is nothing even to guarantee that the work will arrive. Some works seem to set an ETA—there is a sense that it will take them years to make their arrangements, overcome the obstacles of an unprotected journey, get past the false reception desks blocking their paths. In the more assured and seductive version, these works follow the itinerary of Walter Benjamin's secret rendezvous—targeting the *geheime Verabredung* that a work has made with the singularity of a destination: in the form, perhaps, of a future reader. The reader or receptor from the future assumes the responsibility of being addressed, of signing for the work when it finally arrives, helping it originate. Yet, little tells us how many hits a work will have taken on its way or whether we will be there to receive it. Perhaps the work will be prevented from showing up at the appointed time, but some works barrel toward their destination, causing a lot of trouble for a lot of Daseins. Heidegger once said that it can take 200 years to undo the damage inflicted by certain works—I think he was evaluating Plato. For my part, I cannot tell whether *The Gay Science* has arrived or even, really, where it was going when Nietzsche sent it on its way. Still, I am prepared to sign for it. That is to say, I have prepared myself for it. I am not reluctant to assess the damage for which it still may be responsible—assuming the work has arrived and I can find its points of entry—or whether (but this is not a contradiction) this work has fashioned essential trajectories that provide existence with ever new supplies of meaning. I am using *work* here in the widest possible sense because Nietzsche—well, Nietzsche was the absence of the work.[1] He continues to pose the dilemma of the most unauthorized of authors—so many signatures, styles, shredders. Nonetheless, something keeps arriving and returning under that name, something that addresses us with uncommon urgency. So. *The Gay Science.*

To the extent that science is meant to promote life, Nietzsche makes it his business to put demands on its self-understanding. For Nietzsche, science—or, more to the point, the scientific interpretation of life—owes us an account of itself, if only to give us access to its overwhelming use of force over diverse discursive populations. It would not be stretching things too far to say that in Nietzsche's estimation science needs to be audited at every turn, each year. The philosophical pressure is on for science to come clean, to declassify the language usage and rhetorical combinations that have supported the prodigal domination of science over other interpretive interventions and possible worlds. If Nietzsche wants to keep it clean, this in part is because he *needs* science in order to make some of his most radical claims. His relation to science is by no means driven by resentment but rests on appropriative affirmation. As with all appropriations, things can get rough at times. Yet it is from a place of exorbitant responsibility that Nietzsche wrote up his version of science and, against the many pronounced inclinations of science, made joyousness a new prerequisite of scientific endeavor. Not one to get tangled in obsolesced subjectivities, Nietzsche at times saw himself as a scientific object. Thus, in an effort to explain himself as a prophetic human being he writes: "I should have been at the electric exhibition in Paris" as an exhibit at the world's science fair.[2] Elsewhere, as we know, Nietzsche comes out not so much as man but as dynamite. Taking these articulated mutations seriously—one of his masks will have been the scientific object—how can we make sense of Nietzsche's call today?

1. TESTING 1 . . .

If we are prepared only now to receive his version of the question concerning technology, this is because he ran it along the lines of a delay call-forwarding system. He made us wait, holding back the scientific punch he wanted delivered. The call put out by Nietzsche remains the urgent question of a text that bears the burden of an enigmatic encounter with science. Nietzsche gives us science as an assignment, as a trust to be taken on unconditionally. Neither the first nor the last to make science part of an irrevocable curriculum, Nietzsche saw in science the potential for uncompromising honesty in terms of understanding who we are and what we can become. At this point, only the scientific interpretation of life is capable in principle of zapping those dubious mythologies and bad drugs that keep things hazy, enslaved, grimly pessimistic. On some level, science does not owe anything to anyone; it does not have to bend its rules to suit this or that transcendental power broker. In principle, science does not have to rhyme with nation-state or God but should be able to bypass the more provincial tollbooths of ever narrowing global highways. Science, if it wanted to do so, could in principle travel its zones with a free pass. More imposingly still, science could kick its way out of any religious holding pen and put down deadly fanaticisms in a flash of its idiomatic brilliance. In his rendering and genealogical breakdown, Nietzsche did not mean for science to become a servile instrument of a corporate state, though he saw how that could happen. But when Nietzsche takes on science, commanding its future—Nietzsche had first dibs on at least one or two of the possible futures allotted to the domains of science—he addresses the promise of science according to altogether singular categories, drawing up new amendments to its manifestly powerful constitution.

Nietzsche continually offers a model for cognition that cannot simply account for itself or maintain its results within the assumed certitudes of a controlled system of knowledge. At some level, the correlated acts of discovery and invention exceed the limits of what is knowable or even, as Derrida has argued, strictly recognizable.[3] The meaning of scientificity that concerns Nietzsche and that can be seen to dominate the technological field in which we moderns exist embraces the qualities both of destructive and artistic modes of production, involving an ever elusive and yet at the same time tremendously potent force field. Our being has been modalized by the various technologies in ways that have begun fairly recently to receive serious attention in the domains of ontology, ethics, political theory, cybernetics, critical thought, and artificial intelligence. Yet, what concerns Nietzsche belongs neither literally inside nor outside any of these domains but has nonetheless infiltrated their very core—something, indeed, that Nietzsche's Gay Sci was first to articulate succinctly. Nietzsche variously motivates the scientific premise of his work by terms that indicate the activities of testing, which include experimentation, trial, hypothetical positing, retrial, and more testing. If anything, Gay Sci signals to us today the extent to which our rapport with the world has undergone considerable mutation by means of our adherence to the imperatives of testing. The consequences of this grid are considerable, involving, to say the least, our relation to explanatory and descriptive language, truth, conclusiveness, result, probability, process, and identity. Testing, moreover, implies for Nietzsche very specific temporal inflections. Henceforth everything will have to stand the test of time, which is to say that, ever provisional, things as well as concepts must be tried and proven and structurally regulated by the destruction of a hypothesis that holds them together. The logic of the living as much as the inscription of decline has to go to trial. If it were not too explosive, one could say that Nietzsche laid the fundamental groundwork for corroborating Karl Popper's theory of falsifiability.

Nietzsche marvels at a science that, like a warrior, can go out and test itself repeatedly. If today's world is ruled conceptually by the primacy of testing—nuclear, drug, HIV, admissions, employment, pregnancy, and DNA tests, the SAT, GRE, and MSAT, "testing" limits, "testing a state's capacity for justice," as I just read in today's paper, and so on—then this growing dependency on the test is coextensive with Nietzsche's recognition of the modern experimental turn. The experimental turn as we now know it from a history of flukes, successes, and near misses, in its genesis and orientation, travels way beyond good and evil. Its undocumented travel plan—there are so many secret destinations of which we remain ignorant—is perhaps why experimentation is a locus of tremendous ethical anxiety. No matter how controlled, we cannot know where it is going. One could argue that nowadays, since the fateful advent of the Gay Sci but perhaps not solely because of it, there is nothing that is not tested or subject to testing. Let us set up this phase of our inquiry by discussing Nietzsche's unprecedented emphasis on experimentation, which is what I believe provides the crucial access code to the possibility of a gay science.

2. TESTING 1 . . . 2 . . .

A vaguely threatening insinuation, the challenge sparked by the utterance "Try me!" could come from any number of places. It could be the case that it speaks from the place of an action hero, a mundane bully, a girl gang member, a new appliance, a car, or whomever your buffed-up interlocutor might be today. In fact, "Try me!" is very likely spoken from the essence of technology—a shorthand formula intended to establish a tone of defiance, enjoining the other to test a limit. "Try me!" may challenge you to "see what happens" if the line is crossed. It also allows one to encounter the subject on a trial basis: there is something yet to be seen or recanted in the field of the encounter with the other. A call to test the space between us, "Try me!" however soon reverts to a faux experimental generosity. For while it gives the green light to go ahead and probe limits, it switches on the glare of a red light as well, protecting a designated turf. It does both at once: invites an experimental advance and, intimating caution, averts its execution. One throws one's body in the way of an advance. Nietzsche's gesture moves the challenge in a different direction when he invokes *Versuchen wir's!* As if in response to the tapered challenge, his work often says "Let's try it" or "Let's try it out"—let us *give* it a try. Turning the trial into a gift, Nietzsche creates a space of recessive limits, at least as concerns dogmatic assertions and cognitive boundaries. He makes his conditions known. In order to earn Nietzsche's praise, a given assertion must be trial-ready, inviting the type of responsiveness that allows for the experiment—what Nietzsche sees as a highly responsible stipulation and structure. Nietzsche, the thinker of the test site—from the selective test of the eternal return to Zarathustra's trials and the experimental language shots of the aphoristic texts—insisted on these very conditions. *Versuchen wir's!* circumscribes the space of an unceasing series of audacious experiments: "I favor any *skepsis* to which I may reply, 'Let us try [*versuchen*] it!' But I no longer wish to hear anything of all those things and questions that do not permit any experiment. . . . [F]or there courage has lost its rights" (115). Under the flag of courage Nietzsche henceforth closes his ears to anything that disallows experimental probity. One could argue that, in *Human, All-Too-Human* (1878–79), *The Dawn* (1880–81), and *The Gay Science,* Nietzsche sets up a lab in which he performs "the countless experiments on which later theories might be built" (231). Each aphorism is set up as an experiment to be tested, observed, and, where necessary, rescinded. Performing a kind of antisublation, rescindability is the true test of courage. Where Hegel might gather and hold in *Aufhebung,* Nietzsche, in and on principle, discards, lets go. His work depends on the bounce of rescindability, on the ability to mourn that which cannot prove or seriously legitimate itself. Such acts of letting go have nothing to do with wimping out or with simply betraying what has been; instead, they provide a way of articulating the enhanced capacity to take the cuts of criticism, basing nothing on faith or mere durability. It is a mark of vitality that points to the minimally paranoiac path, if that should be conceivable, of scholarly pursuit.

The demands put to us by Nietzsche, in the articulated forms of the autobiographical traces as well as in the various inscriptions of his thought, prompt a number of questions. Sometimes the questions that he makes us ask evoke the quality of an "unthought" layer of sketches he proposes, for as much as he thematizes it explicitly he also appears to take testing's pervasive pull for granted. What, finally, is the nature of the test? Does it have an essence? Is it pure relationality? How does it participate in Nietzsche's great destabilizations or prompt the nihilistic slide of values? Why today is our sense of security—whether or not we are prepared to admit this—based on testability? We *want* everyone and everything tested (I am not unaware of the sinister resonance of this observation, but since when has a desire signaled by humanity not been pulled by a sinister undertow?). Testing, which our Daseins encounter every day in the multiplicity of forms already enumerated—ranging from I.Q. to cosmetics, engine, stress, and arms, and "testing 1–2–3–" broadcast systems, not to mention testing your love, testing your friendship, testing my patience, in a word, testing the brakes—was located by Nietzsche mainly in the eternal joy of becoming. Becoming involves the affirmation of passing away and destroying—the decisive feature of a Dionysian philosophy.

Testing, which we read as one of the prevailing figures of our modernity, still makes claims of absoluteness (something has been "tested and proved"; we have "test results") but in the form of temporariness. It opens up the site that occurs, Nietzsche suggests, after Christianity has fizzled, arriving together with a crisis in the relationship of interpretation to experience. No longer is it a question of interpreting one's own experience as pious people have long enough interpreted theirs, namely, "as if everything were providential, a hint, designed and ordained for the sake of the salvation of the soul—that is *all over now*" (307). Now we godless ones test; we rigorously experiment. We are the Christian conscience translated and sublimated into a scientific conscience. Converted to scientificity, we still however carry a trace of Christianity because what triumphed over the Christian god was Christian morality itself, "the concept of truthfulness that was understood ever more rigorously" (307). As it became more refined, Christianity forced "intellectual cleanliness" upon us (307); it came clean by pushing science as the sublimation of its own murkiness. Now man's *conscience* is set against Christianity; it is "considered indecent and dishonest by every more refined conscience" (307). The Christian god in sum split off from Christian morality, which necessarily went down a transvaluating path less traveled and turned against its recalcitrant origin. The truth march required Christian morality to give up the god. What interests me is the additional twist of transvaluation that Nietzsche's shadowhistory sketches, namely when the value urging truth converts into the currency of testing. Henceforth, in strictly Nietzschean terms, reactive positings will have to stand up to the scrutiny of recursive testing.

With the spread of technology, testing lost some of its auratic and exceptional qualities and started hitting everyone with its demands, that is, anyone who wanted to gain admission anywhere, and all institutions started testing to let you in and let you out. If something weird happens, you are taken in for psychiatric testing. Technological warfare belongs to the domain of testing as well, and does much to support the thesis that there is little difference between testing and the real thing. To the extent that testing counts as warfare today, it marks the steady elimination of boundaries between weapons testing and their deployment. The test already functions as a signal to the enemy other. What this means, among other things, is that the Cold War *was* a war. It also means that W. could at once invoke and scramble these codes by announcing, on the evening of 9/11, that the attack on the World Trade Center was, in his words, a test. How does his language usage work here? Appearing to introduce a new rhetoric of justification for imminent military action, the president in fact reverted to a citation of pretechnological syntagms that capture the auratic pull of the test. In this context the term sparkles as an anointment; the president bears the mark of election by virtue of the test. If a few months earlier he was elected by dubious political means, he is now elected by divine mandate to meet the demands of a terrific test in order to create history, which he begins to do by reinscribing the Crusades. Saying that the terror attack was a test, President Bush leaves no room for the undecidability of Abraham, the contestability of Job, or the intricate martyrdom of Christ in the desert or on the cross. Disturbing the codified usage of the trial to which "test" alludes, the utterance subverts the condition of *being tested* by offering that, at the moment of its mention, the test has been passed. The test will already have made sense and turned in the result: one would not have been chosen to withstand it, the logic goes, if one had not *already passed* the test of history countersigned, in this case, by God.

Reinscribing and repeating the wars of his father, this little Isaac jumps at the chance to return to traumatic sites. Like Isaac, neutralized and silenced by the father's package deal with the sacred, this one wants to dig into the earth, signing a legacy to which he was and was not called. Part of the "vision thing" that we call testing, the first gulf war was conducted primarily as a field test; but it also, phantasmically, displayed the characteristics of a national AIDS test in which America scored HIV-negative, owing to the "bloodless" and safe war.[4] The gulf war set out to prove the hypothesis that no technology will ever exist without being tested; but once it is tested, we are no longer simply talking about a *test*.[5] Nothing will be invented, no matter how stealth, nuclear, or "unthinkable," that will not be tested, that is, realized at some level of calibration. Hence, in addition to related issues of deployment, testing is always written into treaties. The necessity of treaties, conventions, and regulative discourses in itself underscores, in the manner demonstrated by Kant and Benjamin in their critiques of violence, the extent to which testing, like war, has become naturalized and can be only provisionally suspended by treaties that try to ban it.

3. TESTING 1 . . . 2 . . . 3 . . .

Prototype America—since we have established temporary residency in the philosopheme America, or at this point one might almost say in the hypothesis of America, I would like to migrate to another territory that Nietzsche draws up, if only to satisfy his desire for the punctuality of the brief habit and the multiple departures that his work prescribes. Once again, the line of flight takes us to one of the futures of Nietzsche's Gay Sci.

To the extent that the experimental disposition emerges from constant self-differentiation, which is also to say that it can simulate itself and, as Nietzsche suggests, wears many masks, it unquestionably belongs to an experimental site that Nietzsche calls in a crucial moment of development "America." I say "development" because Nietzsche for once offers thanks to Hegel for having introduced the decisive concept of development into science. The gratitude is short-lived: we learn quickly that Hegel "delayed [the] triumph of atheism most dangerously for the longest time" by "persuad[ing] us of the divinity of existence" (306–07), where Schopenhauer's "unconditional and honest atheism" at least made "the ungodliness of existence . . . palpable and indisputable" (307). America becomes an experimental site because it is the place of acting and *role-playing*—a concept developed by Nietzsche for America or by America for Nietzsche. At this point or place Nietzsche links experimentation with the development of improv techniques. The principal axioms underscoring the gay science are related to dimensions of exploration and discovery; discovery is not seen simply as sheer "inventing" but, under certain conditions, as a way of discovering what was already there, inhabited, which is why Nietzsche sometimes takes recourse to the discovery of America—an event, an experiment, a unique stage for representing the serious historical risk. If Mary Shelley saw the discovery of America as an event that occurred too suddenly, without the stops and protections of gradual inquiry (in sum, as a world-historical shock of violence that disrupted all sorts of ecologies, material and immaterial, conscious and unconscious), Nietzsche studies the profound disruption to thought that the experimental theater of America directed. Taking off for America, he redefines the place of the experimenter, letting go of familiar mappings and manageable idioms. The experimenter must give up any secure anchoring in a homeland, allow herself to be directed by an accidental current rather than aiming for a preestablished goal. The accidental current becomes the groove for a voyage taken without any helmsman, without any commander, Nietzsche insists. As exemplary contingency plan, America allows for outstanding reinscriptions of fortuity. Its alliance with unprecedented applications of the inessential—the complicity with risk—gives everyone the hope at least of having an even chance. The fate of America, or this aspect of it, was written into its constitution as a land of discovery. And now we turn to the accidental discovery of America, where Nietzsche goes on a job hunt.

There have been ages when men believed with rigid confidence, even with piety, in their predestination for precisely one particular occupation, "precisely this way of earning a living, and simply refused to acknowledge the element of accident, role, and caprice" (Nietzsche 302). Nietzsche adds that "[w]ith the help of this faith, classes, guilds and hereditary trade privileges managed to erect those monsters of social pyramids that distinguish the Middle Ages and to whose credit one can adduce at least one thing: durability (and duration is a first-rate value on earth)" (302). Uninterrogated durability and rigid social hierarchy will be thrown over by what Nietzsche calls "America":

But there are opposite ages, really democratic, where people give up this faith, and a certain cocky faith and opposite point of view advance more and more into the foreground—the Athenian faith that first becomes noticeable in the Periclean age, the faith of the Americans today that is more and more becoming the European faith as well: the individual becomes convinced that he can do just about everything and can manage any role, and everybody experiments with himself, improvises, makes new experiments, enjoys his experiments; and all nature ceases and becomes art. (302–3)

A disfiguring translation of the Renaissance man, the jack-of-all-trades *is* an American symptom rebounding to Europe, changing the configuration of the want ads that erase natural constraints. One is up for anything, open to the identity du jour, capable of ceaseless remakes and crucial adjustments. The American athleticism of identity switching has marked politics everywhere, brushing against ideologies of authentic rootedness or natural entitlement. It also means that anyone can in principle try anything out, on the bright flipside of which we count the art of improv and experimentation, including performance art and jazz (music was always with science on this point, from at least Bach's *Inventions* to computer synthesizers and the communities of their beyond). Nietzsche's focus rests upon the individual's incredible conviction that he can manage any role. The refined profile for role management, by the way, Nietzsche locates in the Jewish people, who have had to rigorously play it as it comes, go with the flow, adjust and associate. The experimenter is at once the experimentee: there is little room here for the security of scientific or artistic distance, or, more precisely, he supplies just enough slack to let one try oneself out. Everyone turns himself into a test site, produces ever new experiments and, significantly, enjoys these experiments. This plasticity does not match the solemn lab for which Dr. Frankenstein becomes the paradigmatic director, beset as he is with Germanic gravity and remorse over the meaning of his relentless experiments. Nonetheless, oppositions should not be held too rigidly, for Europe and America are sharing needles on this one, contaminating one another according to the possibilities of new experimental *jouissance*. In the end Victor Frankenstein, too, was carried over the top by his brand of *jouissance,* by a level of desire punctuated by grim determination.

Clearly, there is a price to be paid by the experimental player. One cannot remain detached from the activity but finds oneself subject to morphing. One grows into one's experimental role and becomes one's mask. America's increasing obsession with actors—now actors have political views—has roots in Greece and can be connected to Nietzsche's observations on nonsubstantial role-playing:

> After accepting this role faith—an artist's faith, if you will—the Greeks, as is well known, went step for step through a rather odd metamorphosis that does not merit imitation in all respects: *They really became actors . . .* and whenever a human being begins to discover how he is playing a role and how he can be an actor, he *becomes* an actor. . . . It is thus that the maddest and most interesting ages of history always emerge, when the "actors," *all* kinds of actors, become the real masters. As this happens, another human type is disadvantaged more and more and finally made impossible; above all, the great "architects": The strength to build becomes paralyzed; the courage to make plans that encompass the distant future is discouraged; those with a genius for organization become scarce: who would still dare to undertake projects that would require thousands of years for their completion? For what is dying out is the fundamental faith that would enable us to calculate, to promise, to anticipate the future in plans of such scope, and to sacrifice the future to them—namely, the faith that man has value and meaning only insofar as he is *a stone in a great edifice;* and to that end he must be *solid* first of all, a "stone"—and above all not an actor! (303)

Nietzsche enters the zone where actors become the ruling part—"the real masters"—with the irony of mimetic dissuasion. This theater of politics and value-positing stunts should not necessarily be imitated. In this passage of paradoxical reversal, experimenting gradually becomes associated with America and the impending rule of actors. Nietzsche comes to see experimenting in the negative light of project paralysis, inhibiting acts of promising, calculating, or anticipation—acts by which the future can be nailed down, as it were, and "sacrificed" to the performatives that bind it. The future stone age has been compromised, however, by new human flora and fauna, which, Nietzsche asserts, could never have grown in more solid and limited ages. So the experimental disposition, cast in soft metaphors, waters down the solid reputation of the ages, showing the experimenter to be not quite solid as a rock but rather absorbed into a soft present that recedes from distance or future. Nonetheless, Nietzsche considers this age as one without limit—of unlimited finity; the age of actors encompasses the maddest and most interesting of possible ages. It is not clear how the loss of this hard rock faith ought to be evaluated in the end because Nietzsche elsewhere tends to emphasize the need for shedding such faith and, when taking on new forms spontaneously, he becomes somewhat of an American himself.

Nietzsche is well within his comfort zone when the personal technologies of shedding and softening take hold of existence, when brevity becomes the correct measure of a given stage of life. He is attached only to brief habits, he writes, describing a fluidity that allows him to get to know many things and states:

> I love brief habits and consider them an inestimable means for getting to know *many* things and states, down to the bottom of their sweetness and bitternesses. My nature is designed entirely for brief habits, even in the needs of my physical health and altogether *as far* as I can see at all—from the lowest to the highest. I always believe that here is something that will give me lasting satisfaction—brief habits, too, have this faith of passion, this faith in eternity—and that I am to be envied for having found and recognized it; and now it nourishes me at noon and in the evening and spreads a deep contentment all around itself and deep into me so that I desire nothing else, without having any need for comparisons, contempt or hatred. But one day its time is up; the good thing parts from me, not as something that has come to nauseate me but peacefully and sated with me as I am with it—as if we had reason to be grateful to each other as we shook hands to say farewell. Even then something new is waiting at the door, along with my faith—this indestructible fool and sage!—that this new discovery will be just right, and that this will be the last time. That is what happens to me with dishes, ideas, human beings, cities, poems, music, doctrines, ways of arranging the day, and life styles. (237)

Beyond the motif of farewell and Nietzschean gratitude, the passage inventories the things that offer themselves to experimentation, testing, and structural rearrangement, ranging from dishes, cities, schedule, and music to Nietzsche's unquestionably Californian invention of lifestyle. The existential range of motion allows for time to press upon pleasure, to mark the end with a mastered violence. Nietzsche says, and sees the day when, with a feeling of satiety and peacefulness, the time comes for good things to bid him farewell. This reciprocal scene of departure invites the relation to things to evade the punishing rhythm of violent and constant improvisation. Something stays with him—the brief habit does not overthrow a certain habitual groundedness that supports brevity and experimental essays. In fact the excess of habitlessness would destroy the thinker and send him out of America into Siberia: "Most intolerable, to be sure, and the terrible par excellence would be for me a life entirely devoid of habits, a life that would demand perpetual improvisation. That would be my exile and my Siberia" (237). Carried to extremes, the homelessness of experimentation turns into radical exile—into the horror of being—when it demands nonstop improv. Still, the opposite of horror is odious to Nietzsche, a kind of political noose around his delicate neck:

> *Enduring* habits I hate. I feel as if a tyrant had come near me and as if the air I breathe had thickened when events take such a turn that it appears that they will inevitably give rise to enduring habits; for example, owing to an official position, constant association with the same people, a permanent domicile, or unique good health. Yes, at the very bottom of my soul I feel grateful to all my misery and bouts of sickness and everything about me that is imperfect, because this sort of thing leaves me with a hundred backdoors through which I can escape from enduring habits. (237)

The experimental disposition, then, has to dismantle its internal and material lab frequently to keep the punctual rhythm of the brief habit going—a philosophical policy that bears significant implications. Nietzsche never places the experiment on the side of monumentality or reliable duration; it cannot be viewed as a project. Nor is he attached to a particular form of experiment—this is not the scientist obsessed with an idée fixe—but one capable of uprooting and going, for better or worse, with the diversifying flow of ever new flora and fauna. This degree of openness, though it does have its limits and points of closure, necessarily invites ambivalence—those moments, for instance, when Nietzsche stalls, dreaming of immense edifices and the permanence promised by contracts written in stone.

Although he at every point invites such a register of understanding, the Nietzschean ambivalence toward experimentation cannot be reduced to the personal whim or contingent caprice of Fred Nietzsche, even when he experiments on himself or writes in a letter to Peter Gast that Gay Sci was the most *personal* among his books. What he means by "personal" has everything to do with the nature of scientificity that he expounds. In Nietzsche as in Goethe, scientists are at no point strictly or simply outside the field of experimentation; part of the thinking of personality, they cannot extricate themselves from the space of inquiry in the name of some mystified or transcendental project from which the personhood of the scientist can be dropped out or beamed up at will. The test site can always blow up in their faces or make ethical demands on them—this eventuation, for Nietzsche, would remain a personal dilemma.[6] But let us leave for another time the question of where this takes us in terms of the personalized cartography of the Gay Sci.[7]

Notes

1. "L'absence de l'oeuvre" is the formulation of Phillipe Lacoue-Labarthe in *Le sujet de la philosophie: Typographies I* (Aubier: Flammarion, 1979). See Christopher Fynsk's translation of the relevant sections in *Typography: Mimesis, Philosophy, Politics* (Cambridge: Harvard UP, 1989). More recently, Derrida, has linked Nietzsche to the technological grid: "[T]he name of Nietzsche could serve as an 'index' to a series of questions that have become all the more pressing since the end of the Cold War" (*Negotiations: Interventions and Interviews 1971–2001*. Trans. Elizabeth Rottenberg. Stanford: Stanford UP, 2002, 253).

2. *The Gay Science: With a Prelude in Rhymes* (Trans. Walter Kaufmann, New York: Vintage, 1974), 251n42.

3. See Derrida, *Psyché: L'invention de l'autre* (Paris: Editions Galilee, 1987), 60–92.

4. The status of the gulf war as test is a working thesis in my *Finitude's Score: Essays Toward the End of the Millennium* (Lincoln and London: University of Nebraska Press, 1992).

5. In the case of the gulf war, weapons were deployed that had been amassed against the Soviet Union but fell under the risk of never being tried out. As clear as the logic of engagement may have seemed with the justificatory chatter of a new world order, the gulf war was, strictly speaking (in terms of the essence of technology that is pushing these buttons), little more than a field test. While the unstoppable relation of technology to testing may still require considerable theoretical scrutiny, it comes as no surprise to the so-called military establishment(the distinction between military and civil technologies blurs increasingly). In any case, the trade fair held directly after the gulf war tagged certain weapons as "combat proven" and boosted sales. Finally, war, as it increasingly becomes the technological and teletopical test site par excellence, has lost its metaphysical status as meaningful production—at least since Hegel's discussion of war as a sort of pregnancy test for historical becoming. If we no longer know how to

wage war, in other words, how to legitimate and justify its necessity in history's unfolding (we desist at times from calling our interventions war—they have become police actions or humanitarian runs), we still hope that it may yield some test results.

6. The involvement of the personal in the logic of scientific discovery is a problem that has been tried by Derrida in his analysis, for instance, of Freud's place in the discovery of *fort/da* as well as in the trajectories of Lacan's return to Freud, or Foucault's massive reading of desire and power. Yet it is Derrida who is most often cast in the role of experimenter. Indeed, Derrida's relation to improvisation and invention is something that still needs to be understood *scientifically,* if one can still say so, if only to clear away the blindness that has addressed some of his boldest experiments. For this is the age of experimentation, and we have not yet learned to read its protocols.

7. Departing from the American trope, I discuss this and related matters in *The Test Drive* (Urbana and Chicago: University of Illinois Press, 2004).

Koan Practice or Taking Down the Test

I stand on light feet now,
Catching breath before I speak
For there are songs in every style,
But to put a new one to the touchstone [*basanôi*]
For testing [*es elegkhon*] is all danger.
—Pindar, *Nemean* 8 (19–20)[1]

For once
In visible form the Sphinx
Came on him and all of us
Saw his wisdom and in that test [*basanôi*]
He saved the city.
—Sophokles, *Oedipus Rex* (498–510)[2]

Prototype 1.0

Testing the limit. In the interview accorded to Salomon Malka, Levinas announces, "I prefer the word *épreuve* to *expérience* because in the word *expérience* a knowing of which the self is master is always said. In the word *épreuve* there is at once the idea of life and of a critical 'verification' which overflows the self of which it is only the 'scene.'"[3] When Lévinas overhauls experience or experiment with the type of endurance implied by *épreuve,* he opts for a kind of trial: a test site in which the self is placed at absolute risk. The call for 'verification'—the quotation marks indicate the provisional character of verification—announces a life submitted to incessant probes, unfaltering revision, what in Nietzsche is governed by the principle of rescindability. In *The Gay Science* every proposition, every subproposition, and life find themselves subjected to the rigors of the *épreuve.*

• • •

307

"Knowing is not the way."[4]

The exquisite discipline and daring askesis of certain types of non-Western practice challenge the limits of what we understand by testing. By slackening the finish line and undermining the ideology of sanctioned results in favor of another logic of rigor, a number of Zen and yogic teachings at once suspend and resurrect the constitution of the test. Zen does not merely erase testing but holds it in reserve, situating it otherwise. Vast and imposing, Eastern relations to something like testing reconfigure yet steadfastly enforce the warrior poses that pervade Western registers of testing. The value of contest also shifts. In Tai Chi one learns to step aside when a hostile energy is on the loose: one is taught to let the menacing lunge collapse against the stubborn velocities of its own intentions. The engagement with opposing forces (which can no longer be conceived as opposing since, by a slight shift in energy and position, the commensurate reach is broken, the flow diverted)—indeed, the very concept of testing limits, undergoes fateful innovation. All the same, Eastern practices, including those associated with the martial arts, hold back from completely writing off the test; they do not simply oppose the West-test. In a sense, the test becomes even more pervasive because it can at no point be satisfied by a conclusive answer or a definitive response to the probe that has been put out. The difficult boundaries of the Zen trial, the characteristics of which can be at once asserted and equally disputed, are especially evident in the case of *koans*—the problems or inner challenges with which Zen masters traditionally have confronted their pupils. The Occident has put up other fronts, obeying quickening velocities: If such acts as going after the grail or attempting to reach a metaphysically-laden Castle can be viewed as exemplifying narratives of the Western test drive, then the Eastern "test" (this quality has not yet been established) is, by comparison, shatterably slowgoing.

The grail, there is no doubt about it, must be found, if only to mark out the end of a narrative journey. The Castle, at least in Kafka's takeover narrative, cannot be properly located or possessed, though it remains the sign toward which K. strives, hoping to conclude his trial. The scenography of the Eastern counterpart tends to be characterized by that which is immobile, though pupils and monks travel to sit with one another, and there is the phenomenon of the Zen warrior to contend with as well or, in yet another tradition, one encounters the implacability of the bold-spirited Samurai. No one ranks as a weakling in these traditions, even though a place of honor is accorded in Eastern practices to the inaction hero; the koan recipient may sit for years, meditating on a word or puzzle, weighing a persistent enigma posed by the master. In view of these descriptive attributes, K. may be looked upon as a high-strung Zen pupil (not in itself a contradiction), for his journey is abbreviated by sittings in which he tries earnestly to study and solve unyielding narrative puzzles. Nonetheless, the Kafkan warrior remains an effect of the West, even if his territory is at one point evoked as "Westwest," suggesting the overcoming and acknowledged excess of westerliness. He is going nowhere fast. And while it would be foolish to talk too readily about interiority for this lettered being, his goal is posited outside (this gets complicated) and goes under the name of "Castle" or homes in on the boss man, Klamm. K. cannot look inside for the answer, in part because Kafka has evacuated internal metaphors. The Zen pupil looks inwardly, but this is not the same as a subjectivity: the pupil is led to an inner experience without interiority, to understanding without cognition, without a history. K. had a history prior to entering the Castle territory, which does not serve him in his search; the Zen pupil enters the space of distilled performativity for which there is no outside. Reference has become immaterial, though effects of reference may occur indifferently, almost by accident. There is nothing to look for outside an always emptying self. This becoming-empty is what K. undergoes as he searches for a reference that could be tied to the empty signifier of the Castle. He scales the walls of recalcitrant signification but clings to the territo-rialization of a promised outside, a space occupied by the sacred signifier—just as Parsifal goes out to a site where the allegory of his search would be collapsed into a figure. Meanwhile, the Zen pupil, often a wanderer, listens differently, stilling herself to consider the sonic eventfulness of growing grass.

Responding to the demand of the koan prompts a colossal if barely traceable event. This means, among other things, that understanding no longer crowns the end of a labored process of appropriation. In fact, the Eastern concern for the koan tradition lies with enlightenment, which may or may not be closely tied to sudden understanding or to the arduous example of trial by error and the lessons of incessant failure. When one considers Zen practice seriously, it is another seriousness that appears. Yet once we begin thinking and figuring this other seriousness, this other rigor, Western narratives of testing themselves begin to incorporate the Orient. The story of the grail turns out to be even more intricate, more self-doubting, than that of a search conducted under the authority of the commanding signifier. Thus Parsifal's journey already marks the aftermath of the true test he failed to pass. The quest for the grail comes about as a pressing retest, something on the order of a punishingly sustained make-up quiz. The true test, which was never given out or formulated as such, required that an innocent simpleton produce a question motivated by compas-sion. Parsifal, for his part, was too dumb to fill the role of the innocent simpleton, having frozen at the sight of the ailing king. The test required him—innocently, without knowing he was being tested—to ask why the king was suffering. Instead, Parsifal gawked, unable to utter a word of compassion. In this case, the unspoken test was not asking for an answer but for a question. What does this have to do with us?

The failure to ask the compassionate question has brought about the test as we know it—formulated, set, a delimited field governed by a figure of the final limit: the grail. The paradoxical structure of this test should not be overlooked. Parsifal is made to undergo the experience of many trials in order to gain . . . innocence. This process resembles anything but the trajectory of the *Bildungsroman*. (It already engages the Kafkan impossibility of producing, through experiential motions, the effects of innocence.) Experience is not meant to lead to maturity or ethical comprehension but to a kind of aporetic term, eliciting a dispossession of self linked to absolute innocence. *Bildung*, by contrast, climbs different rungs of self-dispossession as it takes on ethicity and the state. Parsifal's process or trial falls back to an originary acquiescence, to a disposition that precedes even the possibility of saying "yes." Something has to be returned to what never happened, prior to happening or to the early grammars of affirmingly absorbing the other. The hero chases down a first place that hasn't yet taken place. As a notion, experience is shown to fold in on itself: destroying its inherited concept, it rolls persistently backwards. Even at the start, as early as the sagas associated with the name Parsifal. It is a stripping down, and in this sense it begins to seem Eastern. Yet, while Parsifal's quest after the holy grail is intended to achieve nothing if not non-knowledge, it takes another turn in the nineteenth century by offering a share of redemptive bonuses. The promise of redemption underscored by Wagner's resumption of the medieval tale has made Nietzsche wretch. Innocence was sidetracked by priestliness. The saving Elsewhere, another time zone—that of transcendence—will have been the goal, dissipating the here and now, bound to an increasingly spirtualized altar. The elusive materiality of the grail, reduced to symbolic qualities, henceforth belongs to the Christianization of world. Still, the force that is gathered under the name of Parsifal—or, in Chestian de Troyes, *Perceval*, in Wolfram von Eschenbach, *Parsifal*, in Richard Wagner, *Parzifal*—establishes an entire paradigm for Western self-testing, for the administration of a test with no preexisting conditions.

Prototype 1.1

> "Soen-sa said, 'Where does that question come from?'
> The student was silent."[5]

The Thousand and Ten Doubts. We might have become accustomed to viewing the test as a way of mobilizing courage, revving our engines, gaining on a problem, or increasing speed as a technological limit is tried. Designed to provoke doubt and shake attachments, the koan slows things down—as if psychic layering had kicked everything into reverse warp speed. The slow motion of a barely codifiable procedure, the koan instigates the other logic of testing, or testing's other logic, to which it at once remains similar as well as unassimilable. If it could be made to represent anything at all—a distinctly Western problem, the drive toward representation—the koan "represents" the emptiness of Zen practice where it cuts across the edges of testing. Koan practice explicitly engages the limits of psychic endurance, providing testing grounds upon which mind and body (there are different mind domains and several bodies to account for, but this is another story) are said to wrestle for a solution. Yet, wrestling does not offer a match for what we are seeking: any effort must be superseded by exorbitant exercises of patience, colossal restraint. Extreme surrender and relentless focus must somehow meet in koan practice. Koan provokes an unceasing assault on the fortress of human reason. Western forms of testing have some of that too, the mind/body collaborations, I mean, as when Oedipus was questioned by the Sphinx. The Sphinx marks the porous boundary between Western and Eastern domains of questioning and tells of bodies menaced by pulverization: should the riddle not be solved, either the questioner or the questioned must go. Passing the test is a matter of survival of the species for Oedipus, as it is for the interspecial dominatrix of the riddle: la Sphinx dissolves when the young man offers the correct answer. In the case of the koan a body must offer itself up for any possible inscription of a response; pressed into service when a question is issued, a body belongs to the writing of an answer. It is as though the very possibility of response required a permanent yet decelerated olympiad of the various flexes of mind and bodies. Still, in preparation for receiving the koan, the all too ready contenders must be wrestled down, disqualified in the preliminaries: rational and discursive thought must be vanquished if the incommensurate, which koan demands upon receipt, is to be discovered. Another site of thinking beyond thinking is being sought, where operations of sublation and annulment coexist, calling for the different experiences of saying.

A site of thinking beyond thinking, testing is not eliminated but takes place beyond the parameters of a test subsumed under codifiable attributes. The largely internal contest of koan is intended to secure an experience of extreme dispossession. But the themes and topoi of inside and outside, of internally and externally determined categories, do not mean much here except for the dependence that koan practice implies on concepts of opening. A draft for scheming radical exposure, the koan, offered by the teacher—the "master"—is meant to "open" the pupil to the possibility of saying. The master is responsible for initiating the call of such an opening. Often this opening, which in no tradition escapes the suspicion of violence, is attained by the administration of a shock. Thus the master, in texts devoted to the koan, is frequently figured as beating, hitting, or slugging the pupil. The hit seals a sort of "compliment" conferred by the attentive master, who prods the physical body for the purpose of uninhibiting a scene of contemplation, new and unanticipated. The shock is crucial to the experience of the koan: it stages the opening of thought exceeding itself in the jolt. Although the temptation may exist to read such protocols of saying in a mood of estrangement, one would be wrong to envision the choreography of violence as something foreign to Western forms of thinking about thinking. There is the Heideggerian *Stoss* (jolt) in *Being and Time* that, awakening to its own beat, still needs to be contended with; nor should one overlook the destructive passivities of Blanchot puzzling out Levinas. Some passages of the *Infinite Conversation* or *The Writing of the Disaster* stunningly converge with the abandonment to which the koan consigns passive bodies, particularly where the koan burdens the student with the strictures of responsible saying:

> Where passivity unworks and destroys me, I am at the same time pressed into
> a responsibility which not only exceeds me, but which I cannot exercise, since
> I do nothing and no longer exist as myself. It is that responsible passivity that
> is Saying. For, before anything said, and outside being . . . Saying gives and
> gives response, responding to the impossible, for the impossible.[6]

The exposure that occurs in and with language does not abandon the body (there are often up to ten bodies to count, to honor, to nurture, including the subtle, back and energetic bodies) or its psychic traces. Perhaps such a thinking of exposure approaches in several ways a kind of Blanchotian destruction. Though the vocabulary of his insight cannot easily be made to pull together other spaces, Blanchot, situated between literary and philosophical thought, offers us a bridge, a passageway, when he writes of tremendous passivity in conjunction with exposure.[7] The "passivity beyond passivity" that Blanchot shares with or retrieves from Levinas may not entirely communicate with the

Zen center of articulation that it nonetheless remasters; still, the themes of persecuted exposure, of the other (*autrui*) who "weighs upon me to the point of opening me to the radical passivity of the self,"[8] of the pursuit of an enigma that troubles all sense of order, cutting into and interruptive of being, appear to converge with the eccentricities of the koan. And where Heidegger's famous description of the "pure night of anxiety" in *What is Metaphysics?* resonates lexically with the writings of the great Zen master, Ta-hui, there is still a deeper cut of askesis, a different eloquence of piety—an altogether other ex-stasis—and still yet another mortal exposure of vulnerability to be dealt with here.

What these names and texts share is the sense that the awakening, regardless of an increasingly imposing degree of intensity, is never quite sufficient to itself—not for Blanchot, not for Kao-feng Yüan-Miao, Heidegger or Levinas. The passivity is never passive enough. Or in Derrida's terms, the responsibility for bearing the enigma is never responsible enough. But if cver the limits of such disclosive insufficiency had been put to the test, it was surely in the koan tradition which, though recorded abundantly, resists the more familiar protocols of discursivity. A teaching without pedagogy, it is a practice; a rapport to thoughtfulness, its practice is dedicated to the obliteration of thought. Calling for the dissolution of time, it takes time. It beats the clock while slowing down the minutes. This teaching takes more time than Heidegger, when after going through the sections on Nietzsche in *What is Called Thinking?*, clocks in and tells his students that they must now turn back and spend the next ten years studying Aristotle.

Passive and constricted, one is responsible for one's koan, which is always related to a public space of notice or inscription. Koan, which comes from *ko*, "public," "public announcement" and *an*, "matter," "material for thought," involves extreme manipulations of exposure. Tremendous feats of rigorous nothingness are accomplished with intractable discretion. Koan is a matter of responding thoughtfully beyond thinking to the call of a master's question—the logically insoluble riddle—in a manner which, becoming public, exposes the student to the outer limits of (not-) knowing.[9] Neither students nor master can be said to possess knowledge: Having no interior, the master is not predicable. This condition in no way demobilizes the *effect* the master produces on the restricted theater of the koan. Unleashing the question, the master may strike the student, regulate the degree of psychic tension, functionally subsidize the pervasiveness of great doubt, and withhold or cede acknowledgement in a series of discrete interviews. The shock that accompanies the field of knowing beyond knowledge, startling the student into different rosters of articulation, has become condensed and displaced onto the figure of the koan itself. The *OED* cites fairly recent usages that assimilate the koan's shock effect to the semantic quality of the term, rendering the nature of the problem the cause of shock: "A less physical shock technique is the *koan,* a problem designed to shock the mind beyond mere thinking." A letter written by Aldous Huxley on 11 January 1969 observes: "They might act as Zen koans and cause sudden openings into hitherto unglimpsed regions."[10] Ruth Benedict avers: "The significance of the koan does not lie in the truths these seekers after truth discover."[11]

The sudden openings to which Huxley's letter alludes, and which the major part of texts devoted to koan interviews confirm, indicate that something like a direct transmission of the Zen hermeneutic can occur outside the sutra. The experience of "getting it" described by the Zen tradition comes closest in re-cent Western articulations to Heidegger's *Ereignis,* perhaps, in the sense that something occurs, bursts forth at a given moment; it is marked as pure eruption without a lead in or back up. What occurs is an a-temporal interruption or a "fold" in time, something that Heidegger draws from the archaic German word, *Eräugnis,* which establishes a link between Being and light. Christopher Fynsk calls this accession to language a blinding of sorts, referring to the opening, in relation to the sudden fulguration of what Hölderlin (and some traditions of Zen Buddhism) designated as a "third eye." It points to an awakening, to a watch that will never be watchful enough.[12]

After years of incessantly working the blindspot, there is still some place where one fails to see, a limit in perception. The koan does not quarrel with its own stain of blindness. It stays with the question, suffers blindness. With time, it becomes evident that the awaited answers are not about their discursive content or levels of perception but about the ever-harassing experience of answering. Answering to the call of the koan, you discover that you are not judged for the quality of the rightness or wrongness of your answer but are turned back upon the ungraspable experience of seeking to answer. Floundering has its own life. At the same time, as the sutras show, one is not given an automatic pass to the failing regions of trying to answer; there exists a hierarchy of flunking out: pupils proffer so many incomplete or wrongheaded answers, to which the master replies with a whacking.

The event of being slugged in the stories and histories that narrate them func-tions to evoke an equivalency to enlightenment. The hit—no doubt severe and to a more Western sensibility, humiliating (yet unflinchingly offered as compliment and gift)—has to be worked between the literal and figurative points of occur-rence in the stories that field them. The teaching words, "I hit you," are punctually invoked by the Zen master. These blows are delivered as semiotic units that are meant to inflict a wound or run interference from a domain that exceeds the experience of reading—if such an untroped domain can be understood to take hold. The body that has submitted itself to the task of answering gets hit. When one is hit by the master's rod linguistically, psychically, or referentially, the terms of relatedness to the question and quest switch. Engaged in dharma combat, you are being reminded by this exercise of scarring that there is something possibly other than reading the sutras, another reading, a different experience of writing that is calling you to answer. The switch: it stings, bringing you back to the question without consolation—no safety net or protective gauze, no institutional binding to hold or heal you. The switch or slug, the cutting that occurs as one gets comfortable with the question and takes on the koan, belongs in fact to a long history of conflict between traditions of the north and south, wealthy and poor practitioners, the readers and nonreader: each time it revives the problem, debated over the centuries, of whether enlightenment can be attained solely by reading, of whether studying the sutras can of itself bring about enlightenment. It may depend on how you read.

The scene of the proto-pedagogy involves only two persons. The master and pupil together produce an allegory of being struck, enlightened. Though the journey is solitary, one cannot arrive at a solution by oneself: there has to be another, someone who functions as limit in a persistent sting operation. The experience of enlightenment has little (nothing) to do with self, with triumphal narratives of self-gathering, or with the bloated accomplishments of successive sieges of alien territory. (It is difficult by contrast to imagine a Western hero, even one that goes under the name *Weltgeist*, who, when facing the master, would go away so empty handed, without succeeding—that is, without *stealing* that place for himself according to the precepts of a familiar parricidal maneuver.) The master stands, or rather, sits, as a reminder that there has to be something there to read, something outside a self, a being, a registrar of expectant saying—something from the get go of trying to get it already emptied, depropriated, even if it occurs in the switch of a whiplash.

What of the master? This word weighs heavily on Western vocabularies. The philosophical, teaching master, often appears as an impoverished cipher. The withdrawal of the exaltation of the master may recall but bears only a vague relation to the Socratic counterpart, the cruiser and prodder, who could give us traction here, as a Western complement to the minimalist figure of mastery. The experience of enlightenment will have nothing to do with what the master has to tell you. The locution, "the master knows" amounts to an absurdity. Without interior or predication, the figure for mastering as such—or rather, in the absence of suchness—the bareness of figure cannot warrant the solidity of hierarchy or the permanence of a superior claim on knowledge. From the texts that treat these relations, we discover that dharma combat equalizes everyone: whoever wins it, has won. The master in any case cannot confer, or confers only the occasional "compliment;" he (sometimes she: there are such stories) repeats, punctuates, helps constitute the experience of enlightenment as he (sometimes she) accompanies the collection of thought (*sesshin*).

The koan, a kind of contemplative story, a riddle or question, might take anywhere from three to fifteen years to answer. One is called upon steadily to go on with the koan every moment of one's life. The problem, at a first level, is how to live with one's question. Some efforts to live with the question are seen as dead in the water, or in any case, as being part of a bad passivity. Against Hung-chih's "silent illumination Zen," Ta-hui offers criticism of what he sees as the extreme passivity of false practice. The root emptiness of Zen practice should not be taken for a dead, lifeless emptiness; nor should practitioners pass their time lifelessly liked "cold ashes or a withered tree."[13] Ta-hui is among those Zen masters who vigorously promoted the use of koan. His teaching was patterned after the koan. Koan practice, the most assured path to the attainment of enlightenment, was required of every Zen student. Once the question had been posed, the puzzle formulated, the student was expected to hold fast to it. However, the koan resisted such a hold. It was meant to summon up terrific doubt, and brought practitioners to the edge of endurance. A number of masters, not to say students, suffered appalling breakdowns, some of whom recorded their shattering experiences. The koan "makes its central point through doubt. Doubt bores into the mind of the practitioner and leads to enlightenment."[14]

For Ta-Hui, the koan elicits doubt but doubt must function neither as a stimulant nor should it undergird drivenness. It belongs to the region of non-negative negations, a patient abiding with the existential of *withoutness.* Your attention should be fixed on the koan without yielding to the sense of enchantment that accompanies a discovery, without fascination for the multiplicities of possibilities it may imply, without the thrill of infinite interpretability and, on the other hand, without the guilt of nontotalization. Nor must material indices from a world putatively outside the dilemma of the koan intrude upon the contemplating mind. In other words, all traces of *striving* must be stilled, although the striving nature of the quest remains largely intact. This structure is in communication with the Faustian valuation of *streben,* the redemptive human quality inscribed in the West-test, though the effort takes on a decidedly different amplitude, insinuating a different measure of achievement. The hold of the koan is barely comprehensible in terms of Western techniques of endurance testing. There is for instance the story of the monk who failed successively to respond to his koan; bringing an answer to the master, he was several times rebuffed. He left the monastery, traveled far until he found a huge wall before which he stood for nine years straight, contemplating the question. After nine years, enlightenment struck, he returned to the monastery where the master was able to acknowledge the response. A second koan sent him out for another fifteen years.

Besides laying claim to incalculable stores of patience, the koan regulates and meticulously increases the dosage of anxiety by which it prods the student toward enlightenment. Kao-feng Yüan-miao (1238–1295), a highly respected master from the Yang-chi lineage of the Rinzai School, emphasized the necessity of inducing anxiety and doubt in his magesterial work, *The Essentials of Zen.* The three crucial traits that inform the practice are "a great root of faith" (Jpn., *daishinkan*), "a great tenacity of purpose" (Jpn., *daifunshi*), and "a great feeling of doubt" (Jpn., *daigijo*).[15] In order to convey its principal cast, he illustrates the *feeling* of doubt by summoning forth a criminal's anxiety. A cousin to Nietzsche's pale criminal, this character is caught in the moment of greatest anxiety: gripped by suspense, thoroughly terrified, he wonders whether the heinous crime committed earlier will be found out or not. The lapse between the abomination and its discovery pinpoints the feeling for which the master seeks duration. Trekking alongside faith and purpose, then, there is the excessive anxiety of being caught out, hunted, humiliated. The necessary hinge with the questioning of the question involves the extreme persecution of the respondent, who is held by the master over the edge of pained endurance, a criminal's suspense. (To make a Western or at least a Freudian intervention here, such a criminal houses a super-ego: the master has already broken in and entered the psyche, bitten by remorse. As Dostoevsky and current psycho upgrades have decisively demonstrated, not all criminals shiver with terror or avoid discovery.)

Ta-hui's teaching of doubt as an essential characteristic of koan practice remained the norm throughout Chinese Zen from the end of the Sung period. Doubt must have its long day without the stabilizers provided by longing or goal. Ta-hui repeatedly warns against the intrusion of a conscious desire for enlightment and so presses for the removal of all imaginative and discursive thought. To underscore the pungency of Zen practice, Ta-hui evokes Wu-Tsu Fa-yen, the teacher of his own master, Yüan-wu K'o-ch'in. Ta-hui returns to the "grandfatherly" teacher, an innovator of rigorous koan practice, after having burned and incinerated the *Hekiganroki,* the work of his own master. The only explanation to help us grasp the reportedly pious act of destruction runs as follows: "Most likely he destroyed the text because he found that its literary beauty was preventing students from the painful struggle with the koan on nothingness, which for him was the only true koan."[16] The self-annulling relation to text in koan history creates significant tensions that parallel metaphysical attacks on writing in the West. Rhetoricity and literary excess are suspected of distracting the contemplator from the objectless object of a prior speech. An allegory of nothingness, the koan cannot at times tolerate the very materiality of its transmission, the linguistic intrusion on which it nonetheless depends. The famous koan on nothingness, which assumes an important place in Zen history and which Wu-men Hui-K'ai set as the opening of the *Mumomkan,* concerns the absolute nothingness of the Buddha nature that transcends being and nonbeing.[17] The opening koan, which carries as title, "Choa-chou's Dog," counts among the few koan to which he attached a long commentary. Here, too, Wu-men locates the essence of the koan in its ability to stir up doubt. The character *mu* is, he explains, "the gateless barrier of the Zen school." He asks, "Do you not wish to pass through this barrier?"[18] The other barrier, that of text, must continually be erased so that doubt can be positioned as the sole partition put up before the ever faltering reader. "Do you not wish to pass through this barrier?" If so,

> Then concentrate yourself into this "Mu," with your 360 bones and 84,00 pores, making your whole body one great inquiry. Day and night work intently at it. Do not attempt nihilistic or dualistic interpretations. It is like having bolted a red hot iron ball. You try to vomit it but cannot . . .

> Now, how should one strive? With might and main work at this "Mu," and be "Mu." If you do not stop or waver in your striving, then behold, when the Dharma candle is lighted, darkness is at once enlightened.[19]

Swallowing the unreleasable red hot iron ball, one strives to become one's "Mu;" one yields to the searing implosion of the incorporated question.

Much as in Plato, the case against writing (and reading) was organized around the theme of passivity. But even writing (and reading) were displaced as acts on to a notion of "gazing," so much are these acts abjected. The Rinzai school, which dominated Chinese Zen during the Sung period, gradually absorbed all other houses and fringe movements with the exception of the Soto school, where the influence of Hung-chih survived. Historians of Zen Buddhism tend to underscore the schism between Hung-chih's "silent-illumination Zen" and Ta-hui's "koan-gazing Zen," an apparent extension of the conflict between the Northern and Southern schools, particularly since Ta-hui's "abusive attacks against the quiet sitting practices by the disciples of silent illumination are reminiscent of Shen-hui's assaults on the 'quietism' of the Northern School."[20] At the same time, it would be wrong to sum up the history of Zen from the time of Bodhidharma to the present in terms of only two opposing operations. Nonetheless, the divide between the Rinzai and Soto schools continues to dominate the issues under discussion, and it is continually reasserted in the controversy between Hung-chih and Ta-hui as well as in subsequent disputes. Let us briefly consider their main features. Those in support of Rinzai reproach the Soto school for tending excessively toward passivity: "Only to sit in meditation, they say, dulls the mind into inactivity and engulfs it in a sleepy twilight."[21] While Soto adherents do not deny the dangers of a bad passivity, they counter that their purpose lies elsewhere: "Authentic Soto teachers cultivate an extremely alert and objectless form of meditation. Moreover, koan are used in the Soto school, albeit not in the same dynamic style as in the Rinzai school. The manner of meditation in the Soto school is more calm, but it certainly does not exclude the experience of enlightenment."[22]

Another significant criticism that Ta-hui directed against Hung-chih concerns the experience itself of enlightenment (Jpn., *satori*). The Rinzai school watches for a flash experience, an abrupt opening that suddenly sparks a profoundly reorienting conversion. "The quickest and surest way to this kind of experience is through the extreme tension-in-doubt produced by the Koan exercise. Both koan and *satori,* say the Rinzai followers, are neglected by the Soto school."[23] The criticism seems hyperbolic, for Soto also recognizes sudden enlightenment, "for which koan practice can be extremely helpful; not a few of its masters underwent powerful, shattering experiences."[24] The value of such explosive experiences and the difficulty of determining their difference from enlightenment, requires some further commentary. For the breakthrough is always shadowed by a breakdown; the ascension can also be a fall, though the discipline requires for its legitimate practice the affirmation of a mark of harmony—a palpable measure of control and another conception of clarity that flows gently from serenity. It may appear to duplicate what we might "recognize" as a manic crisis; still, the breakthrough is constituted otherwise, and has a different temporal run. Wait. In fact it does not run. There is something like a passive shattering that seems to be at the root of the debate, reminiscent of Blanchot's discussion of destructive passivities.[25]

There may be a restraining order put on running or on any fast-paced discursive activity; yet, to the extent that it implies tremendous discipline, the restraint itself disrupts the orders of passivity and activity that have seemed opposable to one another. Once again we see that the athletics implicit in koan practice are not entirely dissimilar from the wrestling matches in Plato or the strained leaps that Heidegger coaches; nor even do they outrun the parameters set by the decathalon that Rousseau charts in the *Reveries of a Solitary Walker.* The athletic contest, no matter how masked or disseminated, has always been lodged in the Western thinking of thought, in what Robert Musil consistently calls our "thought sports." Metaphysics and athleticism often work out on the same track, sharing a field house of language, play and determination. Even as Heidegger negotiates at the limits of metaphysics, he measures jumps and prescribes unprecedented leaps. The leap is favored by Heidegger for nearly two, arguably Zen, reasons: a phenomenal exertion, it goes essentially nowhere. The jump is a movement of departure and return, moving often to the same place, which no longer claims to be the same. Something will have happened in the interval. Something passed from one place to the same place, which leaves the very notion of place in suspense. The leaps and bounds, the breakthroughs and light converge on a barely measurable marker.

Whether rooted in Rinzai or Soto, the discipline behind the practice is incontestable. Whether we can call the pursuit of enlightenment ("pursuit" is too strong a word—too weak in some ways, as well) a *contest* remains an open question, for the terms are perpetually contested as they arise. The rapport to the koan in any case entreats athletic resolve. The body and mind train on the possibility of answering to the task of thinking beyond thinking.

The master gives the student a koan to think about, resolve, and report back on. The procedure, simple yet incalculable, implodes the concentrated student body. During the time devoted to the uncodified test, concentration intensifies to a breaking point. It is however said that only when the mind is relaxed, free from ego and purpose, fully devoted to the question at hand, can it open itself, up, pressing beyond the boundaries of prescribed thinking, stretching beyond the temptation of reason. In his early works, Suzuki subsumes the process under three terms: those of accumulation, saturation, and explosion. These terms are law; they cannot be evaded but serve to indicate an ever present scale of danger. Accumulation and saturation, when feeding a state of high tension, often lead to serious harm. A sense of danger in fact accompanies the whole ordeal, particularly since it is harried by the delicate timing of explosion. In some instances, the explosion, intended in the best of cases to abide by the rules of organic becoming, does not always follow the model of the opening of the skin of a ripe fruit. "There are plentiful examples from the past and present showing how the practice of the koan can lead to a bad end. It is not without good reason that Zen masters sound their warnings. The suppression of reason can throw one's psychic life out of balance."[26] Language falters, the student body cracks. A way to catch the fall, in some histories of its recounted occurrence, is to throw down a distinctly Western alibi and brace it with the grid of psychotherapy. "In the Zen practice called 'private interview' (*dekusan*), in which a student makes a progress report to a master, situations may arise that are like those that can take place in the psychotherapist's office. The student utters broken, incoherent words and gives expression to other spontaneous reactions."[27] The student, battling with narrative, is down for the count.

Body-broken, martyred to an overstretched capacity so as to engage the quest, the practitioner of the koan negotiates with absolute risk, testing and erasing limts that inevitably grind down the prospects of a thinking beyond thinking. Even where the raw nerve of exertion is subdued or denied, the strained condition of a testing without predictable end asserts itself. The intrusion of the test obtains as well in the relation to the master, where the koan figures as the thirdness that emerges between them, as that which cleaves the Conversation, in and beside language.

The significance of the trial of the koan was not lost on some Western philosophers or analysts. Martin Buber became fascinated by the master-disciple relationship in Zen, and focused part of his work on those koan that explicitly thematized this couple. He also compared the koan to the "legendary anecdotes" of Hasidism.[28] Jung was led to identify the "great liberation" in Zen with the emancipation of the unconscious.[29] The psychological structure of koan practice is seen by Jung to open a primordial (if still undeconstructed) space, prior to difference and division. "Under the enormous psychological strain of trying to force a solution for the insoluble koan, enlightenment is experienced as the dawn of a new reality in which the boundaries between the conscious and unconscious disappears, so that conscious and unconscious alike are laid open."[30] The passive construction ("enlightment is experienced") attests to the abiding contest between the possibility of a passive overture and the strain of "trying—"another way of relating the sheer openness of the unconscious to that which enables it: the experience of the test, the trial. It is important to note that, when he enters the zone of the unconscious, Jung emphasizes the strenuous efforts of trying, forcing and experience. He is cornered by that aspect of the koan that clings to the subjection of tested being.

In the end, though the end is not in sight, submission to the koan describes a critical syntax of our being, whether mapped according to Eastern or Western indicators. Something has forced one's hand. Prior even to the question, the posture of submissive assent to the koan, as a kind of primordial acquiescence, a form of consent, welcomes the advent of the question ahead of any determinability, before any dubitative or skeptical interjection, opening the field of a closely held language to what remains to be thought. This openness, it is sustained by the tremors of doubt. As for the adjustment of mind to this persistent downshift in the disposition of a test drive: "Make sure that you do not allow your mind to run off, like an old mouse that ran into the horn of an ox."[31]

321

Notes

1. *Pindar's Victory Songs* (Trans. Frank J. Nisetich, Baltimore, London: Johns Hopkins University Press, 1980), 218. On the Pindaric tradition and the significance of this poem see William Fitzgerald, *Agonistic Poetry, The Pindaric Mode in Pindar, Horace, Hölderlin and the English Ode* (Berkeley: University of California Press, 1987), 55ff.

2. Cited in Page du Bois, *Torture and Truth* (New York: Routledge, 1991), 16.

3. John Llewelyn, "Amen," in *Ethics as first Philosophy: The Significance of Emmanuel Levinas for Philosophy, Literature and Religion* (Ed. Adrian T. Peperzak, (New York: Routledge, 1995). Interview in Salomon Malka, *Lire Lévinas* (Paris: Cerf, 1984), 108.

4. "The Mahayana Sutras," in Heinrich Demoulin, *Zen Buddhism: A History* (New York: MacMillan, 1974)

5. *Dropping Ashes on the Buddha: The Teaching of Zen Master Seung Sahn,* (Ed. Stephen Mitchell, New York: Grove Press, 1976), 134.

6. Maurice Blanchot, *Ecriture du Désastre* (Paris: Gallimard, 1980); *The Writing of the Disaster* (Trans. Ann Smock, Lincoln: University of Nebraska Press, 1986), 37/20. See also Christopher Fynsk's discussion of this passage in terms of the Heideggerian "es gibt" of Being.

7. See in particular Christopher Fynsk's treatment of these questions in *Infant Figures: the Death of the Infans and Other Scenes of Origin* (Stanford: Stanford University Press, 2000).

8. Blanchot, *Désastre,* 43; *Disaster,* 24.

9. For a discussion of related forms of non-knowledge in Eastern and Western thought, see Keiji Nishitani, *Religion and Nothingness* (Trans. Jan van Bragt, Berkeley: California University Press: 1982), 162ff.

10. *Oxford English Dictionary* (Oxford: Oxford University Press, 2000.)

11. See Ruth Benedict, *The Chrysanthemum and the Sword* (Boston, Houghton Mifflin Company, 1946) xi, 246.

12. Ibid., 19.

13. Ibid., 258. See also the introduction to Hsing-hsiu, *Book of Serenity* (New York: Lindisfarne Press, 1990), translated and introduced by Thomas Cleary, ix-xli, and Koun Yamada, *Gateless Gate* (Tucson: University of Arizona Press, 1979), 93–169.

14. Benedict, *Chrysanthemum,* 258. Heinrich Dumoulin, *Zen Buddhism, A History: India and China With a New Supplement on the Northern School of Chinese Zen* (Trans. James W. Heisig and Paul Knitter, New York: Macmillan, 1994).

15. Ibid., 382.

16. Ibid.

17. Ibid.

18. Ibid., 259.

19. Ibid.

20. Ibid.

21. Ibid., 260.

22. Ibid.

23. Ibid.

24. Ibid.

25. While the contradictions and disputes between the two principal schools appear to be bound by a differend—the irreconcilable differences between "silent-illumination Zen" (*mokusho-zen*) and "koan-gazing zen" (*kanna-zen*) cannot be resolved—it is perhaps of some consequence that each school also regarded the other as a genuine form of Zen Buddhism. Zen histories refer to documents which reveal the consistently friendly, cordial relations enjoyed by Hung-chi and Ta-hui. "When Hung-chih died in the monastery of Mount T'ien-t'ung, which through his persevering efforts had become one of the important centers of Zen Buddhist monasticism, Ta hui hastened to attend the funeral rites of his deserving colleague, and we can be certain that Hung-chih would not have hesitated to show the same respects to Ta-hui." Benedict, *Chrysanthemum and the Sword*, 260.

26. Ibid., 262.

27. Ibid.

28. Martin Buber, *Werke III, Schriften zum Chassidismus* (Munich, Heidelberg: Kösel-Lambert Schneider, 1963), Vol. 3 of the collected works, 993ff., also 883–94.

29. See his introduction to Daisetz Teitaro Suzuki's *Introduction to Zen Buddhism* (New York, Philosophical Library, 1949), also included in C. G. Jung, *Collected Works*, Vol. II (London: Routledge and Kegan Paul, Ltd., 1969), 538–57.

30. Zen Master Torei Enji, *The Discourse on the Inexhaustible Lamp of the Zen School* (Trans. Yoko Okuda, with commentary by Master Daibi of Unkan, Boston: C. E. Tuttle Co., 1996), 254.

31. The advice comes from Chinese Zen Master Ta-hui: "The thousand and ten thousand doubts that well up in your breast are really only one doubt, all of them burst open when doubt is resolved in the koan. As long as the koan is not resolved, you must occupy yourself with it to the utmost. If you give up on your koan and stir up another doubt about a word of scripture or about a sutra teaching or about a koan of the ancients, or if you allow a doubt about worldly matters to come up—all this means to be joined to the evil spirit. You should not too easily agree with a koan solution that you have discovered, nor should you think about it further and make distinctions. Fasten your attention to where discursive thinking cannot reach." *Ibid.*, 257–258.

"Is It Happening?"

You're making it up, you're faking it, you can't prove it! As cruel and common as they are, these statements offend not only because they come from a hostile or institutionally appointed space of contestation. They belong to another curl of conspiratorial anguish. The disbelieving persecutor is not the only one who tries to reduce an inassimilable reality to a matter of testability. You yourself, as lacerated victim, cannot believe this has happened, *is still happening* to you. To *you*. Language fails you. It is not as if one has mastered trauma so well that one can get out from under its flaying machine or see or speak or know or understand. That severe, ego-built, part of you responsible for reality-testing shudders to a halt. Remember, K. from *The Trial* could not tell what was happening to him; he tried to play by the rules of cognition, went to court, submitted to the test, if that's what it was, until he was a dead man walking metamorphosed into a piece of executed dog. What I am trying to say is that the victim is rolled into an ongoing surprise attack, shaken down by a sudden spread of anxiety that bears the caption, "Is it happening?" Can this be true? This "*Arrive-t-il?*" of which Lyotard writes hits you in and as the foreign language region of your being, even in its most homegrown aspect of terror. What I am trying to say is that the persecutory reality continues to slap the victim around and does not come with a "how to tell and get over it" kit. There is only something that Lyotard calls a *feeling*—a terrible, startling feeling for which philosophy needs to find a phrase, a link, a support. Philosophy has to stop testifying for the institutionally self-satisfied controllers, stop kissing up to state-sanctioned power plays, and instead get into the untested regions of new idioms, new addresses, new referents; it has to abandon its conciliatory habits. Rather than continue its traditional pursuit of conciliation, philosophy, more or less according to Lyotard, needs to be invaded by new inconsistencies and to saturate itself with the *feeling* of the damaged. The differend must be put into phrases with the understanding that such an act cannot yet be accomplished. In sum, philosophical thought must come up with a link to the feeling-tone of the unaccounted for and offer privileged protection to the unaccountable refugees of cognitive regimens. The

Platonic model, setting truth as an invariable—as that which remains detached from the plight of the addressers and addressees of phrases—serves no useful, pathbreaking purpose in light of the task that Lyotard sets for a philosophy of dignity and activist commitment. How can this new mutation in philosophical engagement stay intimate with those throttled by a dependency beyond dependency? If I am getting this right, Lyotard asks that contact be made with the real ravages of the impossible and that one move with the incessant punches of untameable horror. Even if the object seems elusive (especially when it eludes): one has to go there, be there, stand there.

Not always available to translation or in the least bit comprehensible, the "Is it happening?" tells you only that the impossible has become a real possibility. Adding shock to wonder, this dazed state of troubled residue that cannot be seized or comprehended reverts in Lyotard to a stuporous *Grundstimmung*, to a traumatic stupidity that resets the cognitive levers according to which we respond to catastrophic eclipses, inhibited by that which cannot as such be presented according to classical values of presentation. There is something senseless in the heart of things, provoking "a bewilderment, a stupid passion" that can no longer be resolved into tragic representation or protected by any recognizably edifying recuperation.[1] This is why, among other reasons, Lyotard is determined to offer a redefinition of the sublime as that which is no longer opposed to the beautiful. The task of philosophy no longer consists in neutralizing or domesticating the senseless, in rounding up the savagely unintelligible but in staying with the stupor of unaccountable excess and regressive brutality. Gasché comments: "The task of thinking set by the stupor at the realization that non-being could prevail, cannot be fulfilled by schematizing the unpresentable into facile intelligibility. Thinking absolves its task of witnessing only if it encounters the unpresentable without resistance. The sublime feeling in which the impossible possible is acknowledged can therefore no longer be a sublime that plays by the rules of the beautiful."[2] The evacuated site of non-being, of the nothing, and the senseless "is only truly and properly acknowledged in a feeling of sublime stupor. In such stupor alone, philosophical thinking is true to its task."[3] It is not as though the "proper" of philosophy has now migrated to stupefying figures of the unpresentable. Lyotard does not originate a call for a new mystification, even in the form of some "truth of a task." Nor would he be likely to concur with his commentator that something like non-resistance is possible, given the irreversible vocabularies of psychoanalysis and rhetorical deconstruction. The sublime stupor is meant to stem the enticement of philosophical overreach, calling thought back to the sting of the unsayable: this is where phrasing, each time anew, stunned and dazed, begins to s-crawl.

Notes

1. Jean-François Lyotard, *The Inhuman: Reflections on Time.* (Trans. Geoffrey Bennington and Rachel Bowlby, Stanford: Stanford University Press, 1991), 202.

2. Rodolphe Gasché, "Saving the Honor of Thinking: On Jean-François Lyotard," *Parallax,* 6.4 (2000): 127.

3. Ibid.

Index

Abraham, 110–25, 126n17, 126n20, 127n21, 299; Kafka on, 117–25, 269; Kierkegaard on, 117–18

"Abraham" (Kafka), 117–25, 269

Acker, Kathy, xxxvn44; *Blood and Guts in High School*, 230; community and, 231–32; Derrida and, 227–28; friendship and, 98, 227–38; *In Memoriam to Identity*, 229; *Kathy Goes to Haiti*, 228; medical benefits and, 229; memory and, 229; *My Mother: Demonology*, 237–38; *Pussy King of the Pirates*, 229; reading and, 228, 237–38; university and, 229

addict, xxvii, 129; cocaine, 130; De Quincey's, 135; Freud on, 130–31; heroin, 194; Kantian subject and, 135; Lacan and Burroughs on, 131; morphine, 130; the writer and, xxix

addiction, 131; to the cure, 106; drug, xvii, 131, 134; *jouissance* and, 131; oil, 39, 46; psychoanalysis and, 131; rhetoric and, xxxiii; studies, xvii, xxiv, xxxiiin8, 128; telephonic, 7

address: as apostrophe, 224; direct, xix, xxi; Heidegger's Rectoral, 223

addressee: of the Greeting, 213; future reader as, 293; improper, 122; as Other, 150; presumptive, 120; random, 143; split, 116; temporal predicament of, 116; thinker as, 33; writer as, xx, xxvii, xxvix; of writing, 150

Adorno, Theodor, 215, 277

Agamben, Giorgio, 89, 90, 232

AIDS, 161–66

Alderman, Harold, 34n11

Alferi, Pierre, xxxvn44; on Blanchot and James, 265, 288n18

allegory: ethical, 148; of impossible survival, 147; of the impossibility of reading, 73; irony and, 234; of nonclosure, 39; of nothingness, 318; of politesse, 207

alterity: demanding, 134; extrahuman, 208; extreme, 225n20; internal, 75, 94, 279; narcissism and, 234; relation to, 148; stubborn, 229; test of, 147; thinking's, 214; ungraspable, 207

America: as dead body, 184; experimental disposition in, 300–304; as faltering empire, 50; fascination with actors in, 302–3; homeless, 67; as pathology, 196; role-playing and, 300; technological discourse in, 7; as test site, 300–304; war on drugs in, 129

Améry, Jean, 278, 292n53

amnesia: hypermnesia and, 85–86

anal-sadistic military penetrations, 44

anal-sadistic zoning laws, 36

"Andenken" (Hölderlin), 206–24

answerability, 5, 7, 16, 108, 166

answering machine, 8

anus: connection to ear, 23; in teaching, 160

Frisk (Cooper), 185n1, 191
Fynsk, Christopher, 208–9, 314, 322n6, 322n7; *Heidegger: Thought and Historicity,* 298

Gasché, Rudolphe, 235
Gay Science, The (Nietzsche), 293, 294, 295–307
Genealogy of Morals, The (Nietzsche), 7, 23
Gender, 99, 141, 153, 214, 221
Genius, 102
Gestell, 33n11, 165
Gibson, William, 293
Gift of Death, The (Derrida), 116
Gilman, Sander: *Inscribing the Other,* 167n2
Goethe, Johann Wolfgang von: Freud and, 146, 151; the Great Health and, 153; as killer-text, 153; signature of, 145; on textual survival, 146, 153
"Goethe-effect," 146–47
Graffiti: monumental, 267–68; subway, 262
Gratitude, 148, 250, 303
Greeting: the call and, 208; as going-with, 212; memory and, 213–14; nonappropriative, 206–24; parting and, 212
Grigoryevna, Anna, 183
Guattari, Félix, 131
Guide (Cooper), 197, 198
Gulf War, 38–59, 244; 9/11 and, 89; AIDS and, 163, 299; Rodney King case and, 65, 71, 73, 83; survival of, 76, 83; television's response to, 75–76; virtual reality and, 202

Hallucinogenre, 70, 197
Hamacher, Werner, 160
Hamlet (Shakespeare), 23, 124, 136, 137, 245
Hardly feel it going in (Scher), 90
Hegel, Georg Wilhelm Friedrich, 178,

192, 275, 297; on *Erinnerung* and *Gedächtnis,* 86; Nietzsche on, 300; racist assignments of, 101; struggle for recognition in, 142; on war, 186n6, 240, 305n5; on women, 241
Heidegger, Martin, xxv, 5; action and, 202; *Being and Time,* xvii, xxv, 8, 21, 25–27, 70, 79, 106, 110, 237, 312; Blanchot and, 23–25; on the call, 8, 21; on the call of conscience, 70, 106, 110; de Man and, 47; Einstein and, 21–22; ethics and, 17; Freud and, 26; *Gestell* and, 108; guilt and, 17; on Hölderlin, 10, 205–24; Husserl and, 16, 21; on illness, 166; Laing and, 6–7; language and, 6; laughter and, 17; on the leap, 320; mother and, 22–27; National Socialism and, 8–12, 17–18, 21, 23, 24, 209; Nietzsche and, 22–23, 26; "Origin of the Work of Art," 208, 224; *Question Concerning Technology, The,* 31n11; the *Spiegel* interview and, 15–17, 27; on teaching, 149, 159; on technology, 8, 9, 10, 11, 18, 31n11; the telephone and, 8, 16; television and, 68–69; on thinking vs. philosophy, 175; the uncanny and, 26, 33n11; on unshieldedness, 47; on the voice of the Friend, 237; *What is Called Thinking?,* 8, 22, 24, 175; *What is Metaphysics?* 313; on world, 188
Heidegger: Thought and Historicity (Fynsk), 208
Heimat (1987), 11
Heller, Dana, 144n2
Herf, Jeffrey, 29n9
Heroin, 129, 138n5
Herr, Michael: *The Dispatches,* 63
Hill, Anita, 73
History: vs. History, 47; phantasmatic, 41
Hitchcock, Alfred, 79
Hobbes, Thomas, 90
Holbein, Hans, 92, 175–76; *Christ Taken from the Cross,* 183; *Dead Christ in the Tomb,* 92

Schizophrenia: drugs and, 131; the tele-
phone and, xx, 6
Schlegel, Friedrich von, 191, 192, 278
Schmitt, Carl, 207, 234, 246–47
Scholarship, 147; stupidity and, 260
Scholder, Amy, 230
Schopenhauer, Arthur, 287n5
Science: Christianity and, 298; determi-
nate judgment and, 108; genealogist
and, 162; historical, 34n14; medical,
164–65; Nietzsche on, 294–305; tech-
nology and, 34n11
Scoptophilia, 91
SCUM Manifesto (Solanas), 141
Security: democracy and, 90; the enemy
and, 243; Hobbes and, 90; masochistic
probes and, 91; state, 89–95; techno-
logical seduction and, 90; testability
and, 297
Sein und Zeit (Heidegger). *See Being and
Time*
Shakespeare, William: on falling sick-
ness, 172; *Hamlet,* 23, 124, 136, 137,
245; *Julius Caesar,* 172, 245; Nietzsche
on, 245
Shelley, Mary, 2, 33, 300; *Frankenstein,*
33, 159, 302
Socrates, 5, 101, 159, 160
Solanas, Valerie, 141–44; *SCUM Mani-
festo,* 141
Speculative prolepsis, 40
Spiegel, Shalom, 126
Spliterature, 230
Steiner, George, 114
Stupidity (Ronell), xxi, xxv, 256
Stupidity, xxv, 197, 198, 199, 259–86;
Barthes on, 266–67, 269, 289n21; of
being, 198; the body and, 174, 184n1;
Derrida on, 268; Enlightenment and,
277–78; error and, 256, 274; ethics
and, 257; Flaubert on, 267–70; Jean
Paul on, 270–74; knowledge and, 261;
Musil on, 276–77; poetic act and, 256,
261–65; politics and, 276–77; reflexes

of, xxx, 268–69; sacred, 197; secret
beneficiaries of, 277; transcendental,
256–57; traumatic, 325; the university
and, 229; war and, 251, 270–74; writing and, 266–67, 279–83
Subject, the: active, 202; addicted, 131;
amnesiac, 86; analysand and, 45; the
"arche-teleological domination" of,
221–22; Cooper's, 188–90; Dasein and,
27; the death drive and, 110; death of,
291n50; debilitated, 257, 274; de-situ-
ated, 208; distressed, 282; Heidegger
and, 10; of illness, 166n1, 181; ironic,
94; Kant's vs. De Quincey's, 135; the
law and, 83; legal, 132; in memory
of, 229; minoritized, 281; primordial
aggression of, 76; seized, 181; split,
230; stupidity and, 266, 270–71, 274;
responsibility and, 63; technologized,
7, 163; telephonic constellation of, 22;
universal, 276, 291n50; writing, 266
Sublime: Lyotard on, 325
Supramoral imperative, 128
Sur Maurice Blanchot (Levinas), 138n1,
138n4
Symptom, 41
Szondi, Peter, 206

Taboo: oedipal, 42
Taubes, Jacob, xxxiin5
Ta-hui, 313, 316–19, 323n25, 323n31
Tai Chi, 284–85, 308
Teaching: impossibility of, 158–61; non-
maieutic, 150; without pedagogy, 312
Technology: atopos of, 38; Being and,
3, 21; body and, 61n21; desire and, 3;
drugs and, 79, 193; essence of, 296,
305; God and, 40, 48, 49, 241; mourning and, 18; Nazism and, 2; posthumanism and, 2–3; science and, 34n11;
seduction and, 90–95; the test and,
163, 298, 299, 305; war and, 40
Technosymptomatology, 94
Telephone: (dis)connection and, 11, 12,

cal, 91; reading and, xxiv, 136; reflective judgment and, 108; stupidity and, 289n22; television and, 2; violence and, 278; withdrawal of, xv

Unmournable, the, 40

Video: as call of conscience, 70, 74, 76; the frame in, 64; vs. human memory, 79; as surveillance, 69, 74; television and, 63–86; testimonial, 63–65, 74; as witness, 80

"Von der Dumheit" (Paul), 270–74

Wagner, Richard, 23; Nietzsche and, 235, 245, 249–53, 262; *Parzifal,* 110

War: finitude and, 52–53; God and, 40, 42, 240; just, 41, 240; Kant on, 54–59; mothers and, 241; poetry and, 261; stupidity and, 259, 261; technology and, 47; telephone and, 38, 47; of teletopologies, 38; as test site, 305n5. *See also* Cold War, Gulf War, and World War II

Warhol, Andy, 141–43

Weber, Samuel, 31n10

Western logos, 41, 52, 53, 163

What is Called Thinking, 8, 22, 24, 175

What is Metaphysics? (Heidegger), 313

Will: supplement of, 107

Witnessing, 80

Women: as enemy of community, 241; holiday and, 215–24; as seducers, 110–12; psychoticization of, 143; war and, 241

Woolf, Virginia, 179

World, the: worlding of, 188–89

Work, the, 293–94

World War II, 39–42, 51, 52, 66

Writer: the addict and, xxix; as called, xxvii–xxviii, xxx; the invalid and, 169; mortification and, 263; stupidity and, 266, 279–80

Writerly being, xxviii, xxix

Writing: a deux, 150; allegories of, 190; the ass and, 194; body and, 280–83; as call to the other, 150; death and, 146; as dictation, 150; drugging and, xvii, xxviii; essential, 145; excremental nature of, 198; haunted xxvi–xxvii, 147, 149–51, 154; minority-becoming of, 153; parricidal, 147; philosophy and, 193; rimming and, 190; responsibility and, xxix; stupidity and, 266–67; trauma and, 284; women-becoming in, 152

Writing of the Disaster, The (Blanchot), 312

X, big, 108–10

Zen hermeneutic, 314

Zen master, 315. *See also* Zen practice; Koan, the Zen

Zen practice: Buber on, 321; controversy between Hung-chih and Ta-hui over, 318–19, 323n25; emptiness in, 312, 316; *Ereignis* and, 314; Hung-chih on, 318; "I hit you" in, 314; Jung on, 321; master-disciple relationship in, 311–12, 321; "passivity beyond passivity" in, 312–13; private interview in, 320–21; Ta-hui on, 313, 316, 317, 318–19, 323n31; testing in, 308–9; "third eye" in, 314. *See also* koan, the Zen, and Zen master

AVITAL RONELL is a professor of German, comparative literature, and English at New York University, where she codirects Transdisciplinary Studies in Trauma and Violence. She has taught at Berkeley, Princeton, and Paris VIII; she regularly teaches at the European Graduate School, in Saas-Fee, Switzerland, where she holds the Jacques Derrida Chair of Media and Philosophy. Her most recent books include *Stupidity* and *The Test Drive*.

DIANE DAVIS is an associate professor of rhetoric & writing, English, and communications studies at the University of Texas at Austin and Ronell's colleague at the European Graduate School. She is author of *Breaking Up [at] Totality: A Rhetoric of Laughter*.

The University of Illinois Press is a founding member
of the Association of American University Presses.

Design based on original books by Richard Eckersley;
adapted by Copenhaver Cumpston. Composed in
Adobe Minion Pro with Myriad Pro by Jim Proefrock
at the University of Illinois Press. Manufactured by
Thomson-Shore, Inc.

University of Illinois Press
1325 South Oak Street
Champaign, IL 61820-6903
www.press.uillinois.edu